PENTONVILLE JOHNNY

My life as a drunk

By John Carter

PENTONVILLE JOHNNY
My life as a drunk
By John Carter

Copyright © John Carter, 2000

Published by:
Cotswold Marketing
Taitshill Industrial Estate
Dursley
Glos GL11 6BL

ISBN 0-9548877-0-0

Printed in England by
Antony Rowe Ltd
Chippenham, Wilts.

This book is dedicated to my wife Christine

God grant me the Serenity

to accept the things I cannot change,

Courage to change the things I can

and Wisdom to know the difference.

Foreword

I have written my drinking story in the hopes that it might help some people or even one person to recognise that they may have or be developing a booze problem. It is not only the rich and famous or the people on skid row that get hooked, the majority of alcoholics are 'ordinary people'.

Since I stopped drinking back in the mid sixties, I have lived what I hope can be construed as a worthwhile and constructive way of life.

In my story I have tried to tell how I was gradually and unknowingly, but very willingly robbed of the ability to love and care. This along with the disintegration of all my other mental and spiritual emotions made me a very sad and lonely person.

Although I have regained all my feelings and faculties since stopping the booze, thirty odd years later I am still a firm member of the fellowship of AA. Alcoholism is now registered as the third killing illness in the world and affects one in fourteen people who drink. If you take into account all the drunken car crashes and other types of booze related accidents it really should be listed number one.

In the fellowship of AA we follow a simple voluntary program that at this present moment is working long-term for over three million people world wide.

During the years I have been sober I have related my life story to many thousands of people in the hope that it would help them to achieve some sort of sane way of life. I have attended conventions in many different countries and addressed audiences of thousands. On many other occasions I have been called upon to talk one to one. Without exaggeration I have been told by over a thousand people that I should put my story on paper.

So here it is!

PENTONVILLE JOHNNY

CHAPTER ONE

In Africa, Gambia, to be more precise they have the perfect description of my mum "Boss Lady" this description really says it all. She was a big woman, I don't mean in terms of weight or height although she was over weight all the part of her life that I knew her. The relationship between my mum and me was slightly different from that she had with of my brothers and sisters; being the first son I was always her favourite. She was a very strong lady and eventually became matriarch to many of my cousins and other relatives.

Being a born and bred Cockney she was very down-to-earth I don't think that she'd had a very good education. What she learnt and knew about life came from working and living among her peers, the only job I ever heard her talk about before she met my dad was making rope in a factory on the other side of Rotherhithe Tunnel. As far as I know she left that job to get married and was from then on fully occupied producing and raising a family of seven children. She could however fight like a man whenever the need arose, and it often did. Many times she came to our rescue sometimes when we didn't need rescuing. Outside of the family she never really got very emotionally close to anybody. I never knew my grandmother on my mums' side of the family; however, I did get to know my grandfather quite well. Through this relationship I could see she had inherited a lot of his characteristics.

Nobody ever took too many liberties with us as kids, because she would sort them out very quickly, she had a very dominant but not demanding personality. I always felt that it was better to obey than to argue with her. My dad had two sisters, Molly, and Bridget who were never my mum's favourite people, I know for a fact; she held a grudge against them for over fifty years. My mum was definitely a woman with a strong character and a short fuse; very often she would get into a temper because she hadn't heard clearly what had been said. I remember once being down Petticoat Lane market

1

looking around the second-hand goods stalls. On one of the stalls I saw a type of twisted nail puzzle, which I picked up to, take a closer look at, as most kids would do. When the stall owner told me to put it down again, my mum thinking that he had accused me of trying to steal it, immediately walked around the stall and punched him in the face. The poor man never had a clue what had hit him or why there was a sixteen stone women tipping his stall and all its contents over on him. "Don't you ever call my son a thief again," she screamed at him.

When it came to religion she neither encouraged nor discouraged us. We were a mixed family, my two elder sisters, Cathy, Jean and myself were christened Catholics but at the age of ten I was confirmed in a Protestant Church because I liked Father Drake, the Vicar. My younger brothers and sisters were christened in the Protestant Church. Being of Irish Catholic descent my Mother like many of her generation lived in fear of Priests and Nuns, whenever she saw one or the other approaching she would either cross the road or pretend to be looking in a convenient shop window. Like many Catholics I knew she continually carried a guilt complex about not attending church. She didn't preach to us but she did keep up some of the Catholic traditions, like not eating meat on Fridays and Wednesdays.

I believe that the only real fear my mother knew was emotional rather than physical, I am not too sure that even my dad fancied his chances if it ever came to stand up fight between them. Although they had many arguments and outright rows I can only remember seeing them actually physically fight each other on one or two occasions. Their marriage may have had its ups and downs, which most relationships do, I never ever heard them say they loved each other, but they stayed together until my dad died fifty odd years later.

We spent the first part of the war running between our home and the large basement of Charringtons Brewery, which they had opened for the local people to use as a shelter 'during the air raids'. A very loud siren would alert all the people within hear shot that an air raid was imminent. On hearing this very foreboding sound, men, women and children would come running from every direction, all desperately hoping to reach what they believed would be a safe haven before the bombs began dropping. The East End had quite a large and very busy dock area, which the Germans considered a vital target. But unfortunately the sophistication of their bombers and rockets in those days was very limited which, often caused the whole of the East End to be sprayed with all manner of explosive devices. These were made up of buzz bombs, incendiaries and unmanned rockets.

Throughout the war the unfortunate people living within an area of five miles or so of the London Docks got the full blast of the bombs, that were only supposedly intended to destroy the ships and warehouses along the banks of the River Thames. The very worst type of killing machine I can remember was the Doodle Bug! An unmanned plane or rocket that made a very high pitched, frightening sound as it flew overhead. When the engine ran out of fuel, the noise would suddenly stop then this would be followed by a deafening silence as it fell out of the sky. From the time the noise stopped until the thing exploded on impact nobody breathed or moved a muscle. Even the kids as young as I was could feel the tension and fear and became motionless and quiet. This state of in-animation seemed to go on forever until eventually the sound of thing exploding in the distance reached our ears. This was always followed by a loud in or exhaling of breath as hundreds of people let out a joint very large sigh of relief. I was told that the Doodle Bugs were primed with just enough fuel to reach the London docks. In reality, it could and often did come down anywhere within twenty miles of its intended target. Looking back I think we would have been far safer taking shelter in the docks!

Every time the siren went off, sheer panic ran through my mother, she would grab the three of us by whatever part of our bodies she could catch hold of and haul us off to the shelter. In her blind fear for our safety she would drag us, sometimes forwards, sometimes backwards. Very often she would wallop us for not moving quick enough! Looking back it must have been a very comical sight. Quite why we rushed off to shelter at the Brewery still remains a mystery to me because if any of the bombs had landed on it no one would have survived and it would have taken months to dig out our remains. My mum, however, believed that this was the safest place on earth, I suppose she needed to believe this because as an adult she would have been very much aware of the real dangers we were living in.

Being children I don't think the real impact of war or life and death really meant much to us, as we were never openly exposed to bloodshed or the horrific scenes that the adults must have witnessed. Every time we came out of the shelter and looked at the landscape there was always something different. We saw the remains of buildings shattered and torn apart as a result of the bombing raids, houses were still on fire, and bits of smashed up furniture were spread across streets. I never really knew what to expect in the aftermath of an air raid, there was always lots of smoke and debris, often I saw people screaming, crying, sometimes totally panic stricken.

During the time we spent in the shelter I saw the very best and the very worst of people, some would share their very last food and drink with you while others would steal anything they could lay their hands on. There was lots of entertainment in the shelter, because radio (or wireless as it was called in those days) wouldn't work underground all sorts of people would get up and sing. Old songs and modern songs of the day, I can still remember most of them. One girl who used to sing to us in the shelter was called Valerie Masters; she went on to be quite a famous singer with the Ray Ellington Band who performed regularly on the BBC. Light Programme and for many years toured and performed in the bigger dance halls around the United Kingdom.

Although I was told we had lived elsewhere in the East End my earliest memories start at Number Fifteen Stepney Green. The house we lived in was a three bed-roomed, mid-terrace built in yellow brick. There were 18 houses in this row, all identical. Number One had had its front room converted into a shop that sold sweets and tobacco and was run by a Jewish lady named Rosy, next door to us at Number 17 was a Barbershop run by a man named Henry. Stepney Green formed a T-Junction with Mile End Road, always referred to as THE MAIN ROAD, which we as children were forbidden to cross unless accompanied by an adult. On the opposite side of the main road stood Charrington's Brewery, which made the distance between our house and the air-raid shelter less than half a mile.

I remember leaving the shelter with my mum one-day and being very surprised when we arrived home to find all the windows in our house had been blown or sucked inwards. The entire frames looked as if they had been gently lifted and placed ready for fitting. All the glass was still intact. It was many years later before the thought of how strange this was dawned on me, but it didn't seem very odd at the time. Even the curtains weren't damaged and were still as my mum had hung them. The street door had been blown inwards but was still hanging on its hinges not really damaged.

A German rocket had landed in front of the house flattening the kerbstones and bounced over the roof into our back garden, burying itself in the earth with only the tail fin exposed. It had missed the Morrison shelter by less than two foot; luckily we had given up using this when the brewery started allowing us to use their basement. I think this finally made up my mum's mind up to get us evacuated. I don't know how or when she arranged this but during a break in the air raids, without warning we were marched off to a school in Redmans Road where we were given gas masks and issued with identification labels that were tied or pinned to our clothing. From there we were taken to a mainline railway station and put aboard a train that was leaving London, destination unknown but anywhere safer than the East End would do. The rocket stayed in our garden for the duration of the war until finally my Dad called in the bomb disposal squad to remove it. For many years after the war finished there were unexploded bombs and rockets lying around the East End.

The passage of time was really a bit of a mish-mash in those days; I don't how long it was between the start of the war and our evacuation from the East End. I have no memory of the journey, but I do remember arriving at the house we had been sent to. It looked so big I thought it was a castle, there were several families already staying there. Strangely when I went back only a few years ago to look around the area I had trouble finding this house, I was looking for a mansion but it turned out to be a very ordinary detached country house, my childhood eyes had made it seem so much grander. From the sound of voices it soon became plain that not all the people in England spoke with cockney accents. It was strange to hear so many dialects but when we got to know people, our accent was the one they mostly mimicked. We stayed at this house for some time and I still remember one particular lady that my dad took quite a shine to. As I speak the memories of her flood back, it took me some long while after the war was over to fully understand what went on between this woman and my dad.

My dad had been medically discharged from the army after Dunkirk; I think he had been wounded in the legs but not very seriously. One day he arrived at the big house on a motorbike with a sidecar. Every body seemed to get exited about his arrival; the women wanted to know all about him and several of them asked if they could have a ride on his motorbike. I think my mum got a bit jealous. That evening there was a lot of sexual innuendoes flying around especially as everyone had drunk a considerable amount of alcohol. "Will you send him down to us when you finish with him." and similar comments were flying around. Men were in short supply at this time! All the adults seemed to enjoy themselves that night.

Dad stayed with us for a while and during this time my mum drank quite a lot, often being put to bed very much the worse for wear. I came to realise that my dad encouraged her to drink more than she normally would as he had started a relationship with the woman downstairs. We often saw them kissing and cuddling. Sometimes she would send her children up to our room knowing that my mum being drunk would be unaware of the 'extras'. Then in the early hours of the morning my dad would return and get into bed next to her. I say 'bed' in reality they were just single mattresses, which were placed on the floor alongside each other. Rough, hard, grey and black striped mattresses! Eventually my mum got very suspicious about what was happening and after many heated discussions and rows that nearly came to blows, we left Youldesy Hall.

We moved into the very first house on the edge of a town called Wisbech, which I think is on the borders of Cambridgeshire and Suffolk. We shared this house with a woman called Dolly Parry who had a daughter named Lily; they occupied the basement and the first floor. We had the two upper floors, one of which was really the attic space. I was the same age as Lily, we became playmates simply because there were no boys around for me to play with. We were mainly confined to the garden but whenever an opportunity presented itself we would make a bid for freedom. This didn't happen very often but when it did we would make the most of it. I don't know how we got to know about it, but a plane had crashed into the orchard, which bordered the fence at the bottom of 'our' garden.

We must have overheard somebody say that there was a dead German pilot still sitting in it. Our curiosity was overwhelming; this just had to be investigated. So Lily and me climbed out of the garden and made our way down the orchard. I remember saying to her, "Look at all the apples on the ground, lift up front of your frock and I will put some in it." This she did, it was at that moment in my life that I found out the difference between boys and girls, Lily wasn't wearing any knickers

"Where is your Willie," I asked her.

"I haven't got one" she replied.

"Why haven't you got one?"

"Because I'm a girl!"

My curiosity was aroused but then we saw the aeroplane and all else was forgotten for the moment. As it had crashed and ploughed through the apple trees its wings had been torn off. We climbed up on to the cockpit and were very disappointed to find it empty, no dead German pilot!

We clambered all over it, I found a glove in the cockpit, it was rather large for me but I put my hand inside it. Surprisingly I don't remember feeling any sickness or revulsion when I discovered part of the pilots' hand was still in it. I remember thinking he would come back for it when he discovered that his fingers were missing. I just threw it back into the cockpit and carried on searching around. I soon lost interest in the plane, disappointed not to find a 'German pilot' in it, and told Lily we should collect some more apples. We returned to our garden both knowing that if our absence had been discovered we would receive some sort of telling off. Lily and myself had many more adventures and got into a lot of childhood scrapes.

Dolly was beginning to leave the house almost every night and sometimes would not come back for a couple of days or more. My mum, being the sort of person she was got very on edge at being left in such a big house alone with four children to care for. She was used to the hustle and bustle of the East End, but not the comparative quiet of the country and it unsettled her nerves. It was obvious that Dolly liked the company of men more than just a little, her husband was serving abroad in the army and she was making the most of his absence. Several times my mum asked her not to go out so much because it meant that she was neglecting Lily who was living with us most of the time. After these confrontations she would stay at home for a while but she had managed to let most of her men friends know where she lived and invited them to visit her. Sometimes there would be two or more. On these occasions she would try to encourage my mum to join her, this always finished up with them arguing.

After a while Dolly began to stay away for even longer periods, which resulted in my mum becoming a nervous wreck. Her agitated state escalated when she heard anybody knock on the front door. I don't know what spurred her into action but late one night she got us all out of bed, dressed us and then marched us across town to where she had been told Dolly was staying. We always went everywhere in convoy; she never left us behind! On reaching the house she bashed on the knocker very loudly and continued to do so until the door eventually opened. On seeing Dolly my mum went berserk, she caught her by the hair and dragged her into the street. I had never seen grown ups fighting like this, men or women, the sound of Dolly's head being bashed up and down on to the pavement was quite sickening. She was soon bleeding from her nose and mouth and large chunks of her hair were being ripped from her head. Dolly was trying to fight back but really was no match for the frenzy my mum was in, who was also bleeding from the nose and forehead. The fight seemed to go on forever.

I suppose I was about five years old when this happened. One of the neighbours or passers by must have called the police who came and pulled them apart. Then they took my mum away, I don't know how long she was gone for as all us kids were taken home and cared for by a policewoman until she was released. After a day or two Dolly came back to live at 'our' house and took up exactly where she had left off. Once again men friends began to visit her. I remember one of them came up the stairs to visit my mum, when she heard him knock on the room door she picked up a poker from the fireplace, held it behind her back and then opened the door. As the man tried to come into the room she hit him on the head, he

9

ran off screaming and calling her a lunatic, he never came back again.

On one occasion, a big Irishman tried to chat her up, but unfortunately his timing was a bit out and my dad overheard him, and told him to piss off, but he wouldn't leave and challenged dad to a fight. They agreed not to fight in front of the women and children and both went down into Dolly's basement. My dad told mum that she must not come in no matter what happened. Awful noises and a lot of swearing started coming from the other side of the door. After what seemed like an eternity the door opened, we could see the Irishman lying flat out on the floor; my dad was cut just above the left eye but apart from that nothing else seemed to be wrong with him. Because there was so much blood scattered around, we all thought the Irishman was dead. During our stay at this house I was exposed to more violence and bloodshed than I had seen back in the London air raids!

Amongst the few other memories I have left of Wisbech is the Catholic school I attended for a while. I knew it was a Catholic School because the teachers were nuns, apart from that I knew nothing of or about religion. The only thing I ever remember being taught at that school was fraying. We seemed to do nothing else but fray and pray that seemed to be the order of the day, every day. Although I could read infant books I was told that I was too young to really understand reading and writing. I certainly became a top of the class frayer.

My life seemed rather blurred for some time; I've strange little memories popping into my brain. I recall once my dad came home from work looking very strange. He was by that time employed by a company owned by a chap named Frank Williams. Dad had been put in charge of this company; I think it was some sort of fruit and vegetable distribution centre. Very often he wouldn't come home for a week or more and on this occasion he had been missing for about ten days. During that time he had grown a full beard. To us kids it all seemed very odd. We thought mum would be glad to see him after his long absence but she was very upset. She was convinced that my dad had stayed away because he was messing around with one or two of the girls from the factory. I don't know if it was true or not but I certainly know that they rowed quite a lot during that period of time. It's only now thinking back that the truth of what my dad got up to in those days as really come into my mind. I certainly didn't consider him as an adulterer before now. I believe that all his philandering stopped when we came back to London.

My next childhood memory is about my sisters and me playing in a park in Stepney Green, things were very tough in the days following the war, rationing was still going on. My sisters and I would go to a little park nearly every day where we could play on the benches or among the bushes and trees. There were four parks or what we termed parks; in reality they were four very beautiful flower, shrub and tree gardens. One day while we were playing in the park nearest our house a man came up to us and asked where we lived and what our names were. Cathy told him who we were and where we lived. He then asked us what school we went to she told him that we didn't go to school. He wrote down what she had told on a piece of paper, said thank you and then walked away.

My Sister Jean told my mum what had happened, and what the man in the park had said to us. My mum went mad.
"It's the bloody school board" she said "you should never talk to strangers, this could get us in a lot trouble".
I didn't know that it was illegal not go to school and that our parents could be taken to court for not sending us. The reason we never went was because mum did not think our clothes were tidy enough for wearing at school. I remember I had to wear my sisters' shoes because we couldn't afford to buy new or even second hand ones. I knew then and now that even if I had been sent to school, I certainly wouldn't have gone wearing girl's shoes. I didn't mind

playing in the park in them but in no way would I be seen in front of other boys wearing them.

I don't really know how she managed but my mum must have got me some boy's shoes from somewhere. As she had so often done in past she took us on one of her famous marches to register at the nearest school which was very conveniently situated about half a mile down the street we lived in. We were taken to see Mr. Goodland, the headmaster, and much to our surprise it was the same man who had questioned us in the park. It was quite lucky for us that we had been reasonably polite to this man as even this early in life we were pretty wild and normally would have given any body that spoke to us a mouthful of abuse. Swearing was quite common in the East End among adults and children, nobody seemed to think that using swear words was wrong. So as I say we were lucky because we had not sworn at the man or rather the headmaster on our first encounter. From then on against my will I attended school.

The school was called Red Coat, it was a Church of England school and by pure coincidence my first lesson on the very first day I attended was learning to fray! As I had already been given expert tuition in this field I soon became the best frayer around. I had a woman teacher whose name was Miss Ingram, I don't know why, but I became her pet pupil. I don't have any idea how long I remained in her class but even when I passed up into another class Miss Ingram would send for me to come and see her. She would often give me an apple or some other piece of fruit. Some of the boys in my new class did not like this very much and often would try to take whatever she had given me. This meant that I had to learn another skill, one that teachers did not really approve of. I learnt how to fight. I wasn't really brave; I just found out that I was braver than some of the others. I soon became a bit of a bully to anybody that would allow me to bully him or her; however, once I settled down I did make many friends at school, which I attended for many years, passing through infant and junior school to secondary modern.

You were taught, if you wanted to be taught reading, writing and arithmetic. You passed from class to class simply because you grew older not because of any academic achievements that you may have picked up on the way. Red coat School had quite a reputation for boys that could look after themselves when it came to gang fights. There were several other schools in the area and whenever pupils from any of these crossed our path mini wars would break out. On three occasions when I was involved Redcoat boys laid siege to Hallie Street School once, and to Senrab Street twice. We were armed with pockets full of stones and serious injuries were inflicted on the enemy. Because I was what I was and am who I am, I was always in the thick of these battles sometimes I got hurt and sometimes I hurt others; looking back I inflicted more injuries than I received.

In Stepney Green there were only two other Christian families the rest of the population were Jewish. Opposite our house there was a Jewish bakers, the lady who owned and ran it was called Mrs Gottlieb, it was from her that I learnt about Jewish bread, Bagels, Motzas, Pretzels, and proper cheesecake. Being a Christian, so called, I was asked on many occasions to switch on the lights and light fires for my Jewish neighbours on their religious days. I did this quite willingly as I was very often financially rewarded and having money meant that I could buy cakes, sweets, doughnuts and the like. It was about this time in my life when I realised that I liked to be liked by everybody and I believed it was possible to make everyone want to like me. It was to this end that I would share my cakes or money with people not realising that I was buying friendships.

I remember a time, when, along with a couple of mates, I decided to become a member of the Arbour Youth club. We took part in all sorts of different activities, for a while I joined the Sea Scout troop, which used one of the clubrooms as a meeting place. This was fine until the leader told me I needed a uniform before I could go on any of the camping trips with them. When I asked my dad if he would buy me one he said it wasn't worth spending money on me because I wouldn't last more than 10 minutes and would soon lose interest like most other things I had taken up in the past. At first this upset me but like a lot of other things that the lack of money deprived me of in those days, I soon got over it. I asked the club leader what could I do that would enable me to travel around and see different places, that did not need a uniform or cost lots of money.

He suggested that I could take up boxing, because it would mean that I would only need a pair of cheap shorts and a vest. When I asked him if I could be any good at it, he said to me, because you don't weigh much you should be very fast. If you can throw four or five hard and quick punches and then quickly step out of the way when your opponent tries to retaliate, you should be very good. I went home and told my Mum and Dad what the bloke had said. At first my mum was dead set against the idea but dad was very much favour of it. He said if I could learn to accept the discipline of training that was needed to become a boxer, it might help me to be a more responsible and better-behaved sort of person. I never really understood who or what my dad wanted me to be, or what he meant by more responsible, better behaved sort of person; most of the boys I hung around with carried on just like me.

On the following Saturday morning my dad took me up Whitechapel Waste, which was one of our local street markets. He approached one of the stallholders, who among many other things sold sports wear and asked if he had any boxing trunks. The man showed him several pairs that I liked, but being a West Ham supporter, my dad chose a pair of claret and blue ones made of pure silk. The man on the stall said, "Don't hold them up too high John, because the lorry they fell off, ain't got out of sight yet". After that he took me into a shoe shop and bought me a pair of bumper type slippers. He put the shorts and bumpers in a brown paper carrier bag and gave it to me. As he stuffed the bag in my hand he added that if I lost interest in the boxing before I'd given it a real trial, over a decent period of time, I would have to work and pay him back the money he had spent.

When I started going to the training sessions I refused to wear my new gear or show it to anyone because I wanted to save it for my first proper fight. I stuffed the brown paper bag, which held my treasures, under my mattress. I didn't care in the least what I looked like, running and skipping around the gym in my everyday clothes and bare feet. For days I felt so proud of myself knowing that, for the first time in my short life, I would have the right kit that was needed to do the job. My little brain told me that I was going to be the next Randolf Turpin or Freddie Mills. After about a week in which we had had three very short training sessions, six of us were told that we were going to represent the club in a match that would take place at the York Hall Baths in Bethnal Green.

Before this could happen, however, we would each have to fight a member of our own club so that we could gain some experience of actually being in the ring under competition conditions. I was matched against a boy of my own age called Harry Applegate. He was the biggest built of twin brothers, but I was quite pleased about this draw because I had knocked hell out of both of them in the school playground. I said to him if we just pretend to spar with each other for a couple of rounds neither of us will get hurt or look stupid in front of our mums and dads. Harry not being the brightest boy in our school agreed with my idea. What I actually said and what I intended were two totally different things; my plan was, as soon as they rang the bell, I would attack him as hard and as fast as I could.

When the big night finally arrived, the gym where the ring was set up, was packed with spectators, they were crowded in so close to the ringside the front row people could touch the ropes without

15

leaving their seats. I could see that my mum would be sitting less than two foot away from me when I got in the ring; I found it all a bit overwhelming. For the first time since my dad bought my kit I opened the brown paper bag, took out my shorts and shoes, and with all the pride I could muster, laid them out in full view of the people in the changing room. I wanted all of them to see my most treasured possessions. The trainer kept telling us to relax because it would stop us feeling nervous, I couldn't understand what he meant, as it would not have bothered me to fight both Harry Applegate and his brother Billy at same time. I was going to be a world champion there was no doubt in my mind Harry Applegate was just a stepping stone in my life's plan.

When we were told it was time to get ready, I took off my clothes and for the first time put on my shorts. It was only at that moment I realised that when my dad had asked for a pair of boxing trunks, the man on the stall had taken it for granted that he wanted them for himself. As I stepped in to those bloody shorts the waistband came up under my armpits and the bottoms went down below my knees almost reaching my ankles. I could have fitted my whole body down one leg of them and they still would not have been tight enough to stay up on their own. The trainer saw my predicament and, once he had stopped laughing, took off his tie and tied it around my waist; he then pulled the waistband of the shorts down over my hips. They were so bloody big that the part he folded down made it look like I was wearing a full-length, ladies' skirt.

I could hear Harry Applegate and his brother laughing at me, which made me feel very angry, I couldn't wait to get in the ring and carry out my intention of knocking his bloody head off. When the referee called out our names the crowd cheered and clapped. The applause surrounded us as we walked across the room and got into the ring but when the audience saw what I was wearing everybody started laughing at me. I heard a man who was sitting in the next seat to my mum say quite loudly that skinny looking little thing looks more like a girl than a boxer, he could do with a lot of bread pudding and some big dinners, not a boxing match.

I saw my mum stand up and face the bloke, in one motion she lifted him off his seat by the lapels of his jacket and pushed him over backwards into the crowd, then she picked up his chair and hit him with it. The crowd went wild and started cheering and stamping their feet, they obviously thought that my mum, fighting with a man was definitely going to be much more exciting than anything that was going to happen in the ring that night. The crowd was shouting for her to take him into the ring and finish him off. My dad, looking very embarrassed, grabbed hold of her and pulled her back to her seat. He then turned to the man, who didn't know what time of day it was, and helped him into a seat a safe distance away from my mum.

Whilst all this was happening Harry and myself had been quietly sitting on our stools in the ring. The bedlam gradually calmed down and it was then that the bloke acting as my second decided that I needed cooling down. To help me do this he started flapping a towel in front of my face. Unfortunately he flicked it a bit to close, it caught me across both eyes which immediately sent me temporarily blind, accompanied by floods of tears. The referee came over and examined my situation, without further ado he declared Harry Applegate the winner of the fight on a technical knockout. I could not see what happened next but I could hear my mum shouting and swearing, and the referee begging for someone to let go of him. When I was finally able to open my eyes the bloke who had caught me in the face with the towel was flat on his back inside the ring. It wasn't until I got home that I found out exactly what had happened.

It turned out that my mum had become so outraged at what she thought was a deliberate plot to make me lose the fight; she could not contain herself. My dad told us that she had punched the referee, knocking him out and then run round the outside of the ring and attacked my second, my dad said she catapulted him over the ropes into the ring where he landed flat on his back. After that she had bashed up Harry Applegate's mum and dad just because she suddenly didn't like them! Needless to say that was the end of my quest to become a world champion boxer.

It wasn't long after my boxing career finished that my next memorable escapade took place. I was going around with three Jewish boys, one of them was called Harry Whipple and the other two were brothers named Gerald and Lionel Ostermire, we would normally hang around St. Dunstance Buildings or in one of the parks along Stepney Green. I think that it was during the school holidays when I persuaded them to come with me for a ride on the Underground. At first I didn't tell them what I had in mind because I thought hat they wouldn't do what I wanted them to. Bunking on to the London Underground had become a very simple exercise to me; one of my favourite pastimes was to ride the Circle Line all day. Very often I would go on my own and over a period time I visited all of the various tourist attractions around London.

But on this particular day I fancied a new adventure. When I told the boys that we would be going to Southend and riding on all the amusement park attractions.
Harry asked, "How can we do that with no money?"
"Don't worry," I told him, "My Uncle Tom works in the Kursaal, (which at that time was the biggest amusement park on the coast) and he will give us tickets for all the rides."
This boosted the boy's enthusiasm for my plan. It was very simple we would get on the tube at Stepney Green, change at Upminister, which was a mainline station, cross the platform and catch a steam train to Southend. Nothing could be easier.

All went well until we got to Upminister. When I had made this journey in the past there had always been a steam train waiting just across the platform from where we got off the tube, but on this particular day there weren't any waiting steam trains. Not having tickets I felt that if we approached any of the staff to enquire which platform we needed they might get suspicious, so we just waited around until a train pulled in. At our tender age all trains looked very much alike so therefore logic told us it was only natural that they should all be going to the place we wanted them to. Because of our lack of knowledge about time and motion I would normally count the stations as we passed them. As I had often done this particular journey on my own, I knew that if we were at the back end of the train when it pulled into Southend our carriage would be far enough down the platform to be out of the sight of the ticket collector. Then we would be able to slip out through the exit used by the postmen for loading and unloading the Royal Mail vans.

We passed several stations that from my limited memory of the route I thought we should have stopped at. Lionel had also done this journey before and said, "Maybe this is what they call a straight through train." I didn't know what he meant but even at that age I did not want to feel inferior in thought, word or deed so I agreed with him and we continued to look out of the window. After some time and passing many more stations we came to the conclusion that we had somehow made a mistake and that not all trains went to Southend. We were in a single compartment, non-corridor carriage with no access to a toilet, which the youngest of the Ostermire brothers became desperately in need of, as time passed and the train didn't stop his painful discomfort made him cry.

Harry said to me, "That sign up there says in an emergency pull this chain to stop the train."
We all agreed that wanting to go to the toilet so badly was definitely an emergency; I climbed on the seat and pulled the chain. After what seemed like forever the train stopped but it was too late for little Ostermire, he just hadn't been able to control his bowels? At that time in my life I didn't know what Jewish people ate but whatever Gerald had eaten for lunch that day certainly made him smell like it had been dead for a very long time, before it finished

up in his stomach. We pulled the leather straps that released the carriage door windows and put our heads out so that we could breathe in some fresh air. We were all laughing at poor Geralds' plight when the engine driver climbed into our compartment through the door at the opposite side of the carriage from us.

He looked at the communication cord and asked us why we had pulled it and did we know that there was a fifty-pound fine for doing so if it wasn't an emergency. I told him that it was an emergency because Gerald had shit himself and the smell was making us all feel very ill.

"I'm sorry but that is not what we call an emergency; stop swearing and show me your tickets," he said.

"I'm not swearing, I just said he had shit his trousers." I replied in all innocence.

The fact that we had bunked onto the train without paying suddenly dawned on me. The driver reached up and turned a dial, which in turn took up the slack on the emergency chain. He told us we shouldn't be on a train without a valid ticket and that we weren't old enough to be travelling on our own.

He climbed back down on to the lines, slammed our compartment door and walked towards the front of the train. We watched him climb into the engine, the train whistle blew twice and we gradually pulled away. The train finally stopped at a station called Bath, I'd never heard of this place but in my mind I thought that it was just what Gerald needed. Once again our compartment door was opened and a man with a very strange accent, which I now know to be West Country, asked us to get off the train. We did as we were told like little lambs and followed this person to his office.

He introduced himself as the Station Master and wanted to know where we were travelling to and also where we had boarded the train. Before we could answer any of his questions he must have got downwind of Gerald because he looked straight at him and told him to go and stand outside the office door. Harry and myself just laughed, but Lionel didn't think the situation his little brother was in was at all funny and he told us so in no uncertain terms. Arguing amongst ourselves however, didn't impress the Station Master; he wanted to know our names and addresses.

When we told him that we were from London and that our destination was Southend he almost had a fit.

"However did you get from the East End to Bath on that train".

We hadn't told him about the tube journey to Upminister and changing trains; we were just acting dumb.

The wafting scent of poor Gerald cut short our interrogation.

"I'm sorry," he said, "But I can't stand the smell of your little friend any longer, will one of you please take him into the toilet and clean him off."

When none of us rushed to do what had been suggested, the Station Master asked us if we were related. I had to admit that I wasn't, but as Lionel and Gerald were brothers I thought it only right that Lionel look after his younger brother.

"I don't care who does it as long as someone does it soon," the man said to us.

Lionel took Gerald to the toilet, which was a great relief to all our nostrils. When they came back we were taken to the station buffet where we were given tea and biscuits. The Station Master told us that because we were so young we were not going to be allowed to travel back to London on our own. I asked him what he meant and he told us that the railway police at been in touch with the Metropolitan Police who in turn had informed our parents of our whereabouts. This gem of information didn't exactly fill us with joy.

My dad was pretty strict but he was nowhere near the disciplinarian that Lionel and Gerald's father was. Harry's dad always seemed to be a very nice bloke; a cabdriver, and was blessed with very Jewish cockney sense of humour. When all our dads arrived at the Police station where we had been taken none of them bore any resemblance to the people we knew and loved. They were all in very foul moods and if it hadn't been for a policeman being present I am sure that we would have been beaten up immediately on sight. Harry's dad as a cabby had a very great deal of knowledge about the streets of London but once outside the city he was completely out of touch with distances.

My dad had often worked as a long distance lorry driver and had told them that Bath was over hundred miles from London but this didn't seem to register with Harry's dad as he had insisted on bringing them in his taxi. This was all brought up in the discussions that took place in the cab on our way back to London. The boys and me were being barraged with questions, which we weren't being given time to answer in between being slapped around the head and sworn at. Mr Whipple was moaning about all the driving that he had done and how much money it had cost him; my dad said he was quite willing to share the cost.

"So you should" butted in Mr. Ostermire, "It was your son that pulled the communication cord".
Mr Whipple said it would be nice if all three of them would share the expenses including the £50 fine that they had been told that the railway police were going to impose on us. After listening to several more conversations it became obvious to me that I was definitely going to get the blame for everything that had gone on. Even when Mr Whipple had almost driven off the road into a tree they tried to make me responsible.

Eventually in the early hours of the next day we arrived back home. I was greeted by my mum who was just leaving the house to go to her part time office cleaning job, which she'd taken very much against my dads will; it was a welcome that I really could have lived without. First of all she hugged me and seemed delighted to see me, and then within two or three seconds I felt that I had been knocked over by a bus as she clumped me up the side of my head. I often wonder how I never got brain damage from all the wallops

I received as a kid. The next time I saw the boys they told me that they had been forbidden to speak to me ever again. They did speak to me and for many years we stayed friends, but from then on Gerald Ostermire was affectionately called 'Smelly Gerry'.

It took some years after the war ended before people started putting their lives back in order and doing the things they had done previous to it. This meant that once again sometime around the end of August or the very beginning of September each year, Stepney and the surrounding areas would become almost deserted of women and children due to the annual migration of East Enders down to the hop fields of Kent. For many years we went to Crow Plain Farm, which was owned, by Frank Highwood and his son Peter. It was situated three miles from a small town called Yalding, a typical Kentish town, which was built on the banks of the River Medway just above where it came to a bottleneck as its current carried it over a man-made weir. They had built several sluice gates to control the speed at which it flowed, then it swept gently over a sloping waterfall and on under a bridge that dated back to Norman times. After that it was allowed to meander freely through the rest of the Kent countryside and on out to the sea. This area where the sluices had been installed was known as both the Lees and Yalding Common, to my mind it was a place of great beauty and for many years after hop picking had stopped it continued to draw me back to that part of Kent.

I loved going down to Kent with my family but hated the reason we went. Hop picking was the most tedious, boring thing that anybody could be asked to do. My memory of the years and the incidents that I got involved down in the hop gardens, have merged and turned it all into one long fantastic sunny summer's holiday. As I grew older I went back many times to Kent but never to pick hops.

In the street where I lived there were lots of boys and girls of my age but I never liked staying too close to home. I made pals with several lads who lived some distance away from me; two or three of them lived in Jamaica Street a good half a mile from Stepney Green. I got to know them through a mate who went to my school his name was Roy Wendelkin. He introduced me to Terry Wilson, Norman Garnett, Billy Jiggins and Martin Olsen plus lots of others. Norman, Billy and me went around together and for some time we were deemed to be inseparable.

By this time my dad had started his own scrap and salvage business in a yard behind our house on, which had previously stood a block of flats called Paragon Mansions. These had been badly bombed during the war and occupied for some time afterwards by one strange old lady who was always dressed in black and attacked any women who walked past the flats. Rumours abounded about her but no one ever knew who she was or where she went when the flats were demolished. We were all about the tender age of 11 when, one weekend, the three of us climbed onto the roof of a single story workshop at the back of my dad's yard. Once up there we found some stones, which we picked up and started to throw idly at various targets. Norman decided to start aiming at a small window in the side of a printing factory; he missed several times so I thought I would show him how to do it. I picked up a larger stone and flung it straight through the window, on hearing the sound of breaking glass we ran away. A little while later after summoning up our courage we returned to the roof from where we climbed down into the printers' backyard. Norman said if we reached inside the broken window we would be able to undo the bolt and let ourselves into the factory.

At first I was a bit concerned about this as the people who owned the printing factory were friends of my dad's, both Norman and Billy assured me that no one would know it was us that had broken in. I didn't take much encouraging in fact I was first through the window. It was a wonderful, strange place, all sorts of things that I had never seen in my life, great big rubber rollers all different colours and when we touched them our fingers would stick to the surfaces. We searched around in the workers private lockers and desks; I must have collected at least ten penknives. There were boxes and boxes of lead type, which we tipped out all over the floor. It was great fun at the time. When we got fed up playing around in the factory we left and went over the roof looking for other premises that might be of interest to us. It didn't take long before we had broken into five shops; in a matter of three hours or less I'd gone from being a bit of nuisance and a petty vandal to a thief. From each shop we entered we stole different things, groceries, shoes, penknives, tools and lots of other stuff. We made trips from each of the premises to a derelict house where we hid the spoils.

On the Monday, I went to school as usual, having no guilty feelings or thoughts about what we had done over the weekend. At about three o'clock in the afternoon a monitor came into my class and asked the teacher if I could go with him to the headmaster's study. On reaching the headmaster's room, I was introduced to two policemen who asked me what I had been doing on the previous afternoon, "Nothing" I said, "Only been playing with my mates." "Where were you playing," one of them asked
"Up the park," I replied.
The policeman then asked me did I know Norman Garnett or Billy Jiggins or Terry or Roy. When I said I did, he asked if I had been playing with them on Sunday. I said I'd been with Norman and Billy but not Terry or Roy. He whispered something to the headmaster who said "Of course". "Will you come with us John," the other policemen said more by way of an instruction than a request.
"Where to?" I asked.
"To the police station."
"Why?" I said.
"To help us."
" How can I help you there anymore than I can help you here?" I asked.

25

"We'll let you know that when we get to the station" they replied. The headmaster told me to go with them so I did.

I'd never been in a police car before, in fact I'd never been is such a posh car in all my life. The journey to the police station was over quickly, far too quickly for my liking; I enjoyed every minute of it. I was taken into the station and put in a cell where Norman; Billy, Terry, and Roy were already inside. After the policeman closed the door behind me I asked them what was going on and how did the Old Bill get my name and know what school I went to. Roy told me that Norman and Billy had taken him and Terry to pick up our loot. This didn't bother me, as I had no interest in the stuff outside of stealing it. I looked on it as just a prank; something to do, the gear held no value or use to me. I repeated my question, how did the police know about me? Norman said someone had seen us and recognised me, it was some time later that Terry Wilson told me how they had gone to pick up the stuff and that the police had been laying in wait for them. When they got to the station, Norman had given the police my name and address along with Billy's. So at the very young age of 11 I'd gone from petty vandal to shop breaker, factory breaker to thief and had been grassed on by one of my best pals!

When our parents arrived we were all allowed home. My mum was so ashamed knowing that she had to face the people from the factory. Unbeknown to me the boss of the printing company had lent my dad quite a lot of money to start his business and was also the landlord of the yard he was renting. My mum was crying in anger and smacking me round the head at every given opportunity. I kept saying sorry but it really didn't make any impression on her. About a week later we were taken to the juvenile court at Toynbee Hall on Commercial Street. While we waited in the corridor to go in front of the beak we heard several other kids talking about what had happened to them the last time they came before Basil. Henreques. On hearing that name my blood turned to water as I had heard that B.M.R. was notorious for sending little boys to very nasty places a long way from home. For the first time ever in my life I felt fear, whatever was going to happen to me. I was absolutely terrified, how could I possibly undo what I'd done how could I get out of this mess?

"Please mum take me home," I begged.

"You've made your bed now lie in it," she answered.

Suddenly the two policemen who had come to my school were pushing us through a large pair of doors into the courtroom, where we came face to face with a fat grey haired, bespectacled man sitting behind a large desk. When he had finished reading whatever was on the papers in front of him he looked up at us and asked, "Did you break into these shops and the Printing factory?"

I didn't reply, I just kept on crying I really was very frightened. I didn't know what prison was and I wasn't over keen to find out, somehow I knew this man could send me there. My tears and distress had no effect on B.M.R. whatsoever.

"Stand up you snivelling little wretch," he said to me. "I haven't decided how I am going to punish you yet so therefore I am going to remand you in custody for 10 days."

On hearing this my mum began to beg Basil not to send me away she told him she would be able to punish me in any way that he would like to suggest.

He was unmoved, "Madam we cannot have children like your son running wild, with a total disregard for other people's property and personal effects. I do feel for you but in this case I feel that a far greater lesson is needed, and I intend to see that one is given."

All five mothers were crying as we were led away to a small bus in which we were driven to Shepherds Bush Remand Centre, officially named Stanford House, where there were boys of all ages awaiting sentence for all manner of juvenile offences.

On reception we were greeted by two masters whose sole intention was to terrify anybody who had been sent there, in my case they did a perfect job. I was frightened witless for the entire 10 days I spent there, every day I prayed to go home. There I was a cheeky little cockney boy, who was by no means stupid even at that age and yet I had no idea why I was there. I knew that I had done wrong, a very serious wrong, but nothing in my tiny mind could justify what these people were doing to me. The teachers never spoke in any sort of encouraging tone; they shouted and threatened us from morning till night.

Each day they would try to find different things that would make us even more frightened. One method they had was in the main dining hall, which doubled as a gymnasium, we were made to play a game with a medicine ball which weighed about twenty pounds or more and two rough coconut mats which were placed one at each end of the room. I think there must have been at least 50 boys aged between 11 and 16, we were divided into two teams and the medicine ball was thrown into the centre of the room. There were no rules; it was the biggest and hardest free for all I would ever see in my life. The game lasted forever or so it seemed, no one ever got the ball on to the coconut mat, which was as far as I understood the object of the game, without someone suffering some sort of injury. Another of their sadistic plans to make us even more obedient was a game loosely based around cricket. A master would stand in front of a wicket with a bat and each boy would bowl one ball to him which he would then hit as hard as he possibly could straight at us, yelling, "Well held!" when the ball hit one of us. My pal Billy Jiggins had his kneecap dislocated in this way. I have never, ever liked cricket since.

As I said I spent 10 days at Stanford House; I promised myself that I would never ever do anything wrong again! Eventually when we came back up before the beak, from the way he was talking to us I thought he was going to send us away forever. I did some of the most serious crying I have ever done in my life. I was so relieved when he told us we were going to be placed on probation for a period of two years; it felt like all my Christmases had come at once.

PENTONVILLE JOHNNY

CHAPTER TWO

On our return to school we were treated by some of the lads like returning heroes, which didn't go down too well with the teachers, especially Mr. Waring. He made us take our chairs out to the front of the room and stand up on them facing the rest of the class. When he was satisfied that he had got us standing at attention he went into great detail of what he thought about our despicable behaviour. Eventually he finished his character assassination of us by telling our schoolmates that we were no better than little thugs, who should never be trusted to go out on our own again. The embarrassment of being ridiculed in this way, together with the memory of my stay at Stanford House remained in my memory for many years, and helped to stop me doing anything illegal for a very long time. From then on, whether or not those events had anything to do with it I can't say, but I suffered from a serious guilt complex, which manifested itself whenever the police or any figure of authority visited our school, as they often did. These feelings came over me whether I was in the wrong or not. Consequently I always seemed to be looking and acting guiltily even when I hadn't done anything wrong.

Shortly after the remand home episode, I passed my 11 plus examination with flying colours. I was graded in the top seven of my year; my parents were told that I had achieved a good enough standard of marks to get into a Grammar School. Unfortunately my family couldn't afford to buy me the uniform that it was compulsory to wear at our local Grammar. Looking back, I would have loved to be a student at that school, if only for the very posh name it had, Raine's Foundation. It was one of the best schools in London at the time, but it wasn't to be. Once again my future was determined, by lack of finances; my life might have been so different.

I must have been about thirteen years old when some of my schoolmates dared me to go into the girls' playground and kiss a girl called Iris Cross. Not being one to turn my back on a dare I did this without thinking too much about it. She didn't seem to mind at first, but later I was summoned to the headmaster's study where I was confronted by

29

one of the lady teacher's the headmaster, and Iris Cross. I certainly wasn't expecting anything like the accusation they threw at me; in fact I was quite shocked at what they said I had done. When I look back on those days I really was quite immature and ignorant in sexual matters. Iris had accused me of touching her breasts. I didn't really understand the significance of this allegation, because little girl's tits were of no interest to me at that age, I was only responding to a kissing dare! I certainly knew then and now that I didn't touch Iris Cross anywhere below her neck and shoulders.

My mum was sent for and I was told to wait outside the headmaster's study where, unbeknown to them I could overhear their very deep and meaningful discussion about my immediate future. At the end of the debate I was instantly expelled. I never got a chance to defend myself against Iris's allegation. My mum just marched me off to a school further down the road, which was named after the explorer, Sir Martin Frobisher but the kids called it Allie Street. It was some years on before I realised that I had been expelled for sexual assault. I still don't understand the reason why Iris Cross, told lies, as she was found out to have done on several other occasions that I was told about sometime later. None of this really meant much to me at the age of thirteen.

On my first day in my new school at playtime I was greeted by several lads some older and some younger than myself, who were no strangers to me because we had been stone throwing enemies for years. There I was, alone, with the odds very much stacked against me when and if it came to a fistfight. Lucky for me one of the older boys decided I should have a one to one with someone my own size and age, it turned out I had to fight a boy that I had already beaten in the past. His name was Terry Lee, we struggled back and forth until one of the teachers intervened, after that I was accepted as an Allie Street boy. The next problem I had to overcome was passing my old school on the way home every night. To my old schoolmates I was now the enemy, I think they call it running the gauntlet, which I did until I left school a year or so later.

PENTONVILLE JOHNNY

My first job was working for my dad, by this time he had another yard where we reduced railway sleepers into small bundles of kindling wood. We started work around about five o'clock each morning our first job would be packing the bundles of sticks we had chopped the previous day into boxes, then loading them on to the lorry. My dad would then drive slowly around the streets while I went knocking on the doors selling the bundles of wood. We didn't finish until very late at night, after doing this for a week my dad gave me the grand sum of six shillings from which he deducted four shillings for my keep; he really was one of life's most generous people. Talk about slave labour, it worked out that I had done sixty hours work for two bob, which was less than one old halfpenny an hour.

On the Sunday following my first weeks work I met a old school mate named Kenny Buckle who told me that I could get a job working with him in Rectory Square at a packing case manufacturers, who paid a starting wage of four pounds and ten shillings a week. Understandably my dad wasn't very happy about me leaving his employment so I told my mum I could pay her at least two pounds a week and also have money left over to start buying my own clothes. She was easily convinced and she in turn persuaded my dad that it was a good idea.

I went for an interview and got the job, as luck would have it by the time I began working there the starting wage had gone up to four pounds fifteen shillings a week. I felt like a millionaire when I received my first pay packet, I gave my mum two pounds on the Friday night and then went out to meet the world with more money than I had ever had in my life. I really can't remember what I did that night but I certainly know that by Sunday I had no money left and nothing to show for it. I tried to borrow some back from my mum but she said, "A fool and his money are soon parted", an oft-quoted phrase. I never have learnt about saving money so she was probably right!

It wasn't long before I heard of another job that paid more money. It was in the Minories in a distillery where they bottled and packed

Gordon's and Booth's Gin. One of the things that made the job look and sound attractive to me was that you could fiddle quite a lot if you got onto the right gang, which didn't prove to be a problem for me when I started working there. My first job at the distillery was to stand at the receiving end of a bottling line, examining and packing the bottles of gin into crates. Then placing the crates onto a set of sloping metal rollers, which would carry them down through a covered shaft, past an electric beam that counted each crate as it emerged into a bonded warehouse. I don't know why they didn't seal the crates before I put them on the rollers. It was so easy to put an extra bottle or two in each crate, which would be taken out, at the other end of the shaft before they were bound with metal straps. At the end of each week and according to how many men worked on the gang, we could each have at least two bottles of gin to sell. The security at the distilleries I am glad to say wasn't very efficient.

It was while I was working at this job, I found out about the true nature of women, my education about the fairer sex started one day as I was pushing a trolley load of empty crates into a service lift. Four or five women of various ages jumped on me, after relieving me of my trousers and underpants; they painted one of my nuts green, the other one blue and my Old Chap black. Then they all went about their business, leaving me naked from the waist down, with nowhere to hide. I made sure that I was never caught like that again but I certainly enjoyed watching other young lads get the same treatment. It took weeks for the dye to wash off my body and every day the women enquired as to how clean my testicles were; could they have a look at them? Since then I have always been of the opinion that a crowd of women are far and away ruder than a crowd of men!

I did try drinking some of the spirits we bottled but I never really acquired a taste for Gin. Eventually I got the sack from the distillery because I began using the factory like an extension of my old school playground, a place to have fun. The management finally realised that for some time I'd been going from department to department laughing and joking with the women and having a splendid time but not actually doing any work. I always tried put on a phoney show-off sort of childish attitude when I was in the company of the women, which I used a means to cover up my true inner feelings towards them, which were mainly the ones of fear of rejection.

One memory I have that is clearer than most is about one of the girls who drank too much and became very sick. I was told to stay with her until she was capable of getting home under her own steam. I escorted her around the streets until she suggested that we could go to the local park, as I was being paid to stay with her I didn't really care where we went. When we arrived at the park known locally as Itchy Park she took me by the hand and led me behind some bushes. It was entirely at her suggestion that we had sex. In my ignorance of all matters sexual and of the physical requirements a woman might have expected from intercourse, I took it very much for granted that she found the entire minute or so of bliss as enjoyable as I did. The next time she got drunk in the factory they gave her the sack. Being a caring sort of person I thought if I walked around with her once more the same thing might happen again, so I offered to look after her. The foreman told me I was welcome to go with her but I wouldn't get paid for the time I took off. Being that it was pay, day I decided against it. Although I never saw her again she still remains a slightly embarrassing but very pleasant memory.

My next job was at a cabinetmakers factory called Glendales. As I had learnt a little bit about working with wood at the case makers, I felt I was very well qualified to start as a cabinetmaker. The money was good and the people seemed to be quite nice. In those days there were no women wood workers or cabinetmakers so it was an all-male factory, perhaps a safer environment. Glendale's was owned by three Jewish brothers, Morris, Jack, and I think the other brother was called Sidney. The person I took most of my orders from was Morris or Morrie, as he liked to be known. He was a very likeable, balding tubby little bloke, and wore thick horn-rimmed glasses. At first I worked in the machine shop or mill as they called it, where all the wood was cut and moulded by machines called spindles, planers, and circular saws.

A couple of months after starting this job I reached my sixteenth birthday, convinced that sixteen was as grown up as one could get, I decided to celebrate it in a pub. With every intention of being served over the bar like an adult I went into The Brewery Tap public house, which was alongside a cinema called The Troxy on Commercial Road in the heart of London's East End. I'd been in pubs before but this was the first time I was going to present myself to the bar staff as a grown up. My ego was lifted sky high when the barmaid served me without a second glance. Perhaps I looked old enough or maybe they didn't care.

I had had the odd sips of drink before, in the darkest corners of pubs out of sight of the landlord and also at family parties, but never enough to have any real effect on me. This time it was totally different, more exciting, much more grown up! Some of the older people in the bar knew me as I was friendly with their sons or daughters or they were people I worked with. I started drinking Watney's Brown Ale; after swallowing three pints in rapid succession I began to feel very good. I could feel myself growing in stature, I started talking much louder. Thinking along the lines that the more I drank, the better I would feel, I ordered several more Brown Ales and gradually became the life and soul of the party. This was my first real experience of what alcohol could do to and for me. The more intoxicated I became the more my confidence grew, witty and sexy innuendoes verging on the very vulgar flowed freely from my mouth. I made a whole lot of 'new best friends'.

All the negative emotions, that I had suffered since my childhood began to drop away, I felt a strange wonderful feeling of mental freedom descend on me. Why couldn't my life be like this all the time? The inferiority complex that had been a constant companion disappeared along with the insecurity that I had accepted as part of my nature. How long it lasted I don't really know, an hour or two maybe, but I felt magic and wanted it to last forever. Of course I didn't stay slightly intoxicated; in this heady atmosphere I went overboard and got roaring drunk. Before that evening I'd always been nervous and shy with girls on a one to one basis, but during those wonderful few hours, I wasn't only chatting them up and talking to them as equals I was acting superior and ordering them, 'to get their knickers off!' Talk about going from one extreme to another. The older people in the bar were laughing at my antics and I began to feel that I was becoming someone they would respect and feel privileged to be able to call a friend; in fact they would surely want to be my lifelong friends.

Suddenly, I felt something was going wrong in the pit of my stomach, my brain went into turmoil. No! No! This couldn't bloody well be happening to me. I was going to be sick and I couldn't stop myself, nor could I get to a toilet in time. Everybody was staring at me as I vomited all over my new found, lifelong friends. The embarrassment I felt as those people watched me shrink in humiliation is indescribable. I made for the nearest exit, and as I left I could hear my ' new best friends' laughing at me, they were no longer laughing with me. I went home feeling very ill and so ashamed of myself. That's how it all started the very first time that I took a serious drink. I wish I'd been wise enough to heed the message that rang out very loud and clear that night.

Forty-eight hours later, on the following Monday morning, I went back to work still feeling very shaky and hung over. The memories of the Friday night were still very vivid in my mind but the embarrassment was beginning to fade and almost seem worthwhile. Because I now knew in my mind that for one brief period of time, I had felt wonderfully free of all mental and moral restrictions. I had discovered the real me. For a short time I had become what I really wanted to be, the person I really believed that I was. I had been the life and soul of the party. I decided that I must unlock this inner person from his emotional prison. I would practise drinking until I didn't get sick! Those thoughts and feelings stayed with me for rest of my drinking life. I didn't immediately get a craving for alcohol but that first session and the transformation I went through always sat at the back of my mind.

My initial job at Glen Dales was to stand behind a machine called a four planer, the machine was set up by the machinist who fed pieces of wood, two foot long by two inches square into it. When it emerged at my end it had been moulded into a shape that would fit on the edge of the cabinet doors. As the pieces of wood slid out I picked them up and stacked them onto pallets. Doing this for eight hours a day soon became very, very boring. The charge hand wasn't a very bright sort of a bloke, he couldn't see that if he varied the work, even slightly, it would cause less tedium among the boys minding the machines and they might pay more attention to what they were supposed to be doing. On one occasion through boredom and because I was day dreaming, I didn't pick up the wood fast enough and it came in contact with the wall at the end of the bench. This caused the timber to jam, then shoot up into the air, my machinist Lenny warned me that if it ever happened again, he would throw something at me to keep me on my toes.

Well it did happen again and he did throw something at me, it was a two foot piece of wood, I turned to avoid being hit but was too late, it caught me on the back of the head. I was unconscious for some time. As I was coming round I heard Lenny telling his pal what he had done. There was blood on the floor and all over my clothes. I was taken to hospital where I was stitched up and then sent home. I went back to work the next day wearing an unnecessarily large bandage around my head. When he saw me arrive Lenny came running up and asked if I could remember what had happened? I said of course I could, but told him not to worry, he was safe because I wouldn't grass on him, I'd pretend it had been an accident, to save him losing his job. We made up a half true story about the timber jamming against the wall and being forced to fly into the air and catching me on the head as it did so.

I was then transferred into what they called the chip hopper room, which was another glamorous occupation. My job was to hook sacks on to the bottom of a large Silo or hopper as it was called. Every wood cutting machine throughout the factory had a suction pipe attached to it, which would suck up the sawdust and shavings and carry them through miles of tubes all culminating in my hopper room. When each sack filled up it was my job to unhook it and replace it with another one. It wasn't very long before I became bored with this occupation and very often wouldn't bother to change the sack, causing wholesale blockages and machine stoppages throughout the factory, or at other times I would just let the sawdust fill the hopper room.

When this happened, I just shovelled the sawdust up off of the floor and put it into the sacks. Morrie, my direct boss was not too keen on me operating this way so I was offered my cards or a transfer to the polishing department. I took the latter; at least it was more interesting than the machine shop. I learnt a lot about French polishing and furniture assembly, I stayed with the company for some time, and eventually I was sent to work with the dispatch gang, which meant doing overtime and earning lots of extra money. Every Saturday lunchtime the dispatch gang would go for a drinking session in the Royal Duchess, a little pub just around the corner from the factory. As soon as I joined the gang I was invited to go along with them.
I hadn't drunk alcohol seriously since my initial episode in the Brewery Tap so when I first joined in the dispatch gangs drinking sessions the memory of how that night had finished was still fresh in my mind. This made me start very slowly, only drinking one or two beers in a session but as the weeks went by my tolerance for alcohol grew. On several occasions I became quite dizzy but not sick, as the weeks turned to months my confidence grew more and more. I became more part of the Saturday ritual than the rest of the gang; I would never miss a Saturday lunchtime drink. While my capacity for drink went up, my wages stayed low, which meant I couldn't afford to buy as many rounds as the others, did. When the dispatch gang tumbled that I wasn't buying an equal share of the rounds, they dropped me from their circle. I found this very upsetting, because my strong desire for alcohol was now on par with that of a millionaire but my pockets were still the property of a pauper.

It was around this time I first met the Barrett brothers, Tony, Mickey, and Ken, who had an old van parked on the corner of Wellesley St, and Gold St opposite to where a friend of mine called Alex Warren lived. I didn't know the Barrett brothers at the time but I often saw them painting their van. It was while I was knocking around with Alex and occasionally calling at his house that I noticed that the Barrett's van changed colour every week.

Then there was Jamie Collins and his wife Jean. Jamie was the oldest brother in the only other Christian family that lived in Stepney Green. The Collins clan consisted of Jamie, Johnny, Terry, Henry, Paul, Kitty, and Martha. At the time I'm writing about, Jamie had recently married Jean and they had moved out of the family home into a small flat in Cressy Houses. Both of them had spent several years in the army, in fact that's where they'd met. Jamie and Jean being very open and friendly people would often invite Alex and myself to visit them. It was on one of these visits that they introduced us to Ken Barrett, who had recently moved in to the flat opposite them.

I had often seen Ken, 'who was six foot six tall and weighed between seventeen and eighteen stone', walking around the neighbourhood wearing a very sharp looking white suit. As you can imagine he well stood out from the crowd, especially as most East Enders still thought that black gabardine and dark blue serge was the 'in' thing. I recognised him as one of the three blokes I had seen painting the van near Alex's house. Jamie introduced him as 'Kid Barrett' the boxer. While the introductions were being made his two brothers Tony and Mickey came up the stairs. Ken invited us all into his flat, which was brightly lit with very modern ornate wall and ceiling fittings, but very sparsely furnished. It looked more like a workshop than a home, because leaning around the walls were at least a dozen partly built tiled fire surrounds.

Ken explained that as a professional boxer starting out he was quite short of money, so to bolster his income he was making and selling tile surrounds. Also, along with his brothers Mickey and Tony he did painting and decorating plus any other type of work that would earn them some money. I asked them why they kept painting their van a different colour every week? Tony answered me and said, " We're doing it because we're learning how to apply and spread paint correctly," he went on to tell us how laying on paint properly was quite a skilful thing to learn.

It wasn't long after meeting them, Ken asked me if I would like work with him and the boys. When I asked him what I'd be doing he said that his father lived in a town called Faversham down in Kent where, between the two of them, they had acquired a contract to demolish several houses for the local council. I then asked him when would I be expected to start? He told me he'd let me know in the very near future. There was also a lad around at the time called Alan Saunders who I had known for some time, he wasn't an old schoolmate or anything like that, he was just somebody that I had met in my travels. Alan, Tony, Mickey, and myself struck up a friendship and started hanging around together.

The Barretts had a strange family history, their parents were separated but not divorced Ken, Tony, Mickey and a sister called Yvonne were from one union. Then the father met and moved in with a woman called Rose, between them they produced a further five children who now lived in Faversham. The mother after being abandoned had taken up with several men and had also increased the world's population of Barretts by giving birth to another five or six children. One day Tony told me that he had heard news that his mother was very seriously ill in a Sheffield hospital and asked me if I would like to go with him and Mickey to visit her. Because I never ever considered that taking time off of work for no reason was wrong, I said yes. While we were talking Alan Saunders came up and asked us what was happening. When Mickey told him our intentions he asked if he could come with us.
"No problem." Tony told him.

"What we should do is catch the tube out to the North Circular Road and start hitch-hiking." Alan said. As I had never tried thumbing a lift before this all seemed very attractive and exciting to me and without further delay, or telling anyone of our intentions, we set off for Sheffield. When we got off the tube on the Watford side of London we started walking along the North Circular trying to hitch a lift. None of us really understood that going on a journey like that needed proper planning. As I said neither Alan nor I had informed our families that we were going, nor had we taken into consideration that we might need a change of clothes.

We walked all rest of that day and way into the night, all of us were feeling very tired and more than just a little bit fed up. We were quite aimlessly trudging down one country road after another, not knowing if we were heading in the right direction or not. I was quite relieved when Mickey broke the silence we had fallen into with the suggestion that the next time we see a house with a light on we should knock and enquire if there was anywhere locally we could sleep for the rest of the night. The people we woke up were not very pleased but they did tell us that there was a place called ' Spike', not much further along the road.

Following their directions we soon came to the place not one of us the remotest idea what a 'Spike' was. We went through a pair of wooden gates and followed a narrow path until we came to a large single storey building with big double doors. On one side of the doors was a very shiny, ancient looking brass bell-pull that Alan immediately gave a yank to. In the quiet of the night it sounded like we were inside the clock tower with Big Ben. All of us were feeling very nervous about the situation so we allowed some time to pass before daring to ring the doorbell again. On the third occasion we had to ring it we allowed an even longer period of time to go by, but still there wasn't any answer. Alan said he thought that we had waited long enough and for the fourth time yanked the handle of the doorbell, this time he did it with such force he very nearly pulled it out of its socket.

There were two small windows in the doors through which we saw a light come on exposing a very long corridor, in the distance we could see what looked like a very small man making his way slowly towards us. Alan decided that the man wasn't walking fast enough and shouted through the doors for him to get a move on. With the internal lights switched on we could all see very clearly through the windows in the doors and watched the man growing taller and wider the closer he got to us. Ken Barrett was a very big heavy weight boxer but this bloke, when he arrived and stood up next to us, made anyone Ken Barrett's size, look like a boy (he was a massive!)

"Why are you making so much fucking noise you ugly little bastards?" he roared at us. Our words of apology rang out in unison. None of us could raise enough courage to tell him we were neither bustard's nor ugly and readily accepted that if he thought that's what we were, then, so be it?

"What do you want?" he roared again.

"We were told that we could get a bed for the night if we came here" Mickey said.

"I don't suppose for one minute that any of you have you got any money?" the man said.

"Not a lot," we replied.

"So you want to stay here for nothing?"

"That would be nice," Alan said to him.

"That ain't how it works here," he replied.

"Well how does it work?" I asked.

"Firstly you are all required to take a bath, then you can go to bed and when you get up in the morning you do some work around the buildings or in the gardens to pay for your lodgings. Is that OK with all of you?" he asked.

"Yes," we replied.

"Come with me then," he said. We followed at a distance, no one among us really wanting to get too close to him.

After what seemed like a long and very invigorating walk we eventually arrived at some sort of store room where the giant went in for a second or two and then came out, carrying four of the biggest shirts I had ever seen in my life. He gave us one each and then told us to follow him again.

41

"Put your night shirts on those stalls over by the wall," he said. Like lambs we did as we were told. He then pointed at some walk through showers and told us to remove all our clothes and go and stand directly under the nozzles. Like slaves we obeyed his every word, one at time he slowly turned on the taps of the showers. The weather out side was very wintry and cold and as the water from the shower nozzle came down over my head and started running down over my body my skin turned blue. I'd never felt anything so cold, as the nearly freezing water reached my lower half, my nuts shrank so fast I thought they were coming up through my body and out the back of my neck. Our reactions to the cold water seemed to amuse the giant no end.

Before undressing we had been told to hand over our cigarettes and matches. Not wanting to be without a smoke all-night and expecting to bath not shower, I'd hidden my cigarettes and matches under my armpits. I didn't stay under the water long enough to get them wet. The small white towel we were given to dry ourselves wasn't really very adequate but none of us mentioned it. The next instruction we received was to put on the nightshirts, after completing that little task we were each given a wire basket to put our clothes in. When we had done this, we were told to place the baskets on shelf type racks, inside a large metal cage, come locker, which we were told would remain securely locked all night to protect our property against thieves.

The next instructions we were given was to be very quiet and follow our host who then led us into a dormitory which, if my memory serves me right, was furnished with about thirty beds each with a side locker. As our eyes adjusted to the light we could see that some of the beds were occupied.
"You can get sheets and blankets off of the shelves at the end of the room and then find yourselves an empty bed," the big man said.
With that he turned and walked out, closing and locking the door behind him. The light was just bright enough for us to be able make up our beds. I took the nearest one to me and very quickly got between the sheets. Tony, Mickey, and Alan did the same but on the other side of the room, we were all pretty much worn out. The beds were a lot

narrower than the usual single beds and the gaps between them were less than eighteen inches. When I struck a match to light a cigarette I saw, lying in the next bed to me, one of the most frightening sights, I had ever come across in my short life. I knew it was human because it asked me for a cigarette.

I leapt out of bed, gathered up my sheets and blankets and made up another bed on the other side of room alongside the boys. Mickey asked me why I'd moved.
"I am not sleeping next to that fucking beast over there," I told him.
Alan got out of bed and went over to look at who or what I had been frightened by. I heard him let out the sort of sound that you make when something very unpleasant gives you a nasty shock. The poor unfortunate bloke in the bed was covered all over in thick black hair like a gorilla, his face was pitted with smallpox scars and he had lost an eye which had been replaced with a false one which didn't close while he was asleep. I was never very much afraid of violence but people with deformities like this poor bloke had got, always made me feel uncomfortable.
I am afraid that in spite of several people rather pointedly telling us to be quiet and threatening to get us slung out nobody got much sleep that night. At about eight o'clock the next morning we were woken up by the giant and given our clothes back. He told us to get dressed and follow the others into the dining room. When we got there we were each served with a breakfast, which consisted of a very thick, almost solid dollop of porridge, two chunks of un-sliced stale bread and a large knob of frozen margarine. All this was served up on the same plate and because there were no knives, forks or spoons we had to use our bread to scoop up the porridge. We were told by one of the other lodgers that after breakfast we would have to work in the gardens to pay for our night's board and lodgings.

As they hadn't said how long we would have to work for my suspicious mind told me that we could be forced to work all day. So when I saw the path leading to the exit gate I decided to put my running ability to the test and it didn't come up wanting. Both Tony and Mickey saw me leave and followed suit and it didn't take Alan many minutes to discover that we had gone. We met up some distance down the road where all of us agreed that hitchhiking wasn't the best or quickest way to get to Sheffield.

Between us we had less than five pounds so I thought it was time to show them how I used to bunk on the trains.
"What a good idea," Tony said.
We asked the first person we saw for directions to the nearest station, our luck was in because it was less than a mile away. Arriving at the station in very high spirits we bought four platform tickets and waited for the next train going north to arrive. After the experiences I'd had in this was a corridor train, which would at least afford us half a chance of escape if things came on top. We boarded the train found an empty compartment sat down and I very soon fell asleep. I don't know along I slept for but it certainly didn't seem anything like long enough before I was being very unceremoniously woken up by Mickey shaking me. He told me that he had been to the toilet and on his way he had seen the ticket inspector heading in our direction.

Trying to think quickly and clearly wasn't exactly what we did best, so using the limited amount of intelligent brain cells distributed among us we decided to go to the nearest toilet, lock ourselves in and hope that the inspector wouldn't check it out. Four blokes squashed into a railway carriage toilet, wasn't a very comfortable situation to be in for any length of time. Tony, who always turned out to be the impatient one among us, decided that he wanted to go and hide in the toilet in the next carriage. When we opened the door to let him out there, larger than life, right in front of us was the ticket inspector. "Can I check your tickets please?" he said to us.
It must have looked like some sort of comic opera when all of us started frantically searching our pockets for our imaginary tickets and not one of us being able to find them.
"Oh dear," the inspector muttered. "How unfortunate that all of you have lost your tickets, what a strange coincidence. Follow me to the guards van."

At the next station we were taken off and marched into the stationmaster's office, which immediately brought back some very pleasant memories of my younger days. During my minute or so of reverie Mickey explained to the Stationmaster about his mum being very ill and promised that if we were allowed to continue our journey he would pay the fare as soon as he could afford to. After the Stationmaster had rung the hospital to check our story and found out that it was true he told us we would be allowed to carry on with our journey. Ten minutes or so later we were each given an open return ticket to London, then put on the next train to Chesterfield, which was where we had, been told the ex Mrs Barrett lived.

When we got to Chesterfield Station, Tony rang a bloke called John Sherwood and asked him to come and pick us up. He arrived sometime later and drove us to the mother's house which was no mean feat as she lived about fifteen miles from the station along some very narrow, winding, mountainous country lanes in a little village sited on the very highest point of Derbyshire. The village was called Appenole and consisted of seven pubs, one shop and six houses. When we got to the house we were greeted by two friendly teenage girls, one of who was carrying a very tiny young baby. Behind them was a very miserable looking bloke, who didn't seem at all pleased to see us?

Alan asked if it was okay for us to have a wash and brush up before we went to see the mother. The bloke told us it wasn't at all possible, as there wasn't any soap because the shop hadn't delivered the week's grocery yet.
"That's all right," Alan, said, "Water and a towel will be sufficient."
Tony then introduced us to the bloke, John, Alan, "Meet the bloke my mum lives with."
That was it, no names no pack drill I thought. We were then told that the hospital visiting hours had finished for the day so we couldn't visit Mrs Barrett until the next morning. Being only a two up two down property it wasn't a big house but that night it was a very crowded

house. The four of us, plus the mother's boyfriend had to sleep on two mattresses in one of the rooms and the girls and baby in the other.

It became obvious that Mickey and Tony didn't care very much for their mother's lover and he cared even less for them. The next morning Mickey told us he was quite concerned that there wasn't any food in the house, and asked the eldest girl, who was about sixteen, when they had last eaten. She told him that when the mother's bloke had found out we were coming, he rang the shop and told them not to deliver anything until after we'd left. Mickey suddenly flew into a rage; it took all the strength we could summon up between us to stop him inflicting serious injuries on his mum's boyfriend. A couple of minutes later the bloke left the house and we never saw him again. He did however go in to the shop and convince them that they wouldn't get paid if they delivered any food to the house. We found this out, when we visited the shop and asked for the groceries.

"You can take them with you if you pay cash now," the shopkeeper said.

Tony immediately replied that we could buy groceries anywhere for cash and this particular order wasn't for us but for his mother and her children.

The shop owner said, "I know who the order is for but I'm not willing to let it go before I get paid". It was very obvious that there was no future in trying to talk this man around to our way of thinking.

John Sherwood's car was full of petrol so fortunately we didn't have to spend any money on transport when we went to visit Tony's mother some thirty miles away in Sheffield. After the introductions, Alan and myself just sat and listened while Mickey and Tony told their mum about the situation back at the house. The mother was a big fat woman who didn't stop talking long enough to inhale the proper amount of breath she needed between sentences, which meant that she was constantly grasping for words or gasping for breath. It soon became obvious to me that she very much enjoyed being one of the world's victims. She went into the greatest of lengths and the smallest of details telling us just what we could all do to make life so much more comfortable for her. Not once did she even hint at an enquiry about the health or wellbeing of the two young daughters or her small baby.

Mickey and Tony asked us to stay for a few more days, while they tried to sort things out for their family. I suggested that as we had no money left, it might not be a bad idea if we went into a food shop where one or two of us could create a distraction or disturbance of some sort while the others nicked some food. Alan said he had a better idea and explained that as it was Friday, which was pay- day for most of the people in the locality, we could wait until the evening and then go into Chesterfield and rob someone. Mickey butted in and said he didn't think it would be very wise for him and Tony to take part in a mugging because they had both grown up around the area and were very well known.
"That won't matter," Alan, said, "Because it will be dark and we can choose the place where we do the robbery."
Between us we decided to go for the heroic option of snatching a woman's handbag. I drew the short straw and was appointed the one to do the actual bag snatching.

John Sherwood drove us into Chesterfield and dropped us off near the church with the Crooked Spire. From there we looked around for a likely darkened alley to hang about in until some unsuspecting person or persons came along. I felt quite nervous about mugging a person but carried on in the hope that the boys wouldn't see through my bravado, causing me to lose face with them. When I got the signal from Tony that someone was coming down the alley I started slowly walking towards him or her. My intended victims turned out to be two women.
I thought, "This is going to be easier than nicking milk off a doorstep."
Neither of them gave me a second glance as I walked past. I could see that one of them had a leather handbag tucked under her arm, I turned quickly, stepped up behind her, grabbed the bag, put my legs in gear and took off at a hundred miles an hour. I don't know who was more shocked, me or the woman. When I first grabbed the bag it slipped

out from under her arm quite easily but then suddenly stopped as the shoulder strap, which I hadn't noticed she was wearing diagonally across her body and around her neck, nearly jerked her head and my arm off.

"Let go of my bag you fucking thieving bastard," she screamed.

"You let go." I shouted back at her.

Her friend, after taking a second or two to size up the situation joined in the act by grabbing hold of the shoulder strap. I was pulling and they were holding on and screaming at me.

"Please let go of your bag," I begged the woman. "I desperately need money."

"So go to fucking work and earn some like I have to," she screamed at me.

While all this very heated conversation was going on we were still playing tug of war with the handbag and turning around in circles. Realising the noise of the disturbance I was causing might attract unwanted attention, I said to the woman, "Keep your fucking bag." I let go of it and then turned to walk away but by this time both of them had got over the initial shock and started attacking me. The handbag was now being used as a weapon against me; the woman who wasn't carrying the bag was kicking, punching and scratching me.

I looked around for my mates and saw that all three of them falling about laughing at the two women beating me up and I really mean beating me up. As I was only trying to defend myself and didn't want to hurt them I decided that my best and safest course of action was to run away, so I did. The last I saw of the two women they were both looking very pleased with themselves and shouting for me to come back if I wanted any more. Sometime later, when we met at the place we had pre-arranged my pals were still laughing and began describing in very exaggerated details all the left hooks and uppercuts that I had received.

"Lucky you ran away when you did, otherwise those two little girls would have killed you." They said.

"Very funny." I replied.

Alan pointed out that our situation had got even worse because John Sherwood had decided that we weren't the sort of people that he wanted as friends and was refusing to let us get into his car again. When I told them that I was going back to London right away, Alan made the strangest suggestion that I'd heard for a very long time, which was, and I put it in his words. "If we make our way back to the house I will dress up in one of the girls frocks, put on some of their make up and go out to find a man who will pay me to have sex with him!"

Neither, Tony, Mickey or myself fully understood what he meant nor did we want any part of it.
"I don't really care what you do," I said to him. "I've got a return ticket to London and that it is where I am going right now."
I asked Tony to point me in the direction of the station, when he did I started walking away. Just then a car pulled up beside them and someone shouted what sounded to me like a friendly greeting to both Mickey and Tony. They called me back, said that they had been offered a lift back to the house and asked me to stay one more night then they would come back to London with me. I agreed and that night because we thought both of the girls had gone to stay with friends I slept in the mother's bedroom. I was more than just a little pleasantly surprised when some time in the middle of the night, one of the Barretts teenage stepsisters got into bed with me.
Early the next morning, just as we were about to do something rude but enjoyable, for the second time, someone started banging on the Street door. I can only assume that Tony opened it and let whoever was there into the house. One by one I could hear people going downstairs to see who had been knocking, when I heard raised voices my curiosity got the better of me I couldn't help myself, I just had to follow everyone else's lead. To my surprise our guests were two policemen who were accompanied by Alan's dad and uncle. Because Alan hadn't told them about our trip his parents had got worried about him, and they had reported us to the police as young runaways! The police went to see Ken Barrett who had told them where we were.

They passed the information back to Alan's parents who decided that the dad and uncle should come and take him home.

When I saw Alan's uncle it all suddenly became very clear to me where Alan had got some of his strange ideas. His uncle had travelled all the way up from London to Derbyshire wearing a pair of bright powder blue trousers and a ladies' matching twin set, plus a two string pearl necklace. He was also wearing make up and bright red nail varnish. All this along with his outstanding permed tinted hair did nothing to hide the fact that he was a man, who was making the two policemen look and feel awfully embarrassed at being in his company. Alan said his goodbyes to us and left with them, I never saw him again. After he had gone, Mickey, Tony and myself got a lift into Sheffield to see their mum who told us that she was being discharged in a day or two. After four days with very little to eat I was so desperate that on the way out of the hospital I went into the kitchen and stole a loaf of very hot bread and scoffed it down in no time flat. From there we went to the station and caught the first train back to London, where on our arrival I went home to my parents house and the boys went back to Ken's flat.

A couple of days later we were all visiting Jamie Collins and talking about our recent misadventures when there was a knock on the door which Jean opened and greeted a Police Sergeant friend of theirs.
"Is this a social call, " she asked.
"It is and it isn't" he replied. "I am trying to find out if the four little run away boys all got back home safely."
Jamie Collins said to him, "I would hardly call these three great lumps 'little' boys."
The copper took off his coat and helmet sat down on the sofa next to me. We told him it was because Alan's parents had been so worried that they lied to the police about our ages. They thought that if the police knew how old we really were they wouldn't help to find or fetch Alan back. The Sergeant found it very amusing and as he had met Alan's uncle he said that it would be a waste of police time pursuing the matter any further.

CHAPTER 3

Due to the Sheffield trip and various other inconsiderate unofficial holidays I took, I eventually lost my job at Glen Dales, and started working for a company called Ross and Klug who were under contract to manufacture wooden bookcases for the Friendly Library Association. Their factory was in Handbury Street, just off of Brick Lane. Not long after I had started work there Mickey and Tony Barratt, who I had now been with friends for some time, told me that they were looking for a job to tide them over until the tender Ken had submitted for the demolition work in Faversham came through. When I recommended them to Frank the mill foreman, he gave them both a job. We soon got into the swing of things and within a couple of weeks, we were operating a sideline in stolen bookcases. Because the factory only had a single house-door type entry, it made stealing assembled bookcases quite impossible, so we had to take single panels and assemble them ourselves. Taking into account, our ignorance of time and motion, plus the risk and work we put into our operation, it was never going to be a very lucrative venture, nor did it ever turn out that way.

Occasionally and mainly out of boredom, just for something to do on a Friday night, Tony, Mickey and myself would walk along Commercial Road looking at the prostitutes. I don't know why we did it; I think being a bit immature for our age, we thought it was all very exciting and very grown up to walk past the women and see how many of them would approach us with offers of sexual favours, for money of course. On one particular Friday evening, we had been home and got changed and then couldn't make up our minds what to do with our time. Tony looked at me and said, " Let's go up to Aldgate and if any of the girls offers us a good time, we could have sex with them."
My inner feelings of shyness, and my outer feelings of a show-off, were totally at odds with each other about going along with Tony's idea. Not wanting to be looked on as some sort of whimp by either of them I agreed to go along with the suggestion. At about half past

51

nine we started casually strolling along Commercial Road trying to look as nonchalant as we possibly could. At first I wasn't too sad to see that there weren't many girls out plying their trade, and out of those that were present, there wasn't any we fancied. We walked up and down for a time and then decided to go into a Café and wait for a while. We ordered coffees and took as long as possible to drink them. While we were wasting time, we talked about our intentions, during the conversation Mickey made it quite clear that he wasn't going to have sex with a prostitute.

"Come on," I said to Tony, "Let's see if there are any good looking ones about."

"Alright," he said.

We left the cafe and started walking towards Aldgate tube station. We hadn't gone far when an attractive, brassy looking, young girl asked us if we wanted to do business with her.

Tony said, "Yes, how much is it"?

"Ten bob up against the wall or a pound if you come back to my flat," she said.

Tony looked at me and asked what I wanted to do, I said, "Ten bob's worth".

"How about you," he said to Mickey and got a stinging reply telling him not to be disgusting, and that we could catch all sorts of diseases from this type of girl. We both laughed at him trying to cover up the fact that we felt embarrassed. The girl asked Tony how many of us wanted to do business. "Just us two," he replied.

"All right then I'll call my friend." She looked along the street and shouted to a woman who was standing about hundred yards or so away from us who answered to the name of Rosy.

She said to Tony, "You come with me and your mate can go with Rosy when she gets here." Without saying anything else she turned caught hold of Tony's hand and led him away. When her friend got closer to us I recognised her from one or two previous visits I had made to the dives and cafes along Commercial Road. She was known as Cross Eyed Rosy, for very obvious reasons. As well as having a very bad affliction in both eyes, she had large thick misshapen lips and a figure that bordered on the grotesque. What made me feel most uncomfortable about going with her was being able to see through the almost transparent blouse she was wearing, I could see that her tits weren't exactly the shape of melons, in fact the only fruit they reminded me of were extra long bananas. They started in the same place as an average everyday woman's would, but finished only an inch or so above her midriff.

I felt completely trapped when she grabbed hold of my arm in a vice like grip and then started leading me very firmly towards the alley where I had seen Tony and his partner go. I felt very uncomfortable in two ways, firstly I didn't want to have sex with this monster and secondly I was too frightened to say so. This will do she said to me as she stopped beneath a streetlight and lifted up her skirt. Before I could count to three she had got my Willie out and was putting a condom on it. I must admit this woman was very professional and knew exactly what she wanted us to do, she opened her legs and directed me in, it all happened very quickly.

"Come on," she said, "We aint got all bloody night, start fucking."
"Alright," I said and tried to go through the right motions.
"Come on, come on," she said "Time's money, time's money". I tried to close my eyes and think of someone else, but in my mind I could still see her cross-eyes and ugly face, which took away and kept away any incentive I had to reach a climax. In fact the longer I tried the worse I felt. She was holding me around the waist and started to kiss me on the cheek, I jerked my head away to avoid having any more physical contact than was absolutely necessary.
Suddenly she smacked me around the head and said, "Hurry up you little bastard and cum."
"I'm very sorry," I said, "But because I don't fancy you, I can't do it".
"You'd better fucking cum," she said, "Because you are not getting your bloody money back."

I stepped back out of her grasp and said, "I'm very sorry you don't do anything for me and you can keep the fucking money." I felt so embarrassed when she smacked me around the head again and told me to piss off. She then went on to say how she had satisfied thousands of better looking and more grateful men than I'd had hot dinners.

Just then Tony came round the corner and could see what was happening, he suggested it might be a good time to leave. I was still standing there trying to protect myself from being walloped and wondering what to do with the condom I had taken off.
Rosy said to Tony, "Next time bring a proper man, one that knows what to do with a woman." I really felt like saying you don't even look like a woman, but I just dropped the condom on the ground, zipped up my trousers and walked away. Thinking about all the wonderful things that I'd been told about adult sex and how much better it was going to be with a women instead of the usual schoolgirls I had messed around with. I felt that most boys of my age, just having finished their first grown up sexual encounter would be feeling very proud of themselves not be walking away feeling as humiliated as I did.

The wages at Ross and Klug's weren't very good; even if they had paid me well, I still wouldn't have had a clue how to handle money. Just around the corner from the factory, in Brick Lane there was a Greek cafe where I had my lunches on credit, and being sort of person I was, I had to have the biggest and best meals that were available. So it was no wonder that not long after I started the account, it was working out that after I had settled my bill at the end of each week, I hadn't got any money left, outside of what I paid my mum for my board and lodgings. Plus I did find out that Tony Barratt was having the occasional meal on my account. Why the cafe owner had allowed this I don't know so I refused to pay my last bill and told him to collect it from Tony. I took my account to the Curry house a little way further down the road. Which turned out to be better for me because this café stayed open until late at night seven days a week and I could eat on tick during the evenings and at weekends.

PENTONVILLE JOHNNY

Twice a week a lorry came to Ross and Klugs to collect the sawdust and wood chippings; on its arrival all the Factory workers would be told to assemble in the basement. Once there, they would form a human chain to pass the sacks of sawdust from the hopper room, which was located at the back of the building, to the front and then push them up through a small pair of doors that opened out on to the pavement. From there two blokes would lift them on to the back of the lorry. One day while we were performing this task I was passed an extremely damp and heavy sack. As I tried to lift it and failed, I felt something click at the base of my spine, there was a quick twinge of pain and then it passed off, I thought nothing more of it at that time.

As I hadn't been warned about the extra-heavy sack, my reaction caused some merriment among my workmates and I realised that it had been done as a practical joke. The next day I felt quite a lot of pain in the base of my spine and down my left leg. I worked for several hours until, without any warning, I blacked out. When I regained my senses I was in the London hospital and didn't have any memory of how I got there. After several days of lying flat on my back and complaining about it at every given opportunity, I was told that if I took things very easy I would be allowed to go home. Two days after my discharge from the hospital I went to the factory to let them know that I was up and about again, but unable to return to work. They told me that I wouldn't be receiving any wages until I was signed off the sick. This was bad news because I had never signed on the sick, and was totally ignorant of how to go about doing so. That was until Frank the mill foreman explained it all to me. My back did improve but was never a hundred percent ever again; I never went back to work for Ross and Klugs. After a very long spell on the sick which I mostly spent hanging around the Clubs and Dives, I got out of the work habit. When the doctor signed me off, I just went and signed on at the local Labour Exchange and was paid a pittance but it suited me as I had grown to like the idea of not having to work for a living.

One day when I went to sign on, one of the officials called me into his office and wanted to know my exact age, When I told him I was 18, he asked me why I wasn't in the army.

"I don't know," I replied.

All boys between eighteen and 21 should be doing National Service he told me. Then he poked a piece of paper under my nose and said, " Sign this form."

When I asked, why? He said, "If you don't sign it we will no longer be able to pay you unemployment benefit."

I signed immediately, and then went home and told my mum what had happened.

She called me a bloody fool and said, "I bet they come and take you away within a week."

I knew about National Service but it wasn't something I felt very concerned about, quite a lot of my pals hadn't bothered about it so it was natural that I didn't. My mum was right, however, within a couple of days a letter arrived telling me to report to the army recruitment centre at Wanstead the following Friday.

When I arrived at the centre the recruiting sergeant who met and warmly greeted me at the door seemed like a very genuine and nice sort of person; he went out of his way to personally direct me into the examination room. After being pushed, prodded, 'drop em, and coughed', I was told that I was A.1. Fit. My friendly sergeant reappeared, "How did you get on," he inquired.

"Fine," I said.

He then told me about all the benefits that could be gained if I signed on as a regular soldier. The least of them being that I would get more money and much more time to prepare my uniform and boots, plus I would stand a ninety nine percent chance of being posted abroad to a warmer climate. As my mum always said, I was very easily led. Like a fool I signed up for three years serving in the ranks and four years with the reserves or with the colours as they called it.

Two minutes after signing his form, the very nice sergeant had a complete change of personality and was telling me in no uncertain terms, the sort of man that he and his friends were going to turn me into. He explained that by signing the piece of paper as I had done, I had handed my life and soul over to the army, and they had total control over me for the next seven years. I felt a sudden chill go through my body, and thought whatever had I done? I did check around just in case he was telling me porkies. Unfortunately, he was telling me the truth. My mum was right again; the following week another official letter arrived, informing me that I had to report to Blandford Army barracks on the Monday of the following week. I had signed on to serve my time with a regiment of the Royal Electrical and Mechanical Engineers. I travelled down to Dorset by train and on the journey I managed to inform everybody in my carriage that I was an army volunteer this met with some approval from my fellow travellers, one kind gentleman bought me several drinks.

On my arrival at Blandford Forum I made my way to the nearest pub where I teamed up with a bloke I had met at the Recruitment Centre. Among many other valuable bits of information, he told me that in Dorset there was a drink called Scrumpy, which was made from rotten apples. Here I was, a hard drinking 18-year-old, soldier of the Queen who didn't know the first thing about drinking cider! When I ordered my very first pint of scrumpy the kindly publican told me that if I wasn't used to it I shouldn't drink too much of it in one sitting as it was very potent; that was like waving a red rag at a bull. My fellow comrade in arms and I soon polished off four or five quick measures after which neither of us admitted to being drunk, however, for several hours we had to remain sitting on a bench outside the pub because we had lost the use of our legs. We were both hoping this was only a temporary set back. Eventually an army lorry pulled up near us, the soldier driving it knew my drinking pal and offered us a lift to barracks.

My letter of instructions said that I should report to the officer in charge, so when I saw the sign for the Commanding Officer's office I took my newly found mate in to meet the man. I don't have to go into very much detail when I tell you that somehow the Colonel In

Charge wasn't overjoyed to meet his two newest recruits on such a personal level, especially as we were obviously more than slightly the worst for drink. As he was ordering one of his staff to show us where to go I could feel the effect of the drink wearing off and the fearful reality of my situation began to dawn on me. We were taken to a barrack room and allocated a bed, and a locker. Neither of us possessed much gear, only what we could cram into a small suitcase and the clothes we were wearing.

At differing intervals during the rest of the day and into the early evening several more blokes arrived and each in turn allocated themselves a bed and locker. On the arrival of a man wearing a uniform with stripes on it we were told to form two lines. Then we were further told, to march to the Quarter Masters stores. (I had only ever heard this term in a song, sung in Charrington's shelter, when I was a kid) From the Q.M. stores we each drew three uniforms, a mattress, a Billycan, a mug, a pillow and pillowcase, a kit bag, a backpack, plus sheets and blankets. It was all issued for the wearing of, for the sleeping of, or the walking in of! As a cockney I had grown up with loud voices all around me, but even with my background the unnecessary screaming and shouting that went on all the time, I felt was totally out of order.

After marching back to our barracks, carrying what felt like a ton of equipment, a Lance Corporal introduced himself and told us he was going to be in charge of the platoon, as we were now called. He like me was a cockney from Stepney but that is where the similarity between us ended. He walked around the spider (barrack room) shouting at each of us in turn and telling us how important he was and each time he mentioned his own importance he pointed at the one solitary little stripe he wore with great pride on the sleeves of his tunic.

Eventually he arrived at the foot of my bed. "And where are you from," he barked at me.

"Stepney Green," I answered.

"Scum of the earth," he replied.

PENTONVILLE JOHNNY

My blood boiled. I was about to swing a punch at him when he jumped backwards and started screaming abuse at me. Two of the other lads got between us and one of them said that if I walloped a non-commissioned officer I would be sent to an army prison for the rest of my service. He went on to say that by allowing prat's like this corporal to shout and scream at us, the Army and all the wise men behind were convinced that it was teaching us discipline. It was very hard to control my temper but I let the moment pass. The Lance corporal told us that we had two weeks to get our kit ready for the Commanding Officers inspection.

When I was younger I had often wanted to go into the army or air force, because I had read about various members of the different military services who had received lots of medals for performing heroic deeds. In my childhood fantasies I was more than sure that I would be awarded with at least the Victoria Cross. Now in reality this skinny fucking corporal had destroyed my desire to be an ordinary soldier, let alone a hero. During the fourteen days we were given to prepare our kit for inspection we were put on fatigues, for my first assignment I was sent to the officer's mess. I arrived before daybreak and stayed until after midnight. I must have peeled three hundred weight of potatoes, scraped one hundred weight of carrots, shelled thirty pounds of peas, washed and sliced fifty cabbages, and cried buckets of tears as I skinned and chopped up bag after bag of onions.

The regular kitchen staff seemed to take great joy in informing me that on every other occasion that rookies had been assigned to them there were always at least two or three people to share the work. I must say this information wasn't helping my morale, I was getting more and more pissed off with the army, and even more so when some effeminate looking and sounding officer came in and told me what a wonderful job I was doing, and all on my own! When I arrived back at the spider all the lights were out which meant I had to find my way to my bed and locker in the pitch dark, this caused me to disturb all of the fifteen lads I shared the billet with.

The next day I was sent back to the officer's mess, where once again I was working on my own. My fatigues for that day were washing and polishing the regimental silver. I don't mean the cups and shields from the Battle Honours Trophy cabinet; I mean the officer's everyday knives, forks and spoons the sugar bowls, the teapots the milk jugs and coffee pots. Each officer had a personal set of silverware and there were over a hundred and fifty of the stuck up silly bastards. Once again I didn't get back to my billet until after dark, waking the boys up for a second time really made me popular. Because of my two very early morning assignments I had been woken up by the duty corporal and gone off to work missing the official reveille on both occasions. In my pre-army days, I had conjured up a vision of a lone bugler, in the middle of an empty parade ground, playing a very brisk but pleasant tune on a shiny golden bugle. In my imagination he would be standing under a flag of the realm that would be gently fluttering in a warm breeze, just like Montgomery Cliff in 'From Here to Eternity'. Well the yanks might have been woken up in that way but us British lads were made of sterner stuff. We were brought back to life each morning by a fucking horrible little Scotsman bashing an empty dustbin and its lid together, and then throwing it up the centre isle of our billet.

I discovered this method of British wakeup calls on my third morning, when I was allowed to stay in bed a little longer because some other poor soul had copped for the officers mess duties. I was told that the last man out of the ablutions would have to clean and polish the offending dustbin and its equally offensive lid. This just about shattered every good illusion I ever had about the army; even the rifle I was issued with was rusty on the outside and the barrel-blocked solid with almost immovable thick toffee like gunk. My bayonet had firmly rusted itself into its scabbard. I don't know if the Lance Corporal was issuing the assignments or whether it was just my bad luck, but due to the fatigues I had been ordered to do, I just never had enough time to prepare any of my kit. Everybody else seemed to have cleaned and pressed their uniforms. Highly polished their brass buttons and shone their boots until the reflection was of mirror quality, or as the Lance-jack said you could see to shave in them. The next time I was ordered to polish the reveille dustbin and lid, I knew that the army was no place for me. I decided to test out a piece of very important information that I been carrying at the back of my mind, which was that all three branches of the Military services would discharge a sick regular volunteer, far sooner than a sick conscript.

In a way my second consignment of fatigues was a sort of demotion because I was put to work in the Sergeants mess, which was the identical to the Officers mess but without the silverware. On the third consecutive day of being sent to do fatigues in the Sergeants mess, I just couldn't take anymore of the British Armies' stupid rules and pointless regulations. As I bent over and pretended to pick up a sack of potatoes, I let out a yelp that sounded just like an injured puppy. I then put on a very elaborate show of great pain, at the same time indicating that it was emanating from my lower back. I threw myself on the ground and wriggled about trying to recreate the movements that I had seen a bloke do, when he was having an epileptic fit. I was immediately taken by Red Cross ambulance to Tidworth Military Hospital, where I was put into bed and given painkillers. It was at least a week before anybody came to examine me.

When a Doctor did eventually show up the first question he asked me was "Are you are a regular soldier or a national serviceman"?
I told him I was a regular. I assumed that he had read my records and knew that my stay in the army so far had been less than a week. He asked me if I had any objections if they sent for my civilian medical records. I had no qualms about letting the army see my papers as they would prove that I'd had trouble with my back in the past.

Gradually over the first week I pretended that the pain was easing, mainly so that I would be allowed to use the proper toilet facilities instead of a bedpan. My overall stay in hospital, lasted several weeks during which I was X-rayed hundreds of times from every angle they could manoeuvre my body into. When my civilian medical records eventually arrived they no doubt swung the probability of a discharge very much in my favour Most of the other lads in my ward were swinging the lead, we actually had bets on who would get discharged first. One day I was sitting on my bed when four or five officers swept into the ward, accompanied by the duty sister who pointed at me and told them my name and rank. One of them, who appeared to be in charge, gave me a clipboard with form on it.

"Sign here" he said.

I did and then he told me that it was my medical discharge and as of twenty-eight days from that moment I would no longer be a soldier, serving in the British Army.

The next day I was given a railway warrant and about thirty pounds in cash and told I could spend my four weeks discharge leave at home. The next train was due to leave Tidworth station for London was in two hours, I arrived on the platform with an hour and half to spare. I had been instructed to go back to the barracks in Blandford to change my clothes but I didn't bother, which meant that the only clothes I had to wear was my army gear which I continued to wear for several weeks. I was quite disappointed when the army sent my civilian clothes back, and asked me to return their uniform, as I had been having an above average, successful time with the girls while I was wearing it. I did seriously consider buying another uniform and carrying on the pretence of still being in the army, but I never did.

The army sent my discharge papers and pay book, along with a £200 cheque to my parents' address, where my mum was hoping that I would give her some of the money to pay for my keep. I told her as soon as I found someone to change the cheque for me I would come back and share my good fortune with her. I can honestly say with my hand on my heart that it was a very sincere intention on my part when I told her I would give her a share of the money. But once the cheque had turned into cash all the good thoughts in my head, immediately became all selfish ones. With money in my pocket and no work to do, it was easy for me to hang around the all night cafes and dives along Commercial Road. All types of people began to come into my life; nobody actually worked for a living around the area. The prostitutes generated sufficient money to keep a lot of pimps happy and they in turn spent it on the people who hung around them.

I think nearly every race in the world was represented in the square mile between Cable Street and Brick Lane; it was really a very early melting pot for all nationalities. As I came towards the end of my teen years I was pretty ignorant about life, I knew very little about sex, drugs, and drink, and even less about being a opportunist petty thief, which is what I told people I was. My biggest problem was trying to get enough money to maintain this way of life on a permanent basis and stay among the night people. Once I got my army cheque changed I never went home for a week. When I did eventually put in an appearance it was because I had run out of money and was suffering from lack of sleep. As soon as my mum caught sight of me she went berserk, all I had to show for my £200 was one new but very grubby college boy style pullover.

Because I needed sleep and I mean desperately needed sleep I tried to explain or rather lie my way into my mum's good books hoping that she would let me go to bed. During the entire week I had been missing the only time I'd slept was in a cafe sitting on a chair with my head resting on a table. Eventually after much cajoling she allowed me to go to bed. All was well until my dad arrived home from work and started ranting and raving. He told me several times to get out of his house but thanks to my dear old mum talking him round I was allowed to stay, but only on the condition that I promised to find a job and start contributing some money for my board and lodgings. For the millionth time, I promised that I would. My dad also said that while I was living under his roof I wouldn't be allowed to hang around the cafes and dives. At that moment because I was so desperately in need of sleep, I would have agreed to do anything they asked of me.

After two days, most of which I slept, I felt refreshed and told my mum that I was going out to find a job. In fleeting moments of guilt I tried to stop myself from becoming the horrible immoral person

I knew that was turning into, especially when I realised that I was finding it so easy lie to my parents, who did nothing but care for me. As soon as I stepped into the street outside of my mum's house that day I found it impossible not to be drawn back to Aldgate and the dives. Once I got back amongst the night people, I was once more overcome with the illusion that I could live a completely carefree way of life. Around the dumps and dives of Aldgate everyone seemed to be taken on face value. No one asked questions or worried about how much money you had, or what property you owned, neither did they care how you dressed or even how often you washed.

This time I was missing from home for about three weeks, sleeping rough on the streets as well as in the cafes. Drinking cheap plonk, taking uppers and downers and hanging around the dives was becoming a way of life to me. My mum must have nagged my dad so much that one day he searched all around the dives to find me. I don't know how but he did find me and took me home with him. On my arrival there my mum, seeing the filthy state I had let myself get into, burst into tears and pleaded with me once again to stay and get a proper job. To avoid upsetting her any further I agreed to do what she wanted. I tried very hard to stay at home on my parent's terms but there was always something that cropped up that I couldn't live with. I just wanted to be free to come and go as and when I liked without fear or favour. Of course I knew that this was totally unacceptable to my mum and dad, even over a short period of time, they soon got over the novelty of having me back at home. They were beginning to get more than a little fed up with me using their house like a hotel. My dad told me that if I didn't get a job and start contributing to my keep they were no longer going to tolerate my selfish behaviour.

It was during this period of re-civilising myself I met up with the Barrett brothers again, who told me that the contracts for the demolition work they had been waiting so long for had at last been finalised. When Ken asked me if I was still interested in working for him, it seemed like the perfect solution to appease all parties. I told my parents I was going away to work in Faversham with the Barretts.

PENTONVILLE JOHNNY

My mum looked very disappointed and asked me why I couldn't just get a job locally and behave like most of my schoolmates. I told her that this would pay much better money and would also give me a chance to see a part of the country that I had never seen before! She reluctantly agreed for me to go, but my dad was so pleased that I was leaving he couldn't stop smiling and almost started cheering.

The Barrett brothers had arranged to meet me at their flat, where on my arrival I met two other blokes who I was told were coming with us. I didn't know them very well, but when Tony told me their names, I realised that one of them was Ken's girlfriend's brother, Terry Chapman; his mate was called Michael Burke. Within a couple of minutes of arriving outside the Barretts flat, we all piled into the multi-paint-coated van and set off for Faversham. The trip down to East Kent, was quite an interesting experience and not only because of the scenery. The really interesting part was that Tony had decided this was the time that he was going to learn to drive properly. He informed us that although he had often driven the van before, he had never actually been on the road or in traffic with it, or with any other motorised vehicle for that matter.

After travelling in fear for many more hours than was necessary we finally arrived in Faversham, where we were taken straight to the job site, which I found quite surprising because I thought that we would go to our promised lodgings and change into our working clothes. Ken, who was already on the job, explained to us that we were going to lodge in his father's house, so what time we got there really didn't matter. He then pointed out that there was a good couple of hours more daylight left and he was rather hoping that we could start stripping the lead from the roofs of the houses that we were going to demolish. Which would mean that as soon as it was sold we would all get a quick couple bob out of the deal. This sounded sensible so without much ado, we got stuck in. By the time we had finished it was quite dark and very late, we were all looking forward to the hot bath and cooked meal, we had been promised.

Having got to know the Barretts as well as I did, it came as no surprise to me, when they told us on our arrival at their fathers council house that all six of us were going to share one pokey little room. To add insult to our disappointment they had neatly laid out on the floor three piss-stained, double mattresses that we were told had 'especially' been bought for us to sleep on. The look of horror that came over the faces of both Terry and Michael when they heard and saw what was being expected of them was a picture to behold. It was obvious that they had never experienced anything remotely like the awful conditions they now faced. We were then introduced to Harry Barrett, who bore no family resemblance whatsoever to any of his son's. He was short and thin with a nasty weasel like face and in a matter of minutes we discovered he had a very greasy, unpleasant nature that suited his looks. He was one of those people who couldn't or wouldn't look you in the eye when he was talking to you. From the things he was telling us, or rather bragging about himself, within the first hour or so of meeting him, I knew that he was never to be trusted.

The next day we were all back on the demolition site at the crack of dawn, after working for an hour or so Terry, and Michael walked off of the job saying that they were going to find a cafe to have breakfast. What they said and what they did were two totally different things, because when they returned to the site an hour or so later, both of them were carrying their suitcases. It was quite obvious that they had been back to Harry's and packed their gear. When they asked Ken for some money so they could return to London. Harry butted in and said because they were letting him and Ken down, he didn't think they should get any money. He also went on to say how expensive it had been to bring them down from London, and the use that they had already made of the lodging's would cost them much more than they had earned!

The show of indignation that Harry put on was worth a round of applause, the opinion I had already formed of him was proving to be very accurate. I also thought, that this wasn't a very reasonable or sensible way to treat his future daughter-in-laws brother. It became obvious to me that if things were left up to Harry no one would get paid for the work they had done. I put on an act of nonchalance to show that I wasn't too concerned or frightened of either the father or his sons, hopefully conveying to them the message that it wouldn't be wise to try the same trick on me. Then I walked over and very publicly gave Michael and Terry enough money to get home. At the same time I made sure that I was looking at both Ken and Harry as I said I would get it back from them when they sold the lead we had stripped the previous evening. Both of them nodded in agreement, I think Harry had read all the signs that I had sent out and realised that I wasn't afraid of any of them and in no way were they going to be able to treat me like a fool.

On the following Friday I collected my wages, plus what I had given the two boys and was very much looking forward to getting back to London for the weekend. Tony and Mickey told me that they were going to Herne Bay, to stay with their granny and their dads' two stepsisters. For the first time in ages I gave my mum some money for my keep. I had made myself a promise that I would do this, because I hated suffering from the pangs of guilt that came into my conscience whenever I caught a mental glimpse of sort of person I knew I was becoming. This way of thinking and self promises to make up for the wrongs I had done always came into my mind whenever I stayed off the booze for any length of time, as I had done during my first week in Faversham. In my early days down in Faversham, drinking played very little or almost no part in my every day activities. So my honest attempts to become a reformed character stood a much better chance of reaching their goal; sometimes during that week, even though I say it myself, I felt that I was well on the way to becoming a good person.

That weekend went by very quickly, before I knew it, it was Monday morning and I was bunking on the train to Kent. As I was making my way from the railway station to the demolition site, I began to notice that building-wise Faversham was a very attractive place. On my walk

I also discovered that it had several other even more eye-catching assets scattered around. Most of these appeared as I deliberately dawdled past a factory called the East Kent Packers, where a crowd of very lovely young women and teenage girls were sitting on a lawn enjoying an alfresco tea break in the morning sunshine. I slowed down from a dawdle to a snails pace so that I could soak in all the pleasures that a young red-blooded youth like myself could glean from such an encounter. As my dirty little mind was contemplating how and what I would do if ever I had the good fortune to get my hands on any of these beauties, some of the younger ones actually whistled at me.

The houses we were demolishing were in a little street called Tanner Street that was situated in the lower West Side of the town, by lower I mean downhill. Before I'd left on the Friday I had asked Harry to bring my working clothes to the site for me as it would save me a journey out to the house and back again. While I was getting changed we talked about the weekend, I let it drop into the conversation how attractive I thought some of the townswomen were. Mickey asked me where I'd seen these good-looking women.
I said to him, "If you come for a walk with me at lunchtime I will show you."
That day and for the rest of that week, the three of us took to walking past the Packing Factory as often as we possibly could, hoping to catch sight of all the nice, sexy looking young ladies.

I worked with the Barrett's around the Faversham and East Kent area for several months, over all we demolished more than 50 council owned houses and several private ones. I earned a lot of money but I'm sorry to say that as soon as I started to frequent the clubs and pubs my resolve to become a better person was quickly forgotten. I met and went out with quite a lot of the local women and girls, and being so preoccupied with all the free love that was available I rarely saw any reason to go back to London. How the women of Faversham thought and felt has always mystified me; by mystify I mean their behaviour towards strangers, like the Barrett brothers and myself were at the time when we first arrived in Faversham. Most of the ones I fancied were married but it didn't seem to make any difference to them whether they went out with me or not. As and when they came out with me they certainly didn't have any intention of staying sexually faithful to their husbands. Because my mum had always drummed into me her Victorian type morals, it naturally made me feel a bit guilty whenever I slept with a married woman. So as soon as I found out that quite a lot of the single girls didn't put up too much of a struggle to keep their knickers on, I tended to leave the married one's to the boys.

During the months I lived there I got to know and the area almost as well as I knew the East End. Most of the population around the council estate where we lodged were gypsy families. Who had given up travelling and settled down to live in houses. I got to know many of them very well, some of them through the pubs and others through various fights or bits of trouble that I had got in to during my stay there. There was one particular family that I got on very well with even though we had started off on a very bad footing.

The White Swan pub was on a T-junction where the two main roads in and out of the town centre met; it was situated about a hundred yards along from the Market Square. As in many other similar sized country towns this area was used by the townsfolk for both business and pleasure activities. On most days of the week, directly under the town hall, sheltered from the weather, they held a small market where you could buy vegetables, clothing, and the usual array of goods that can be found in most street markets. The actual Town Hall was built on stone pillars, which from some of the old drawings I had seen had at one time been very ornately carved, I think the building dated back to Norman times. Unfortunately over the years most of the once very delicate designs had been worn away, mainly due to erosion from traffic fumes and the constant brushing past of men, women and children. From the ground up to a height just above 6 ft the rounded columns now looked like they were just plain shiny stone.

It was in the White Swan that I met Henry Crichton; at the time both of us were slightly the worse for drink, which obviously wasn't the ideal circumstance for us to come together. We immediately took a dislike to each other and it was inevitable that we were going to argue or fight before the end of the evening. Very often on previous occasions I would get a record from behind the bar, put it on the record player, and let it automatically play it over and over. On this particular evening I chose 'The Heel' by Eartha Kitt and played it more than ever. I wasn't actually listening to it as I had an ulterior motive for doing what I was doing. From where I was sitting I could see that Henry was beginning to get hot under the collar, which was just what I was waiting and hoping for. Eventually he walked over to the record player took the record off and smashed it on the floor. Facing up to him I said, " Why did you do that."

"Because I fucking wanted to," he answered and immediately started to swing a punch at me, I ducked and the same time punched him in the stomach, several of the customers jumped in and pulled us apart. The landlady told us if we didn't stop fighting she would call the police.

As neither of us wanted to get nicked we stopped and very civilly arranged to continue the fight early the following evening in a field just out side the town which was used by locals as a sports and recreation ground. During my tea break the next morning I was sitting on the site watching the traffic and people pass by when I spotted Henry coming towards me, I thought to myself, why wait, went up to him and punched him in the face. After throwing and landing punches on each other for a minute or so I began to feel that I was getting the better of him, which made me really got stuck in kicking, biting and head butting. Suddenly without warning Henry turned and ran away shouting as he went that he would be coming back with his brothers.

"You can bring anyone you fucking like," I shouted in return. I then went back to work on the site. It wasn't long before a bloke called Thomas, who was a friend of Henry's and who had heard about the trouble between us, came on to the site and told me that Henry was the youngest but one of sixteen brothers. Including Henry all of them came in over six foot tall and were well built.

When I explained my predicament to the Barretts it was quite plain that they knew the Crichton family and most certainly didn't want to have any trouble with them. I don't know why I showed up at the field that evening, but I did. When I saw the entire Crichton clan my stomach muscles put all the butterflies they could gather to work on my bowels, putting put it politely I felt shit scared, and seriously thought my time had come to die. It looked like a scene from an old western movie where Wyatt Earp met the bad guys in the OK Corral. As I walked towards them I saw that they had brought their mum with them. Looking at the crowd of them I thought this family are seriously abusing the privilege of being ugly. I stopped at what I thought was a safe enough distance from them and the mother walked up to me and asked if I had beaten her son up on my own or had my friends helped me? Where I got the cheek from I don't know, but when I finally summoned up the courage to answer her, I said, " If I ever needed help to knock the shit out of a prat like your son, I would give up and die." My brain was racing along six to the dozen trying to come up with some plan or excuse to extricate myself from this very frightening situation, without losing face.

Old mother Crichton turned and told Henry and one of his brothers to come and join us, when they had done so she said to Henry, "You are not going to bring unnecessary trouble or shame to this family I want you to shake hands and apologise to this man." To my surprise, Henry without question did exactly what as his mother had told him to. I can't find the words to explain the relief that came over me when I realised that these people lived by a sort of old-fashioned code of honour, at least as long as their womenfolk were around. When the family began to disperse the oldest Crichton brother invited me to go for a drink with them. The elation that I was feeling made me want to accept his invitation but some little semblance of sanity told me that if I went drinking with them and had too much the trouble could start all over again. I declined his offer and went back to Harry Barrett's house where I watched T.V for the rest of the night.

For a while I began courting a young blonde girl named Pat Saunders, whom I grew very fond of, much to the dismay of her parents. Several times before I found out how much her mum and dad disliked me, I thought but wasn't certain that her father had unnecessarily insulted me, I couldn't understand why as I was never discourteous to him or his wife. Whenever I met old man Saunders in a pub as I often did he was always very jolly and carefree and never let the opportunity of me buying him a drink pass by. One day I asked Pat if she would like to get engaged, she smiled and said yes. I went directly off to local jewellers and bought a very cheap ring and that evening I went around to meet Pat, to put the ring on her finger. After I had done this, we went into her parent's house to let them know about our engagement.

On hearing the news, her father suddenly went into what I can only call describe as a Blue Fit. This came as quite a shock to both Pat and myself, as we had actually spoken to him about it, in the pub on the previous night. As I've already said he had often insulted me in the past but this time there was no mistaking it he was right over the top, so much so that Pat lost her temper and swore at him. Immediately Pat's mother heard the swear words she turned around and pushed her face into mine until our noses almost touched, and then told me exactly what and how little she thought of me.

To say that I was taken by surprise by her very insulting outburst would be quite an insignificant explanation of the way I felt. Apart from going out with her daughter, I'd rarely had any contact with Mrs Saunders. I certainly didn't feel I deserved to be treated in the manner which both of Pats' parents were now treating me. It would have been quite easy for me to punch old man Saunders or inflict some sort of injury on him but once again my sober Victorian way of thinking told me to keep my cool. Thinking that one day these people, when they had got over the initial shock of their daughter's engagement, might forgive me for whatever they thought I had done wrong, and take me in as their son in law. Not only did I have a Victorian upbringing I also had a very vivid imagination.

Pat's father forbade her to see me again as he was still convinced that I was the one who had called him a fucking miserable old bastard, even though Pat had told both him and her mum that she was the one that had said it. For a while I continued to see her, but as I wasn't allowed to see her in or near her house it became very difficult pretending that we weren't together. Gradually the relationship began to peter out and when I wasn't with her I started going out with other girls. For some time I carried a real sense of injustice around in my mind over what had happened between Pat and myself. It was around about this time that I first met Harry Swan who was a member of another very well known local family. I was introduced to him by Ken Barrett who afterwards told me that the Swan family, were not the sort of people to get on the wrong side of. As I had fallen foul of most people in Faversham and the surrounding areas Ken's warning went totally unheeded.

The earlier incident and outcome of my confrontation with the Crichtons had unfortunately gained me a false reputation as some sort of hard man. This I was unaware of until one evening when Tony Barratt got drunk in his girlfriend's house and her father asked me if I would go and talk to him. I had never seen Tony in the type of mood that I found him in when I arrived at his girl friends. He looked straight at me and said, "I am going to prove that the reputation you have got is a load of bollocks." With that he lashed out at me. All I saw was a flash or glint of light reflect off of whatever he had in his hand, the next thing I knew, I was blind in my right eye and through my left one all I could see was blood spurting all over the place. Before I could recover my wits about me and catch hold of him, he had run out of the house.

When I got up enough courage to look in a mirror I was relieved to see that the cut was above my eye and not through it as I had first

73

thought. Sarah's mother gave me a towel to cover the wound and told her husband to drive me to the local hospital where they stitched me up and asked what had happened. Without thinking too much about what I was saying, I told them what had happened and who had done it. Sarah's dad had been cut across the backs of both his hands when he had raised them to protect his face. I asked him what had made Tony so angry, what he told me wasn't very pleasant to listen to. It turned out that some people had been saying all sorts of nasty things about me, helping my unjustified reputation to spread and this was making the Barrett family feel very uncomfortable being around me, especially Tony. Someone had told him, that I had said I was so hard and in control that if I wanted to sleep with his girl friend, Sarah, there would be nothing he or his brothers could do to stop me. None of the Barretts were what you would call stupid but it did come as a bit of a shock that they believed the sort of crap people were coming out with. They surely must have known that it was all bullshit

It wasn't long after this incident that I told Pat what I had been doing behind her back and that it was over between us and within a matter of days I returned to London. Where I drifted back to the cafes and dives and also started hanging around one or two clubs in the Soho area. During this period I spent a long time sleeping rough, what I mean by rough is sleeping on or under the tables in one or another of the dives. It didn't matter very much if there were good or bad things happening to me during this part of my life because I just wanted to avoid the reality of being alone with my confused thoughts and feelings. To achieve this numbness of my emotions I smoked dope, drank lots of cheap wine and also started taking pep pills, the effect I got from them me made feel so safe I accepted that it was the right and natural thing to do. Sometimes I would strike lucky and one or other of the prostitutes that I had got to know would take home me for the night, but this didn't happen on a regular basis.

In one particular cafe called the 41, which was in Dean Street, a narrow road that still runs between Shaftsbury Avenue and Soho Square, I met and started hanging around with a large crowd of

Irishmen all about the same age as myself. Although a woman named Kathy managed and ran the café singled handed it actually belonged to her husband, who nobody outside of a very select few ever got to know. I did see him on several occasions but never got to speak to him, Kathy had a daughter also named Kathy who, with everybody, using his or her inventive intellect to the full, was later in life re-christened Young Kathy. She and I became very good friends through one of the Irish boys who called himself Pongo. He was an excellent dancer as was young Kathy.

One night in Thomas's Club in Frith Street, Pongo was dancing with Young Kathy and openly showing off his skills as Rock and Roller. When he saw me watching him he stopped dancing, came over and asked if I thought I could do better. It must have been the way I was looking at them that made him feel that I was in some way disapproving of him, which wasn't actually true. Many times in my life the way I've looked at people has been misconstrued as some sort of insult or criticism but I can assure you that most of times this has happened it has been a mistake, as it was on this occasion. I did take up his challenge, however, and started dancing with young Kathy, the way we immediately picked up each other's moves and rhythm made it feel like we had been dancing partners all our lives. Several people put money in the jukebox to make sure that the music didn't stop and asked us to keep dancing.

We must have danced for about 20 minutes or more each time a record finished we got a round of applause, this didn't do much for Pongo's ego but it certainly did a lot for mine. For several months after that night, whenever Kathy and I were in seen together in any of the clubs or dives, people would ask us to dance for them. One night as we were dancing and amusing the crowd down in the Batty Street Club, I swung around as I usually did, but because the dance area was a bit over crowded there wasn't really enough space to go all out as I had done. The restriction caused my elbow to hit Young Kathy in the eye, which immediately started both swelling, and closing.

She looked like she was going to pass out so I carried her up the stairs to the street to get some fresh air. Young Kathy was a great favourite among the Irish population in both the West and East End of London. When the false rumour was spread around that I had deliberately injured her, I had to sit in the '41' cafe for several weeks or more always in the company of both Kathy and Young Kathy, just to prove to all and sundry that it had been an accident and to show that we were still very good friends. If I wasn't in her company for any reason during this period, I found myself fighting and arguing with a lot of drunken Paddy's. Sometimes some of them only wanted an excuse to fight me because my friendship with Kathy had upset their mate Pongo.

Every night in one or another of the dives in both the East and West Ends of London, there would be some sort of confrontation and a great deal of violence. This was mainly caused by the suspicious jealousy of the foreign pimps who liked to be thought of as hot-blooded Continentals. People were being wantonly stabbed or slashed for little or no reason at all, and it was happening almost continuously. Some of the prostitutes deliberately caused trouble; just to become the centre of attention. Because of my overwhelming need to be wanted and liked, I wouldn't hang around with the same crowd of people for too long, just in case they got to know me too well and uncovered the two faced, 'everything to all men' side of my nature. I didn't always judge the timing of my departures from one group of friends to the next correctly, and was quite often ejected from the social gatherings with a 'if you come back here you're dead warning.' This wasn't the case when I changed my allegiance from the West End Paddies back to a small English crowd of people who I had known from school days, one or two of them were pimps and the rest were opportunist or petty thieves like myself.

If anybody had asked me what attraction there was in the way of life I was living, there was no way on earth I could explain it. It was more to do with the crazy way I thought rather than felt about it. Even to this present day I still have shudders when I remember the grip it held me in. My parents obviously cared very much for me, their home was always clean and tidy and most of time very welcoming. I was never allowed to go hungry or dirty while I lived there. Yet those were the very things I chose to do and did, to maintain my existence in the painted sewers I called cafes, clubs and dives.

It became inevitable that I would be arrested sooner or later. The first time it happened I don't think it was entirely my fault; one of the boys I had grown up with, named Peter Molineau had stolen a car and then picked up a young, attractive, unattached prostitute. Two other lads and myself were standing chatting on the corner of Commercial Road and Batty Street when we saw Peter drive past. We shouted for him to stop and pick us up, he spun the car around and skidded to a halt along side of us, jumped out of it and told us his dad bought it for him the previous day. We all knew different but did not disagree with him, none of us really cared that much.

One of the boys whose name was George, held a sort of Indian sign over Peter, even I had beaten him up in the past so it wasn't very difficult to persuade him to take us for a ride in his new car. The ride turned out to be rather more than we bargained for. Peter in his eagerness to impress the girl and us revved up the car engine and pointed it at the open road. He actually drove us at break neck speeds all the way down to Kent, Dover to be more precise. On the journey each of us tried our luck with the girl who was passed from lap to lap in turn. She allowed each of us kiss her and fondle her tits. When it was my turn, I, being I, naturally assumed that she had chosen me to be the first one she was going to go all the way with. However, just like the other two before me, I got so far and then she told me the same as she had told them, which was that as much as she wanted to, we couldn't have sex, because she had caught VD.

It certainly stopped all my sexual desires and intentions when she whispered that little sentence in my ear. My knowledge of VD was zero. I knew just enough to know that it wasn't very advantageous to catch it. Not wanting the girl to think that sex was the only interest

I had in her, I made up the excuse that I had a touch of cramp and pushed her on to George's lap. He obviously went into the same routine as the rest of us had done. We laughed quite loudly when it came to the part where the girl whispered to George about having VD, because his reactions were very different from ours, he called her a dirty fucking cow and just pushed her on to the floor in front of him.

"I can't help it," she said, "I will see all of you alright when I'm cured, you won't be sorry then." None of us made further sexual advances towards her; she just became a passenger in a stolen car, the same as the rest of us.

Just as we arrived in Dover the car engine spluttered once or twice and then cut out, we coasted for a short distance and came to a halt, very obviously out of petrol. It was then that Peter admitted to having nicked it.

George said, "It doesn't really matter, just go and get a can of petrol and get us back to London". Peter told us he was broke and asked if one of us we would mind buying the petrol? It came as no surprise to find out that none of us had any money.

George punched Peter in the head, saying, "Fancy driving us all the way down here you silly fucking prat."

At that precise moment a police car came down the street, shone its roof lamp on us and then parked directly in our path. My ability as a runner had for many years and on frequent occasions saved me from being nicked. On seeing three large constables emerge from their car and then start running towards us, I fully intended putting and testing my athletic talents to their uppermost limits. When I took off Peter followed me. We ran for a considerable distance turning left and right, in and out of very unfamiliar roads and streets. Although it was beginning to get light, neither of us saw the hole in the ground, Peter ran past me and fell, straight into it, I followed suit and landed on top of him.

Neither of us were hurt, just winded and gasping for breath, at the same time trying not to breathe too loud because we could hear what we thought were the police searching around above us. The hole we had fallen into was a disused cellar measuring about eight-foot deep and ten wide, strewn with piles of rubbish, which luckily had broken our fall. After waiting for things to go quiet we emerged from the hole and took stock of our situation, no money, dirty clothes and at a guess we were fifty miles from home. Our prospects weren't exactly what you would call good. When Peter suggested that we should nick another car the thought of it made me feel a bit nervous but taking into account the plight we were in, I soon accepted the idea. We felt really lucky when a couple of minutes later we came across an unlocked car with the key in the ignition.

As it was parked very close and directly outside a house we decided it would be a wise move to push it along the street some way before starting it up as we didn't want to disturb the owner by turning over the engine. When we got in the car, Peter turned the ignition key but nothing happened.
"Try it again," I told him. He did, still nothing.
"Let's try to bump start it," he said.
"OK," I replied.
Peter remained sitting behind the steering wheel while I started to push it. Just then a postman came walking down the street towards us.
"Give us a shove," I called out to him. He immediately came over and started pushing along side of me. He said, "Tell your mate to turn left when we reach the corner because that street runs downhill."
Peter did as he suggested and as the car reached the top of the, both the postman and myself jumped in. The hill was long and steep, which soon helped the car to pick up speed.
"This should do the trick," Peter said.
"Yes," echoed the postman.

As I looked down towards the gear stick I cringed, because there for the entire world and his brother to see, was a large open space where the engine should be sitting. I could quite clearly see the road passing at a great rate of knots beneath us. "What a pair of bright prat's," I thought to myself. By this time the car was travelling uncontrollably at more than thirty miles an hour and getting faster by the second, which meant that without having any brakes at our disposal our only two means of stopping were either to crash head on into something or to run it alongside a wall. The second of these options is thankfully what Peter took, causing considerable damage to the car and the wall in the process. Eventually the car scraped to a halt about ten yards from a stationary police car, unfortunately for us, one of old Bill was a personal friend of the owner of the car we were trying to steal. They arrested Peter and the postman and told me follow them; I still can't explain why I just followed them like a lamb and never even thought about running away. The postman went into a complete state of both shock and panics and was trying desperately to tell them that he was innocent and how he had unwittingly got involved with us.

When we arrived inside the station, the desk sergeant recognised the postman, and after getting him to write out a statement let him go home. As I hadn't been caught or involved with the police since my school days, I believed them when they told me that if I made a statement admitting the illegalities that I had been involved in, things would go much easier for me in court. One of policeman questioned me and wrote down all the answers I gave him on an official looking form which, when he had completed, he pushed across the table and told me to read and sign. Without thinking I signed my own name, not the false one that I had given to him earlier. As I handed the paper back to him I saw my mistake standing out like a beacon. When he brought it to my attention I just told that I had decided to be honest with him.

When Peter and I had finished giving the police all the information they needed to convict us we were put into a cell. Neither of us were overly surprised to see that George and the other chap were already there (I never saw the girl again). After several hours we were taken out of the cells put into a police van and driven to Canterbury Magistrate's Court, which we saw was attached to the local prison. It was the first time I had stood in a proper Dock charged with an adult criminal offence. The memories of my juvenile court appearance flooded back to me, the thought of crying entered my mind because I thought it had worked so well for me when I was a kid. A kaleidoscope of ideas ran through my head, which coincided with the fear running through my body.

The four of us looked as if we had been dragged through a hedge backwards, the Magistrate didn't seem to hesitate for a minute. He listened to the charges against us and immediately remanded us to Canterbury prison. Not many minutes had passed before we were handcuffed and led out of the courthouse, along the street and in through the main gates of the nick. It was the first time I'd actually seen an adult prison close up. It looked and felt pretty ominous. My brain was reminding me of how stupid I had been not to run away when I'd had the chance, instead of inanely following like a lamb to the slaughter.

My memory is slightly confused about this prison and its lay out, all I remember about my arrival there was being given a bedroll, consisting of two sheets one blanket and a brown and green knitted eiderdown plus a piss pot. On receipt of them, I was taken on to B wing and told to go up the stairs to the top floor. As I walked along the landing in the direction I had been pointed in I started to wonder why each level had very heavy duty wire mesh strung across it stretching the entire length and breadth of the cellblock. The officer escorting me to my cell seemed very unexpectedly polite when he told me that the second cell from the end on my left, would be my home for the duration of my stay.

As soon as the door closed behind me, I felt very securely locked in the first proper prison cell I had ever been in. I slung my bedroll on to what passed as a bed and burst into tears just like a child. As the acute sense and feeling of loneliness descended on me, I began to cry uncontrollably and unashamedly. This went on in both the privacy of my cell and in the open public areas such as the workshops and exercise yards and continued, on and off, for the entire ten days of

81

my remand. I also allowed the unknown fear of what my appearance at court was going to bring deprive me of sleep. The prison food made me feel sick just to look at it. It didn't help my time to pass any quicker, having to listen to the clock of Canterbury Cathedral, (which is less than half a mile from the prison), chime every fifteen minutes and strike every hour throughout the my entire stay.

While we were on remand, Peter's dad came to visit him and told him to ask me if I would tell the police that I had stolen the car we had travelled down from London in. He said if I agreed to take the blame, he would pay me X amount of money. For a time I thought about agreeing to do it but the idea that I might have to stay in prison a second longer than was absolutely necessary certainly helped me to decline his offer. By the time we got back to court I had lost a considerable amount of weight and as I was very skinny in the first place this extra weight loss made me look very skeletal. I think the magistrate took this into consideration and decided that the ten days remand had been sufficient imprisonment. It turned out that Peter's dad had been worried that his son, being the original car thief, was going to be the only one of us to be disqualified from driving. Hence the reason he had told Peter to offer all three of us a bribe to take the blame. As it turned out it didn't really matter because we were all convicted of the same offences and each given a two-year driving ban plus a year's probation.

A reporter who worked on our local paper and who was supposed to be a friend of ours had a field day writing about and naming two, Big Time London Car Thieves, who went down to Kent and stole a vehicle without an engine. Both Peter and myself had been to very great pains not to mention the missing engine to anyone, but when all and sundry read it the East London Advertiser, we became the subjects of many long cruel jibes.

CHAPTER 4

There followed a rather unfortunate and very sad period in my life that started one day when I walked into Vincent's club. This so-called Club was really a shop basement that consisted of two rooms each about twenty square feet in area. The entrance was just an ordinary street door next to a café, if you weren't actually looking for it or knew of its existence you could quite easily miss it. Immediately inside the door was a very steep flight of wooden stairs that dropped about eight feet below pavement level. At the bottom of these you had to turn sharp right through a narrow doorway into the first room, looking to your left, in the far corner was a Jukebox that not only played music, it created the only source of light in the room.

Directly opposite the entrance to the so called music and dance room was another small doorway that led into what was called the snooker room, this consisted of a bar on the right hand side and a single unisex toilet in the furthest corner on the left. In the middle of the room was a three-quarter sized snooker table that was lit up by a six-foot long fluorescent tube that was hanging from the ceiling on a crudely converted toilet chain and fed electricity through two exposed bare wires. There were also several chairs and three or four card tables randomly spread around. Snooker was never played in the club; the primary and only use I ever saw the tatty green baize table used for was marathon crap games. A single, forty-watt bulb dimly illuminated the bar. All the walls were painted from the floor to the ceilings in a very bright yellow gloss; the floors were covered in black asphalt and the entire place was desperately short of ventilation. Sometimes I had seen as many as sixty people crammed into the two rooms, all taking part in illicit drinking, gambling, and on rare occasions in those early days, drug taking.

I feel that I must explain a little bit more about the dives. For several years most of them were owned or rented by Maltese people who opened them up as drinking or gambling clubs. Due to the illegality of them the people who ran them were often, after a short passage of time, forced by the police to either close down, or pass on whatever

83

legal or moral agreements they held on the premises to their mates. Each time this happened the dives would be rechristened to whatever the new owner or tenants name was. For instance, Batty Street had been named Tony's, Paul's and Peter's, among numerous others, at this particular point in time it carried the title of Vincent's. Vincent was a large man who had, at some time previous to my getting acquainted with him, accidentally or otherwise lost his left arm. This disability didn't in any way prevent him from being able to take care himself when faced with any sort of violent confrontation.

When I walked into Vincent's, on that ill fated afternoon I was surprised to find about half a dozen of my old school pals drinking in there. It was obvious that some of them had had more than just a little taste of booze. Billy Mac as we called him was quite a big bloke, so was his best pal Billy Fisher, these two were both acting in a way that showed they were very high. As well as my mates, I estimated that there were at least thirty people in the place, the majority of them being Maltese pimps, several of who were accompanied by their prostitute girlfriends. Some of the girls were dancing with my mates and being subjected to some very rude suggestions and the occasional bit of groping.

I stepped to the left side of the entrance and leant against the wall, watching what was going on. I didn't take much notice, when a fairly well built Maltese bloke came in and stood in the doorway next to me. That was until he took one or two paces into room and hit Billy Mac on the back of the head with a Coke Cola bottle. When Billy turned around and asked me who had hit him, I pointed at the bloke. With that Billy swung a punch that landed squarely on the Maltese bloke's chin, rendering him instantly and completely unconscious. Within seconds the entire place was pandemonium, bottles, glasses, chairs, knives and coshes were being used. We did the best we could to put up a defence but it was pretty hopeless because we were outnumbered two or three to one. Somehow we managed to fight our way up the stairs and out into the street. Even when we got out in the open we really hadn't got a dog's chance of winning the battle as quite a few more Maltese blokes arrived on the scene and joined in the fight. One of our mates ran down the street and got his car and then drove back to pick us up. As we scrambled into the car, we made very sure that the Maltese pimps knew that we would be coming back.

When my pals dropped me off, I made my way to the St Louis club, which was about a mile from Vincent's. I stayed there drinking until Martin Olsen, who had also been involved in the fight, came in and told me that the trouble at Vincent's was going to start up again. I went with him to Batty Street where there were about twenty or more of our friends as well as those who had been there in the afternoon. They were all milling around waiting for the trouble to start. Mickey Holland, Bobby Woodford, Billy Mac and Billy Fisher were discussing what would be the best way to get at the Maltese pimps who they thought were waiting in the club. When Martin and me joined in the conversation one of the group suggested that we should all rush into the club as fast as we could. One of the other boys said, "It would be suicidal to do that because the narrowness of the doorways at the top and bottom of the stairs would only allow one or two of us to enter at a time, giving the Maltese a chance to pick us off too easily".

As I'd been drinking most of the day my courage was at a peak so I bravely volunteered to go down into the club and see how many of the Maltese blokes in there were on our 'wanted list'. As I looked through the doorway of the music room, I became strangely calm and very sober. I could see upwards of 40 people there, I tried to be as casual as possible but it was obvious to me that they were ready and waiting for us. There were blokes there that I knew were hardened gangsters from around the West End and Soho area, several of whom were openly carrying guns. Luckily for me most of them were standing on the opposite side of the room. I did a very smart about turn, and made what I thought was a dignified but hasty exit. I felt very relieved to get out of the place with all my bits and pieces still attached to me.

When I explained the situation to the boys they agreed with me that it would be stupid to make any attempt to get into the club.

Terry Wilson said, "I think we should blow the cowardly bastards up!"

On hearing that, Bobby Woodford went to his car and came back with a can of petrol, some paper and a box of matches. I took the can and poured some of its contents down the stairs. Terry was holding the paper while Bobby tried to set light to it but the draught going down into the basement kept blowing the matches out.

I remember saying, "Don't waste your time with the fucking bit of paper, and give me the matches."

I flung the can, which still had a considerable amount of petrol in it, down the stairs and then struck a match, as it flared I threw it onto the spilt petrol. Because I had never seen petrol ignited this way before, I wasn't in any way prepared for what happened next.

There was an almighty flash followed by a sound very akin to a hurricane blowing through a large tree. I was almost sucked down the stairs as the flames drew the oxygen from the street into the club. My eyebrows and the front of my hair were singed; the screams from below sounded inhuman. I closed the door and started to run away. I hadn't covered more than 10 yards, which was about half the distance to the corner of the street, when a policeman came charging past me.

"What's going on," he shouted, as he rushed towards the club door.

I stopped and watched him push the door open, which allowed in more oxygen causing another furnace like burst of flames to shoot into the cellar. Although it seemed like it had only been a matter of seconds, lots of things had happened. One of the people inside the club had been trying to get out; he was standing half way down the stairs when the copper opened the door. Suddenly to his horror he became engulfed in flames and to make matters even worse he was carrying the petrol can, which began to act like a flame thrower whilst at the same time there was burning petrol spilling out of it splashing all over his body.

He slung the can across the street and pushed the policeman out of his path, screaming for help, threw himself down on to the pavement and started rolling over and over trying to put the flames out. Someone came out of the cafe next door and covered him over with a blanket. When I looked around and saw that there was a very large crowd gathering I slipped away and went back to the St Louis club, where I spent the rest of the night drinking and talking. I remember telling a girl about the fire at Vincent's, not only did I tell her about it, I insisted that all the Maltese bastards in it deserved to be burnt to death. She argued that it wasn't right and that it should have been the English blokes who got burnt. I called her a dirty old slag, threatened to slap her and walked away, found a comfortable place to sit and promptly fell asleep. First thing the next morning I went to the public baths, where I slept for several more hours, until the water turned cold and woke me up.

About two days after the fire, I went into Barney's café, which was only about 50 yards around the corner from Vincent's. It was a long narrow place with the tables and chairs set out like a railway buffet car. I ordered two bacon rolls and a cup of tea, which I was very much enjoying until a small crowd of Maltese blokes came in and stood blocking the doorway. One of them was Vincent, the others I had seen around but didn't know very well. Apart from them and me there were quite a few other people in Café, most of who were strangers to me.

A chap named Dennis came over to me and said, "If I were you John I would try to get out of here because the malts have sent for the police."

When I looked around for an escape route I saw that there was no way out, other than through the main door which the Maltese were securely guarding and from the way they were looking in my direction, I knew that I wasn't going to be allowed to get through it in one piece. I finished my bacon rolls, drank my tea then sat back and considered my situation. Feeling quite sure that Vincent and his pals couldn't bear witness to me taking any active part on the night of the fire I decided, rather than to run the risk of getting seriously injured trying to fight my way out, I would take my chances with the police. The Maltese blokes seemed to be getting more and more agitated. Dennis, who spoke their language, told me that they had just heard that the chap who had got burnt on the stairs was now on the critical list and getting worse. This piece of information was causing these blokes to get even more upset, Dennis went on to say that one of them was carrying a gun and was about to shoot me. I was very relieved when the police arrived and Vincent pointed me out to them. I put on what I thought would be an Oscar winning performance of surprised innocence, as they led me away.

I was taken to Leman Street police station where I had had the dubious pleasure of being a guest on many occasions in the past. At first the police acted as if they weren't really interested in me, they said that anyone who could burn that many Maltese ponces in one go was more of a hero than a criminal. As my opinion of the Maltese was based purely on the attitude and life style of pimps I had got to know around Aldgate and the West End, I didn't particularly hold the entire Maltese race in very good esteem. Because I thought they shared my prejudice I was almost convinced that what the police were saying to me was genuine. The desk Sergeant told me that I would have to wait in a cell until it was time for me to be questioned by some Senior Detectives. Several hours later a Detective Inspector and his Sergeant came into the cell. The eleven by eight-foot cells in Leman Street were just white glazed bricks from floor to ceiling with a six-foot by two-foot, wooden board raised eighteen inches above the asphalt floor on a solid concrete block, which served as both a bed and a seat.

I was sitting on the board when they came in. I knew the Inspector from past dealings that I had had with him, he wasn't a man to be trusted or taken for a fool.
"Well John what have you been up to now," he said to me.
"Nothing that I can think of," I replied.

This wasn't the answer he was hoping to get from me. I realised this when his expression changed from a welcoming smile to a threatening grimace as he punched me in the face.

"I would like you to co-operate with us John, because any one who burns Maltese bastards is OK in our book, aren't they Sergeant?" he said.

From then on they played Good Cop, Bad Cop. The good cop gave me a cigarette and the bad cop punched or kicked me, some of the time even the uniformed officers took turns slapping me around. My clothes were taken away for so called forensic testing which left me standing in just my vest and underpants. There was a short spell when they rolled up some wet towels and then used them to beat me around the body. I was determined that I wouldn't admit to anything. I was now a very sober thinking person and fully realised the seriousness of what I had done plus the consequences that I would have to face if I opened my mouth. The police told me that there was going to be at least twenty charges of attempted murder and maybe one of actual murder.

I lost track of the time I spent in the police station, I don't remember whether it was three or four days that they held me. I was eventually released on what they call a bench summons; this meant that they could call me back any time they wanted to, without having to go in front of a Magistrate to apply for extra holding time. I didn't care about any terms and conditions they placed on my release, I just knew that under no circumstances was I ever going back to that police station. Suffering from considerable pain I went to the London Hospital emergency department where the doctor who examined me said that I was lucky that the internal workings of my stomach hadn't been ruptured; I didn't tell him how or why I had received all the bruising. He gave me a prescription for painkillers and told me to go home and rest for at least a week.

In those days my mum kept newspapers for two weeks or more before she threw them out so while I was resting and recovering I caught up with the news about the fire. Six of my mates had been arrested and charged with all sorts of offences. Somehow my dad got to hear through the grapevine that I wasn't going to be charged, where I had summoned up my resolve and determination not to talk from I don't know but it certainly paid off. I read in one of the papers that my friends were due up in court about a week later. When I went there to see what was going to happen to them, I got the biggest and most hurtful shock of my life.

It happened when Terry Wilson's mum walked up very close to me, looked me straight in the face, spat on the ground between my feet, and then called me a fucking dirty little grass. I'd taken a lot of physical punishment in the police cells but this untrue accusation hurt me more than anything I had ever known. To be a called a grass in the East End was worse than being a child molester. Before people found out differently, I was threatened with death and many forms of torture, but nothing they could physically do to me, could possibly compare with the emotional hurt of being labelled a grass. Not to be trusted by your closest and longest friends meant that you hadn't got any friends. The tortured feelings I suffered during the following months were and are still indescribable.

It was at this time that I met up with a girl that I knew from my childhood days spent in the war shelter, she was a Jewish girl named Edna. Fortunately she knew nothing about the life I had led in the years since I had last seen her. It turned out that she had had a baby out of wedlock, which she was bringing up in an area where she wasn't known. This was to hide from the shame that relatives and neighbours showered on single mothers in those days. We had seen each other a few times over the years as we were growing up but this chance meeting was a Godsend, I couldn't believe my luck when she invited me back to her flat for a meal. After we finished dinner we talked for several hours and did some serious petting, followed by very enjoyable sex. She asked me if I would like to stay for the weekend; not wanting to appear pushy I suggested that as I had missed both the last bus and tube back to the East End maybe I should stay, but only until the next morning.

However, I did stay for the weekend and the four or five weeks that followed. Edna's flat was in Muswell Hill not far from Archway station where I often caught the tube back to the East End. On a trip back to see to my parent's one day I met a bloke named Salvo, who was half-Maltese and half-English. He asked me what I was doing in that part of London, he seemed very concerned, even worried that I had seen him. I told him that although I hadn't grassed on my pals I was still staying out of their way because I couldn't prove I hadn't. He suddenly seemed very eager to tell me that his Maltese dad had been told by some of the pimps, who had been in the club on the night of the fire bomb, (as they now called it) that they were so upset at my being released without being charged, that they had purposely started the rumour that I was a grass in the hopes that I would be shot dead or seriously injured by my own people. I am sure that this would have happened had I not met Edna and been able to stay away from the East End.

I carried this information around in my head until I couldn't bear it any longer; I just had to go and confront some of my mates who I had heard were now out on bail. Terry Wilson and Mickey Holland had had all the charges against them dropped because they had been able to prove that they were at the London hospital at the time of the firebomb having treatment for the stab wounds they had received in the afternoon. When I told them what Salvo had said both of them told me that it had been hard for them to believe I was a grass and then they told me they were sorry if it had caused me any harm. The other four blokes who had been charged were still in custody so I had to wait until they came up at the Thames Court to be committed for trial at the Old Bailey.

On that day, I went to the court and listened to all the witnesses giving evidence, both for and against them. One very big surprise I got was that Salvo; the bloke I'd met on Archway tube station, was one of the main witnesses against them. I realised then that, like me, he had been in hiding when I had seen him. My friends were allowed out on bail, when I got to talk to them outside of the court I asked them how they could have possibly believed that I had grassed on them. Knowing that I couldn't push the matter too far, I accepted their apologies and walked away, feeling like the loneliest person on earth. Thinking to myself how could or would I ever know if they believed me, or would feel they could ever trust me again.

During that period I drank quite heavily using the effect of the booze not to get drunk, as I had always done in the past, but to counteract my low self-esteem. I lost track of Edna when she moved and never gave me her new address! It was about then, I became an almost permanent resident in the St Louis Club. The St Louis was an Afro Caribbean Club mainly frequented by black Americans who were stationed at the various army and air force bases around the U. K. The owner of the St Louis was called Serif, commonly called Sheriff by the club members. He was a very sneaky African, however, after having dealings with Salvo I was quite use to sneaky bastards. Sheriff was always very grateful to any one that could get him a white woman to use for sexual purposes and knowing all the prostitutes that I knew enabled me to keep him well supplied. Out of gratitude for my services he gave me a very well paid job as his club doorman.

The Club opened every afternoon at three o'clock and remained so until the early hours of the next day. For several months I rarely saw any white people, which, suited me, very well as I was still suffering a lot of emotional hurt over being called a grass. Working on the door as a bouncer, part of my job was to search the Americans and their bags removing any weapons or alcohol I found. It didn't take long for me to get to know the ones that carried the drink, and it became very easy for me to do a deal with them, whereby if I didn't relieve them of their alcohol, sometime later they would share it with me. I became very friendly with two particular black Americans who were named Burns and Allen.

The way this friendship started was a bit out of the ordinary. One of the girls that used the Club often made out that she was a German and pretended that she could only speak a few words of English. Why she did this was a mystery to me in fact her entire situation was rather crazy. She was a white prostitute that would only solicit and have paid sex with black men; a very elderly lady always accompanied her. Her pimp was a bisexual white bloke who I had got pissed with on several occasions.

One night in the Club she convinced Allen to go back to her flat with her, for what she told him, was going to be a very good time! When he asked his mate to wait for him, he said that he would be back in about and hour or so. After Burns had waited most of the night and realising the Club was about close, he asked me if I could tell him where the woman lived. I said that I would take him to her house and stay with him because I didn't want to cause her any trouble. When we got to the place, we saw Allen standing outside shouting and waving his fists at the upper windows. He looked very distraught and dishevelled. At that particular time I didn't know Burns and Allen very well, but whenever I had seen them, they had always been dressed and groomed immaculately so seeing Allen as ruffled and as untidy as he was now came as a bit of a surprise.

Burns told him to cool down and asked him what was wrong, after a while Allen began to calm down slightly. He explained that while he had been in bed with the girl, someone had come into the room and stolen his wallet from his jacket which he had left hanging on the back of a chair. He told us that he knew who had done it and wasn't leaving until the wallet and all its contents had been returned. He was threatening to call the police if didn't happen. This was a situation I really didn't want to be involved in so I took my leave and went back to the Club. By this time it was almost empty, I ordered a drink and sat at the bar for a while. I wasn't there very long before, I was joined by the pimp of the make-believe German bird, who seemed to be quite pleased with his self and offered to buy me a drink, which I accepted. I noticed that he paid the barman in American dollars.

Before we had had time to down the drinks, Burns and Allen came in and on seeing the pimp Allen ran up and grabbed him by the throat, demanding his money, wallet and ID cards back. While they were struggling two policemen arrived.
"This is the bloke I was telling you about," Allen said to the coppers, "This is the bastard that stole my wallet."
The police asked the pimp if he had any objections to being searched.
"I most certainly do," he told them.
"Well then you won't mind accompanying us to the police station."
"Why should I?" he said.
"This man has laid a serious charge of robbery against you, surely you want to prove him wrong?"

With that the pimp tried to sneakily ditch a wallet behind the bar which both the coppers saw him do and one of them said, "That was careless Sir, you seemed to have forgotten where your pockets are."
They grabbed hold of him, forced his arms up his back and frog marched him away. For some weeks following Burns, Allen and myself hung around together, making quite a lucrative friendship on my part. They were both very highly paid officers in the American Air Force. I knew that whenever they came up to town, they would bring several bottles of very strong American Booze with them; I always thoroughly enjoyed being in their company. When the pimp came up in court he was found not guilty, because the police said the evidence 'got lost'.

After a period of heavy drinking and lots of physical confrontations, I decided it was time for a change in my life. I started to stay away from the Commercial Road and Cable Street dives. While I was going through this change I renewed my friendship with some old school mates, who were totally different from the people in the dives, but like me, were fascinated by their way of life. One of the boys called Danny lived in a cafe in Cheshire Street just off Brick Lane. His father had run the café for many years, in partnership with his wife

PENTONVILLE JOHNNY

(Danny's mum) until she had walked out leaving him to bring Danny up on his own. The cafe was opened religiously at five o'clock every morning so that the Brick Lane and Cheshire Street stall owners could have breakfast before they started their day's work. Danny's dad would leave him to close up at two o'clock every afternoon, which meant that we could sit around in the cafe for the rest of the day planning what to do with our lives.

There were four of us. Harry Parlour, George Gudge, Danny Reed and myself, sometimes Danny's girlfriend Joan would hang around with us. Very often we would sit around the cafe planning robberies. On several occasions we went out to look at premises (mainly shops) that we thought could easily be broken in to. One day it was decided that we would actually do some jobs. The first one we selected to do was a little grocery and tobacconist shop next to Allie Street School. We all knew the shop very well as they had been selling us cigarettes since we were little kids. Our plan of action was that we would go into the shop wearing identical Duffel coats with hoods on, which we could pull over our heads to hide our faces. Once we were in there one of us would ask for something that we knew was kept in the back room. When the person behind the counter went to get it we would jump over the counter, lock him in and then take the money from the till. In theory we reckoned on getting as much as a hundred quid each especially if we left it until late on a Friday afternoon when most people would have paid up their weekly credit accounts.

On the day we chose to carry out the robbery, we borrowed a car and parked around the corner from the shop. After watching for some time we came to the conclusion that the shop was empty of customers. The first thing that happened when we got into the shop was I had a lapse of memory; I forgot what I was supposed to ask for that would have sent the shopkeeper into the back room. I also felt the reality of the situation descend on me. To carry out our intentions would be termed as robbery with violence and I knew that this sort of offence carried at least a seven-year prison sentence! The real truth of the matter was I'd lost my nerve. I ordered five cigarettes, which luckily I had just about enough money to pay for, then turned and walked out of the shop, closely followed by my three would be partners in crime. I knew that, like myself, none of them had what it would take to use the sort of violence that would have been necessary to steal the shopkeeper's money.

On another occasion we planned to rob the offices of a firm that both Harry and I had worked for some years previously, both of us knew the layout fairly well so it all seemed very simple. Over a period of a week or so during the daytime we went past the premises many times trying to assess the easiest way to break in. As the factory wasn't very far from Danny's cafe we decided to do it on foot. There was a small window above the street door of the offices, which I recalled the office girl often getting a bollocking for forgetting to shut it when she locked up at night. Once again we had to decide on the best time to do the job. I told the boys that I had always been paid on a Friday morning when I worked at the company; this gave them the idea that there was a chance of the wages being left in the safe over the Thursday night.

At about half past eleven on the following Thursday we met up in Danny's café as usual and then walked down Brick Lane to the Ross and Klug factory. We had previously agreed that, as Harry was the smallest of us we would lift him through the window, if we found it open. At first he said it was a good idea, but by the time we got there, he thought differently. I sighed with relief when I saw that the window was partially open. I turned, lent my back against the factory door, stooped down slightly and cupped my hands together between my legs thinking that Harry would use them as a foothold when he reached up to release the side brackets. This would then allow the whole of the window to be removed, giving him plenty of space to climb through.

He said to us, "Before I go in I want all of you to promise me that if I get caught you won't object if I give the police your names and addresses."

"What did you say?" asked George.

"Can I give your names if I get caught?" Harry replied.

"Bollocks!" said George, and with that Harry suggested that one of us should get through the window first. I said it doesn't matter who goes through the window because if Harry gets caught he will grass on us anyway. He didn't deny it.

So it was back to the drawing board once again, all of us were about the same age, in our late teens to early twenties and if the truth was known none of us really had strong enough nerves to make good thieves. Nevertheless we started planning another job. By this time I think each of us knew that we had to pull a job, just to prove to ourselves that we meant business. For a while it looked like we were becoming a joke among the people who knew what we were supposed to be up to. Sometime before our feeble attempts at being thieves started, I had overheard two blokes in a café, discussing a robbery they intended doing. The boys thought that 'my' idea to do this job was original and I never gave them any reason to think differently. For egotistical reasons alone, I became determined to prove that I had the bottle to do the job.

As it was 'my' idea they were following, I assumed that I was the leader of our little gang. The job we intended doing was a small chemist shop located on the west ticket booth area of Aldgate East tube station. None of us had any idea what we were going to do or how we were going to do it. In fact formulating the plan of action just fell in to place; what I lacked in education I made up for in intelligence (or so I liked to believe). Aldgate East station was closed at midnight every night just after the last tube passed through it. Sliding metal trellis grills covered all four of the entrances, which were then securely locked with very strong steel and brass padlocks. It was obvious that to try to break in through any of these entrances would be virtually impossible, not least because the station was so close to Leman Street, home to one of the most notorious police stations in London. Every policeman going on and off of duty would have to pass very near to one or other of the station entrances.

PENTONVILLE JOHNNY

I don't know how the idea came to me but when it did it just made such common sense. "It's so simple," I told the boys, when I saw they were beginning to doubt our ability to do the job. "There's a door we can use at the back of Whitechapel station where the porters and line workers go in and out of when the front of the station's locked."
All of us had by this time been to Aldgate tube station to check out the chemist shop. Being a lock-up shop it didn't have a very large window display all we could see was about a dozen or so very expensive cameras. Danny decided we would need a larger car than usual, to carry away whatever goods we were going to steal.

On the night before we were going to pull the job we stole a Riley Pathfinder, which was the top car of its range at the time, we felt reasonably secure in our choice because it was the same type of vehicle that the Police used. We parked it at the back of Whitechapel station in the afternoon, not too far from the workers access. Danny in his wisdom reckoned that the door would be locked after a certain time each day, but it wouldn't cause us any trouble because all we had to do was lift one of us over the wall to unlock it from the inside. That night I felt there was more determination among us than I had felt at any other time. Danny suggested that I should be the one to be lifted over the wall. Before you put me over the wall do you mind if I try the door?" I asked.
We were delighted when I turned the handle and the door swung open.

We had given George, who was bigger than the rest of us, the honour of being in charge of the gang's sacred crowbar. We walked down a metal staircase that led us to the side of the track. When we were sure that there were no signs of life other than our own, we started walking through the tunnel. I didn't have a clue how the other three felt but I found it a very strange and eerie experience as we walked the mile or so through the gloom and semi-darkness of the tube tunnel. We seemed to be getting deeper and deeper under ground. The atmosphere was dry and warm but felt very dirty. I could hear and I was almost certain I could feel a vibration from the hum and power of the electricity drifting up from the conductor rail and circulating in the stale air around us.

Walking quietly behind the others, my mind began to question my motives and actions; suddenly I didn't want to be there. Why was I doing this? Why did I do any of the crazy things I did? Every nerve throughout my body was sending signals to my brain telling me to run away; I was getting so close to breaking into a panic it was making me feel physically sick trying to keep control of myself. I promised myself there and then that I would never, ever get into this sort of situation again without a good, strong drink inside of me. As we rounded a bend the lights from the platforms at Aldgate station came into sight. I had ridden on the tubes most of my life but never once had I realised that the tunnels went round bends or up and down inclines. These were strange thoughts to have when walking along next to a set of rails carrying enough electricity to send you to meet your maker should your concentration lapse long enough for you to take the slightest wayward step.

It seemed to take forever to cover the last hundred yards or so to the platforms. The chemists shop was not actually on the platform but on a landing one flight above, on the same level as the ticket booths but still one level below the streets, at the far end of the station. We stopped to discuss what we should do when we reached the shop. George said he would take the responsibility for prizing the locks off and opening the shutters. We suddenly realised that an empty tube station was a very hollow sounding place; any noises we made would easily carry up to the street and beyond. Danny suggested if we waited for some traffic to pass overhead, we could use the noise to cover any sound we needed to make. We tried to do it this way but somehow, someone had sent all the traffic to another part of London.

Time was passing and pressing, one of us, I don't know who, said if we wrapped one of our sacks around the crowbar, it would make far less noise, which is exactly what George did. Suddenly there was a loud bang as the padlock broke and shot away from the door. The hollowness of the station magnified the noise until it sounded just like a cannon being fired. Harry took off like a greyhound being released from the traps, very closely followed by myself, with Danny and George bringing up the rear. The platforms were about two hundred and fifty yards long, no professional sprinter then or now would have had a cat in hells chance of catching us over the first hundred yards or so. George called for us to stop running. He couldn't shout very loud because of the sound carrying too far, nor could he whisper but some how he got his message across.

All that had really happened was that, following Harry's lead we had just run away from our own noise. It was obvious that George was slightly braver or maybe just slower than the rest of us, he was also one of those people that gave more thought to things before he did them. Using all the courage we could muster, we nervously walked back to the chemist shop, listening very carefully for any sound that might indicate we had been discovered - none came.

George pulled up the roller shutter that acted as the door and each of us in turn filled our sacks with whatever goods we thought worthwhile. I pressed a button on the cash register and was delighted to see a pound note and some coins in the drawer. I immediately started helping myself to what I thought was a single note and was very pleasantly surprised to discover that the single pound note was sitting on lots of other single pound notes. Three of us were fully occupied filling our sacks and hadn't noticed that George had slipped away and broken into the kiosk next door. This place was full of cigarettes and cigars. I didn't stop stuffing my sack until it was brimming over with cameras, perfume, cigarettes, and whatever else I had been able to push into it.

When Danny told us that it was time to leave, we each picked up our sacks and started for the tunnel. Taking into account the length of both the platform and the tunnel we had a considerable distance over which to carry quite heavy loads. Harry led the way, setting a pace the rest of us found very difficult to keep up with, I couldn't understand where he was getting his energy from.

Just as we were reaching the surface near Whitechapel, feeling the fresh night air and a sense of relief, two blokes walked across the lines about 50 yards in front of us. We all ducked down instantly. My brain went into overdrive telling me to do what I do best, run away, but after carrying a heavy sack for so far my legs were telling me something totally different. I saw George get the crowbar ready. Again my brain clicked into overdrive, surely we're not going to kill them, I thought! Just then they turned and walked off in the opposite direction. Before we knew it, we were up the stairs and into the car and Danny calmly drove us back to his Cafe. We unloaded our sacks in Danny's bedroom where his girlfriend Joan was lying in the bed. I took out the money from my pocket and chucked it at her, she smiled and then we all laughed as the tension melted. It looked like quite a lot of money as it spread itself over the bed but there was only about a hundred and twenty five quid.

Harry placed his sack on the floor looked around at us and asked were we keeping our own sacks or were we putting all the gear together to sell. We all looked at him strangely.
"Why the fuck do you want to know that," asked Danny.
"It's just that the stuff that I've got I especially selected for my girlfriend," he said.
"Everything we brought out with us belongs equally to all of us," said Danny "Anyway what was so special about your gear."
"It's especially for girls," Harry squeaked back at him.
"This is all beginning to sound fucking stupid, let's empty the sacks out," George chimed in.
"I thought I'd leave mine in the sack and just take it home with me," said Harry.
"Come on, open up your bloody sack," I said.
"I don't want to, not in front of Joan it will embarrass me," he said.

With that George asked Joan if she would mind turning her head, which she did, George then emptied Harry's sack on to the bed and twenty boxes of Tampons tumbled out.

"What are they?" I asked. Joan, who had now turned around, was laughing quite loudly. She explained to me what they were and what they were used for.

"Harry, you fucking idiot," I said. "You have risked at least five years of your life for about £20 worth of sanitary towels! I can't believe it, your bloody birds pregnant anyway and she won't need anything like that for the next nine months."

We then realised why Harry had been so far ahead of us in the tunnel, the tampons couldn't have weighed much more than a small bag of sugar. When we emptied the other sacks it really did look like quite a big haul. Joan got out of bed, which was rather a pleasant sight as she was wearing only knickers and no bra. Danny, looking a bit embarrassed, told her to get dressed.

Over the time period that we had been going into Danny's cafe we had all seen Joan in various states of undress, she certainly wasn't a shy person.

I turned to Harry and said "Well Harry I think that your idea was a good one you keep the tampons and we'll share the rest of the proceeds".

"You can fuck right off, " Harry replied.

Danny pointed out how much of a risk we had all taken and how very little the value of Harry's contribution was going to be. Harry was by now getting very uptight and beginning to believe that we were really going to cut him out of his share. By the time we had finished winding him up he was almost crying with temper. He got so angry that eventually George threatened to punch his lights out if he didn't stop acting like a kid. The air was tense with excitement. All of us realised that we had carried out our first proper job from beginning to end, without completely losing our nerve. We reluctantly had to admit that once or twice during our escapade we had been very frightened, especially when the lock came away from the door with such a bang.

The next day on the second page of the Evening Standard we made headlines, not for what we had stolen, more for what we hadn't stolen. It turned out that the ticket booths had not been emptied of the day's takings and there had been more than £30,000 left in them overnight. None of us had even considered that there would be any money in the booths therefore we hadn't bothered to look. George being what he was just shrugged his shoulders and said, "What we didn't have, we wouldn't miss." For a lad of twenty George was quite a philosopher. Locally we became infamous, again not because of what we had stolen, but because the police didn't have a clue as to how we had gained entry to the tube station and carried off so much gear.

We did tell a lot of our friends that we had done the job and how we had bravely walked through the tunnel. Our reputation as a gang soared; around the local pubs we had become quite a talking point. However we now faced the problem of selling our ill-gotten gains, which wasn't proving to be a very easy task. Because of the headlines in the East London Advertiser the following week making our gear so hot no one wanted to be seen dealing in cameras. So here we were with lots of loot but no money, the hundred and twenty five pounds we spent in little or no time at all.

Feeling very confident we decided that we would do another job, but this time we would make sure that whatever commodity we stole would be more readily exchangeable for cash. Finding this sort of thing was quite difficult but eventually we decided to steal a large van and take the entire contents of a grocery shop which Danny could sell to his dad, who in turn would be unaware that it was bent, sell it through his Cafe. Danny's father was a strange bloke he never really got over his wife leaving him and each day when he finished in the cafe he would go up to his room with a pint bottle of gin and drink himself to sleep. He never had a clue what we got up to in his premises.

The first part of our new plan was, as I have already said, to steal a decent sized van. Harry said he knew of one that would be parked on the Mile End Waste, very near the Blind Beggar's pub. George who also knew about the van agreed to steal it. I was by now suffering from a very overblown ego and really forgot that the tube station robbery was pure chance, with a great deal of luck thrown in. I was going around issuing orders to the other three, I was actually telling them what they should be doing, what they should be looking for and how they should report everything they did back to me. I began to get lots of silly little superstitions creeping into my mind, one of which was about Danny's dog.

Somehow I had worked out in my thinking that every time the dog left the café at the same time as us, we were going to have bad luck. I never realised that my phoney superior behaviour was causing a lot of ill feeling among the boys. It was very much brought home to me one day when both Danny and George forcibly insisted that either I changed my attitude or they would change my face and also chuck me out of the gang. I said that I was sorry and that I would try my best to change. We shook hands and agreed to forget about it.

Stealing the van was quite easy; George got into the driver's seat and Danny in the passenger's seat, one of them hot wired the ignition while Harry and myself forced the side, panel door open and tried to climb in. We hadn't considered that there would be anything in the van so when we found out that it was almost full of eggs, cheese, butter and margarine plus lots more groceries we were delighted because it meant that we wouldn't have to break into any shops. We drove the van back to Danny's Cafe and parked outside his front door.
"Go and stand on that corner," Danny told Harry, "And watch out for the police."
I told them that I was going to that corner and sent Harry to the one down the other end of the street, which was much further away. George and Danny began unloading the van and Joan also came to lend a hand. They hadn't been working long when I saw a police car coming towards us. I ran and warned them, George jumped into the back of the van closing the door behind him and Danny got into the front and lay across the seats so that he couldn't be spotted through the windscreen. Harry like always took off, like a greyhound.

Pulling Joan into the café with me, I closed the doors and waited for what seemed like an eternity for the police car to pass. It did eventually go past but then I heard it stop, reverse back and then stop next to the van. I whispered to Joan that she should go up to bed and that I would go out the back door, climb over the wall and make my way home. After pulling myself up onto the dividing wall at the rear end of yard I balanced along the top of it until I reached the alley and was just about to jump down when I saw the flash of torchlight. I looked along the alley and discovered that there was a copper standing at the open end having a quiet smoke and amusing himself by switching his torch on and off. I turned around and scurried back along the wall on all fours, climbed back down into the cafe yard and hid behind the door of the outside toilet.

By this time the police were banging on the front door and, after what seemed like an age, I heard Joan shouting for them to keep the noise down as they would wake up the neighbours (she was a very good actress).
"We are very sorry to disturb you love but we would like you to tell us if you know the two men in this van."
I heard a slight scuffle and then Danny's voice saying, "Of course she knows us, you know as well as I do that she lives with me."
I could hear the police getting closer to where I was hiding and then suddenly the door of the toilet was slammed into my face so hard it broke my nose.
"Hello my son," one of the policemen said to me. "You live here as well?"
"No," I answered. I was then invited to come out and join them, for a little chat.

Coming face to face with George and Danny I pretended not to know them. I first thought that I would make up a story about Joan and myself having an illicit affair behind Danny's back but I knew somehow that this wasn't going to work so I just kept quiet. The police then started questioning us about the van and its contents, half of which were now in Danny's passage. All the commotion had woken Danny's dad

who came downstairs asking what all the noise was about. One of the policemen who knew him said, "I'm sorry to disturb you Mr Reed but could you tell us if all of this property is yours?"
He looked around and said it was. We knew that he was confused because some of our groceries had been stacked on top of a legal delivery that had arrived earlier in the day.

We were all placed under arrest except for Joan. By this time there were at least a dozen policemen searching the premises, as they went from room to room it began to look more like an Aladdin's cave than a café. With all the proceeds from the tube station being discovered, the police thought that all their Christmases had come at once. We were then taken to Commercial Street police station where George and myself firmly denied knowing anything about any of the stuff outside of the groceries and the van they came in. We could hardly plead innocent to that being caught red handed as we were.

George asked one of the coppers why they had driven past, and then come back?
"When we drove past the van we saw the side lights go off," he replied.
Danny told us later that while he was lying flat in the front of the van he thought it might look suspicious a van having its lights on while it was supposed to be parked up for the night, so he switched them off. Due to his thoughtful bit of action we were all going to be locked up. As we were being driven away from the café, I looked back and saw Danny's dog wandering around loose, which proved my theory about it, was true! For my part in those crimes I was remanded on bail for three weeks and then put on another two years probation, George Gudge got three months in Brixton and Danny Reed got a one-year bind over. We never reformed as a gang; in fact I have never seen Harry Parlour or Danny since those days.

CHAPTER 5

After making many more false promises about going straight and becoming an upright citizen, I let my mum and dad down once again by returning to the dives where this time I had become friendly with two Scotsmen, who told me their names were Stewart and Murrey. By now the reputation and way of life of the people using the dives, had attracted a large gang of deaf and dumb people, who I along with my two Scottish pals, occasionally teamed up with. The deaf and dumb crowd formed a very formidable gang, I never saw less than 20 of them hanging around together, I think it was because they firmly believed there was safety in numbers. Very often they would go into cafes or restaurants, order food and drinks all round and when they were given the bill or asked to pay they would put on a wonderful performance of not understanding what was wanted of them. If and when the waiter or owner insisted that they pay their bill, they would just simply smash the place up.

I was taught how to use sign language by one of the gang members called John; he told me that he liked the idea that we shared the same Christian name. He introduced me to his deaf and dumb girlfriend, Pamela, who immediately took a shine to me and lost whatever interest she had had in him, from then on she became my constant companion. Wherever I went she followed me, I did explain to John that it wasn't my fault. He told me that he didn't care if she went off with someone else, as he didn't want her anymore, mainly because she liked having sex too much, especially with all his mates. He also told me that at one time he had tried to put her on the game but because she enjoyed it so much, she'd had sex with blokes just for the thrill of it. He said he had bought her several packets of condoms, but due to the delight she got from having sex she hadn't taken enough money off the punters, to cover the cost of them.

John told me that he was now looking for a proper prostitute to pimp off of and if I wanted to take Pamela off of his hands I was very welcome to her. I never really had a choice in the matter; Pamela stuck to me like glue. Everywhere I went I had to explain to her in sign language what I was going to do and who I was going to do it with. Sometimes things got very embarrassing because she wanted to follow me everywhere, even into the gents' toilets. I became the brunt of what I thought were callous jibes, such as "Johns cocking a deaf'un." Or " Johns talking his fingers to the bone", and many more. At first I found all the attention Pamela showered on me very flattering but after a while it began to wear a bit thin. What, deaf and dumb John had told me about her was very true, she was a nymphomaniac. Very often we would go to bed and spend hours having sex and then when I fell asleep she would wake me up again, usually by sucking my Willie.

Whenever I left her on her own, she would instantly start looking around to find some other bloke to have sex with. For a time I hoped she would go off with someone permanently, unfortunately it didn't happen. There was a period of about four days when she disappeared without trace, I thought or rather hoped that it was the end of our relationship, but no such luck. I walked into Vincent's Club one night and there she was, as large as life and looking very delighted to see me again. Most men I know would probably be delighted with the situation I was in, but I am afraid that the amount of physical attention that Pamela needed and demanded was way beyond my capabilities.

On the weekend following her four-day absence, the hop-picking season began so I decided that I would take her down to Kent for the weekend to visit my parents. I also felt it would be good to get away from London for a while. We travelled by train down to Paddock Wood and then by bus to Five Oak Green. On the Saturday afternoon and evening everything was fine, my mum and dad seemed to like Pamela and played all sorts of childish word and sign games with her. She looked and acted very much like she was enjoying herself. My mum seemed to be delighted that I'd taken the time to learn sign language because she kept telling me to use my hands to say something to Pamela.

On the Sunday morning I wandered around renewing my acquaintances with my Mum's friends and relations and at the same time introducing Pamela. While I was doing this, one of the women that had been friends with my mum for many years said to me, "Is your girlfriend from a place called Burnt Oak in north London and is a her name Pamela?"
"Yes," I said.
"Oh dear," she muttered, "I don't think your mum is going to enjoy reading the front page of the News of the World today."
"What are you talking about," I said, "What has Pamela got to do with the front page of a newspaper."
The woman, who's name was Jesse passed me the paper pointing to the slightly smaller of two very large headlines, covering at least three columns in what looked to me like extra large bold print.

The story in the paper told how a very attractive, blue-eyed, blonde, deaf and dumb girl named Pamela had been arrested for soliciting. It went into details of her family background and lots of personal things that I didn't know about. When they arrested her, she had resisted very violently. It said that as the policeman tried to take control of her, she had stripped all her clothes off and run down on to the platform of Aldgate East tube station, where she started kissing and cuddling a complete stranger, who happened to be a West Indian doctor. When the Policeman tried to drag her away she put what he described as a death lock grip around the doctor's neck and was holding on so tight that the copper felt obliged to ask the Doctor if he would help them to get her to the police station.

I was hoping that my mum hadn't read the paper and that I could make good my escape before she did but my luck was out, I could see by the look of shame and anger in her expression as I walked towards her that it was to late. I didn't know what to do or say, I really couldn't mentally come to terms with it at all. She walked over to me and without saying a word, using all the strength she could summon up she punched me full in the face. I went down like an empty wet sack, before I had time to gather my wits or get up again she had put the boot in landing a very painful kick on the side of my head. By this time Pamela had read the paper and was beginning to look very happy about the fact she had become famous. She was holding up the paper to show my mum's friends who, on hearing the commotion, had gathered around us; Pamela was pointing to the story and then to herself.

The best I could do was crawl away on my hands and knees, hoping to get far enough away so that I could stand up and leg it to safety. Once again I was out of luck, I had never seen by mum so angry, especially with me, she kept kicking and calling me all the filthy names she could lay her tongue to. She kept asking me what she had done so wrong in her life that I should bring such disgrace and shame to the family. The main thing on her mind that kept her attacking me was she thought I had become a pimp. I knew that both my parents considered getting money by pimping was about the lowest thing on earth, a man could do.

I told them that I didn't know anything about Pamela being arrested or any of the very unpleasant history of her family, nor was I a pimp. My mum was so upset and ashamed about the whole episode she just wanted me out of her life and Pamela out of this world and into the next. We packed what little stuff we'd brought with us and headed off back to London. I went round to see Stewart and Murrey and asked if we could stay at their flat for a while. They both readily agreed and suggested that if I needed money I could go with them to break in a shop they planned to do that night. After what I'd been through I thought it would make a pleasant change to do something entirely different.

They had stolen a car the previous night with the intention of using it to do the job. Both of them were very surprised when I told

Pamela what we were going to do and she insisted on coming with us. Although they were surprised they didn't object. We drove to Head Street, which was just off Commercial Road, about mile or so from their flat. The shop they had chosen to break into was a tobacconist's come grocers; it took us nearly an hour to prise the back door open. When we eventually got into the main part of the shop we discovered that there was not very much in the way of stock, in the darkness we just loaded what ever boxes came to hand until the boot and back seat of the car were full. Stewart and Murrey drove back to their flat where we had pre-arranged to meet. By the time Pamela and I got there they had finished unloading and had also got rid of the car. Thinking that I wouldn't have to do anything other than to sell my share of the spoils, I went into their flat feeling very good.

Pamela sat herself down in an armchair and promptly fell asleep. We started opening up the boxes to find out exactly what we had nicked. There were 90 steak and kidney pies, a hundred and fifty fruit pies and 25 ounces of Golden Virginia. All in all, the Anglo-Scottish shop breaking association had spent about two hours risking our freedom in order to steal sufficient goods to make us all extremely sick! Just as we had finished discovering what our haul consisted of there was a knock on the room door and someone demanding to be let in. Stewart told me that it was their landlord, who lived downstairs, without waiting or thinking Murrey opened the door and let him in.

He was a tubby, very Jewish looking bloke, who had enough savvy about him to be able to take one glance around the room and comprehended the complete situation. Looking at Stewart he said, "You're not going to turn my house into a storeroom for stolen goods, I've telephoned the police and they are on their way."
Before he had finished issuing his warning I had crossed the room grabbed hold of Pamela, pushed him to one side, and taken off like a bat out of hell, thinking to myself I'm not going to prison for stealing a few poxy fruit pies. The very thought of standing on a

prison landing among some of London's finest villains and having to explain why I was there, sent shivers of embarrassment down my backbone and made my legs work like pistons.

As my family was still down the hop gardens I took Pamela to their house because I thought they wouldn't know that we were staying there. Why I hadn't gone there when we first got back I don't know. For the following week or so we just stayed there, keeping a very low profile until eventually I thought it was safe enough to go down Vincent's Club to find out what had happened to the two Scotsmen. When we arrived at the club, a Maltese bloke that I knew told me the police had been around looking for a man with deaf and dumb girlfriend. You didn't have to be an Einstein to fathom out how the police knew that Pamela was deaf and dumb. The landlord of Murrey and Stewart's flat certainly couldn't have known because she was asleep when he came into the room and hadn't made any sound or signs when I had dragged her out past him.

I thought that if Pamela and myself we were going to have any chance of staying at large the first problem we had to overcome was how to communicate with each other, without being seen to use sign language. I also had to explain to Pamela, why we couldn't be seen using it. Life got even more complicated when I told people that either Murrey or Stewart or both of them had grassed on me. It turned out that Stewart was the younger brother of a very well known, one-legged Glasgow hard man, who got his kicks out of going around altering peoples facial features with a cut-throat razor. And peg leg as I christened him was very pissed off that someone, namely me, was going around telling people that his one and only beloved little brother, was a coppers nark. My situation was improving all the time! I was frightened to use the sign language in case the police saw us and at the same time I had to keep looking over my shoulder for some drunken, razor happy, one-legged Scots lunatic.

One evening, I don't know how or why, I got into conversation with a chap in Barney's cafe, who I had known for some time but only very casually. He told me he was going to do a fairly sizeable job that would earn him a lot of money and asked me if I was interested in going in with him. Before meeting him and starting this conversation I had managed to consume sufficient alcohol to give me enough courage not to care very much. I agreed to do it with him and asked him to tell me all about it. He told me that the first thing we needed to do was to steal a car, I thought not another bloody stolen car, but didn't actually say anything. We searched around several streets that were very close to where my parents lived. I showed the bloke our house and told him that my parents were away and also said that after we had done the job we could go to the house to divvy up the spoils.

Eventually we came across an unlocked car, I got into it, pulled out the ignition wires and started the engine. The bloke asked me would I if he did the driving. That's all right by me I told him, I can sit in the back with Pamela. As I got out of the car to change places, three men came running round the corner shouting for us to stop. I really didn't have much option because Pamela, who wasn't facing in their direction and obviously couldn't hear them, had started trying to kiss and cuddle me, which put a stop to any chance of me making a getaway. It turned out very lucky for the bloke sitting in the driver's seat because at the first sound of the shouting, he took off in the car faster than Stirling Moss could ever have done from the starting grid at Brands Hatch. The people shouting turned out to be three coppers and they were suddenly all over me like a bad rash.

When they found out that Pamela was deaf and dumb they were more than delighted to inform me that apart from helping to steal the car that had just sped away, I was also wanted for questioning about a whole list of crimes that had been committed around the area. I felt bloody sick about the bloke leaving us behind and getting away in the car that I had started up, added to the fact I

113

was now up to my neck in the shit again. We were taken to Arbour Square police station where we were charged with breaking and entering plus aiding and abetting the taking and driving away of a vehicle without the owner's consent. I did a deal with the Sergeant in charge of our case, I agreed to plead guilty to all the charges on the condition that if I was remanded I would get out on bail, plus all the charges against Pamela were dropped. The next morning we were both put in the dock of the Thames Magistrates Court. As soon as I told the beak that I was going to plead guilty, the sergeant told him that they weren't offering any evidence against Pamela. When she was told to leave the box she clung to me refusing to let go until, I persuaded her that I would be out very soon.

The magistrate decided that I would be remanded until I could come up for a proper hearing. When he asked the Old Bill if they had any objection to me being released on bail, they told him that they had no objections, as long as I could put up a surety of two hundred and fifty pounds to guarantee that I wouldn't abscond. I felt really cheated, the bastards had put up the conditions and I had abided by them, but as soon as I had put my neck in the noose they had gone back on their word. I was taken down to the cells to wait for the cattle truck, as they were so called, to take me to either Brixton or the Scrubs I didn't know which.

The lady in charge of cell cleaning mistakenly opened my door thinking that the cell was empty. "Oh," she said, "I didn't realise you were in here John."
I looked at her but didn't recognise her. I couldn't understand how she knew my name or who I was.
She said to me, "I don't suppose you recognise me but I am a friend of your mums, does she know you're here?"
I said I thought she was still down hop picking; the woman told me she was sorry to see me in trouble and asked if there was anything she could do for me. I asked her if she would contact my dad and tell him I needed bailing out, she said she would, but I didn't hold out much hope.

Very much to my surprise about an hour later my dad came in and agreed to stand bail for me, he told me that if I even thought about running away he would kill me. I asked him how he had found out so quickly that I'd been nicked, he told me that he hadn't known I'd been nicked. He went on to tell me that the reason he was at the police station was because sometime during the night one of our neighbours had reported someone breaking into our house. The police had contacted him down in Kent and told him to come to the police station to identify some of the goods they had found in a stolen car. While he was in the station, the desk Sergeant saw him sign his name for his property and asked him if he had a son with the identical name, when said he had, they told him where I was and why.

After I'd signed my bail form we were taken to the station yard where my dad collected his property, while he was doing this the copper asked him if he knew who the owner of the stolen car was, he said he didn't. When I saw it I felt really sick because it was the one I'd nicked the night before. I didn't tell my dad what had happened or that I knew the dirty bastard who had broken into our house. He picked up his gear, put it in his own car and then drove us straight down to Kent. When he told my mum about the trouble I was in, she reared up on me again but luckily this time she calmed down a lot quicker and said, "If I hadn't been so keen in sending you and the girl away this might not have happened, but now that it has, we will have to live with the consequences."

I stayed down in Kent for a further two weeks, which gave me time to make a bit of a recovery from all the physical exertion I had been using trying to keep Pamela sexually satisfied. When we arrived back home our next-door neighbours told us that Pamela had been around the house nearly every day, banging on the front door and squealing. She had even made them let her go through their house, so she could look over the garden wall into ours. My mum looked at me and said one-day my son you are going to pay

very highly for your sins I only hope that you will have the time
and the good graces to set things right before they take you up or
down.

During the period I was on bail I had a birthday, which in itself
wasn't very, significant, it fell two days before I was due at Court.
To celebrate it I got drunk and somehow finished up fighting with
the police, who luckily for me didn't find out that I was already on
bail and released me on my own surety. When they did discover
what had happened they just added a charge of assault on to the
two that I was already facing. By the time the big day arrived
my mum had bought me a new suit, shirt and tie, she said you're
not going into that place looking like a scruff and bringing more
shame on your dad and me. I told her not to worry because where
they're going to send me no one would know my family.

On the day I appeared in court, I was once again greeted by the
familiar red and blue mottled face, which unfortunately for him,
belonged to my beloved and regular magistrate, the right honourable
Colonel Batt. As he stared across his courtroom, listening to the
charges being read out, I could hear him tut tut tutting to himself.
The clerk of the court told me to sit down, while the police gave
their evidence. When I was asked what I had to say in my defence
I just pleaded guilty and apologised, trying to look as sincere as
I could. In my mind I was thinking that at least in this court they
couldn't give me any more than six months.

However to my surprise the dear old Colonel had other ideas,
he looked at me and said, "You, Sir have been in my court more
times than I have myself. You have in the past appeared before me
charged with such a variety of crimes, I really think it is time that
you were taught a proper lesson."

I was still thinking that the only proper lesson he was able to give
me was six months out of which, if I kept my nose clean, I would
only spend about 16 weeks behind bars. I nearly fell over when
the Colonel said because it wasn't within his power to send me
away for corrective training or Borstal, he was going to transfer

my case up to the London sessions for sentencing. I though this old bastard's passing the buck; in my mind none of the charges were really very serious. I couldn't believe it; looking directly at him I asked why he was treating me so unfairly.

He said, "In this court alone, you have already been placed on probation five times and not on one of those occasions have you actually completed a period of supervision without committing a further offence. Even now as you stand in the dock before me you are still under a two-year provision order with at least eighteen months to run."
He went on to say that people and their property should be protected from the likes of me and the only way he felt he was able to do this was to recommend a much stiffer and longer sentence than was within his power. I was remanded to Wormwood Scrubs to await sentencing. Sitting in the cubicle of the cattle truck my imagination ran riot, memories of Stanford House kept popping in to my mind and all the tortuous things that they did to me 'for my own good' of course. I was also thinking that I was now a lot older and wiser and much more capable of looking after myself.

Still mulling over what the Colonel's had said I began to wonder how many more times in my life would I have those or similar words said to me. As the cattle truck rattled on towards the prison from the radio in the drivers cab I could hear Nat King Cole singing, 'Too Young'. When I got into the Scrubs reception block the first con I saw was Stewart, my brain went into some sort of auto drive. I ran across the room and kicked him straight in the bollocks calling him a fucking grass. As he went down he looked at me and screamed, "It wasn't me, it wasn't me, it was Murrey, he grassed on all of us, including your girlfriend."
Realising where I was, I looked around to see if any of the screws were going to stop me doing any more damage to Stewart.
One of them said to me, "We always find it better, on reception, to let people fully exercise their grievances against each other, that

way when they are put on the wing it very often follows that there might not be any more trouble between them."
I realised then that this wasn't Stanford House, nor was it anything like it. I didn't bother trying to wallop Stewart again.

I spent the next two weeks on the remand section of A. wing, among a lot of blokes that I'd grown up with. It wasn't long before I was nicknamed 'The Fruit Pie Kid'. Most of the cons in there were waiting to be sentenced for a complete catalogue of different crimes; at one time it looked like half of my old school mates were in there. I found the regime very easy to adapt to, there were cons that would eat me if I stepped out of line, and likewise there were others that I could have for breakfast if they upset me. I was a long way from the top of the pecking order but still far enough up it from the bottom to be shown a bit of respect from most of my fellow inmates.

Time in prison always seems to go faster when you look back at how long you have done, as opposed to forward thinking of how much longer you have got left to do. Eventually I came up to the London sessions to be sentenced. As I stood in the dock my mind began to wander, I was thinking about all the people that had previously stood the box where I was standing and how many years they had been sentenced to. I have been in some very lonely situations in my life but standing in the dock at the London sessions completely sober, certainly felt like one of the loneliest. When the judge had finished reading to himself the recommendations of the magistrate he asked how old I was, the policeman who had read out the evidence against me told him that I was in my early twenty's. The judge looked at me and said, "Unfortunately, I think you are too old to benefit from a period of Borstal training."

I was very relieved when he gave no sign that he had overheard the very loud sigh of relief I let out when I heard those words. He went on to say that it was his duty to make sure that the public and their property were adequately protected from the likes of me, and felt there was no way, he could deal with me, outside of a custodial sentence. It was about then that my brain went off the boil I just thought this prat, is talking for the sake of talking, he must love the sound of his own voice. I have always suffered from a low concentration span and because of it, I didn't hear what he actually sentenced me to, the only words I remember hearing him say were " Take him down".

When I asked the screw how long I had got he looked at me and said, for a bloke with over 16 previous convictions you really have been very lucky because out of the nine months sentence he has given you, you will only have to serve six. I thought to myself that silly old bastard at the magistrates could have quite easily dealt with this and I wouldn't have had to spend the time waiting on remand. When we got back to the Scrubs I saw that at least half of the twenty-five boys I'd travelled on the van to court with, had also come back. Most of them had been sentenced to Borstal Training. During my time on remand, I had heard some horrific stories about Reading, Bedford and various other Borstals. With these in mind I felt really lucky that I was only doing nine months. I felt even luckier when I was put on C wing and was told that there was a spy called George Blake on D wing, doing 45 years.
I was allocated a cell on the ground floor at the furthest end of the wing from the main gate. Just outside my door there was a table tennis table, television and a piano. I thought to myself, the only two things that are missing in here are women and booze. The downside of this was that I had to serve a minimum of 17 weeks before I would be allowed to take part in what they called recreational association. On more than one occasion during that sentence, I could have sworn that some of the people outside of my of cell door enjoying their out of cell privileges were actually women. At that time man on man sex was considered nice, but highly illegal. Quite a few of the inmates on my landing were serving sentences ranging from three months up to two years for having, same gender relationships.

In the cell next to mine was a struck-off barrister who had been caught giving oral sex to a young bloke in a Sloane Square public toilet; outside of his being queer he was one of the nicest people I ever met in or out of prison. Further down the wing I met an ex MP called Baker who was serving time for some sort of fraud, I'm not sure what but I do know that he was very liberal with the advice he gave to people on appeal. Directly opposite me was a Welshman who had worked on the overnight mail train between Cardiff and Liverpool, his employers were the G.P.O. and his job was to hand stamp the time and dates on the post. He had actually been nicked for taking late pools coupons and putting an earlier time stamp on them. Between him and his mates they had put in numerous false claims and received about £7,000 in bogus winnings from Littlewoods or Vernons.

I asked him why he hadn't just filled in one coupon and taken the jackpot instead of lots of silly little claims. He told me that he thought it would be much safer to do it his way, because no one ever checked up on small claims. It passed through my mind how amazing it was that people like him always wasted or missed the wonderful opportunities that fell into their laps. A day or two after my conversation with him I was approached by another Welshman, who told me that I should be very careful who I was seen talking to. When I asked him to explain what he meant, he told me that the first Taffy I had spoken to had been charged with 21 offences and had had a further 16 taken into consideration. I said, to the second Taffy, "Why should I be careful if I talk to him?"
Taffy Two told me, that Taffy One had got the 16 T.I.C. charges dropped in return for giving the names of all the people who had taken part in his little scam. Taffy Two then told me that he was one of the 'T. I. C's.'

Over a period of time I got to know the rest of the T.I.C.s and like all the Welshmen I have ever met in my life they loved to sing. The only time Taffy One was allowed to join the rest of them was when they sang in the Church choir. I did find out later that not only were they a choir in prison they were also all in the same village choir on the outside and believe it or not Taffy One was the Choirmaster. I told one or two of them that I had now had the privilege of seeing both the Crooked Spire of Chesterfield and the Bent Choir of Aberdare. I don't think that the Welsh boys were quite ready for my sense of humour as none of them spoke to me again. There were so many characters on C wing I found it hard not to smile most days.

I was sent to work in the mail bag shop, where sitting on one side of me there was an Irishman called Paddy Connolly who was waiting to go over to Camp Hill on the Isle of Wight to serve a three-year corrective training sentence. On my other side for the first couple of days was Roy Nash. I think he was serving five years for doing something nasty to someone with a knife in a dance hall. I don't know if I said anything to upset him but one-day he refused to work and they sent him back to his cell; I never saw him again, during that sentence.

On the day that I finished sewing my very first mail bag, I had laid it out on the floor for the screw to inspect, a con called Polish Michael walked by with a pair of scissors in his hands making pretend motions to cut up my newly completed achievement. Michael had been a partner in a pig farm and for some reason known only to him had decided that he didn't need anyone to share in the venture. So he murdered his partner, cut up the body and fed it to the pigs. When I saw him approaching my mailbag making the threatening motions and before I had taken the time to think about what I was saying, I had told him to 'fuck off and find another partner to cut up.'

The next instance he was chasing me around the workshop trying to chop me up with his scissors. Michael was such an enormous brute of man, it took about four inmates and two screws to catch hold of him and wrestle him to the floor and a further 10 minutes to convince him that I was joking. He gradually relaxed and began to smile telling the people who were holding him down that he had mistaken what I had said and thought I had insulted him. With sighs of relief all round they released him and helped him to his feet. He walked over to me offering to shake hands, when I did it felt like I had put my hand in a vice. He said to me in broken English, "You are a very funny and lucky boy". I thought that is a lot more than you could say for you're ex partner.

One day as I was walking through the mailbag shop, not really looking where I was going I accidentally tripped over a pile of boxes, which reactivated the pain in my spine. Some of which was genuine but a lot of it I put on. Hoping to be sent to an outside hospital, I became an expert at convincing the prison medical staff that I was constantly in very severe pain. My act was so good they put me in the prison hospital and issued me with a pair of crutches to lean on. The following couple of weeks turned out to be about as good as it could get in prison. I was put on a ward where a blue band trustee called Johnny Lee was in charge, on the outside among many other names Johnny called himself the Tsar of Fulham, he was serving the last few months of a ten-year sentence. Like me Johnny was swinging the lead about his illness and by doing so he was holding down a very cushy job, we got along like a house on fire. There were four other blokes in the ward, none of who were much to write home about. It was rumoured that one of them had worked on a farm in Devon and was serving time for sexually interfering with the farm animals. Looking at him it wasn't difficult to believe.

After several examinations by a visiting surgeon I was asked if I had any objections against going in to Hammersmith Hospital, to have an experimental operation on my spine. Because the uppermost thing in my mind was that I would be out of the prison, the thought of what benefit having an operation would do for me never entered my head. I sent a letter to my parents telling them when I was going into the hospital and asking them to bring me some cigarettes and booze. About a week after I had agreed to have the operation I was transferred into the civvie Hospital. The following day I was operated on and became the first person in England to have that type of spinal operation. For the first couple of days because the pain was so bad I really wondered what I had let myself in for, I could hardly move. One of the nurses told me that I was being injected with more morphine in a day than a drug addict would take in a week. Gradually I began to feel better and was looking forward to seeing my mum and dad. My only disappointment when they eventually came visit me was that they didn't bring me any booze.

Sometime after the operation the surgeon came to see me and asked if I felt any better? By that time my sense of humour had returned, and once again without thinking I said, " Better than what? I think you will benefit much more from the publicity than I will from the actual operation." At that time he was known as Mr Stevens the Royal Surgeon, it really didn't matter what he was, all I know is that like the Taffy's he wasn't ready for my sarcastic wit. Within 10 minutes, I was transferred back to the Scrubs and put in a single cell in the prison hospital. Many years later I was told, that Mr Stevens had been made a Lord.

Fortunately on my return to prison I needed physiotherapy, which meant that I spent most of my time walking around the hospital exercise yard, this continued until I was released. The night before I got out Johnny Lee and two hospital screws came into my cell to say goodbye, and also to get their own back for all the strokes I had pulled on them during my time. Johnny grabbed me around the body, trapping my arms down by my sides. One of the screws caught me around the legs, then the other screw produced a battery driven set of hair clippers and cut a two inch parting through the centre of my hair from my forehead to the back of my neck. After they had finished having their fun they let me go and ran out of the cell laughing slamming the door behind them. I could hear Johnny Lee saying he really is going to look lovely when gets out in the morning. Until then I'd had reasonably long hair but now I looked like a badger, there was nothing else I could do but ask the screw to lend me the clippers and shave the rest of my head.

One of the other cons from the hospital was also released at the same time as myself. I had known him for some time and had shared many hours talking and joking with him in the ward and on the exercise yard. As we were both going in the same direction, which was towards the White City tube station, I naturally started walking along side of him, I had known for some time during our stay that he was doing porridge for some very unsavoury offences.

As we were walking along he looked at me and said "The people we are passing can plainly see from the way your that your hair is cut that you have just been released from the prison. Which is not so in my case so could you please walk on the opposite side of the road or some distance in front or behind me."

I thought to myself this fucking mongrel, who as been serving time for some sort of devious perverted sex act has just told me that I am not good enough to be seen in public with him. The last I saw of him he was sitting on the kerbside with tears streaming down his cheeks and gingerly trying to nurse his very sore bollocks.

CHAPTER 6

While I had been in the scrubs my old stamping ground had changed, there were a lot of new faces hanging around, and several more so-called clubs had opened up. If you took time out to sit around and listen to the different accents and languages being used, which was something I often did, it soon became very obvious that the racial melting pot was certainly working around the East End. In this period of time making superficial friendships was very easy, that is how I became associated with several blokes who I thought were of a like mind to myself. Every weekend the popularity of Vincent's and the other clubs like it within a square mile seemed to be growing and attracting more and more people from all over the London nightspots and vice dens. They all came to drink or take drugs and dance the night away. It had also become the 'in' place for a large group of overdressed transvestite homosexuals; most of who worked in and around the world of show business.

Hard and soft drug taking was very much on the increase; personally I still had a preference for the effect of alcohol. However, during this period I did experiment with lots of different types of drugs. The socially taken, in-drugs of the time, along with the obvious cannabis mixtures, were pills of various descriptions. One variety of the pills I remember taking were called Preludin; a couple of these would give you enough energy to stay awake and dance non-stop for several days and nights. When it first came to the attention of the night people it was being sold openly in chemists as a slimming pill, without the need of a prescription. Taken for the purpose it was originally intended, it worked very well, but as an upper I felt it worked a lot better!

Along with giving me the energy to stay awake for days and nights on end I got several, unwanted side effects from taking Preludin. Firstly it gave me a very strong urge to talk twice as much as I normally did, which was already ten times more than most people could bear. This affliction was accompanied with an almost unquenchable thirst

125

and a compulsion to drink cup after cup of weak black coffee. I tried Black Bombers, Purple Heart's and many others that I can't put a name to but none of them gave me the effect that I was looking for. Cannabis just made me feel very hungry and want to go to sleep all the time. On one occasion I took a couple of yellow tablets called Dexadrine which I was told were going to act faster and make me feel higher for longer than anything I'd ever taken before. When these highly remarkable pills got into my system all they did was make me feel very angry at myself because no matter how much alcohol I consumed, I couldn't get that nice confident feeling of being drunk.

Two of the blokes I began to hang around with frequented parts of the Soho area that up until meeting them I wasn't very familiar with although I had heard of some of the cafes, like the Two Is and the Whisky A Go Go. I quickly got to know these new places very well and the different people that used them. One of my new friends was an Irish boy called Jimmy Makin who told me that he had played bass guitar on Cliff Richards and the Shadows first hit record, I think it was called 'Move It'. During this period I made passing acquaintances with many people who later became household names in the music industry.

For a time I became the road manager to a group that I later learned went on to make up part of Lulu's backing group. It didn't take me long to lose the job though; as I always made a point of getting them fixed up with lodgings much closer to pubs than to the venues where they were doing their gigs. I would then go in to the pub and explain who and what I was, give them the name of the hotel or guesthouse where the group were staying and then run up a tab in their name. I had a free piss up in nearly every town, city or village they played in.

Jimmy Makin changed his name to Del Ward as he was hoping to become a famous singer, in my opinion he had a terrific voice but, when it came to the casting couch for the big shows, he told me that he always kept his trousers up. There were several occasions when he appeared on BBC Television in the Oh Boy Show; I also appeared on it as a Rock and Roll dancer. By modern standards it was a really dreadful show, the up and coming stars in those days were given dummy microphones and told to wander among the audience miming to their latest releases. Sometimes the cameramen would deliberately lose sight of the would-be stars, especially if there were any nice looking young girls wearing extra short mini-skirts or low-cut dresses, who were obviously much more photogenic.

Early one evening somewhere round about mid August, I was sitting in the '41 Club' in Dean Street when Jimmy came in with two other blokes and introduced me to one of them called Norman. Norman told me that he had just finished working as patrolman for the Automobile Association. I knew the other one from the East End, he called himself Alfie Price. The four of us sat around drinking whisky out of teacups and talking about how fed up we were just going from Club to Club every night and sleeping all day, never having enough money to do what we really wanted to do with our lives. After chatting for some time, I proposed that we pool what little bit of money we had between us, then go around and ask anyone we knew to lend us some more, that is if we knew anybody silly enough to give us a loan! I suggested that we could use what was left of the night circulating the rest of the dives, tapping up any likely prospects. Then we could meet up the next day in Barney's Café and do something about changing our way of life.

We met as arranged and clubbed our money together, apart from two five-pound notes I had tucked down my sock for safekeeping or emergencies. Then using Norman's car we drove to my parent's house where I collected my tent and some clothes after which we set off to start our new way life in Kent. Faversham is where I had not only persuaded them that our destiny lay, I had convinced them that there was very rich pickings to be had just by picking fruit or scraping up cockles from Seasalter beach. These were two of the many ideas that I had put to them. All I really wanted to do was go down to Faversham and look up some of my old mates and I couldn't think of a better way to do this than to travel in someone else's car mainly at their expense. In those days and for most of my life I never gave a thought to the consequences of my actions. I just used people as a means of getting my own way, using whatever legal or illegal methods, truth or lies it took. I had a good feeling that this trip was going to turn out exactly the way I wanted it to.

When we got close to Faversham, I directed them to an area of dense woodland, situated just off of the main road between the village of Oare and Faversham itself. After finding a gap in the trees wide enough to drive the car through, we drove in very slowly using the front of the car to push the lower branches aside allowing them to swing back into their natural positions undamaged. This made it possible for us to completely hide the car and the tent from any passers by. It was surprising how far we could get into the woods and still have room to manoeuvre the car whereby it would be ready to drive out again. I didn't know then, nor did I ever find out who owned the woods. After we had finished pitching the tent we drove into Faversham, to the Fleur-de-Lis Café that was situated in the town centre and was very often used as a meeting place by some of my old mates while they were waiting for the pubs to open.

That day we were in luck, several people that I had got to know during my previous stay in Faversham were waiting for the orchard buyers to come and select their work gangs for the fruit-picking season. I introduced my new friends to my old mates and made it known that we were looking for work and also that we were quite willing to do anything, legal or otherwise, for a price. Before the fruit buyers arrived, Harry Barrett, the father of Tony, Mickey and Ken, had convinced Norman, Pricey, and Jimmy that it would be best for all of us if we made up a gang with him and his sons, and let him act as ganger and do the price fixing. At first I tried to dissuade them from doing this but my protests fell on deaf ears. Eventually I let them decide for themselves because I knew in my mind what I wanted to do and it had nothing to do with picking fruit. When the fruit buyers arrived, Harry went into the crafty little act that I had got so used to seeing him perform when I had stayed at his house in the past. I knew that he would get the best possible deal available, I also knew him well enough to know that he wouldn't have the slightest intention of passing the same deal on to the rest of the gang.

Bright and early the next morning we drove to the orchard where we were to start work. When I asked Harry how much they were going to pay us for our labour, I knew from the way he was avoiding making direct eye contact with me that his cheating little brain was doing overtime working out how much he could undercut us on the price the fruit buyers had quoted him. He eventually muttered a price to us. On the one or two previous occasions that I had tried fruit picking it had taken me about eight-hour's non-stop hard graft to earn just over Five Pounds. Even after several weeks' experience I could barely earn enough to pay for my food and lodgings. The price that Harry had told me we were going to get was less than I had been paid a year or so earlier. As none of my three mates had ever picked fruit before they had no idea that working for this price, wouldn't keep them in food.

Jimmy, Norman and Pricey were happily labouring under the impression that they were going to earn enough money to eat the very best of food and live the high life in the nightclubs and cocktail lounges around all the coastal resorts of East Kent. Because it was at my instigation that they were there, I didn't think I should do or say anything to disillusion them. We were each given a ladder and a large canvas bag. The bags were designed in such a way they hung from your lower back over your bum and around your sides, and had the capacity to carry five or more bushels of fruit. After I had picked four bags of apples I climbed down, laid my ladder on the ground and told the boys that I was going into town to do some business. As I left I could see they were all busily working away like the proverbial beavers. I had absolutely no intention of continuing to pick fruit if I could find an easier, softer way to earn money.

My intention when I left the orchard was to look out for one of my old girlfriends or maybe find a new one. To further this cause I went round to see Ken Barrett hoping that he would know the whereabouts of some of my old flames. When I got to his yard there was only his brother Tony there and as we hadn't seen or spoken to each other since he had slashed me with the razor, I didn't think he'd be very friendly or helpful to me. I was very surprised when he put on what seemed to be a very over the top act of being glad to see me. We chatted for quite some time and apart from giving me the information I wanted, he told me nearly everything that had been going on in and around Faversham while I had been back in London. I told him that I come down with three other blokes and that we were looking for any kind of work. He said his dad had already told him that we were doing some fruit picking.

He went on to say that the reason he was hanging around in Kenny's yard and not out picking fruit with us was because he had heard that I was back in Faversham, looking for revenge. Having this thought in his mind, and not wanting to come face to face with me, he had arranged with his dad to talk to me and find out what my intentions were. I laughed because the thought of revenge had never entered my mind; I told him that I had accepted that when he slashed me with the razor he was drunk and didn't know what he was doing, otherwise I would have been back to sort him out long before now. We shook hands and agreed to forget the matter but I knew there and then that I would never trust him again. Tony had been frightened to face me, but given the right circumstances I felt sure he would quite happily stab me in the back. From what he said and the patronising way he had spoken to me I realised that he had an almost identical personality to his dad and that they were both totally devoid of any moral principles.

He went on to say, "When you and your mates are finished picking fruit this evening, if there's still enough daylight, you could all go down to Seasalter beach and scrape cockles like a lot of other people around here do. With what you earn on the fruit picking plus what

you get gathering cockles you should be able to pick up some decent money."
I thanked him for his advice and reminded him that it was his crooked little dad that was holding the boys' purse strings, he laughed knowing exactly what I meant. I asked him if there were any dances or other activities going on locally where I might catch up with the some of my old girl friends. He told me there was going to be a dance at the East Kent Packing factory, the following Saturday and that he and his brothers were thinking of going to it.

When I got back to the tent the rest of the lads were already there, between them they had acquired two washing up bowls a kettle and several blankets, Jimmy had borrowed a Primus stove and a mirror. Pricey had robbed some unfortunate person's allotment of enough vegetables to last all four of us at least a week. Norman had done his part by going to the butcher's shop and buying a chicken and some other meat. I thought all in all we were getting quite comfortable in our new way of life, well at least the first two days of it. After we had finished eating a partially raw, partially burnt concoction of food, we went to the nearest pub for a drink.

The next morning when we arrived at the orchard, we found both Tony and Mickey Barrett had joined their dad. I kept a wary eye on them all day, especially when I was working at the top of my ladder. It was a very uncomfortable feeling knowing that they would be walking close to the bottom of it and at any time could pull it out from under me. Knowing how they had performed in fights I had seen them have when we knocked around together back in London, I knew that if I fell over they would never give me a chance to get on my feet again. Whilst I was concentrating on the Barrett's I was unaware of how hard I was working, and at the end of the day was surprised at the large amount of fruit I had picked. I had been preoccupied with thoughts of not only defending myself against the Barrett brothers but, when and if they started any trouble, I was going to knock the shit out of both of them and their dad.

I knew from my past experience of fruit picking that whenever the fruit buyers came to collect the day's harvest they paid cash on the nail. Before we started work on the fourth day, I asked the boys how much money Harry had paid us for the work we had done so far. Because we had elected Norman our treasurer I had assumed that he had collected some money from Harry on my behalf as well as for himself and the other two. When they told me they hadn't received any money, I explained to them what the procedure was and how they should have been paid at the end of each day's picking. Norman got down from his ladder and went over to asked Harry for our money. Harry staying at the top of his ladder just said. "Sorry! Boys, I took your money home and forgot to bring it with me this morning. Don't worry I'll have it for you tomorrow."

Once again I climbed down from my ladder, laid it on the ground and said I was going into town telling them that I would see them later. Knowing full well that Harry Barrett would try his best to cheat us out of our money. I went to the Fleur-De-Lis Café and had a meal after which I just wandered around aimlessly trying to think of a better way to get money. Eventually I made my way back to the tent where, because it was still early, I was surprised to see the boys.

They told me that earlier in the afternoon they had decided to have short break and had left the orchard to go for a drink and a sandwich in the local pub. They swore on oath that they hadn't been gone for more than fifteen minutes, but unfortunately for them and me during that time all the fruit we had picked had been collected and no doubt paid for. Now Harry Barrett and our wages were nowhere to be found. They'd driven round to his house and to Kenny's yard but no one had seen him. It was quite obvious that the boys were very concerned about their money. They asked me if I thought that Harry would try to cheat them.
I told them, "You could bet your last fucking penny he will."
"Why didn't you tell us this before," they asked me.

I said, "Because on the first day we met him, in the café, you didn't want to hear what I had to say, when I tried to tell you what he was like."

They had decided that they weren't going to pick any more apples until they had been paid for the work they'd already done. I said that I had another idea how we could earn some money and explained the best way I could with my very limited amount of knowledge about gathering cockles. I also told them that we would be able to sell whatever we got direct to the buyers and wouldn't need the services of a ganger or middleman. They seemed very enthusiastic about my latest idea; I can only think it was because none of them realised what scraping up cockles from a beach entailed. When I was in Faversham previously, I'd been taken to Seasalter and shown the rudiments of cockle fishing and some of the telltale signs to look for when you are searching for them.

With almost the last bit of our money we bought two garden rakes and then stole some wire mesh to make a sieve. In my mind collecting cockles looked simple, I thought that all you had to do was to follow at the water's edge as the tide went out keeping an eye out for small air bubbles that came up through the sand. When you saw them, you raked the sand just like you would the loose earth in your garden, heaping it into the sieve, which you then lifted and shook, the shaking motion would allow the sand to escape leaving the cockles behind. It was all going to be so very easy. Two of us used the rakes while the others held the wire mesh. We could see several other people doing the same as us but none of them had had the good sense to work as a team we were doing.

After several hours, apart from aching backs we had very little to show for a lot of hard work, by this time the tide had gone a very long way out and was about to turn. I did notice that every now and then the people working on their own came walking back up the beach carrying large sacks of cockles, which they were stacking close to the where our was parked.

"Bollocks to this," I said, as I threw away my rake and started walking back to the car, it wasn't long before the boys joined me. If anyone looked down the beach towards the water that day, they could clearly see where we had been working, as there were small piles of cockles trailing from the waters edge back to where we had started raking. At this juncture the boys were very quick to point out that my master plan for collecting shellfish had been very seriously flawed because I hadn't taken into consideration that we would need sacks or some other sort of receptacles to carry our catch home in.

As we walked past the neatly stacked sacks of cockles in the car park, I suggested to the boys that if we took some of these it would be a just reward for all the hard work we had done. We picked up a sack each and loaded them into the boot and back seat of the car. Apart from the smell and the tight squeeze, we drove back to Faversham feeling quite happy about how the day had turned out so far. I took them to see Tony Barrett, as I was sure he would know someone who would buy our shellfish. When we showed him our days' catch, he was more than a little bit keen to help us and gave us the address of Harry Swan who I had met in the past but got to know only very slightly. When we got to his place he was working in his backyard, cleaning whelks. We introduced ourselves and asked if he would be interested in buying our cockles. Harry was a tall, blonde, blue-eyed, powerfully built bloke and you could see from the twinkle in his deep blue eyes that he had a wicked sense of humour. Unfortunately for us he had just that day restocked with cockles, or so he said, but he thought his brother Frank might be interested in them.

He said, "As you are all strangers in town, I will come with you to make sure that you find my brother's house and don't get lost on the way."
Norman thanked him and said that it was bloody good of him to put himself out to help people he didn't know and with that we all set off to see Harry's big Brother Frank. When we arrived Harry pointed at a side door and told us not to bother knocking just to go in. The door led into a small yard where several men were working, boiling

and cleaning various types of shellfish. As we walked towards the man that Harry had indicated was his brother, I shuddered and felt a very uncomfortable sensation run through my body. I turned around and walked back past Harry and stood in the entrance with the door open. From the look on his face, it was obvious that Frank Swan wasn't very pleased to see us. It dawned on me then that we'd fallen into a set up, neatly done by Tony Barrett and Harry Swan who'd sent us to the very people that owned the cockles we were trying to sell!

Frank said to us, "I'm sorry but we knew you were coming to see us so we've called the police, who should be here any minute now, if you drop our sacks of cockles and leave immediately you might get away before they arrive."
I turned and ran down the street until I reached the corner and then ran blindly turning left and right through several other streets. Until I eventually finished up at the Fleur-De-Lis cafe in the marketplace. When I had finished drinking my second cup of tea and calmed myself down, I made my way back to our campsite. When I got there the three boys were standing outside of the tent looking quite sheepish.

Jimmy looked at me and then towards the tent and nodded his head trying to quietly indicate something to me, as he was doing this the tent flaps flew open and two blokes I recognised as being members of the local C.I.D emerged.
"Hello John," one of said to me. This copper had been trying to nick me for years, so much so it had become a bit of an obsession with him.
"At last," he said. "I've got the goods on you. Your mates here have told us that this was all your idea."
For a moment or two I lost it and started punching into Jimmy and Pricey but before I could land one on Norman, the old Bill had grabbed me. We were taken to Faversham police station where we were formally charged with stealing four bags of shellfish to the value of £5 each.

I really felt stupid when I heard how much they valued our loot at. Thinking about the amount of time and energy we had put in trying to scrape up our own cockles, plus the money we had spent on tools and petrol. If we had worked night and day for a week we wouldn't have collected enough cockles to cover our expenses. We were each given a bench summons to appear at Canterbury Magistrates court when and if the Chief Constable of Kent decided it was worth proceeding with the charges. On our way back to the tent after leaving the police station the boys decided that they'd had enough of the good life and were going back to London.

I told them that I'd be staying, as there wasn't much going for me in London. I also said that I'd found a Tenner and if they wanted to have a drink on me before they left they were very welcome. Norman said he would be delighted to, as long as I didn't try to persuade them to stay and take part in another one of my crazy, bankruptcy making schemes. We all laughed and then made our way to the nearest pub. After we had been there for some time drinking and laughing about all the stupid things we had done and the silly ways we had gone about doing them, Harry and Frank Swan came in. When they saw us they asked if it they could join us for a drink, we agreed and they did. When they offered to buy us a drink we gratefully accepted and after the usual cheers and icebreaking period we began to tell them about our escapades.

Before we could get settled for the evening the boys decided that they would make their way back to London, as otherwise it would be too late when they got there to find accommodation. Harry asked me if I was going with them. When I told him that I wasn't he suggested that I move my tent into an orchard that belonged to a friend of his who lived just on the edge of town. Frank said it would make more sense to be closer to town now that I wasn't going to have any transport. I agreed with them. The following morning I met Harry who instructed me how to get to the orchard and lent me his pickup to collect my tent. On my arrival at the orchard I was met by a bloke called David, who initially gave me the distinct impression that I should know him, and didn't seem very pleased when I didn't show any sign of recognition. What's more he got very off handed, as he seemed to reluctantly show me where to pitch my tent.

I thought, for a person that I had never met, he was treating me in very strange way. I also thought that if he didn't want me to camp in his orchard, he shouldn't have told Harry that it was okay for me to do so. I pitched my tent and then drove back to Harry's to return his pickup. After thanking him for what he had done I was about to leave when he asked me if I would like to come in for a drink. In my life up until then I had never refused a drink and I certainly wasn't about to start. We went into his house and sat talking and drinking for several hours. During the course of the day Harry introduced me to his wife Peggy and his daughter Jennifer who for some unknown reason, and which was never explained to me, had been nicknamed Butch.

Peggy was a natural blonde and very attractive, physically and mentally, being still to this day one of the nicest people I have ever met. Butch was very much like her but had naturally flame red hair and for a kid of her age she was very polite and well spoken. While I was there I asked Harry about David and why he had offered to let me pitch my tent in his orchard and then made me feel so unwelcome. Harry explained that David was the only English bullfighter in the world and felt that he was so famous that everyone should instantly recognise him as a superstar. If they didn't he would very quickly turn into a super brat. After several more drinks I could feel the nice warm glow of the booze beginning to relax my mind and body. I decided that it was time to leave before I became too familiar with them and said or did something that would cause me to wear out my welcome. I said goodnight, and made my way back to the tent.

As I was passing David's front door, I saw him coming out carrying a shotgun under his arm.
I said, "Excuse me David, I don't wish to appear rude but I feel that I should know you or I at least recognise you from somewhere. Have we ever met before?"

A smile as big as the Moon spread across his face. He took a deep breath and began talking almost as fast as a machine gun fired bullets, he told me in very minute detail why and what he was famous for, at the same time inviting me to come across to the stables and shoot some rats with him. I got to know him very well and he like a lot of other famous people I've known, as long as you continue to pander to their already swollen egos they will forever give you their undivided love and attention.

As I had first sensed, Harry Swan had a real wicked sense of humour bordering on the evil especially when he was under the influence of drink; when the drink was in us we were like twin souls. I began working for Harry delivering and selling shellfish all over the Kent and Sussex coast travelling as far as Brighton in one direction and Clacton-on-Sea in the other. Over the following two or three months I learnt a lot about the shell fish trade, and also got very friendly with several more girls who were very liberal with their sexual favours. Harry didn't pay very good wages and often he would forget to pay me at all but that didn't worry me to much as I was selling quite a lot of his stock and pocketing the money. It was one of those nice periods in my life that I hoped would never come to an end. It was also at this time that I met Mary Scott who I was very deeply smitten with and who seemed to grow very much in love with me.

I had seen her on several occasions at various different functions in the local dance halls but always in the company of a bloke who looked very much older than her. Thinking she was married or seriously attached to him, I never considered trying to chat her up until one night she came to a dance in the Packing Factory with him and two other attractive girls. For most of the evening the bloke danced with each of the girls in turn. Seeing his predicament and being the sort of decent, caring bloke I was, for totally unselfish reasons, I thought I ought to help him out. Choosing my moment carefully I walked over and asked Mary for a dance, with a very lovely smile on her face, she accepted my invitation. While we were dancing I asked if the chap with her was her husband. She told me that he was her sister's husband and that they mostly went dancing together because her sister didn't like socialising in large crowds, although she would always be there to pick them up at the end of the evening.

I asked her name and if she would like to have a drink with me, she said her name was Mary Scott and she would love to have a drink. We walked over to the bar and engaged each other in what felt like a very deep and meaningful conversation during which she asked me if I would like to go with her to see a group that were appearing at the Horse Bridge dance hall in Whitstable the following Friday. I felt delighted and told her I would. She then said that she was quite willing to pay for herself as it was going to be quite expensive. I told her if she wouldn't let me pay for both of us, I wouldn't go. We were really enjoying each other's company when her brother-in-law came over and said it was time for them to leave. I was quite disappointed because I hadn't thought to ask if I could take her home.

By this time I was living in Harry Swan's house and sharing a room with John Sherwood, who had come down from Chesterfield to visit the Barretts, but after staying with Harry Barrett for a couple of days he had decided that he didn't like them very much. While he had been staying with them they introduced him to Harry Swan, who had offered him a job working with me on the shellfish rounds. Peggy noticed on the day that Mary and I planned to go to Whitstable; I was paying much more attention to my appearance than I usually did.
She said, "This girl must have something very special going for her, the way you are preening yourself John, I hope she is worth all the trouble you're going to. Is there any chance that you will bring her back here to meet the us?"
"Only if you're very lucky," I replied.

When I met Mary, we caught the bus to Whitstable where I enjoyed one the best nights out that I'd had for ages. Unfortunately the last bus returning to Faversham was very early. Which meant that our wonderful night was a wonderful short night. When the bus arrived back in Faversham I was very deeply disappointed to see Mary's sister waiting there to take her home. Mary wrote down her address on a piece of paper and gave it to me, saying that she had a friend who lived two doors away from her parents house, whose husband had left her. She told me the number of her friends house and said she would see me there the next evening about seven o'clock. The next twenty or so hours seemed like a lifetime they dragged by so slowly.

When I knocked on the door of the address Mary had given me I was surprised to be greeted by a very attractive blond girl. She didn't look one bit like the sort of woman that any man with half a brain would want to dump, which is what Mary had told me the girl's husband had done. At first I thought that I might have come to the wrong place but she assured me that if my name was John, I was very much in the right place. After introducing herself as Sylvia she invited me in and asked me if I would prefer a cup of tea or a drink?
"A drink would do nicely," I told her.
She smiled and said, "That is exactly what Mary said you would say."
Not only was she a very friendly person she was also quite chatty. During the short period of time that passed while we were waiting for Mary to arrive, she told me nearly every detail about the separation from her husband and how her mother kept arriving, uninvited, to stay with her almost every weekend since he had left.

Eventually when Mary did put in an appearance she was carrying six bottles of beer and three lots of fish and chips. The girls had one beer between them and told me to drink the rest and as I was never shy when it came to drinking I did just that. We spent a pleasant couple of hours talking and fooling around. Sylvia said that she had been working from very early that morning and was feeling very tired. She said she didn't mind us stopping as long as we kept the noise down then went to bed leaving us alone on the sofa in her front room. We were doing some very heavy and serious petting when Mary told me that she had only ever had sex once before and because the bloke had been so rough with her, she felt that she didn't ever want to do it again. We certainly enjoyed being together on the sofa that night, both physically and emotionally.

Some time later Sylvia knocked on the room door and asked us if we would like a cup of tea.
Mary said, "I am sorry if we have woken you up."
"No you haven't," Sylvia answered. "I could hear you having such a good time I got very jealous and was thinking that I could come down and join in with you."
She laughed and then went into the kitchen to make the tea, Mary said to me in a very low voice "I don't think I would like having sex with another woman present."
What I said and thought were two totally different things; I didn't think for one moment that Sylvia had been joking.

The name of the village where the girls lived was Ospringe; it was situated about five or six miles outside of Faversham. At the time Sylvia had decided to make the tea I realised it was too late for me to catch a bus or taxi, which meant that I was going to have a very long walk back to Harry Swan's house. When I began to explain this to the girls, Sylvia interrupted me and said that I could sleep on her sofa. She went on to say that it would be nice, knowing that she had a man in the house and then giggled. Mary said she thought it was a good idea for me to stay, because we could all the catch the same bus into town the next morning. I could see from the way that she was looking at me that she wasn't over keen on the idea of me staying with Sylvia. She kissed me and said she didn't want to go home, but she had to, as her parents would be worried. I stood at the back door, and watched her walk the fifty or so yards along the road and into her house. I walked back into the front room, picked up my cup and drank the remainder of my tea. Sylvia said she didn't think it was worthwhile trying to get any sleep as it was nearly three o'clock which meant that she only had a couple of hours before she would have to get up for work. I said I hope you don't mind if I try to get a couple of hours sleep as I will be working and travelling all over Kent and Sussex that day.

She said, "Of course not, why don't you go upstairs and get in my bed."

I thanked her and said that I would, she started to give me directions to her bedroom but stopped and said, "Come with me it will be easier if I show you."

I followed her into the bedroom where she sat on the side of the bed and began telling me how much she missed having a man around the house. While she was talking, she took off her dressing gown, which proved to be the only item of clothes she was wearing. It was all happening so fast, Mary hadn't being gone more than five minutes and here was her friend trying to get me into bed. It didn't take very long or much persuasion for her to get me to join her between the sheets. At about quarter past six I got up and dressed then took a blanket and pillow and went down stairs and lay on the sofa. As luck would have it, my timing was perfect because within less than two minutes Mary came in the back door and asked if we were ready to catch the bus into town. I didn't make any arrangements to see Mary again because I felt quite guilty about having sex with Sylvia in less than an hour of telling Mary I was falling in love with her!

That day we had to deliver some cockles and other types of shellfish to several of O'Hagens seafood shops in Brighton. On the journey I told John Sherwood what had gone on the previous night. He asked me if I would introduce him to Silvia because he had now been in Faversham some time and hadn't been out with a girl since he'd arrived. I said that if I ever saw the girls again I would certainly put him in the frame. We travelled nearly a thousand miles that week, not really seeing much of Faversham during the daylight hours. On the Friday evening Harry told me that I'd had several phone calls from a girl who wouldn't leave her name, only a message to say if I want it to see her she would be waiting in the White Swan until closing time that night.

I asked John Sherwood if he would like to come with me and told him if the girl who had left the message was Mary there was a very good chance of her friend, Sylvia, being with her. I was pretty sure of my facts because Mary had told me, that she would never go into a pub on her own. John Sherwood was a very pasty faced, bloke who always seem to be living in a different world from the rest of us. He was capable of working very long hours and seemed to need very little sleep. Quite often during the time we shared the room at Harry Swans, he would go to bed very late, toss around for an hour or so and then get up again and start working or doing something to busy himself.

We made our way to the White Swan and as I guessed both Mary and Sylvia were waiting there, I introduced John who instantly seemed to meet with Sylvia's approval. Mary told me that she knew what had gone on between Sylvia and me, because Sylvia had told her how she had enticed me into bed. Mary went on to say that if it ever happened again it would be the end of any relationship that we might have. I told her I was sorry and that I would try my best never to do it again.

"Don't try your best, just don't bloody do it," she said.

We spent the weekend at Sylvia's because for once a blue moon had occurred and her mother had decided not to visit her. On the Monday morning all four of us caught the bus into town. As it was very crowded we had to sit in different parts of the bus. Mary said to me that Sylvia had told her that she was a bit upset with John because on the Sunday night he had got into bed with her, turned over and immediately fallen asleep. Also, she had a problem trying to wake him up in time to get to work.

I said it was very strange because he normally didn't sleep more than an hour a night, perhaps he was pretending because he did not fancy her.

Mary answered me in a very sarcastic tone, "You told me you didn't fancy her but you still shagged her." "Well maybe he's a poof," I said jokingly, hoping that the subject would change.

When the bus arrived at our destination, we kissed the girls and told them that we would see them the following weekend in the White

Swan. Sylvia looked at John and asked him if he really wanted to see her again, he assured her that he would very much like to see her as often as he possibly could. He added that if she didn't mind he would try to get round one evening during the week. Mary looked at me and said it would be very nice to see you as well. These girls certainly knew how to flatter us boys.

When we got to Harry's house, Peggy was waiting for us with a very worried look on her face. She said that she had been given strict instructions to make sure that John took his pills.
I looked at John and said, "I didn't know you had to take pills."
In his deep Derbyshire accent he replied, "Neither did I."
Peggy assured him that Harry had left very strict instructions that she should give John two pills dissolved in a small whisky. John looked totally befuddled, he looked at me and said that Harry always insisted that he should take a small whisky every night before he went to bed to help him sleep, but he certainly didn't know about any dissolved pills. I asked Peggy if she would show us the pills, which she did. I said to John, "In London these pills are what we call uppers, people only take them when they want to stay awake all night."

John informed both Peggy and me, in no uncertain terms, that he wasn't going to go to work until he found out from Harry about the pills. I said that suited me because as I hadn't slept very much over the weekend I would try to get a couple of hours rest. I hadn't been lying on my bed very long when I heard John shouting at Harry and accusing him of trying to turn him into a zombie. I got up and went to see what was going on. John wasn't there but I did hear the front door slam as he was leaving. I asked Harry and Peggy what was wrong; Harry kept laughing and said that John had tumbled to his little game.
"What little game was that?" I asked him.
Peggy said that she didn't think it was one bit funny.

She told me that Harry had told her such a convincing cock and bull story, she believed that John was seriously ill with a sickness that he was unaware that he needed medication for. As I have said before, Peggy was one of the nicest women I had ever met, and to see her in such bad temper was very unusual. She explained to me that Harry had been systematically feeding John amphetamines, disguised in whisky or some other sort of drink. This meant that he could never sleep for more than an hour or two, and that his mind would never really be alert enough to realise that Harry was making him work up to 20 hours a day for practically no money. When she'd finished explaining the things Harry had done to John and it had sunk into my brain, I didn't find it very difficult to believe. I knew that Harry was a very devious person but this really was a lesson to me in just how devious he could get.

Later John told me when he left Harry's house he had gone straight to the East Kent Packers factory to look for Sylvia so he could explain to her why had fallen asleep so heavily. After he had done this, she gave him the keys to her house and told him to go straight to bed and that she would see him when she got home. When I spread the news of what Harry had been doing to John around town. I'm afraid poor old John became quite an object of ridicule. The jokes went from 'sleep worker' to the 'Derbyshire living dead'; most of which, because John was not the brightest star in the sky, went straight over his head. I did hear many years after I left Faversham that John and Sylvia eventually got married and had a family.

I began to get the feeling that Peggy wasn't too keen on the idea that I was bringing Mary into her house, she never said as much but whenever she saw us in the pickup truck together she would walk away without greeting me in her usual friendly manner. I did ask her if Mary had ever done anything wrong to her, she just said that she really didn't know Mary very well. One day Harry bought a small spider monkey to keep as a pet, which we would all take in turns to exercise. It was a friendly little creature and was always be getting up to some mischief or the other. About a week before I left Harry Swan's, Peggy, Harry and myself were sitting in the front room talking and watching the monkey, which was roaming freely around doing its tricks, as it often did. During the course of our conversation, Mary came into the room wearing a low cut summer dress. When the monkey saw her, it ran along the back of the settee and around the room until it came up behind her, then it jumped on to her back and sunk its teeth and claws into the exposed fleshy part of her shoulder.

When she screamed Harry jumped up and tried to pull it off, but as he did the monkey tightened its grip on her until she began bleeding quite badly. The more Harry tried to make the monkey let go, the harder it clung to her until eventually he really had to wallop it very hard to make it release its hold. When it finally did he swung it around by its tail and smashed its head against the wall crushing its scull and killing it instantly. We took Mary to the hospital where she was given several stitches and a tetanus jab. Peggy, who had come with us, told me that she was very sorry that this had happened but that this breed of monkey only ever attacked people who threatened some kind of evil against their families.
I said, "Surely you don't think that Mary wishes you or Harry any harm."
She said, "I hope we never live to find out." It was then I decided it was time I started to look around for somewhere else to live.

About a week after the monkey incident, I was walking across the Market Square when Inspector Bill Gibbons stopped me and told me that I was wanted as a witness in the Magistrates Court. Which by pure coincidence was now sitting in the town hall just above the place where we were standing. When I asked him what they wanted me to be a witness about?
He said "Your friend Tony is up before them on the charge of G.B.H. that we brought against him for slashing you with the razor. Surely you haven't forgotten."
I told him that I hadn't forgotten but I was totally unaware that Tony had ever been charged with any offence. I certainly hadn't made any

complaint against him in fact the only time I had spoken to the police about the matter was the night that it had happened. Even then it was only because the doctor had asked me how I had received the wound. When I told him, he said that he would have to report the matter to the police. I had told him that was his business not mine, the next thing I knew the police had arrived and were asking me to tell them what had happened. I told them that I had been slashed with a razor, but I never told them who had done it.

I followed the Inspector up the stairs in to the Magistrates court and sat in the first empty seat I came to. Just as I sat down, I heard the magistrate tell Tony that he was going to send him to prison for three months. The next minute Tony was lying on the floor kicking, shouting and screaming. The Magistrate ordered the police to pick him up and take him away, which they did in a very unkind manner. As they dragged him past me I told him that I was sorry but there was nothing that I could do to help his situation. He looked at me and said they want people like you and me out of this town and they are going to use any method they can to get rid of us. Bill Gibbons told Tony to stop talking bollocks, and stand up and accept his punishment like a man! A few minutes later we were back outside the Magistrates court standing on the Market Square watching a police car taking Tony away in the direction Canterbury Prison.

With a look of pure delight on his face, Inspector Gibbons told me that some weeks previously, my three London mates had appeared before Canterbury Magistrates court, where each of them had been fined £25 for stealing the sacks of cockles. Gibbons also told me because the police hadn't known of my whereabouts at the time, they hadn't been able to issue me with the court order that would have informed me that I was due in court at the same time as my pals.
He continued to say, " Now that he had located me I would have to appear in three weeks time to face the same charges."
When I told him that I couldn't afford the fare to get to the court, he said, "Come round to Faversham police station the night before and I will personally make sure that you get a lift to the court."

I'm afraid that if Bill Gibbons thought that I was going to give up one unnecessary second of my freedom by staying in a police station overnight he was very sadly mistaken.

The three weeks seemed to fly by, I spent as much time with Mary as I could, Harry promised that he would come to court and speak on my behalf and tell them how his family had forgiven me and that I was now following a decent worthwhile occupation. This all sounded very good to me and I asked him if I received a fine that was more than I could afford to pay at the time, would he lend me the rest of the money. Knowing his sense of humour I expected some sort of sarcastically humorous answer. John he said if money is all it takes to get you to walk free from court, you can have all that I've got. He then said, for the next week or so why doesn't Mary tell her family that she is going on holiday with some of her friends and then you can both come and stay in my house. At that moment I thought that nobody could ever want or have a better friend.

On the day I stood in the Canterbury Magistrates Court, as you know not for first time, I began to feel very uneasy. Bill Gibbons had what I thought was a very unnecessary amount of police witnesses for such a petty crime. Both Harry and Mary told me that I was over reacting because I was nervous; I thought they must be right. I was put in the dock and told to stand up when the Magistrates came in. It wasn't long before a door at the rear of the courtroom opened and in came three of the most miserable looking human beings that I had ever had the misfortune to rest my eyes on. One of the pompous bastards who acted as the chairman looked across at me and sniffed up, what we call in the East End, a dewdrop that was hanging on the end of his very long pointed nose. It was all that I could do to stop myself from laughing out loud; I knew that he could see I was finding something very amusing about him.

When they had taken their seats and instructed the clerk of the court to read out the charges against me, I was asked how do you plead to these charges. If I had pled not guilty it would have meant that

Harry Swan would have been a prosecution witness and would have been legally obliged to give evidence against me. It seemed to make more sense to plead guilty and let him put in a good word on my behalf. Looking at it from my side, if the owner of the property I had stolen was going to speak for me, I thought I would have a much better chance of getting a small fine and walking out of court. Because I hadn't answered right away the beak asked me if I had legal representation.

"No your honour," I replied.

"Do you wish to be represented by legal aid," he asked me.

I told him that as I was pleading guilty I didn't feel that I should waste the courts time.

"You can be commended for that," he said.

"Is there anyone available to speak on your behalf," he asked me.

I told him Mr Swan; the owner of the goods that I was charged with stealing was going talk for me. They instructed Harry to go into the witness box. As he was approaching the witness box, I saw him reach into his inside jacket pocket and pull out a pair of glasses and put them on the his face. I knew very well that he never wore glasses and from where I was sitting I could see that there were no lenses in them! Harry spoke very highly of me and assured the magistrates that the sort of things I had done in the past would not happen again, if I were to be allowed to continue in his employment. The magistrate looked straight at Harry and asked him if he thought that people should have the right to leave their property in a public place without some sneak thief stealing it.

I knew by his tone that this bench of Magistrates weren't going to show me any leniency what so ever. The chairman told Harry that it was very commendable what he had done for me and that it would be taken into consideration, when he was passing sentence. He then turned to Bill Gibbons and asked if I had any previous convictions. Inspector Bill Gibbons looked like he was going to fall over himself with glee as he rushed up to the witness box.

"Yes, your honour," he said, "This man has been convicted of many crimes and at least one of them in this, very court, which you yourself may have had the displeasure to have dealt with your worship."

"I cannot possibly remember every petty criminal and sneak thief that comes before me," replied the chairman.
Gibbons went on to say that several of his colleagues were in court and available to give testimony against me, on several different matters that I had been guilty of, but I had never really been brought to book for. He went on to say that I was a very well known gangster in the twilight world of London's red light districts. Without any discussion with his joint Magistrates, big-nose looked at me and asked me if I had anything to say in my defence. I said that I thought that it was very unfair; to allow Gibbons to blacken my character about things that were of no concern with what was going on in the court today. I was just about to say something else I thought might help to persuade them to look more favourably on me, than what they were doing at that moment.

Suddenly the chairman looked directly at me, and in a very high pitched, tone of voice told me to 'Shut Up'. Without stopping to take a breath, he continued to say, "If you think that by persuading your very gullible but obviously very good friend, Mr Swan, to come into my Courtroom, falsely claiming to be the owner of the stolen property, is in any way going to make this court deal with you more leniently than it should, you are very sadly mistaken. You will be spending the next six months in prison finding out how mistaken you have been."
I said to him "But you only fined the other three twenty-five quid each."
He snapped back at me, "Because you were obviously the ringleader."
Wondering what had happened to all the good feelings that I'd felt when Norman, Jimmy, Alfie and myself had left Barney's café, for the second time in my life I made the walk from the Magistrate's Court, along the street and into the front gate of Canterbury prison.

CHAPTER 7

Canterbury prison is a very small nick; the exercise yards are the smallest I have ever walked around. One afternoon during an exercise period one of the inmates, that we had christened 'Mad Angus' because whenever he came out of his cell he walked around ranting and raving in a very strong, hard to decipher Scottish accent, had decided that he didn't like the trainee prison officer who was in charge of the yard. This poor bloke hadn't been in the prison service long enough to be issued with a uniform, the only identifying difference between him and the cons on exercise that day was that he had a chain with a bunch of keys hanging on it.

Somewhere along the line a very highly intelligent prison gardener had decorated the edges of the flowerbeds and paths with loose red house bricks, resting at a slight angle on each other. Mad Angus picked up several of these and started throwing them with all the strength he could muster at the screw. Most of them narrowly missed the target but when one did make full contact with his kneecap it certainly caused him to sit up and pay attention to what Mad Angus was up to. Most of the cons began to cheer as the screw tried to limp quickly away, at the same time blowing his whistle. One of the cons jumped on Angus and wrestled him to the ground, an action that most of us, because of our hatred of the screws, thought was totally unwarranted.

Over the following three days or so, all the con's that were on the exercise ground during the attack on the trainee, were taken before the governor and charged with aiding and abetting the assault. Each of us was deprived of 14 days remission, pay and privileges. The bloke who had jumped on Angus preventing him from doing any serious damage to the trainee, was given two months extra remission, which gave him an immediate release. On the following Monday morning, Tony Barrett (who was serving his time for attacking me with the razor) came into my cell and told me that my name was on the list of transfers to Pentonville. I asked him if he was coming with me? When he told me he wasn't I laughed and said of course not, they couldn't send you to a man's prison. Two days later, I was safely tucked up, in a Nutters cell in the Ville.

For the first month or two Mary wrote at least two letters a week expressing in very great detail how much she was missing me, and also about the undying love that she would carry in her heart forever. About a month before I was due out she wrote what I thought was a very strange note.

It started with the usual, "My dearest darling," and then went on to say, "If you receive a gossipy letter, telling you that I am being unfaithful, please ignore it because it will have been written by a person who is jealous of the love we have for each other. Please find enclosed the words that Harry (Swan) has told me will express the way I feel."

Enclosed was a typewritten copy of the popular song, 'Aint Misbehavin'.

That letter, containing such a very deep and meaningful pledge of faithfulness, was the last I heard from her until after I came out of prison. I did, however, receive the 'gossipy' letter she had told me about. In it someone accused Mary not only of being unfaithful to me with Harry Swan but also of breaking up his marriage. It went into what I thought were unnecessarily lurid details about their relationship, which made me feel very uncomfortable. It was signed, "From a Caring Friend!" The details were put in such a way that I found it impossible to convince myself they weren't true. After I had got over the initial and very hurtful emotional pains of reading it, I settled down and served the rest of my time planning how I was going to take my revenge on both Harry and Mary.

When I finally got back to Faversham, the first thing I did was to go around and see the person I thought might be the author of the very informative letter. My guess was right, it was a woman named Pat who I had been very friendly with and who was also Peggy Swan's closest friend. She admitted sending the letter, but told me that neither Harry nor Mary knew for certain that she had done so. She had only threatened them with doing it if they didn't stop seeing each other. I asked her not to let anyone know that she had told me, because there might be a very good chance of me getting back with Mary if she thought that I was unaware of what had been going on. Pat promised she wouldn't say a word to any one.

I was full of very mixed emotions when I saw Mary. I knew that my real feelings for her were still as deep and strong as they were on the day I went to prison. She greeted me with a kiss on the cheek, not the sort of embrace that one would have expected between two people who were deeply in love and had been forcibly kept apart for the amount of time we had. I knew there and then that whatever feelings she'd had for me in the past were now gone. I walked away from her feeling that the bottom had fallen out of my world. Not knowing or caring what I was going to do next, I wandered around the streets of Faversham for several hours, trying to get my head back on track. Mary's rejection combined with the emotional pain I was feeling, fuelled my brain with ideas of revenge, my only problem was how to go about exacting it.

Feeling certain that my very good friend, Harry Swan wouldn't be to keen on having me around his place, I decided that I would be much better off if I went back to live in London. As I walked across the Market Square, on my way to the train station, I heard someone calling me, I looked around and was delighted to see the lovely smiling face of Peggy Swan. She hugged me like a long lost son and asked me how long I had been out and why hadn't I been around to see her. When I told her that I no longer had any reason to stay in Faversham and was on my back to London, she insisted that I should go and stay with her and Harry until I got on my feet again. My brain told me that this was just what I needed to do if I wanted to get my own back on Harry and Mary.

From the first day I moved back in with the Swan's, Harry took it upon himself to take me around all the clubs and pubs of West

London and the coastal resorts of Kent that he had discovered and frequented, while I had been away. It was very obvious to me that the reason he wanted me to be his very best buddy and constant companion was to keep me from seeing Mary. As I said earlier, I already knew that she had lost interest in me but I wasn't about to tell Harry, otherwise it would have meant the end of all my 'expenses paid' drinking trips. I don't know how Peggy felt about this but she seemed quite delighted whenever she saw me and Harry going about together, she knew that while he was in my company, he wouldn't be spending time with Mary.

On one of these trips, we went to Margate; Harry said that he was almost certain that I would know the girl who owned the Club we were going to visit. He said it was on Swain Road, in Cliftonville, and added that it was a very upmarket area. He told me that the girl's name was Esther and that she had been well known around the Soho area before coming to live in Kent. From his description of the woman I had no idea if I knew her or not, and really didn't care one way or another, I just wanted to get to the Club and start drinking, at his expense.

My feelings for Mary still ran very deep within me even though I had mentally accepted that our relationship was over. Knowing it was Harry's fault, my devious way of thinking told me that the longer I could hang around, allowing him to ease his conscience by spending money on me, the better my revenge was going to feel. Even without having to resort to the kind violence that I would normally have used to settle these sorts of matters. I didn't hate Harry in fact I quite liked him and really didn't mind being in his company, it was unfortunate that we had both fallen in love with the same girl. At the time of the Margate trip, he was totally unaware that I knew about his affair with Mary. As I said earlier I wasn't going to be one that killed the golden goose.

When we arrived in Swain Road I began to look out for the club, Harry said it didn't have a sign because it wasn't a proper licensed drinking club. I asked him what sort of club it was, he told me it was just like the ones in Soho, only a bit smarter on the outside. I realised what he meant when we stopped in front of a very elegant guesthouse. Like most of the other houses in the street it was a white painted four-storey property. Harry directed me to the basement door that was situated about six foot below ground level, hidden under a flight of stone steps that led up to the main entrance of the upper part of the house.

The difference between this basement club and many others that I had been in was that the dividing wall had being taken out to make two small rooms into one large one. Installed against the far wall there was what looked like a very well stocked bar. There were several small circular tables spread around the room, each covered with a red and white check tablecloth on top of which was either a Cianti or Mateus Rose bottle with partly burnt candles stuffed in their necks. The place smelt of stale cigarette smoke and booze, the ashtrays were full to overflowing and the few people that were propping up the bar already looked drunk. They greeted Harry like a long lost relative, he pointed to an empty table and told me to sit at it, then asked me what I wanted to drink. While he got the drinks I sat down in the seat he had pointed to, which was as far away from the people at the bar as he could possibly get me.

I had got quite used to Harry whispering to most of the people we met, obviously warning them not to mention that he had been in these places with Mary.
On several occasions I said to him, "Do you think that you should go ahead and prepare the crowd for my arrival?" Thankfully he never really caught on to what I was hinting at.
Looking around the club I noticed that the décor was badly in need of attention. It looked like at one time in the not too distant past someone had wasted a considerable amount of time and money trying to make the place look like an old Wild West saloon. The walls were painted bright red and draped with heavy red brocade curtains edged with tassels. The toilet doors were painted to look like the swing-slatted type that you would go through when entering a saloon

in Dodge City. It made me feel like any minute I would see John Wayne come bursting into the bar, looking for the bad guys.

If you stood facing the bar, on your right hand side there was a door marked private, which I guessed was the access to the upper part of the building. I remember thinking the person who had designed this bar must have had a lot more money than sense or taste. I was about to say this to Harry when a woman I had known in London came through the aforementioned private door. Harry stood up, walked across the room and kissed her on the cheek putting his arm around her waist and bringing her to our table. This is the bloke I've been telling you about he said, pointing to me. Before he could say any thing else she said I have known 'Rasher' for many years, from both the East and West End of London. With that she pulled me up from my seat put both arms around my shoulders and kissed me full on the lips and did some very suggestive things with her tongue.

It wasn't the sort of greeting that I would normally have expected from a person who I'd only known on a friend of a friend basis, from various meetings around the Soho and East End club scene. This was Esther the Jewish girl that Harry had been telling me about. I could see that Harry was quite pleased with the way she had greeted me. My brain told me that his plan was if we fancied each other it would be a good way for him to dump me off and then he could go in search of Mary. I had got so used to the way Harry's mind worked I could read it in his facial expressions. Esther was an attractive woman with long black hair and blue eyes. Lots of memories flooded into my head about the time I had known her in London. In those days she had been very fond of giving people who didn't know her very well the impression that she was a scatter brained type of person.

I had known her for some considerable time, but as I have already said not on a very intimate level. Several years earlier she had lived with a friend of mine in the East End, that is how I got to know that she was a long way from being a scatterbrain. My friend had told me on several occasions how shrewd she really was and how she had earned a great deal of money from buying and selling properties around the Victoria area. Seeing her now I began recalling how much trouble my mate had got into when some of the blokes in the East End had tried to pull her. Because of the simpleton act she put on, many of them thought she would be an easy touch for money, sex or both. I didn't know whether she deliberately wanted to cause trouble, but she certainly led a lot of men on to think that she was available. When they tried to get past the chat up stage, she would call on my pal to see them off. She had a fascination for so-called rough diamonds.

At the end of the longest kissing and cuddling greeting I had ever had, we sat down and started to reminisce about the old days in London. When Harry went up to the bar for more drinks, Esther lent across the table and whispered to me, "Do you know that he had been bringing your girlfriend to my Club." I told her that I was fully aware of what had been, and was still going on between Harry and Mary but that I didn't want him to know that I had found out because I was using him as a gravy train. Esther smiled and then asked me did I still want Mary. My little bit of grey matter clicked into overtime, I knew that I had to think quickly and carefully to come up with the right answer.

If I told her I was still in love with Mary, it might spoil any chance that I had of spending the night drinking her booze, and finishing up in bed with her. I felt after the things she had done with her tongue while she was greeting me, my prospects in the bedroom direction were very good. She was a lot older than Mary was, but equally as attractive, plus I thought she might still have money. At that particular time I was still feeling the emotional pains of rejection and my ego was in need of a boost. I told her that I was still very fond of Mary but I wouldn't be able to live with her after what she had done to me. All the time I was talking to Esther, I was watching her face very carefully, hoping that I would be able see in her expression, if this was the answer, she was hoping to hear.

When Harry came back to the table with the drinks, I watched both him and Esther and could see from the glances that passed between them that there had been something prearranged. I thought this would be an opportune moment to go to the toilet and give them some time alone to discuss whatever plans they had made for me. I excused myself and walked towards the gents, I was surprised to see that Harry was following me.

When we got into the loo, Harry said, "I am sorry John but this as all been an elaborate set up between Esther and myself. She told me some time ago that when you were both around the London clubs, she really fancied you very strongly, but because you were pals with the bloke she was living with, she didn't think it was right to tell you."

"It's all well and good you telling me this, but what have you set me up for? You know that I can't stay here for the night as I have got to see Mary early in the morning," I lied.

He said, "If you want to stay with Esther, I'll tell Mary that you have had to stay over for a job interview at the Dreamland Fun Fair Park."

I felt like calling him a lying bastard, as I knew for certain that he would be seeing Mary at the first given opportunity but what he would be telling her was anybody's guess. It certainly wouldn't be anything that could possibly put me back in her good graces. I put on what I thought was a good show of pretending to resist his idea but finally agreed to do as he suggested.

When we got back to the table Esther was holding two bottles of wine and two glasses, she said to Harry, "I hope you don't mind but I have to go back upstairs to see that my children are safely tucked up in bed." The fact that she had children came as a complete surprise to me.

"Would you like to come up and see them," she asked me.

For a second or two I was lost for words, Esther, seeing my dilemma said, "I am sure that Harry won't mind being left out on this occasion, as he as most probably seen them more often than he as seen his own daughter."

I followed her through the door marked private; up a single flight of stairs and along a wide hallway, which led in to a very large lounge situated in the front of the house. I guessed it was directly above the clubroom. It was furnished with two four-seater sofas facing each other over a large glass coffee table; there were also two double-seated matching armchairs. Esther closed the door behind us and turned the key in the lock and then placed it on the coffee table. She put one bottle of wine on the table, handed me the other one, and told me to fill the glasses. She said that she had told a little white lie about checking on the children because they were staying with their grandparents in London for the weekend.

She went on to tell me how many bedrooms there were in the house and how much money she could earn from guests staying during the summer season. She also said that because the town died in the winter months she had converted the basement into a club to subsidise her income. We talked for a while about everything and nothing. I asked her if Harry had been telling the truth when he told me that she fancied me. She giggled, put her drink on the table, took her shoes off, moved along the sofa towards me and kissed me. We continued to drink, talk, kiss and cuddle until she told me that she wouldn't be able to have sex because she was allergic to French letters or rather rubber and she certainly wasn't going to run the risk of becoming pregnant because we hadn't used one. I began to suspect that she and Harry had cooked this plot up between them to get him off the hook. Here I was locked in a room with an attractive woman feeling pleasantly the better for drink and very randy, being told that all this come on was going to lead nowhere. I disentangled myself from Esther poured another drink and sat back on the sofa some distance from her.

She looked at me and said, "I didn't mean that we can't have any sex, I just mean intercourse."
I thought this was a very posh word for shagging, I looked at her and said, "What can we do then."
She said first you can go back down to the club and get a bottle of what ever booze is your preference, when you come back I think you will be surprised at what we can do. When I got back to the room Esther had done what they do in all good films she had slipped into something more comfortable only her version of more comfortable

was naked. My preference from behind her bar was a bottle of vodka, I told her I would pay for it before I left.

She looked at me and said, "I was rather hoping that you weren't going to leave."

"That's up to you," I replied. "It's your house and your club."

"Lets talk about it later," she answered.

I took off my clothes, lay down next to her on the sofa and commenced to take part in every sexual act that I thought was humanly possible outside of penetration. Stopping only for the occasional very large glass of vodka, it was a very pleasurable and in some parts, memorable experience.

We woke up the next morning looking and feeling very hung over but quite content. The first thing she asked me was if I would stay and look after the place, while she went up to London, to collect her children and do some business. I told her that I wouldn't mind doing what she wanted but I had very little money and had been dependent on Harry Swan for food and lodgings.

She said, "Don't worry, you can buy all of the food you need on my account at Gradus' stores in North End Road."

This all sounded very good to me, so I agreed to stay on. Before she left she told me not to open the club and if anybody enquired why it was closed I was to tell them that I was the new Manager and we were doing renovations.

She gave me the keys to her car and said that I could use it around town but as it wouldn't go into top gear using it for long runs would be totally uneconomic. It would use a tremendous amount of petrol running in only the lower gears. It was a two year old black Ford Consul, I couldn't understand why she hadn't had it repaired, it would have certainly have been cheaper than using the train to transport herself and her children backwards and forwards to London.

After I dropped Esther at Margate station I drove back to the house, parked up, skipped up the front steps and let myself in. As I closed the door behind me, from down the hallway I heard a very long low growl followed by a loud feminine command of 'sit'! The instruction was totally ignored and the biggest, blackest Alsatian that I had ever seen had me pinned with my back against the front door. This dog was so big its paws were on my shoulders and I was looking up into its mouth, which was at least six inches above me and slobbering all over my face. I was fully expecting it to take my head off in one mouthful, to say that it suffered from halitosis would be more than polite.

The voice I had heard issuing the command to sit was coming from a woman who I can only describe as a clone of Hilda Ogden. "Get down Jet," she kept saying to the bloody great oaf of a dog, then she looked at me and kept repeating over and over, "It's all right, it's all right he won't bite you."
Apart from feeling too frightened to take into consideration whether he would bite or not, I felt that I was going to die from the smell of his stinking breath. I suddenly realised that this animal was not only dribbling over my head and shoulders he was now trying to shag me with the biggest Willie I'd ever seen on man or beast. I heard the woman say, you must be a nice sort of person because he only does that to people he likes.

Eventually she grabbed Jet by the collar and dragged him off of me, at the same time explaining that she was the cleaner and that Esther had told her I would be looking after the house and dog. Within a matter of three or four minutes I had gone from the elevated position of Manager of a small but select seaside hotel and night club, to a canine sex object and now Zoo Keeper. It was one of those times in my life when I asked myself how the fuck did this happen to me, and why. I never had a chance to get to know this woman because the next thing she did was to give me a set of keys, and tell me to tell Esther that she no longer wanted to work for her. Before I could ask what the situation was and if there were any guests staying, she was outside the door saying goodbye to Jet and then she was gone. I never saw or heard of her again. Jet immediately adopted me, which I found a great comfort because he was the only living creature that I knew throughout the entire seaside resort of Margate.

I walked into the lounge where I'd spent the night with Esther thinking that I was going to work out a plan of action when to my surprise there was a little black boy sitting looking out of the window. "I'm sorry." I said, "I wasn't aware that we had any guests staying in the Hotel."

"I'm not a guest, I am Baby Bubbly, the singer," he told me.

He stood up as he was talking and walked towards me with a look on his face that said I should immediately recognise him and pay some sort of homage for being allowed in his presence. It was like meeting Dave the Bullfighter again. Most of my life, I have hated people who suffer from delusions of grandeur and think they are a station or two above all others. Whenever I've had the misfortune to come across them, I've always done my level best to bring them into the real world, as I see it.

"Well, Baby Bubbly," I said, "It's very nice to meet you, where do you sing in the local pub? Or has Esther been having cheap cabaret acts in the club downstairs."

I could now see in his face that I had hit home, he looked very deeply wounded and began to protest, explaining that the places he sang in did not include anything as low as pubs or basement dives. I let him continue telling me how good he was and how famous he was going to become as soon as he found a decent songwriter. Listening was never my strong point and listening to people talking bullshit, really got up my nose.

I said to him, "You must be one of the other members of the human race that God has made nearly as important as me."

I could see that this had really flattened his ego, because he was looking at me with an expression on his face that said, very loudly and without using any words, I want you to immediately drop dead in great physical pain!

Baby Bubbly must have been about 16 or 17 years of age, but he stamped out of the room like an immature two-year-old. I sat down on the sofa, wondering what sort of weird experience I had let myself in for. Within a couple of minutes of Baby Bubbly making his film star type exit, a giant of a man came in to the room and introduced himself as Jim Ledbetter, he asked if it was okay to join me. When I said yes, come in and take a seat, he told me that Esther had informed him, Baby Bubbly, and several other people who were staying in the guesthouse, that I was the new Manager. If they wanted anything they should see me as I was going to be completely responsible for the running of the place in her absence. Big Jim was a veritable gold mine of information. He told me that in the early hours of the morning Esther had gone from room to room waking people up and telling them about me. I asked Jim what she had actually said.

"Not very much," he replied, "Just that you are a well known villain from the East End, who she has brought in for protection and take care of her business interests."

I asked Big Jim to explain exactly what Esther's business interests were. With a big grin spreading across his face he asked if she had landed me with all the responsibility of the place and not bothered to explain the situation?

"That seems to be the size of it," I replied. "Will you tell me what I need to know about Esther and her business interests?" I asked him again.

He said, "Yes," and began telling me how he came to be staying in the Hotel.

He said, "I was working around the area renting out and installing Jukeboxes and slot machines and arrived here looking for bed and board. When Esther found out what I did she ask me if I would install some of my machines downstairs in the club, which I did."

At that point I interrupted him to say that I hadn't seen any slot machines, only a broken Juke Box.

He said, "That is the main reason she's brought you in."

"I don't understand what you mean," I said.

"It's very simple," Jim replied, "She has been a woman trying to run a club in a town that is dominated by male club owners, who have all lost a lot of good business to her."

"From what I have seen of Margate I would have thought there were more than enough night club punters to go around," I said.
He went on to tell me that Esther, like many of the other dive owners, had never applied for or been granted a licence to serve alcohol on their premises. This meant the business she was taking was the highly illegal but lucrative late night drinking sessions. I told him that I still didn't understand about the missing slot machines.
"That's also very easy to explain," Jim said. "Some of the club owners have employed bully boys to come here and cause trouble. The last time they were paid to do so they took the opportunity to steal the slot machines and smash the jukebox. That was after they had deliberately slung booze all over the walls and drapes."

My brain was working very hard trying to understand the complexities of the overall situation, sitting here in front of me was a man who stood six feet five inches tall, in his stocking feet, weighing somewhere in the region of 20 stone. He was openly admitting to me that he had stood by and watched a couple of little bully boys do several hundred pounds worth of damage and then rob a woman of property that legally belonged to him. When I asked him why he had allowed it to happen, he explained that I was making the same misconception as Esther had made about him due to his size.
"I do apologise, John," he said, "But I don't have any sort of stomach for violence. I am just an every day working chap, who couldn't fight his way out of a paper bag with two mates to help me."
I began thinking about the previous night and all the words and sexual acrobatics that had gone on between Esther and myself. Considering the conversation I was now having with Jim I came to the conclusion that emotionally it had meant nothing to her other than a means of getting me to act as an unpaid bodyguard.

Just then Baby Bubbly and another two other young blokes came into the room and asked, in a very condescending manner, if any of the hotel staff were going to make themselves available to cook and serve breakfast. I felt more than a bit disconcerted about the way they were looking directly at me while they posing the question. Feeling the hairs on the back of my neck begin to bristle with temper, I said, "I'm sorry I have no idea, who or what is going to serve you with your breakfast. The fact of the matter is, I have no fucking idea what the hell is going on in this madhouse and what's more I certainly don't have the slightest idea why I am here!" As I stood there in what I thought was my best George Raft threatening pose, Jet decided that it was time to shag me again.

Mentally I felt quite delighted that Esther had given these people the false impression that I was some sort of hard case. It was obvious to me that none of the people I had seen so far who were staying in the hotel, would be capable of looking after themselves if it came to any sort of violent confrontation. This meant, if I used their fear of my newly appointed hard man reputation I could have some sort of control over them. At the same time, I was thinking that all the hard men I had met in my life, gave off a much better and more convincing tough guy image when they weren't letting a great big dog use their leg to work out its' sexual frustrations.

I pointed to Baby Bubbly and suggested that if I supplied him the groceries he could cook the breakfast for everybody. I could see that he was still seething from our first encounter; this latest put down was really sticking the boot into his ego.
He looked at me, braced his shoulders and pulled himself up to his full four foot two and a bit and said, "I am the lead singer and these people are my backing group. I do not make breakfasts for anybody, especially when they are residents in a run down flea bitten hotel like this!"
"That's okay by me," I told him, "You can make your own arrangements."
Turning to the others, I asked, "Who out of the rest of you is going to make our breakfast?"
They all looked very sheepishly at each other and then at the floor.
Big Jim said, "I will make it for you and me John, but the rest can do what they please."

Baby Bubbly said, "This isn't fair, we work for Esther and part of the deal is free board and lodgings, we are entitled to be fed."
"I am sorry," I said, "that's your arrangement with her not mine. It's bad enough that I've got to feed this fucking great dog, who by now had decided to give his full an undivided love and sexual attention to Baby Bubbly.

It turned out that there was absolutely no food of any description in the place. Even the bar and been cleared of all its stock.
I looked at Jim and said, "She's not even left us a dog biscuit. Do you have a car.?"
"No," he replied, "I've been using Esther's Consul."
"That's all right," I said. "She's left me the keys to it so you can drive us to the shop where she has got an account."
When we got there I was surprised to find out that I knew the proprietor. Some years previously he had owned a shop in the East End and was a friend of my mum's. He told me that Esther had reached the limit of her credit and if it hadn't been for the fact that she was a Jewish girl, no matter how many kids she had, he wouldn't have allowed her to run up a tab.

I didn't tell him that neither Esther nor her children were at home. I took as many groceries as he would allow me to have and promised him that I would make certain sure that Esther settled her account by the end of the week. At that moment in time I really hadn't the slightest idea if I would ever see her again. It had become crystal clear to me that she was skint. Once again my luck was running true to form. Here I was living in a grand house, the sexual plaything, manager and bodyguard of a (one time rich!) attractive widow who now had a thousand enemies, piles of debt at least six desperate dependants and no fucking money.

When we arrived back to the house Jim cooked the breakfast in what seemed like no time at all. I hadn't realised how hungry I was until I saw the big fry up sitting on a plate in front of me. I asked him if there was any condiments or brown sauce available?

He said, "I think I saw some in the kitchen cupboard downstairs, hold on a moment I'll go and fetch it."
"No that's OK." I said, "I'll get it myself." For some inexplicable reason both of us decided to go to the kitchen for the sauce.

When we got to the kitchen the fridge door was wide open and all the food we had bought apart from what was on our plates had disappeared, the only evidence of it ever existing were several shredded empty containers, scattered around the floor. We looked at each other both thinking the same thing, and made a quick dash back up to the lounge, but it was to late. Jet with a smug doggy-type look on his face was just finishing the second breakfast; he'd even knocked over and lapped up our coffees. Jim said how silly of us, we never remembered to get the poor thing any food of its own. Poor thing, I thought to myself, all our food has gone and the only place that would possibly have given us credit to get some has closed the account. The last time I'd had anything substantial to eat had been 48 hours previously. The only money I possessed was in the glove compartment of Harry Swan's pickup and he was by now some thirty or more miles away thoroughly enjoying himself shagging my ex girlfriend! This silly big fat bastard in front of me was calling the big ugly beast that had just swallowed my breakfast, which could be the last one I might have the good fortune to come close to for several days, a poor thing! There was a great list of names that I could think of to call that fucking animal, but a poor thing wasn't anywhere near the top of the list.

There were six people in the house including myself and between us we managed to scrape up less than fifteen pounds. This became a central kitty, which I took charge of and each day we would spend as little as we could on the most food we could get. Early on the morning of the fourth day I was woken up with quite a start when two little boys decided that the best way to get me out of bed was to jump on me. I was still feeling quite fuzzy headed when I heard Esther's voice telling them to get off of me. I looked at her thinking that maybe I had dreamt the past couple of days.

"Surprise! Surprise!" she said "Come on sleepy head wake up I've been travelling most of the night so that I could get here to see you as early as possible."
I managed to groan a response, saying to her, "I didn't think that I was ever see you again."

What ever gave you that idea she replied, "I told you I was only going up to town to get my boys and to do some business."
When I saw that she was heavily laden down with full to the brim shopping bags, the attraction this woman had once held for me instantly returned. I thought there must be some food in those bags somewhere she couldn't possibly be carrying that much luggage, without, there being something to eat. Suddenly the room filled with people, one of who was my old friend Jimmy Makin or Del Ward, as he was now known. All of them were carrying suitcases and pieces of luggage of various descriptions. I asked Esther what the fuck was happening? At the same time trying to explain to her in the politest way I could, how I had just spent four very hungry and angry days with some very objectionable people, while all the time trying to avoid getting shagged by her dog, that she very conveniently had forgotten to tell me about.

And now here I was lying in a makeshift bed in a very public lounge not wearing any clothes surrounded by what looked to me like a crowd of fucking poofs, one of which was telling his or her friend, how attractive I looked. Esther being a bright girl and realising I wasn't in the best of moods she put down her shopping bags and started ushering the people into the next room, at the same time telling me she would explain everything.
"That coming from you would be an excellent and very novel idea," I said.
When she had finished showing everyone into the back room, she came back and told me that the people I had just been so rude in front of were the very people that were going to make us a lot of money. I thought I don't know Margate very well, but a load of fairies going round renting out their bums to the public didn't strike me as a novel

168

way of making a lot of money. Although I didn't exactly put my thoughts into words, Esther read my mind.

She said to me, "I know they must all look like raving homosexuals to you, but at this moment in time they are the most popular rock and roll music group around." Luckily for both you and me I have agreed a deal with them whereby they will pay their own expenses and work on a profit sharing basis around my dance hall circuit."

This was another revelation. "What bloody dance hall circuit are you talking about," I asked her. "Hasn't anybody told you that I run dances in most of the major towns around Thanet and East Kent? The group that arrived with me, that you have just been so disrespectful to are called, Johnny Kidd and the Pirates!" She exclaimed! "They've been on television and have a record in the top twenty, even you must have heard of them."

She was right I had heard of the group and at that particular time they were very popular, I could see that they would draw crowds in to the dance halls. It was just then that Baby Bubbly decided to come back into the room. For some reason known only to him, he had put on his stage clothes and was wearing make up. Some black people I have known in my life were and are able to wear make up very tastefully, but I am afraid that Baby Bubbly just looked like a white-faced clown. He looked at Esther, burst out into tears and started using all the mannerisms of a little girl, it suddenly dawned on me that Bubbly was a poof. Over the four days that I had got to know him he certainly had been able to hide that little quirk in his nature.

He said to Esther, "You told me that John was going to be nice and look after us." As he was talking to her he was burying his face into her chest and by doing so was covering the front of her very smart tailored navy blue costume in make-up that looked more like flour than face powder. I started to laugh; not at them but at the scene they were creating. I was the only one that could see any amusement in the situation.

Bubbly said to Esther, "When I first saw John I almost fell in love with him and was going to steal him from you. Now I wouldn't have him near me if you gave me a million pounds."

At that time in my life the things I hated most were blacks and homosexuals, these prejudices were born of fear. In this particular incident Baby Bubbly had just combined the both and elected himself my personal public enemy number one. I felt that I wanted to kill him, however could he think that he would be capable of making me have any sort of sexual or emotional feelings for another man. The only thing I felt was revulsion and disgust. What was going on in my mind at that moment is really unprintable? I'm positive, that both Esther and Baby Bubbly wouldn't have come within ten miles of me if either of them had had the slightest inkling of what was going on in my head.

It didn't take long for Esther to convince me that she had found a way to renew her fortune and once again she was on the way up. I began to believe that my luck was changing for the better; we started doing the rounds of the dance halls and making serious money. I began wearing trendy clothes and became very well known for my dancing ability. There were at least one or two girls in every dance hall that wanted to partner me. For a couple of months my life couldn't have been better I was receiving money for doing the things that I loved to do most. I was invited by one of the groups Esther hired, to appear on The Oh Boy Show with them, which as I have mentioned earlier I did on several occasions. On two of the show's I was asked if I would run from the side of the studio, jump into the centre of the dance area, grab hold of a girl and start to rock and roll. I must have been so good that they only included my part of the show on special occasions; unfortunately I have never been privy to those occasions. I have never actually seen myself on television. Andy Warhol said that everybody will be famous for 15 minutes I guess my quarter of an hour is lying somewhere on the cutting room floor of some television studio.

However, as they say all good things come to an end. After our initial physical relationship Esther and I didn't sleep together again, firstly I told her that I would get very embarrassed if her children saw us in bed together. She seemed to accept this excuse that was until I stopped going on the dance-hall circuit and began inviting different girls I had met at the various venues to come and visit me back at the house. This mainly went on while Esther was either working or up in London visiting her folks. One of the groups that she hired for the tour left a penniless girlfriend at the house when they went back to wherever they had come from. She and Esther became friends. It was this girl who told Esther what was I was getting up to behind her back. I have no doubt in my mind that she slung in a few of her own little embellishments. Whatever she said didn't really matter because I didn't physically fancy Esther any more, the only attraction she had ever held for me was financial which, since I had left the circuit, wasn't very rewarding.

One Saturday afternoon, I was expecting two girls from Canterbury to arrive at the house; waiting with me was Stanley Gradus the son of the shop owner. I had met him when I was buying groceries for the house, we had joked about being exiles from the East End and seemed to hit it off as friends. When the girls arrived we showed them into the lounge, told them to make themselves comfortable and asked if they wanted a drink, to which they both said yes. Before we had time to get the booze out of the cabinet, the lounge door was thrown open. In marched Esther with her friend Penniless who was saying, "You don't have to take my word any more Esther, you can now see for yourself what he as been doing behind your back."

From the conversation that followed, I could only assume that Esther thought one of these girls was someone that I had been seeing on a regular basis.
She looked at me and said, "I'm going to give you a choice, you either stop seeing this little trollop or we are finished, it is entirely up to you."
Thinking primarily about my board & lodgings and the fact that I hadn't even got to know the girl's name, I found it quite easy to promise never to see her again. Further Stanley and I hadn't even decided which of the girls was going to be with who. For the next week or two Esther didn't let me out of her sight. I went to all the dance halls on the circuit drove her around in the car with no top gear, played daddy to her two little kids and acted just like I thought

a reformed partner would have done. We never slept together nor did we have any more sexual acrobatics.

She had done such a good job at spreading the propaganda about me being a villain; I couldn't see why she needed me around anymore. That was until one night when I was selling tickets on the door of the Horse Fair dance hall in Whitstable. Two thick set, rough looking geezers pushed past me without paying. I grabbed hold of the second man, swung him around and asked him where he thought he was going.
"Where do you think I am going, you stupid bastard," he said.
Before he could say anything else he was sitting on his arse holding his bollocks. I had been taught the hard way, that if any body gets verbally aggressive with you and you didn't respond quickly enough, it wouldn't be to long before they became physically aggressive. So, if an opportunity arises whereby you can land the first kick or punch, at least ninety per cent of what follows should go in your favour.

His friend hadn't seen what happened to him and was still making his way up the stairs towards the dance floor. I told the bloke who was working with me to keep his eye on the fellow on the ground and if he tried to get up, either kick him again or hit him with something. Luckily for me some of the boys that I knew from Faversham had come to the dance and I had let them in free of charge, which meant that if needed I help they were available. When I caught up with the bloke I was chasing he was having a very heated discussion that looked like it would soon become a physical confrontation with Esther.
I heard him say, "You have taken my family's money and signed a contract and now here you are double-crossing us."
Esther replied very calmly, "Can we talk about this outside,"
The bloke said, "What is there to talk about, you have cheated us, you can either leave this dance hall now under you own steam, or accept the consequences and we will still take our money back."
When he turned around and realised that it was me standing behind him, not the person he was expecting to see. We both instantly

recognised each other, this was a mate of mine that I had worked with on the club doors back in Soho.

"Look John," he said to me. "Me and my brother had no idea that you were involved with this woman. We have paid her £5,000 to take over the East Kent dance hall circuit. She is breaking a written agreement."

I asked Esther whether this was true. It was a stupid question because my mate had no reason to lie.

Esther nodded her head and said to me, "If you were any sort of man you wouldn't let this happen to me."

I told her that she was very lucky that my mate hadn't cut her to pieces as he was very well known to have a great deal of talent when he used a cut-throat razor. My old mate and I left the dance hall and went to a local cafe where we sat down to discuss the matter. I apologised to his brother who was still nursing his bollocks but I don't think he was very interested in my apology. It turned out that Esther had sold the dance hall circuit to several different promoters. By using the make-believe reputation that she had spread about me, and insinuating that whenever I was in trouble I could call on the Kray twins to back me up, most of the promoter's had swallowed their pride and hadn't bothered trying to get their money back.

When we got back to Margate, I told Esther that she would have to find somebody else to look after her because I would be leaving as soon as I could find somewhere to go.

She said to me, "What sort of man are you to walk away and leave somebody your supposed to be fond of in trouble. I'm really glad now that I didn't let you have proper sex with me because I'm not allergic to rubber I was going to tell you many times but somehow I knew that you were going to turn out no good."

I said, "I am very sorry you feel this way, because I have always liked you as a friend and I do hate having to part like this. As for the sex I was too busy with the girls of my own age to worry about sleeping with someone nearly old enough to be my mum." (Which she wasn't)!

She went absolutely berserk, at first she tried to set the dog on me and then she started throwing every movable object she could lay her hands on. Luckily she was in such a bad temper her aim was way off so all the precious little missiles she threw missed me by a mile. After a while she calmed down and told me she was sorry for what she had said and done. She asked if I would do her one last favour, and reminded me before I had a chance to say no, that I should take into consideration that she had been very good to me as far as money and friendship were concerned. "I suppose I owe you that much," I told her. "What do you want me to do?"

"Could you keep an eye on the boys for a day or two, while I go up to London and try to raise some money to pay off your friends."

I agreed to do it on the condition that her friend Penniless stayed and did the cooking for her boys, also that she left me the car. She agreed and within half an hour I was seeing her off on the train to London.

Not wanting to go back to the house, I drove to the Clock Tower Club, went in, ordered a drink and sat down at the nearest empty table. While I was waiting for the barman to fetch the drink to my table I looked around the room to see if there was anyone in there that I knew. To my surprise Peggy Swan and Mary's neighbour Sylvia were sitting at the table next to me. When I joined them it was the first time in a very long while, that I had met someone who was genuinely very pleased to see me. After the usual embraces we sat down and began to talk. Peggy told me that Harry was now living with Mary; I could see she was in a lot of emotional pain just talking about it. She had been married to Harry for a considerable amount of years.

She and Sylvia had decided to come and drown their sorrows. They said that had been hoping they might see me. Several times during the course of the evening I suggested that they come back to the house with me, at first they declined but after a few more drinks and some rude suggestions they agreed. Peggy was driving her own car and knew the way because Harry had once taken her to the club. As there were no lights on when we got to the house I took it for granted that Penniless and the boys had gone to bed. There was still plenty of booze left in the house, before too long all three of us were feeling quite merry. Sylvia said she would like to lie down for a while because the drink was going to her head. I showed her into one of the bedrooms and then went back to talk to Peggy. We did kiss once or twice during the evening. I certainly wanted to sleep with her but she felt we would only be doing it to spite Harry. I honestly couldn't disagree with her; eventually she went to join Sylvia in the next room.

When I woke up the next morning they had both gone, I felt very sad because as I have said before Peggy was one of the most genuine and generous people I had ever had the good fortune to meet. I looked out of the window to see if their car was still in sight, it wasn't. I was quite surprised to see a crowd of people standing on the opposite side of the road looking up towards the roof of the house. I dressed and went out to what the people were looking at. As I opened the door I thought I heard a car backfiring and then someone shouted, "Look out, it's a real gun."
I began to wonder what was going on and felt the sooner I got out there the better. I crossed the road and looked back up to the roof. I got a terrible shock when I saw Esther's two sons balancing on a narrow ledge at least 60 ft above ground, not only that but one of them had a gun and was waving it towards the crowd.
I said to the person next me, "Did I hear someone say that it was a real gun?"
"Yes," he said. "You can see the bullet hole it made in that car over there." Then he said, "Its your roof they're on, what are you going to do about it?"

I ran back into the house and up to top floor as fast as I could and I climbed half way out of the dormer window and asked the boys to come back into the house.
The oldest one said to me, "We will, if you promise not to lock us in our room again."
"I'm sorry," I said. "I don't understand. I have never locked you in your room."
"You may not have," he said, "But you told mummy's friend to."

Once again I said, "I'm very sorry but I have never told anybody to lock you in your room, nor would I ever consider doing so." Slowly looking very cold and uncomfortable they made their way towards me. Most of the time, I never felt any emotions for or against these two kids, even though they had given me plenty of reasons to dislike them intensely. At that moment, I felt very compassionate towards them and also found a great deal more understanding how they must have felt. I put my arms around them and took them down into the lounge and wrapped them in blankets. The oldest one pointed the gun at me but I could see that he didn't have his finger on the trigger and I felt sure that he wasn't going to shoot me.

There was a loud knock on the front door followed by the sound of heavy footsteps running along the hallway and up the stairs. When I opened the lounge door and saw that it was a police, I told them that the boys were safe in the lounge. When the first policeman came into the room I handed him the gun telling him that I thought it still had some live ammo in the chambers. We were interviewed for several hours and it turned out that Penniless had tied the boys to their bed with some leather straps, put the light out, locked the room door on them and then left for places unknown. They had managed to get free from the bed and dig their way through the plaster and laths in the sloping ceiling and then by removing some slates they made a hole big enough for them both to crawl through. They told the police they had the found the gun under the bed and thought it was a toy.

The Police asked me if I knew where Esther could be contacted. I felt very strange when I told them that I didn't have the faintest idea where she was nor did I know her parent's address. They took the boys away and said they would place them in care and as soon as I heard anything from Esther I should let them know. It was two days before Esther came back. Once again she was looking very financially flushed. By this time I had done some serious thinking about the relationship I'd had with my parents and how my mum must have really cared for me. Never once in my life did it she ever let me down. The more I thought about these things the more resentful I got towards Esther. Back in the East End I had never known anyone whose parents could so easily abandon him or her into the care of complete strangers like Esther had continually done. What made it more unusual, she was Jewish, a race and religion whose whole foundation was based on and around family unity.

When I told her what had happened to the boys, she said to me, "John, I am very tired and feel that it would be better if I left sorting out my sons until tomorrow."
Coming on top of the thoughts that I had been having over the past couple of days this reaction was too much for me to take. I just had to walk out of the room because if I had stayed I would have physically harmed her. I hated myself when I allowed this type of emotional reaction to control my thoughts. I told myself over and over again that this wasn't my problem. I had no right to interfere; whatever this woman wanted to do about her children was up to her. Trying to control and channel my thoughts in a negative direction didn't help me to get rid of my resentment. I had about ten pounds in my pocket and I knew that if I could drink a sufficient amount of booze it would stop my emotions from making me feel so guilty. I went out and didn't return to the house until the early hours of the next morning and was surprised to find Esther still sitting awake in the lounge.

It was very obvious that she had been drinking heavily and at that moment looked very much like she needed a friend. All the façade had fallen away from her the make up and all the finery that was Esther's mask had crumbled. I watched her go through every sorrowful emotion that a woman could go through.   .
She said to me, "Without my boys I am nothing, everything I do, is for them."
Right then, I felt glad that I had drunk enough to stop me feeling sorry for her. Otherwise I might have got sucked back into the scheming cows games again. I went to bed and like many occasions in the past I was rudely awakened by a loud knocking on the front door I guessed that if anybody was making that much noise that early in the morning it had to be the police. I was right. At first I thought they had

come to see Esther about the boys but when they summoned me into the lounge and asked me if I was the barman who had worked in the club on the night of the raid I realised that this was something else that she hadn't seen fit to tell me about.

I said, "Sorry but since I have lived here the club as never been opened to be raided or for any other reason."

There were two men wearing plain clothes with the Police, who I thought were C I D. Officers, as usual I was wrong. The sergeant told me that they were bailiffs and that if I had any personal belongings in the house, I should pack them quickly because they had a high court warrant to seize the property and contents, plus an eviction order for anyone staying in the house. I said this can't be right the woman will never get her children back if she hasn't got a home for them.

"Don't worry," he said. "We are taking her into custody because she is due to appear in court this afternoon."

When I asked them why they were being so hard on her they told me that during the raid on the club they had found a supply of drugs, some of which were in Esther's handbag.

As well as being charged with illegally selling alcohol; she was also facing drug possession charges. Not once over the five or so months I had been with her, had she had ever given me the slightest hint she was in so much trouble. I was a bit jealous of her in a way because I was totally incapable of holding on to a secret as well as she could. I went into the lounge and packed my belongings. As I was leaving Big Jim came down the stairs was his suitcase and asked me were I was going I told him that I did not know or really care. The two policemen came downstairs escorting Esther between them. She looked at me and said, "Why don't you take the car John it as never belonged to me and I don't think the owner will ever come back for it."

I heard sometime later that she had put on such a wonderful show in court the judge fined her £200 and placed her on probation for six months.

I never saw Esther again.

CHAPTER 8

As we were walking away from the house Jim told me that he had arranged to stay with Ray Scaith, a bloke we had got to know through Stanley Gradus. He told me that Ray's mother owned and ran a guesthouse down on the seafront just at the end of the Golden Mile. I asked him if he thought she might have a room for me? He said, "Because it's still the closed season, most of the guesthouses around here are desperately looking for lodgers to boost their winter income. I think she will be more than delighted to rent you a room."

When we got to the house what Jim had said turned out to be very true, Ray's mum put me in a large double room on the first floor, which had a superb view of the beach, promenade and all the seafront amusement arcades. She was a friendly short dumpy little woman of about 50; she wore very thick make-up, which would have been far more acceptable had it been on the face of a clown. She was a very good-hearted person, but I always got the feeling that she was very lonely because whenever she engaged you in a conversation it was never for a quick chat. She could do a good 15 minutes just talking about something trivial like a duster. As I said she was very good-hearted and was always willing to help you in any way that she could.

For a week or two we just hung around the Guesthouse and along the sea front, Big Jim stayed with us most of the time but he seemed very uncomfortable and was always going off on 'shopping sprees'. One day he came into the lounge and asked us if any of us would like to start working for a living. By this time Del Ward had moved in with us and like me he was quite willing to do anything to earn some money over and above the dole money we were getting. Jim said there was about enough work to keep at least four of us going for a month or so. He told us the job would be wiring out two cottages for electricity and it was up in North Wales. We told him that we would love to go with him but we knew less than nothing about installing electric wiring circuits. He assured us that he was a qualified electrician and that we would only have to do the labouring for him. When he told us how much the pay was, we couldn't wait to get started.

That evening Jim gave Stan Gradus a signed blank cheque and told him to hire a car for our journey. Bright and early the next morning Stan arrived outside Ray Scaith's house, driving a very sporty looking, two tone Ford Zodiac. Along with Del, Stan and Big Jim, I packed my gear into the car and we set off for North Wales. As we were almost passing the door of my parent's house I told the boys I would like very much to call in and see them, which I did and told my mum about our plan to work in North Wales. On our way through Birmingham Del Ward asked us if we would make a detour so that he could see his wife and folks. Del and I had been pals on and off for some years and yet this was the first time I had ever heard him make any mention of a wife.

He was one of the people who had originally come to Faversham with me, and had been nicked along with me for stealing the cockles off of Seasalter Beach. Somehow due to a twist of fate and his musical associations he, like me, had ended up on Esther's payroll. He told us that he hadn't seen his wife or parents for about four years. I was amazed and a bit taken aback at what happened when we arrived at his mum's house. After not seeing each other for such a long time, she didn't show him any sort of convivial or hostile greeting; she never gave the slightest sign that she even knew him. The only sentence she uttered in his direction was, "Have you got any money for me?" Due to what felt like a very heavy atmosphere descending on the proceedings, we made an excuse and left as soon as we possibly could, and then made our way up to Welshpool, which was the next town on our route to Barmouth, our destination.

When Big Jim told us he felt hungry and needed to stop for something to eat we heartily agreed with him and stopped at the first chip shop we came to. Three of us went into the shop leaving

Jim sitting in the car. When we came out again, neither Jim nor the car, were anywhere to be seen. I couldn't understand why had he driven off and left us. After searching around the streets for some time we finally spotted the car parked outside a pub. By now I knew enough about Jim to know that he was nothing more than a big coward which helped me summon up enough courage to go into the pub and threaten to kick fuck out of him if he pulled anymore strokes on us. He said that he hadn't meant to be missing for as long he had, but he'd had trouble finding a 'phone box with a 'phone that worked. He told us that he'd been on the 'phone trying to prearrange some hotel accommodation for us. Feeling relieved that we were reunited with the car and our gear we didn't raise any further arguments and travelled on into the night. Several times during our journey the police stopped us but, after answering all the questions they put to us, we were allowed to go on our way.

As we were travelling along one of the narrow winding lanes, which we later discovered was in Snowdonia Park, the car ran out of petrol. This seemed very odd to me, as we had filled it up between Birmingham and Welshpool only a couple of miles before stopping at the chip shop. I was sure that we had done almost twice the mileage on the first tank of petrol. Nevertheless here we were at about two o'clock in the morning, somewhere on the side of a mountain with no petrol and no idea where or how far away the nearest garage was. At first we decided to push the car back the way we had come, because someone remembered seeing a house with its lights on about a mile or so back. I got out to see how far we would have to push the car before we could turn it round to face the direction we wanted to go in. As I was straining my eyes to see in the inky darkness, I heard some very strange noises that sounded like something very big was breaking through the foliage and heading in my direction. Summoning up all the courage I could muster, I quickly jumped back into the car and convinced the others that it was far too dangerous to manoeuvre it about on such a narrow road and in such total darkness. We decided it was best to wait until daylight, which we did, with all the car doors securely locked.

When daylight eventually arrived, I could see that when I had got out of the car in the dark, I had narrowly missed falling over a sheer drop of several hundred feet. We had stopped less than two feet from the edge of a cliff. I opened my door and squeezed around the car and once again heard the noise that had caused me so much fear during the night. I felt really stupid when I realised that all my mental anguish and overnight discomfort had been caused by a bloody great Welsh ram that was now busily munching the grass on the opposite side of the road. Thinking that it would help me to recover some of my composure I picked up a rock and felt about ten foot tall as it hit the ugly looking beast and made it run away.

Now in the daylight we could see our predicament and decided that the most sensible thing to do was to sit in the car and let it roll down hill as far as it could. After coasting for a mile or two we came to a garage, where we were served petrol by a very dour happy Welshman whose only comments were, "Too bad," and, "There you are then!" For reasons unknown to us Jim insisted that we should only buy two gallons, thinking that the reason behind his insistence was to save money, we agreed with him. Jim didn't seem to be in any hurry to cover the last twenty miles or so to Barmouth and as the views of the countryside we were passing through went from pleasant to breathtaking, none of us seemed to mind him driving so slowly. When we finally got to the town, it was still very early, so we decided to find a café to have some breakfast.

Jim said, "While you are eating, I will go and check on the hotel and the work sight, and also inform the people we will be working for that we have arrived."
It took Jim a lot of what I thought was totally unnecessary coming and going and messing around, to sort out his business. With nothing to do but wait the boys and me just hung around the beach

and the café most of the day. We actually drove in and out of Barmouth several times just to stop getting bored. By the time Jim got around to telling us that he had finished making phone calls and that he had sorted out the work situation, it was getting dark. Then he told us that the only hotel in the town was full and there weren't any rooms for us. I just couldn't hold back from telling him how pissed off I was with all his messing around. I mentally came to the conclusion that he was lying to us, but couldn't for the life of me fathom out why.

Due to our lack of sleep the previous night tiredness was overtaking us and our tempers were getting short but we agreed with Jim when he suggested that we should sleep in one of the cottages we were going to work on. We parked the car up, got our cases out of the boot and then climbed a narrow path up to a small but very attractive little cottage that had been built, defying the law of gravity, on the edge of a cliff. Not having a key was the next problem we had to overcome. I was elected rescue officer and had to manoeuvre myself hand over hand along a less than ample ledge at the side of the house in order to reach the nearest window, which I then had to climb through. When I got inside I switched on the lights and opened the street door to let the others in. It did occur to me that we had been told there wasn't going to be any electric in any of the cottages we had come up to work on.

Much to our surprise the cottage was very well equipped but unfortunately not with any kind of heating facilities. We found it very cold and the fact that we had spent the previous night in the car with very little or no sleep didn't help either. Jim commandeered the only bedroom while the rest of us took up different positions on the living room floor. Del and Stan put on their pyjamas just as though they were at home; I slept fully clothed in case of emergencies. The next morning we were all jolted from our slumbers by the front door being thrust open by a woman who on sight of us started screaming blue murder. One of the lads got up and gently ushered her back out of the door, asking her to wait outside while we got dressed.

When we called for Jim to come down and talk to the woman, he wouldn't answer us, so I went up to see why he was being so coy. He told me that he thought it would be best if the boys and me got out of the cottage and met him by the car. In the meantime, Stan and Del were still doing their best to explain to the woman our reasons for being there. As they were talking I began looking around at the place and could see how modern and recently decorated it was. It was very clear that it certainly didn't need rewiring. Our explanation for being there was beginning to sound as nonsensical to us as it obviously did to women. Because of Jim's reluctance to face her, Del took it upon himself to give the lady his description. She then told us that she knew him, but wasn't too pleased to know that he was in her cottage. She explained to us that Jim had caused a serious incident a year or so previously, but she wouldn't tell us how or what he had done, except that the police were involved and still wanted to see him. On receiving this little gem of information, we did as Jim had previously suggested and went to the car.

We took as long as we possibly could to pack our cases and load them into the car, then we stood around waiting for Jim to appear. I told them that if we had any sense we would leave him and not get involved with the police especially as it wasn't anything to do with us. Out of some strange misguided loyalty the other two wouldn't leave without him. This seemed stupid and pointless to me as he obviously didn't care about all the trouble and inconvenience he had put us to. Somehow like most other con men I had met he managed to wriggle his way out of the situation and into the car, once he was on board we immediately set off back to Margate.

Even this simple journey had its troubles, which started at the first garage where we tried to fill the car up with petrol, Jim told us that he had lost his wallet with his chequebook in it. To be honest I had never seen him with a wallet, and whenever he had used his chequebook in front of me he had taken it out of his inside jacket pocket loose. After a great deal of haggling with the garage owner we got under way. Later when we needed more petrol we had to leave the spare wheel to cover the cost. Del told us that he had decided to stay in Birmingham and get a job on the buses and maybe get back with his wife. It didn't seem to matter to him that he couldn't drive and that his wife had had two coloured children in his absence! Plus all the time he had been in and around the West End clubs and music circuit he had been known as a practising homosexual, That was by everybody but me. It was, in my humble opinion, a very bad choice on his part and being what I am I told him so, but he stayed anyway. With the sort of egotism I had in those days I naturally assumed that, as I wouldn't do as he had decided to do, he must be a very sick and lonely person; I have never seen or heard of him since the day we dropped him in Nechells.

On our arrival back at Ray Scaith's house, we were met and greeted by Stanley's two very anxious parents. Who told us that the cheque that Jim had given Stanley to hire the car had bounced, along with at least twenty others that Jim had issued around the area. Because of their status as shopkeepers and guesthouse owners, plus their popularity among many of the traders in the town, which included the car hire firm, no one wanted to press charges against Stanley, but they were certainly intent on bringing big Jim to justice. Strange as it may seem neither I nor anybody else saw the twenty-three stone giant called Jim Ledbetter get out of the car, take his two large suitcases out of the boot, as he must have done and quietly slip away. As far as I know and because I have never seen or heard of him since, I don't think he was ever caught. It still remains a mystery to me, why he took us on that journey; I don't suppose I shall ever know.

As I had decided I wanted to stay in Margate for a while I was happy to accept the offer of accommodation back at Mrs. Scaiths.

The story of our trip stood me in good stead for many bottles of wine, which I began drinking quite a lot of. The favourite hit record of the day was the Everley Brothers singing 'Cathy's Clown', which was played regularly on the jukebox in the Barbarian club. The Barbarian club was less than a hundred yards from my new lodgings and it became my favourite haunt. I don't know why because they never sold alcohol and most of the people that went there were a year or two younger than me which made me feel very much at home mentally. With two Coca-Colas, a Mars bar and some sixpenny pieces for the jukebox I could dance the night away with some of the best looking young girls in Margate.

It was so convenient, I don't think at that time in my life things could have been any better; it certainly was one of the most sexually active parts of my life. Sometimes one after the other I would take as many as three girls a night back to my room. For several weeks I lived like a Sheikh. Occasionally I would drop into one of drinking clubs and drink too much, boast very loudly about my sexual prowess and how many of the loose women in the Barbarian club I had shagged. When the drink was in me, I could often be heard bragging about how hard I was; sometimes I stood around daring anyone to confront me. Often when I came across some poor soul that I knew to be physically weaker than myself, just to show off I would inflict as much physical and verbal humiliation as I could on them.

The next day I would generally be totally unaware of what I had been doing or saying but I didn't have to wait long before Ray Scaith would tell me every little grotty detail. For all the fun that I was having there was a price to pay, which was a feeling of deep remorse. Frequently I would think to myself, John, you are so much better when you stick to Coca-Cola and Mar's bars and for several days this is what I would do. I was really unaware of other people's feelings towards me although I did have a slight inkling that Ray had grown to dislike me. He never openly showed me any hostility but often I would see a look of delight in his face whenever I was suffering in one of my down periods.

One night as I was coming out of the Clock Tower Club I saw two people heading towards me. I thought that they were going into the club, so I prepared myself to step aside and let them go by. It surprised me when the bigger one of the two placed his hand in the middle of my chest stopping me in my tracks and asked me if I knew him.

I said, "I'm very sorry I don't, in fact I don't think I've ever seen you before in my life."

He looked at me and said, "If that is the case, why have you been going round all the clubs telling everybody how you beat me up in Canterbury prison. They call me Hookey Harris."

He said this in such a way I am sure he thought that it would strike some sort of terror through me. He suddenly took hold of my left shoulder and pulled me around until I was face to face with his mate.

"This is Jock Man," he said.

I said, "I'm very pleased to meet you Jock Man, but I'm afraid I don't know you either. What prison, am I supposed to have beaten you up in?"

I began to feel that this meeting hadn't happened by coincidence, these two had certainly come looking for trouble and it was definitely going to be with me. I began to wonder whether they were going to fight me one at a time or both together. Luckily I'd had sufficient to drink to allay any fears that might have overcome me, had I been caught sober.

I looked at them both, and could see that they would be quite capable of looking after themselves if it came to a rough and tumble. I may have been partly drunk but I certainly hadn't taken complete leave of my senses, what little I had left was telling me that if I took this verbal confrontation any further without someone watching my back it would be a bit futile.

I said to them, "If this conversation is going where I think it is, it really doesn't make any sense. We are three total strangers and I think we have proved that we have all got enough bottle not to be scared of each other."

The Jock came back at me and said, "Surely you don't expect us to be frightened of a fucking idiot like you."

I half turned so that my back was to the club door, which meant both of them were now facing me.

I said, "I don't know you well enough to know what sort of idiot you would be scared of."

I then asked them if they were going to fight me one at a time or were they going to do the real brave thing and both get stuck in.

Harris said you really think that you are some sort of hard case

I looked at him and said, "I'm sorry I don't think that at all. I know I am a hard case."

Just then I heard the door of the club open behind me; my brain told me that it might be a mistake to take my eyes off these two so I didn't look round. Wrong message brain. Before the world closed down, I thought I recognised the voice coming from behind me.

Never having been in the Margate Hospital I had quite a shock when I woke up in what seemed very strange surroundings. Sitting next to my bed were two girls I knew from the Barbarian club, Carol and Maureen. I had been going around with Carol for some time; she was a very attractive girl with long natural dark auburn hair. We had once entered and won a dance competition, which made us the Southern Counties, Rock and Roll Champions.

I looked at her and said, "I knew one day that I was going to heaven but I didn't think you would be there waiting for me."

I then realised that I was covered in bandages and had several tubes going into various parts of my body. Carol told me that I had been found lying unconscious outside of the Clock Tower Club, she went on to say that the medics had told her I had been so badly beaten I was bleeding internally from splintered ribs, which in turn had punctured one of my lungs. Plus they suspected that I had a fractured skull and broken jaw! Which is why I was now in an intensive care ward. The doctors had allowed her and her friend Maureen to sit with me, because they didn't think I had much chance of surviving.

Just then a doctor came to my bedside and told me that he was very glad to see me awake and talking coherently because it gave all the signs that I would have a more than average chance of making a full recovery. It also meant that there hadn't been any serious brain damage. He told me I was very fortunate to have such a beautiful looking Redhead waiting to look after me and then added how she should be a very good incentive for me to stay out of trouble in the future.

As he walked away, Carol looked at me and said, "Right at this moment, John, he has a far better chance of me waiting to look after him, than you do."

I tried to smile but every bone in my body was hurting.

"Do you know why and who did this to me?" I asked her.

She looked at me and said; "I will tell you if you promise not to cause any trouble when you get out of hospital."

It was a very easy false promise to make. For a moment we were interrupted by the arrival of a nurse who gave me several painkillers and said she would come back and give me an injection if the pain got too severe.

It turned out that someone who I had humiliated in bar one night was the nephew of my landlady, which made him Ray Scaiths cousin. Ray and him had got together and hatched a plot to have me 'done over'. I knew Ray didn't like me very much, but I didn't think that he hated me enough to have me done this bad. Carol told me that one of the girls I had been taking back to my room was Ray's Fiancé. The long and short of the situation was, on the night of trouble, when the door of the club opened behind me, the people coming out, were none other than my dear pal, Ray and his cousin. One of them had hit me up the side of the head with a piece of metal, instantly putting me out of the game. In reality

189

I suppose I should have been thankful to him, because it saved me going through all the pain that I would have felt had I been conscious while the four of them were kicking the living daylights out of me.

I asked Carol who the other two blokes were. She told me that they had both been released from Canterbury prison a couple of days earlier and were very well known around the town for causing trouble, especially when they were out of their minds on drugs. Maureen told me that Ray and his cousin had promised to supply a large amount of drugs to both Hooky Harris and his Scottish pal, if they sorted me out. To really get them at it, Ray had slung in the story that I had been going around the clubs bragging how I had beaten both of them up in the nick. She also told me, that all four of them had been arrested for attempted murder. "Are they in custody," I asked her. "No," she said they were all given bail. Which was down to the fact that Ray's cousin was the son of the local Magistrate. She told me that when they had appeared in front of him he listened to the charges being read out, and then said. "As there wasn't another Magistrate available, and because of his personal interest in the case, he was legally bound to stand down, and wouldn't be allowed to take any further part in the proceedings." Carol told me that this was all said and done after he had allowed his son and Ray plus the other two blokes out on bail.

Fortunately, I didn't have a fractured skull, but the injury to my jaw was very painful, mostly I was suffering from severe bruising and a slight concussion. It took several weeks rest plus a course of very strong painkillers to overcome the problem with my ribs. The doctors told me that I should feel grateful for being alive because the beating I'd taken really should have killed me. Gratitude wasn't something that played any part came into my life in those days. When I look back as I am doing now I realise that my attitude was one of, 'because of who I am you should feel lucky that I have made myself available for you to serve me'. Finally I was discharged from the hospital and went back to my room at Ray Scaiths house to collect my belongings. At first his mother was very concerned about me being there, she said she didn't normally let people back into her house after they had run away without paying their rent. It was obvious that she had no idea what had happened between Ray and me. I explained to her that I had been in the hospital and was unable to contact her but I didn't tell her the reason why. When Ray came home I was waiting in the lounge and had been doing so for some time. I just wanted see the look on the cowardly bastard's face when he saw me.

I'd met some cowards in my life, but Ray Scaith took first prize, the fear I saw in his face gave me an adrenaline rush. At first, he plied me with tears and apologies, then he told me how sorry he was for what he had done, so much so, that he couldn't sleep because of the hatred he felt for himself. In the next moment he was pointing the finger at me, threatened to call the Police if I touched him. Then just as suddenly he was on his knees again, begging me for forgiveness. Ray was a well-built bloke and if he had had half the courage of his stature, I am sure that he would have been able to take good care of himself in a fight. By the time he had finished going through the full gambit of a coward's emotions and action I hadn't said a word. Nor did I, my bags were packed so I walked out knowing that I wouldn't gain any satisfaction from giving him a beating.

As I walked away I decided that my time in Margate was over. I still wasn't feeling fit enough to go around and exact any sort of physical revenge on the people who had tried to kill me. For some strange reason I didn't even hold a grudge against them. I just felt that somewhere along the line each one of them would get their comeuppance because I had certainly got mine. On the way to the station I saw several people that I knew from the drinking clubs. I could see in their faces that they weren't feeling one bit sorry about what had happened to me, one of them actually quoted 'The King is dead, long live the King'. I knew then that if I remained in Margate my life would turn into a very miserable existence. Plus I knew that I'd taken all the glory that I could get out of the reputation that Esther had bestowed on me.

I was thinking, that I would call in to the hospital to say thank you, and goodbye, before I left town, because it would be the decent thing to do. I even thought about buying some flowers for the nurses to show my appreciation. I said, to myself thinking about doing something and actually doing it are two totally different things, John, so go and buy a bunch of flowers and get yourself to the hospital. All through my life I have had these talk to myself conversations, and in nearly all of them, I had lost the argument, or made the wrong decision. This time was no different from all the other times. I bought the flowers and went to the hospital arriving just in time to see my favourite Doctor coming out of the entrance holding hands, kissing and looking very much in love with my girlfriend Carol. They were to engrossed in each other to see me so I turned, threw the flowers into the nearest waste bin, walked to the station where I caught the first train to London thinking, who in this world could I trust?

CHAPTER 9

Among the many people I met during my drinking life, Tony Curtis was one of the most genuine and at the same time unusual, even strange, but then most of the people I hung around with had something outside of the norm about them. Tony and I first met in an all night restaurant called the 'Fifty Eight', which was in Sussex Gardens just off Bayswater Road. At the time I was going about with a girl named Eve, who would often ferry me around on the back of her 500.cc motorbike. She was a very tall athletic looking woman with very noticeable, short cropped, platinum blonde hair, which gave her the appearance of being a lot younger than she really was. Eve earned her living working in a near-beer clip joint in Soho. Her favourite place to visit after she had finished work most nights was the 'Fifty Eight'. Back in the late fifties and early sixties it became a popular eating and meeting place for people from many of the various nightclubs and vice joints that had flourished around London. In the 'Fifty Eight' you could be seen rubbing shoulders with film stars and many other types of famous show business personalities. I was first, introduced to the place by Harry Swan when he was doing his best to keep me from seeing Mary Scott.

On the first night I met Curtis, Eve and I had spent some time drinking large Vodka's and smoking several spliffs of canabis in a Soho dive. As usual the effect of the dope made me feel hungry, so we decided to have a meal at the 'Fifty Eight'. Because it was very busy, the waiter, who knew us quite well, asked if we would mind sharing a table with two other people, we told him it would be fine, sat down at the allotted table and introduced ourselves to the two chaps already sitting there. It turned out that they weren't together, but like us they had agreed to share. I'm Tony Curtis one of them said and I am Greta Garbo, Eve replied, we all laughed and then ordered our meal.

When Tony first told us his name, we didn't believe him but eventually he convinced us it was true, he seemed a very genuine person and quite generous. The one thing all four of us had in common at the end of that night, was that we had all drunk enough booze, to make us talk about ourselves a bit more lucidly than we would normally to complete strangers. Tony told us he was a thief and that the type thieving he did was called drumming I'd heard of this term but didn't know exactly what it meant. He explained to us that it was slang for house and flat breaking. "I only break into rich people's places" he said and then asked me if I would like to go with him the next afternoon. I was quite excited and delighted at the prospect of becoming a drummer, as I thought it give me some sort of status among the new people I had started getting acquainted with. I arranged to meet Tony at twelve o'clock the following day, outside Notting Hill Gate tube station.

From there we travelled by tube out to Boston Manor, an area of London that we both considered a bit up market. During the course of that afternoon we broke into four or five houses and netted goods to the value of £1,000, on the bent market, plus some ready cash. In the evening I went with Tony to Ladbrooke Grove, where he was renting a one roomed, grotty attic in Powis Terrace not far from the Portobello Road, he called it his penthouse, I think my description was more accurate. During the day Tony told me about an after hours drinking club that he often went to and asked me if I would like to go there with him that night. Never being one to turn down the opportunity for a drink I very readily agreed to join him. The elation I was feeling about the events of the afternoon was fantastic. On top of which the couple of hundred quid I had in my pocket to spend on what ever took my fancy was adding to the buzz.

When I left Tony's flat I made my way down to Notting Hill station and caught a tube to the Angel from there I walked the short distance round to Eve's flat in Islington Square. When I got there Eve was in a down sort of mood, she said that she was feeling a bit put out with me because I hadn't told her where I was going, or who with. She soon became very forgiving when she caught sight of the packet of cannabis I had bought for her. Eve really was a dope fiend, her flat constantly smelt of burning Joss sticks that were intended to cover up the smell of her cannabis smoking. We smoked quite a lot of cannabis during our time together, but as I said earlier, smoking weed didn't do much for me, other than to give me a ravenous appetite. I often hinted to Eve that she should smoke less and drink more. This suggestion always went down like the proverbial lead balloon When I asked her if she would like come out with me and Curtis for a drink that night, she declined, saying that she needed money and had to go to work.

After I'd washed and changed, I told Eve that I was going over to Paddington to meet Tony. Before I had time to bid her goodbye she rounded on me and said that she wasn't very happy that we weren't going to meet in the club that night, as had become our usual practice. She also said in an almost threatening manner that if I knew what was good for me I would make meeting up with her later, my number one priority. Threats or no threats I had no intention of letting Eve dominate what I did or didn't do.

I didn't live with Eve full time, we just got together whenever we met up, and if I felt like it I would sleep at her place, for a time it was a lot of fun. In my description of Eve I said she was athletic looking what I meant was she was tall, slim and muscular almost masculine with very small tits. What her she lacked in femininity was more than made up for in her very attractive personality, as a friend I liked her very much, but sexually she wasn't the best female turn on I had available to me. As our time together went on I felt that she was, by way of her feminine mood swings demanding more commitment from me in our relationship. Personally I just wanted things to stay on the same friendly and casual basis that they were when we had first got together. Whenever things got too heavy or serious between us, as they often did, I usually walked away and gave her some time and space, to calm down.

I never let Eve's moods deter me from doing what I wanted to do, and that day I wasn't going to make any exceptions. At about seven o'clock that evening Tony and I met up and started drinking in the Elgin Arms, a large pub on the corner of Elgin Avenue that was situated somewhere between Paddington and Notting Hill Gate. From there we went to the Barbi Chick so called because it openly barbecued chickens in public, long before K.F.C. ever became famous for that sort thing. After stuffing ourselves with hot chicken and chips we went to the drinking club he had told me about. It was almost a replica of Batty Street, the only difference was that the stairs in this place went straight into the bar room, even the small green baize covered card tables were the same. This club was intended for serious drinking and very little else.

Some of the people I met there, I had never seen in the flesh before, but I knew of them from newspapers and television, believe me, none them were celebrities or film stars. I could give you a list, of the names, and the crimes to match them, but even now, all this time later, some of them, if not all, are still around and active and therefore might take exception to their inclusion, in my story. However there were some that I became close good friends with, who I know wouldn't have objections to my telling you about them and some of their exploits. The club we were in belonged to a chap called Billy Mannings and his partner Johnny King

It was in this club that I was introduced to and became friends with Billy Gardner and Terry Donnelly, who later became infamous around London for a gangland shooting outside the Mr Smith's club. This happened sometime after I got to know them, I wasn't involved in it, but if I had been invited, I most certainly would have been. Back in the clubs and dives of the East End I'd seen lots of people carrying offensive weapons, mainly knives, razors and coshes and one or two shotguns, but here in Billy's club everybody carried guns. I saw thirty-eight's, thirty-two's, Lugers and lots of the smaller two-two variety. When I say everybody I also mean the women. Billy Manning's partner Johnny was a friend of Tony's;

it was through this friendship that we were accepted into the 'in crowd'. The people who frequented this club, accepted prison records as references, the longer you had spent in nick the better your credentials.

Although we were both still on our feet when we came out of the club in the early hours of the next morning, we were a long way from being sober. Tony said it would be foolish for me to travel all the way across London to Eve's, just to come back a couple of hours later to go out drumming. He invited me to crash out at his place, which was only just around the corner from where we were. We didn't wake up until late in the afternoon to discover that neither of us had very much money left. So going out drumming again seemed like the natural thing to do. This time we stayed local, and did some flats that weren't as lucrative as we had expected them to be. It was no cause for alarm as we both had some pieces of jewellery from the previous day. At about 10 o'clock that evening I left Tony and made my way down to the clip joint where Eve worked and sold two rings and a watch to the owner of the place. My intention was to get clear of the club before Eve arrived for work. Because by then I knew her well enough to know the sort of foul mood she would be in about my overnight absence. Plus I didn't want any sort of confrontation in front of the other girls who worked with her. Knowing most of them as well I did I was certain that meeting up with her could and would become very embarrassing.

Unfortunately before I could make good my escape, Eve arrived and immediately started questioning me very loudly about my whereabouts the previous night. What I didn't know was that she was already well aware of where I'd stayed and who with. Before I could answer her first question she was half way through the second one, which was why I had preferred to sleep with another man instead of coming home to her. The Cheeky cow!
I did manage to squeeze in the question.
"Are you trying say that I am a Fucking Poof?"

"What am I supposed to think, ever since you met that bloke, you haven't left his side for more than ten minutes, you have drunk, eaten and now slept with him, but while you're with me, all you ever do is moan about me smoking a little bit of dope".

It was pretty obvious that she was very angry with me, I could see that there was no way I was going to get the better of her or win any part of the argument so I turned and tried to walk out of the place. For a moment or two I thought I had made a clean getaway but she followed me down the stairs, and out into the street, keeping up a tirade of verbal abuse. I told her that I would come back when she had calmed down.

"I don't ever want to fucking well see you again," she shouted.

The clip joint, we had been in was on the first floor, above a travel agents shop. At this time of night most of Soho was alive and busy with punters looking for prostitutes, theatregoers trying to remember where they had parked their cars, and clip joint hostesses looking for some mugs to fleece.

It felt like and looked like the entire population of London were in Soho that night and all off them were looking and listening to this big blonde sort, giving me some serious stick. When some of the girls from the other clubs along the street heard what was going on they started cheering whenever Eve insulted me. If it hadn't been so embarrassing I might have seen the funny side of it. Much to my relief someone pulled up in a cab, before they had a chance to close the door behind them I had jumped in and instructed the driver to drive off as soon as possible. We left Soho to the sound of hissing, booing and swearing, when the Cabby asked me what I had done to become so popular, we both laughed. I asked him to take me to Portobello road. When I got to Tony's flat, I told him about my encounter with Eve and how she thought we were both queer, much to my mental discomfort he seemed to think that it was a highly hilarious.

PENTONVILLE JOHNNY

The jewellery I'd sold had netted me about one hundred and fifty quid, putting that along with the money that Tony had got from what he had sold we came up with nearly £500, which we decided not to spend too quickly. I suggested that if we bought a couple of bottles of Scotch or vodka to drink before we went clubbing, it would be cheaper and quicker to get pissed. Tony reached under his bed and produced several bottles of spirits, of which we drank at least half a bottle each. Brimming over with alcoholic confidence we caught a cab down to a little drinking come strip joint that we both knew in Greek Street. After drinking several doubles on top of what we had had already we began to get very boisterous and started jeering, booing and hissing at the girls who were going through their strip routines. One of the stripper's came across the raised platform that acted as a stage looked directly at Tony, did a little sexy wiggle and then winked at him. He looked her straight in the face and said," Don't you fucking wink at me you fucking slag or I'll slap you".
On hearing what Tony had said to the girl, one of the club punters came over and told us, in a very threatening manner to fuck off out of the place. Tony looked at the bloke, picked up his glass, drank the contents, and then in one continuous down and upward motion smashed it on the bar and slashed the bloke from the point of his chin upwards across his face to his forehead. At the same time as kneeing in the bollocks.

The events that followed happened so quickly, it was difficult to keep track of who was on or off side among the people we were fighting but because we were so drunk it didn't really matter. We managed to get out of that club with a lot of our bits and pieces cut and bruised but the main and essential parts of our bodies were still intact, fortunately most of the blood we were both covered in wasn't ours. When I asked Tony why he had insulted the stripper, he told me that she was his ex-wife. It was one of those rare occasions in my life when I got stuck for words. As we turned out of Greek Street and into Shaftesbury Avenue Eve appeared, I could see by her expression that she was quite shocked

199

when she saw the state we were in. After giving us both a sort of maternal bollicking she told us to follow her to the place were she worked, when we got there she handed us soap and towels that were followed by instructions to clean ourselves up. Then she gave me the keys to her flat and told me to go home and change my clothes. I didn't like the way she emphasised the word home, but I did as I was told. Tony told me he was going back to his flat, I said good night and I went to Eve's. As Tony and I hadn't, made any arrangements to meet up again, much to Eve's delight, it was some time before I saw him again.

About a week or so after the strip joint fight I was having a drink with some paddy friends of mine in Dean Street the '41' cafe' to be more precise. I was surprised when I looked across the room and saw Curtis sitting in the far corner; my surprise was mainly due to the fact that I didn't think he knew the place. Because he was sitting alone I went over to join him, when he looked up at me I could see that he was in a very distressed state. Although we had drunk and shared several close and exciting times together over the past month or so, I still didn't know him very well. This made me feel a bit unsure about asking him what was wrong, as I didn't want him to think I was poking my nose in to his private business. When I finally did ask what was troubling him he told me that a friend of his had warned him that his ex-wife, the stripper, had paid two blokes to give him kicking.

It was obvious from the way he was talking that he was very worried about it. I asked him if he knew the blokes or where they lived, he told me that they were his ex-wife's cousins. He also said they were both, well known hard men, from the Ladbroke Grove area. The '41' was a four story building which consisted of an empty basement, a ground floor shop, on the first floor was a private drinking club, which was used by theatre critics and sports reporters. On the second floor, Cathy and Musty who owned the entire premises ran a cafe, which was where we were sitting having our conversation. The majority of customers who frequented the café were Irishmen who were either friends or relations of Cathy.

The toilets of the '41' were often used by some of the Irish boys to hide various nasty weapons or shady goods. I told Tony to stay outside the door and keep watch while I searched to see what I could find. There was nothing in the cisterns or the usual places but when I stood on the toilet seat and pushed up one of the tiles in the false ceiling, I found several pieces of lead pipe, each about an inch an half thick, and varying in lengths from 18 inches to two foot. I stuffed one down the waistband of my trousers and took one for Tony. Let's go and find the bastards I said to him. At first he was a bit reluctant but after a little chat and a couple swigs from my bottle of vodka he came around to my way of thinking. Tony told me that when he had first left his ex-wife she had paid the same two blokes to give him a good hiding, which they had done. He said this beating had put him in hospital for nearly a month. For the simple reason that Tony's ex-wife was a very good looking and an all round extremely attractive girl, I had taken the impression that things were the other way around and that she had chucked Tony out. From what I had seen of her I didn't think any man with half a brain and a dick would want to her out of his life.

Feeling suitably armed we left for the address of the so-called hard men. On the way there I suggested to Tony that he should keep back out of sight, as seeing him would immediately tip them off that we were there for trouble and could lose us any element of surprise we might have going for us. When I knocked on the door of the house that Tony had pointed out to me, it was opened by a bloke who at first and second glance appeared to be about twice my size in both length and breadth. I can quite honestly say that it was only the effect of the vodka flowing around inside my brain that stopped me legging it. I took a deep breath gathered myself together and using the most masculine voice I could summon up I asked him if he was one of the bloke's who was looking for Tony Curtis.

"Yes I'm one of them," he said. "What's it got to do with you?"
"Quite a lot!" I replied. "He's my pal and I really don't want to see him get hurt."
Taking another look at size of this bloke, I was hoping Tony was close enough to hear me call him, when the trouble started.
The bloke raised his voice and said, loud enough for anyone in the house to hear, "Why don't you piss off and mind your own fucking business."
"I think this is my business," I replied.
He looked over his shoulder and shouted, "Brian, come up here and help me sort out this big-mouthed, flash bastard who's come looking for trouble."
I was quite relieved when Brian turned out to be much smaller than the bloke I assumed to be his big brother.

As Brian pushed past the bloke who I had now mentally christened Goliath, I saw that he was carrying a piece of wood which was much thicker but shorter than my lead pipe. He came to a stop about two or three paces in front of me, and then lashed out with it; at the same time I saw Goliath pull out a large screwdriver from inside his jacket and then tried to ram the sharp end in my face. Even if I do say so myself, I reckon my fancy footwork that night was magic and served me well as I ducked and swerved to avoid their onslaught. I could see now why Tony was frightened of these two blokes, they certainly didn't care how badly they maimed or injured anybody. But in those days, if I was drunk enough, neither did I. The piece of lead pipe turned out to be a perfect weapon in this situation, it was long enough for me to inflict painful injuries, and at the same time keep a reasonably safe distance away. After fencing around for a while I got a fairly decent blow to the big bloke's head, which sent him to his knees. If all the swear words that Brian used, could have hurt me I think I might have been killed off very early in the fight but as they say sticks and stones will break my bones but names....

PENTONVILLE JOHNNY

I could see that the big bloke was bleeding quite badly and was having trouble trying to get to his feet. He was swaying about like a drunk who had lost control of his legs. Brian was swinging his piece of wood around like a battleaxe; several times he caught me across the arms and shoulders, which was quite painful. Had it not been for the numbing effect of the vodka doing the rounds of my circulation they could quite easily have put me out of the game or at least down on my knees. Out of the corner my eye I saw Curtis running towards us with his lead pipe raised above his head like a sabre. At the same instant Brian also spotted him and started screaming for his brother to get up off the ground, but at that moment in time all the and shouting and hollering in the world couldn't have brought Goliath back into the fight. Tony hadn't yet joined in the melee but I knew that he certainly intended to. When I heard him say to Brian "The odds are in my favour this time you bastard."

I suddenly felt a sharp pain across the back of my fingers as Brian caught me with his piece wood, this seemed to trigger something at the back of my brain which sent me into some sort of black rage. The next thing I remember, was Tony trying to stop me from beating Brian and his brother to a pulp, both of them were lying on the ground begging for me to stop. Luckily for me, I did stop before one of them finished up dead but not before they promised never to interfere in Tony's affairs again. As both of the brothers had reputations for being hard men, when the news of what had happened to them, on their own manor, got around the local clubs and dives it did wonders for my credibility among the criminal fraternity of West London.

After the incident in Ladbroke Grove I went to stay at my parents' house, to recover from my cuts and bruises. This soon became boring especially as both my mum and dad went to bed at about 8 0'clock every night and didn't like the television or radio being played too loud. I sat there night after night missing the excitement of the dives. On occasions like this, I would often be overcome by unwanted and unguarded sober moments, which would allow the guilt I felt about my dishonest and immoral way of life to creep into forefront of my conscience. Eventually the lure of the clubs and the booze got the better of me. I nicked ten pounds out of my mum's purse and headed off to the bright lights once again. The first club I hit was the St Louis, or Cosmopolitan, as some people liked to call it. When I got inside, I met some old mates, who had heard about the fight in Ladbroke Grove. They were now looking at me in a totally different light they were almost forcing drinks down my throat.

I could recall several fights that I'd had previous to that one, where I had come off second best to blokes who were nowhere near as hard as Goliath or his little brother Brian. On these occasions I had either limped or crawled away bruised, battered and rejected, feeling a very lonely person. I knew then that no one respected a loser, even more so, when you came across someone who had bested the bloke that had beaten you up; you certainly were made to feel like a very lowly creature.

The way I was being made up to by the people in the St Louis was a totally new way of being treated, it was almost like hero worship. I loved it. By the time I left the club I was once more in the wonderful state of physical and mental utopia and brimming over with confidence. I remember thinking I wish I could bump into some of the bastards I had lost fight's to in the past. At that moment I felt like taking on the world, it's amazing how a few drinks could make me think and feel that I was super human. I really did love the effect of alcohol. It was about that time I became aware that it would be very stupid of me to let anybody find out that ninety nine percent of my courage came out of a booze bottle. At the same time I was completely unaware that I had a million individual little uncontrollable mental problems running around inside my head or the fact that they were gradually merging in to one almighty big one. My solution to all the hang-ups that I did know about was simple, stay under the influence of the booze, and never allow anybody to see your innermost feelings.

After several days of ducking and diving around the East End I decided to visit Eve at her flat. As I hadn't seen her for some time, I was quite surprised to find that she had left a note asking me to meet her in the Cambridge Circus Club. Being well pissed, my reaction to this situation wasn't very sociable. Firstly, I resented the woman for not being at home when I called, secondly, how dare she write notes telling me! What to do and where to go. Now that this change had come around in my life she should show me a lot more respect. I was beginning to believe that people who wanted to be my friends should ask my permission if they wanted to go anywhere or do anything that might be of the slightest inconvenience to me.

More out of curiosity than care I went to the Cambridge Circus Club to find out why Eve wanted to meet there instead of at the clip joint. As I reached the top of the first flight of stairs, the doorman, who's name was Ray Flack came up to me and said that he had a message from Eve.
After we had exchanged pleasantries, I asked him, "What's it was about"?
"I feel rather embarrassed or more like piggy in the middle," he said.
"For fucks sake give me the message," I growled at him.
He then blurted out that Eve had asked him to talk to me about our relationship. I began to feel a bit uneasy and thought that he was going to tell me he was knocking her off.

Suddenly the jealous possessive part of my nature started to kick in. I didn't care if Eve slept around or not, but if anyone was trying to come between us, I fully intended to show him or her the error of their ways. As I stood facing Ray my mind raced away with an imaginary situation that I my brain turned into pictures conjuring up scenes of what had been going on between him and Eve. In

reality, he was just trying to tell me that Eve was worried I would stop seeing her if she continued to smoke dope. She had asked Ray, who I had once shared a prison cell with, to persuade me to allow her to smoke dope and still stay with her. I disguised my relief with a great show of bravado and told him, "I didn't give a toss whether she smokes dope or not."
As my mood swung I suggested that if he fancied her he should give her one.
He said, "Thank you, but no thank you, we are just friends."
The way I thought and felt in those days was if I decided to break up a relationship that was okay, but if it were someone else's idea I would find it totally unacceptable. For many years I didn't recognise that I had this trait; if I didn't want something it didn't necessarily follow that I wanted someone else to have it.

I stayed in the Cambridge Club for a couple of hours topping up with scotch, and then went round to the to clip joint to have words with Eve. I found her sitting with a punter who had bought her several drinks, a large box of chocolates, plus a white cuddly toy. These possessions meant that this punter had spent over a hundred quid already and looked like he was going to spend quite a lot more money before the night was over. Looking around the club I saw that most of the girls had punters who were spending lots of money on them.

The way clip joints operated in those days was very simple; the hostesses would hang around the street not far from the entrance to the so-called club, deliberately giving the impression that they were prostitutes. When and if a likely punter stopped to enquire as to how much she charged, he would be invited into the club to discuss the matter, during these discussions if he fell for the girl's line of chat, he would be persuaded to buy a drink. Two glasses of very watered down non-alcoholic shandy could cost upwards of ten pounds. There was no actual alcohol sold in the clip joints because this would be breaking the licensing laws and give the police the power to close them down. Each drink that arrived at the hostess's table would have a brass cocktail stick in it, which the girls would keep until the end of the evening. No money would change hands between the girl and the punter. All the drinks and gifts were delivered to the table by a waitress who collected the money and put it behind the bar. If the girl had a persuasive line of chat she could keep the punter buying drinks and other goodies for hours. At the end of some evenings she could quite easily have made as much as three or four hundred pounds

I never failed to be amazed at the gullibility of these blokes, having sex was so important to them they would lose all sense of reality. To impress the girl, who had put them on a false promise, some of them would pay as much as twenty-five pounds or more for a small box of uneatable chocolates. It would definitely cost them over thirty pounds for a little white cuddly teddy bear. Behind the bar in this particular joint they kept about thirty boxes of chocolates and the same amount of cuddly toys. On a good night even this amount of stock wouldn't be enough. When I worked on the doors of these places I saw some unbelievable and unrepeatable things. When the girls began to suspect that their punter might be cottoning on to what they were up to, they would come up with some fictitious excuse for him to leave and arrange to meet him some distance away from the club.

Luckily most of the punters realising they had been conned were too embarrassed to come back, which made the doorman's job quite easy. Unfortunately this wasn't always the case, especially among foreigners, they would often come back with a friend or two, demanding to see the girl. Our plan of action when this happened was a very well rehearsed routine. It was the doorman's job to keep them out of the club and away from the girl. First he would ask them if they were members and did they have their membership cards. When they very obviously couldn't produce one, they were told that it would be breaking the law to let anyone in the club who couldn't prove their membership. This would normally cause the punter to set on us with some sort of verbal attack

Normally you could calm them down by asking them if they would like you to go upstairs and fetch the girl they had fallen in love with, down to see them, they usually went along with this suggestion. Then the doorman would go into joint and return with the waitress or another hostess who would tell the punter that his girl had gone to meet him and should still be waiting for him to turn up. Often they would go away to look for the girl, being unable to find her they would give up and go home. You could guarantee, however, if I was working on a club door, there was always an awkward bastard, it would be my luck to get someone who wouldn't give up until it came to blows, which it very often did.

As I was saying Eve had a real mug punter that night, he was buying her everything in sight. I stood behind the bar drinking a shandy and thinking what a load of stupid bastards these blokes were. I could hear the girls promising them all sorts of sexual variations, from oral to bondage. Eve was telling her punter that, when they met up some time later, she was going to bring a friend, so that he could find out what it was like to have sex with two women at once. She then went on to explain that, as she was a hostess she wouldn't be able to leave the club at the same time as him because the owners might think that she was using the place for prostitution!

The bloke assured her that he wouldn't let this happen.
He said to her, "I will leave now and wait at the place where you said you wanted me to wait."
As he got up to leave I heard her say," I don't finish work until midnight, surely you don't want to wait that long."
The bloke looked crestfallen, Eve seeing his expression said, "Why don't you stay with me for a little while longer and have some more drinks, that way our time apart will be much shorter."
His little piggy eyes lit up with delight Eve looked across to the

bar, smiled at me and ordered two more drinks, which I served them with.

I realised, that she was as high as a kite, "Could you hold on to these for me please, John," she said as she handed me about twenty cocktail sticks worth five pounds each.
How the money worked in clip joints was simple, the waiter or waitress collected the cash when they served the drinks. I have already said. At the end of the evening in exchange for cocktail sticks, soft toys and chocolates the girls would receive about three-quarters of whatever the punters had spent on them. For every punter that came into the club it meant that whatever girl enticed them in would have to pay the doorman a pound out of every ten she earned.

I soon got fed up hanging around, drinking non-alcoholic shandy and decided to go for a proper drink. Eve didn't look at all pleased when she saw me leaving. I intended to visit Terry O'Brien's club in Wardour Mews but being short of money I decided that I would go to the '41 Club' and try to borrow some. When I got there I ordered a cup of tea and then sat down to wait for it to be brought to my table. Like me, most of the people who were in the place knew each other so there was a good deal of piss-taking banter going on among us, which was quite commonplace. I'd just finished my tea and was about to leave when Curtis arrived, when he saw me he came and sat at my table. I was sitting in the corner of the café, with my back to the wall as I often did Curtis sat facing me. Not long after he'd joined me my attention was drawn over his shoulder, towards a fellow I knew as Tucker. He was an enormous Irishman, not very well known for his sense of humour or his deep intellect. Tucker was having a very serious conversation with another large Paddy called Rocky and at the same time was pointing at Curtis, I could see that they were getting very agitated.

Because I knew both of them I wasn't particularly worried for myself but I did feel a bit concerned about Curtis. Tucker had a reputation for being an absolute lunatic; I had seen him take as many as twenty amphetamines in one go. Rocky on the other hand was totally different, he was rumoured to have shot several people back in the old country. Out of the two he was the more calm calculating type of criminal nut case. At one time or another in his life he had been accused of every crime in the book and I believe that he had committed most of them. Eventually they came up behind Curtis and grabbed him around the neck, both of these men were well over six and a half foot tall poor Curtis, being only five foot seven or eight, looked like a little puppet in their arms.

For the simple reason that both of these blokes weighed over a seventeen stone and I wasn't quite pissed enough, I decided not to start any trouble with them Rocky had caught hold of Curtis around the throat and was slowly choking the life out of him.
I said to Tucker, "Why the fuck, are you picking on my mate?"
He growled back at me, "This bastard, and one of his pals, nicked three grand's worth of gear off of us."
"When was that," I asked.
"The last time he was here," he answered.
"I think your making a mistake because the last time he was here, I was with him and I am sure I would have seen if he had nicked anything."
I suddenly realised I shouldn't have said what I just had. What brought this realisation on, was the fact that Rocky had produced a double-barrelled, sawn-off shotgun from under his coat and was holding it under my chin, forcing my head so far back, all I could see was the ceiling.
"So you're the bastard that was in the toilet, while this fucking dog was keeping watch."
I could hear Curtis trying to talk, while Tucker who had by now taken over holding on to him, had one arm round his neck and was rhythmically punching him on the top of his skull.

I managed to get my hand around the end of the shotgun and push it to one side, at the same time telling Rocky to calm down, and explain what he was going on about.

"Don't tell me you don't know," he said.

I knew that my life was in danger and starting a fight with these two people would bring it to a certain and abrupt end. I can also say for certain that my voice had never before or since reached the pitch it got up to when I said to them.

"If I had nicked your gear, do you think that I would be sitting here, with less than five quid in my pocket?"

I had known Rocky for some time and I think this was the reason, he started listening to me. "Tell me," he said, "Were you in the toilet the other week, when this bloke was keeping watch outside."

"That's right," I said. "But I never pinched anything, only two pieces of lead pipe I found above the ceiling tiles."

"Why did take you them," Tucker asked.

I told him about the trouble that we'd had in Ladbroke Grove, and how I'd used them for weapons, and then slung them away,

"Where did you sling them," he asked me.

"Over the wall, down alongside the railway," I told him. I also said, if they wanted me to I would go with them to show them the exact spot.

I was beginning to think that maybe they weren't your everyday pieces of lead and if they were I certainly couldn't see what all the fuss was about as I had left at least five or six other similar pieces in the false ceiling. All four of us travelled in Rocky's car to Westbourne Park station, Where we walked past the ticket collectors box and made our way down onto the platform and then along the lines close to the wall over which we had slung the pieces of pipe. Much to both Curtis and my relief we found both pieces of lead lying within a yard of each other. Rocky and Tucker picked them up and then apologised for roughing us up. They then explained that each pipe contained about fifteen hundred quid's worth of cocaine. Because of the way the pipe ends had been sealed off it looked like they just been cut with a chisel, the fact that they were hollow had never entered my mind.

When the ticket collector saw us coming back towards him, he started waving his finger and giving us a bollocking for not buying tickets. Suddenly when he saw six foot six, seventeen stone Tucker with two pieces of lead pipe in his hand he stopped berating us. I think he showed extremely good sense when he withdrew his objections and just bid us a fond goodnight. Rocky offered to give us a lift back to the '41 Club'. Not wanting to give them any reason to get upset with us again I lied and said I had been on my way to Paddington when I'd called into Dean Street. They drove away leaving me and Curtis standing there. We looked at each other and burst out laughing it worked out that the Paddy's had been hiding over ten grand's worth of drugs inside the lead pipes that they had secreted away above the false ceiling of a publicly used toilet, for safety

Curtis had been out drumming that afternoon and had struck lucky; he'd found ladies stocking that had been hidden away on a nail at the back of a wardrobe, which contained seven hundred pounds. When he gave me half of the money I realised what a genuine bloke he was. We made our way down to Billy Manning's Club and started drinking our way along the optics. Tony's friend Johnny King came over to us and asked if either of us could drive, I was just pissed enough to say that I could. He then told us that he had been given a car, which he didn't know how to drive and asked me if I would do him a favour and drive him and some friends down to Eastchurch Prison on the Isle of Sheppy.

I agreed to do so, thinking that he meant the next day or maybe the following weekend, both myself and Curtis were surprised when within five minutes he asked us if we were ready to leave. He told us that he would explain his mission when we got under way. His explanation was quite simple, he had a friend in Eastchurch prison that he had promised to leave some tobacco and booze for. We picked up John's wife, Maggie and her mate Lucy, and then drove down to Kent. Outside of my bad driving, getting there and back again didn't present us with any problems. When we got there we hid the stuff next to the incinerator inside the prison grounds, within four hours of leaving the club we had made the drop and were back outside John's house in Ladbrooke Grove.

Maggie King had an evil of a sense of humour; her friend Lucy was a very attractive redhead who I fancied something rotten. When they invited us in for a drink, I told them I would only accept their invitation, "If I could sleep with the redhead."
She immediately smiled and said, "My name is Lucy," then added, "Sleeping with me can be arranged but only if it is arranged with me."
What she didn't tell me was that she was the bit on the side, for the very well known local club owner, Billy Mannings, who just happened to be Johnny King's best friend and partner. Whenever, Billy left his club at whatever time he decided to close it, he would come round to see Lucy before going home to his wife. Luckily for me that night the club was very busy, the people we had left there earlier must have stayed drinking until after nine the next morning.

When Maggie came into the room with our breakfast the next day, she told me all about Lucy and Billy's relationship. Lucy then told me that she was pissed off playing second fiddle to Billy's wife and was hoping that he would catch us in bed together, create some sort of a scene, which would give her an excuse to finish with him.
When she told me this I asked her if she wasn't frightened that Billy might give her a wallop?
She said, "You're not the sort of bloke to let him do that."
Knowing Billy as I did, I knew that he wasn't a fighting man, and certainly wouldn't get too upset over losing this redhead. As the situation didn't arise, it didn't matter; this girl was physically and facially very attractive but had a devious evil mind, which

helped me put a stop to any long-term involvement I may have been nursing in my little brain.

Johnny King came in the room and suggested that Tony and I could keep the car, on condition that if he or Maggie needed to be driven anywhere we would do it.
Tony, who had now joined us said," I've got a better idea, back at my flat I've got a Dansette record player that I nicked the other day. I'll give you that in exchange for the car, without any conditions, other than we promise to give you the occasional lift if and when we are available. Can we do a deal?"
I was very surprised when John agreed, the car, we now owned was a one year old, Humber Hawk.

Having the car soon proved to be a great asset, as it meant that we could carry more, and much larger goods away from the houses we broke into. Tony never bothered to drive, I'm not too sure that he could, which was fortunate for me, as it meant that I had it at my disposal all the time. I did for a very short time consider that I might have to cutback on my drinking, and maybe smoke more dope by way of a substitute. Well, that was the theory, in actuality I didn't change at all and went through a period of time when I was extremely lucky that I didn't kill anyone or get arrested for drunk driving. In those days I would often come up with highly moral ideas and plans in my head that my body was totally incapable of carrying out. I now seemed to need progressively more and more drink to salve my conscience, so that I could carry on doing the things that I thought would make me more acceptable to the people I not only wanted to be with, I wanted to be seen to be with.

As I said the car became a great asset, very often, after we had finished an afternoons drumming I would drop Tony off. Then I would go down the East End, pick up a girl and drive down to Margate or Faversham, for what I would tell them was a night out and a meal (bed-and-breakfast). I avoided mixing with a lot of the boys I had grown up with in the East End because they were unaware of the sort of person I was portraying on the other side London. I was never brave enough in sobriety to try to be a hard man around the area where I grew up because I knew that if I ever tried to be a gangster-come-hard man around there some of my mates were quite capable of tearing me apart, so for some time I lived a Jekyll and Hyde existence. In Mile End, Stepney and around Aldgate, I was known as an amicable Pratt and in the West End a violent lunatic.

One night, I was sitting at the bar of Billy Manning's having a nice social drink and a chat with a girlfriend, when two smartly dressed blokes who were sitting on the other side of the room, looking totally out of place, started waving and smiling at me. I was pretty high, but not drunk, I was certainly sober enough to realise that both of these blokes were complete strangers to me. Out of politeness I smiled and nodded back to them, but I didn't make any sort of verbal contact. A little while later, one of them sent me over a drink and then followed it by sending several more, each time he did this I felt obliged to buy one for the girl I was with, which seemed to please her immensely. We weren't actually together in fact we were just passing the time while she was waiting for her boyfriend to show up. Eventually curiosity got the better of me, I excused myself to the girl, as I just had to go over and say something to the blokes, even if it was only to tell them that they were mistaking me for somebody else.

I soon found out that I was the one making the mistake, when he called me darling! A bloody poof, I thought, as I cast a close eye over his expensive suit. However, as the girl I had been drinking with had walked out of the club as soon as I'd left her, I was now on my own, plus these blokes were was offering to buy more Scotch so I accepted an invitation, to join them. After all when the drink is flowing free, it was only right that I should be sociable. During the conversation that followed they asked me if I would I like to go back to their flat in Chelsea for a meal. At first I refused, as I didn't want to go on my own, though the idea did appeal to me, and it wouldn't have been the first time I had mugged a poof. I looked around the twenty or so people in the Club, until I spotted a bloke called Ginger who I didn't know all that well but I had got drunk with him on several occasions. I walked over to where he was sitting and outlined the situation to him; he said, "As I am flat broke your invitation couldn't have at a better time". Within a couple of minutes we were all in a taxi on our way to Chelsea.

Their flat turned out to be closer to Earl's Court than to what I would call Chelsea. When we arrived there I was a bit disappointed to see that they had a porter come doorman attending the front door. The reason for my feeling of disappointment was I thought he might get in the way if I had to make a quick exit. Once we got through the front door the two blokes led us across a wide hallway and up a flight of marble stairs. On the first floor we came to a pair of magnificent solid oak panelled door, with very tasteful, expensive solid brass fittings. Inside the flat, which was bigger than most houses I had been in, there was more luxury than I had ever seen, and that was taking into consideration the contents of all the houses and flats I had robbed. From all the trappings I could see, I soon realised that these, blokes didn't just have a lot of money. They were very seriously rich.

I hoped by putting on my usual act of bravado and ordering them to cook us the meal they had promised I was making it obvious that I was taking charge of the situation. I must say, they prepared the meal very quickly and very well. The plan I had loosely formulated with Ginger was for us to separate the blokes, and then each of us would rob our respective 'partners'. I was left with 'The Smiler' (as I called him) who was the one who had sent over the drinks in the club. In my mind, I had been mulling over several ideas of how I was going to set about robbing him. The opportunity presented itself when I spied a large, ornate oriental dagger lying on a table in the window alcove. When I picked it up and started thrusting it about like sword 'Smiler' began to look very nervous, it was then I that I began to fee I was in charge of the situation.

I searched through every cupboard in the apartment, helping myself to whatever gear would fit me. I rigged myself out from head to toe with the most expensive clothes I had ever worn. As well as the clothes, my collection of jewels was increased when I discovered a small jewellery box containing two pairs of solid gold cufflinks, plus a sizeable platinum chain with a St. Christopher medallion attached to it. It wasn't totally a one-way robbery; because I intended to leave the clothes I was wearing in part exchange. After pouring the remains of a very expensive bottle Scotch down my throat I sat down, thinking that Ginger would soon appear with his loot. After waiting for what I thought was a considerable amount of time, I began to get fed up. Just then Smiler began crying and pleading with me not to hurt him and then he asked me if I would like to feel his dick, and could he rub himself up against me. Previously to this encounter, I had only ever met a couple blokes who preferred to shag men instead of women, I certainly hadn't been this closely involved with any of them.

When I saw 'Smiler' sliding along the sofa towards me and it looked like he was going make some sort of move, I jumped up so quickly to get out of his reach I nearly tripped over my own feet. I was feeling very concerned that he may have sensed my apprehension. I also became very wary about turning my back on him. My brain went into a childish panic thinking about what he would be sticking up my arse if we had a fight and I lost. As he reached out to put his hand on my leg, I slashed at it with the dagger, catching him across the outer part of his wrist. When I saw the blood start to flow down between his fingers, the thought that I might have to kill him came into my mind, which was something I hadn't really contemplated, but my fear of being shagged by a man would certainly have made me do it.

I turned away from him, walked over to the door of the room, where I had last seen Ginger and his partner disappear into and was very surprised when I opened it and saw Ginger, having sex, in the role usually reserved for women. At first I thought the poof was raping him, but listening to the moans and groans of sheer delight coming from him, soon made me think differently. Blimey, I thought, I might have to deal with all three of the bent bastards. I was suddenly covered in the very icy sweat of fear, which was oozing out of every pore in my body. I no longer cared how I got out of that place, as long as I got out with my arse intact. I did eventually escape, carrying all my loot with me, feeling very relieved that I was still a virgin around the hindquarters.

In the taxi on the way back to Billy's Club, the state of panic and fear slowly began to ebb away, and I began to calm down. The cabby must have thought he'd picked up a right loony, because I kept bursting into loud fits of laughter as I mentally relived the ridiculous situation I had just escaped from. Tony did the same when I told him about it, except that he wasn't very pleased that I had exchanged his best shirt and pullover for my new gear. We did go back to the flat to get his stuff, but not too surprisingly, we weren't invited in. I heard some time later that Ginger had taken up semi-permanent residence.

CHAPTER 10

Early one evening not long after the incident with the gay blokes, I was driving from pub to pub, around the Notting Hill Gate area on the pretext of seeking out Curtis, and of course having a drink every time I stopped. I began to get a wonderful feeling that the world was a beautiful place. There I was, with a nice car, money in my pocket, smart clothes, somewhere regular to sleep, and I could say that I had friends in nearly every neighbourhood of the West and East End of London. Feeling a bit peckish, I decided to go for something to eat at the Barbi Chick, which had become my favourite eating-place and I considered the owner to be more than just an acquaintance.

Although I wanted to be known as a hard man and for my violent, evil behaviour, I still wanted to be liked; one of my peculiar traits was that I loved being treated as a welcome regular. I thrived on going into places where the Owner, Manager or waiter would say something personal, like "Will you be having your usual John." I especially liked it if it was a place I considered a bit upmarket, where the clientele was from the middle or upper classes. Whenever I was greeted in this fashion, my working-class snobbery would make me strut around like a peacock and I would tip the staff very generously. I wasn't really aware what exaggerated egotism meant in those days. I just suffered from it.

The owner of the Barbi Chick welcomed me and asked, "Are you going to have your usual John," in a voice loud enough for most people in the place to hear him. I was elated, especially as it was in front of two very attractive girls; I asked equally as loudly if my usual table was available.
"I'm sorry," he said, "We're very busy, but there are some stalls vacant along the wall bar." "Thanks," I said, and then walked across the room and propped myself up on one of the aforementioned stalls, conveniently situated next to the two attractive girls. As I sat waiting for my food to arrive I got quite a surprise when I felt

something hot hit me on the side of the face. I quickly turned and looked at the girl sitting next to me, she giggled and apologised saying that a chip had accidentally flown off of the end of her fork. She reached over and started to wipe my face with her napkin. I was quite delighted that this lovely young girl was paying me so much attention, as the idea of introducing myself, and pulling either her or her mate, had been, and was still the uppermost thought in my mind.

She introduced herself as Frances and her friend as Barbara, and said to me, "We know your name is John because the owner called you by it when you first came in."
They went on to tell me that they were from Birmingham, and that they had initially come to London with some boyfriends for a short visit but had fallen in love with it, so much so, that they had decided to stay, rent a flat and get jobs. Frances told me she was working in Whitley's department store and had a flat not very far from the Barbi Chick. We chatted for some time during and after our food, I was in no hurry, because I had given up on the idea of trying to locate Curtis. When Barbara said it was time to leave, I asked them if they would like to lift, Francis accepted immediately but Barbara was a bit hesitant. I asked the Barbi-Chick owner for our bills and paid them.

When we arrived outside their flat, Frances who had sat in the seat next to me asked if I would like to go up for coffee. I could see from the expression on Barbara's face, that she wasn't too comfortable with the idea, so I muttered something about it would have to be a very quick one. Frances smiled and we went up to the flat, which was on the first floor. It consisted of a small kitchenette and a bed-sitter, which was furnished with two single beds on opposite sides of the room, plus a table and four chairs in the centre. Francis pointed at one of the beds, and told me to sit on it, as it would be more comfortable than using any of the chairs. While we waited for Frances to make the coffee, Barbara sat on the bed opposite me, making sure, that every time she moved, I would get a perfect view up her dress to her knickers. When Francis came in with the coffee, she slid on the bed next to Barbara, also making sure that I could see up her skirt. After talking for a while, I was more than a little surprised when Barbara asked if we would like to play cards.

What a good idea Frances said, we could play strip poker. I thought that the drink had caused me to be a bit befuddled, and that I hadn't heard right. Both of the girls were laughing at the puzzled look on my face, Barbara looked directly at me and said, "Yes! She did, say strip poker!"
"Fine by me" I said.
When Frances produced a pack of cards, we got off of the beds and sat around the table, she began to shuffle the cards like a professional dealer. Just then I heard some footsteps coming up the stairs, my brain clicked into a paranoia mode. Did they think that I had money, had these two nice well spoken girls set me up to rob me? Why should two middle-class, very attractive girls want to invite a rough cockney bloke up to their flat? What could they possibly find attractive about a skinny, six-foot, half-drunk bloke like me? As I heard the footsteps get near and then go past and further on upstairs, I breathed a sigh of relief. I turned to Frances and asked her what had happened to their boyfriends. She told me not to worry because they were both Merchant Seamen and the reason they had originally come to London was to get on a ship out of London Docks bound for America. Apart from that, she said they were just friends, not serious relationships.
We had some more coffee and started playing cards, Frances and I lost the first couple of hands very quickly I had removed my jacket and shirt, Frances had taken off her blouse and then asked me if I would undo her bra.
"With great pleasure," I said but before I could release it Barbara chimed in, "Why are we mucking around, as we all know what this going to lead to. Why don't we just get undressed and go to bed."?

This was the first time in my life that I had been involved in a sexual threesome; I can truly say that it was a very exciting night. Before the girls went to work the next morning Frances pulled me to one side and asked me if I had a friend that would take Barbara out. I said I would try to find someone.

At this time Curtis and myself were sharing a flat in Notting Hill, when I eventually got there he wanted to know where I had been and reminded me that the car belonged to both of us. I was still feeling very excited about the previous night and told him what had happened, and that a very attractive girl wanted him to take her out. Tony said I am sorry mate while you were missing I met a girl myself, and we went back to her place in Fulham. I wasn't totally disappointed; I just thought that I would have to continue sleeping with the two girls until I could find somebody else for Barbara. However Tony did agree to see Barbara and come out for a drink with us that night, after which we went back to their flat where we talked for a while and then went to bed. About an hour or so later Tony got out of bed, got dressed and then asked me if I would drive him to Fulham.

Frances asked if she could come with us, Barbara just turned over in bed and went back to sleep. We arrived in Fulham, at about half past two in the morning. The house he directed me to stop outside of was in Escort Street. It was an end of terrace; yellow brick built property, very similar to my parents' house. Tony pulled out a key and opened the street door and then showed us into the front room where he told us to wait, while he went upstairs to fetch the girl he had met the previous night. When she came into the room with him, he introduced her as Babs, I recognised her as one of the girls I knew from Bayswater road.

She was a very pleasant girl and immediately offered us a drink; Frances and I asked if she had any Scotch, from a cabinet in the corner of the room she produced four glasses and a bottle of Whisky. As she was pouring the drinks the room door opened and two young children came in, Babs told us that they were her kids and that their father was doing a three-year prison sentence, (commonly called a lagging in the trade). Tony must have liked her very much because in my opinion to get out of bed and leave Barbara who was a far younger and more attractive, single girl with no ties, and come to this place seemed a bit daft. There is a well-known saying that there is no accounting for taste or love.

After chatting for several hours, I told them that I had to take Frances back to her flat and I would see Tony that afternoon, I also pointed out that due to our new found responsibilities, we would both need money. When we got back to the girls' flat, after spending an hour or so in an all-night café having something to eat, we found that Barbara had packed all her gear and gone .She had left a note saying that she was going back to Birmingham. It didn't seem to upset Frances at all, she told me that she had been expecting something like it because that months rent was due and they hadn't got enough money to pay it.

"Don't worry about it," I said. "Tony and me are going to work this afternoon and will most probably earn more than enough money to cover it."

As arranged Tony and I met up that afternoon and went out drumming, we did several places and got plenty of gold, jewellery, watches etc but not much ready cash. When I explained to him about the situation Frances was in, he suggested that if we gave up the flat we shared and Frances did likewise with hers, we could all move into Babs' house, which would make things more convenient and much cheaper. When I got back to Frances and told her about Tony's suggestion she was quite delighted because it was such an easy solution to her problem. I began to wonder if Curtis had cleared it with Babs, however, there was no need for me to worry because when we got there Babs told us that it had been her suggestion that we all move in together.

Frances and myself slept in the ground floor front room, the room where we had had a drink the first time we visited the house. Tony and Babs slept in the room behind us, and the children slept upstairs. The room above mine was rented out to a lodger who none of us knew. Tony and I continued to go drumming once or twice a week for the next month or two. I would often go down to Billy's Club and arrive back home whenever it suited me, while on the other hand Tony would stay with Babs and the children most of the time. Frances told me that she was beginning to feel very lonely being left on her own, and that she would like to occasionally come with me down to the club.

I had by this time developed some very strong emotions towards Frances and had mentally set her up on a pedestal. So much so, that the idea of taking her into a dive like Billy Mannings club and letting her mix with the sort of people who went there, gave me a feeling of insecurity. I told her I thought that she should feel above going into those sorts of places. She then told me that she was pregnant and as I was the father of the child, maybe I should rise above going in them too. The thoughts and feelings that came over me at that precise moment are inexplicable, joy, elation, sadness, excitement, and fear all collided in my brain at once. When we told Babs our news, she suggested that we call in her Doctor to make sure that Frances was okay and that there weren't going to be any complications. The Doctor came within a day or so and gave Frances what she told us was a very thorough examination. She said that he'd confirmed what she had thought, which was that she was about three months pregnant.

Tony asked me how long I had been going with Frances. Thinking about it, I guessed about three months.
He said," You must have clicked almost on the very first night you met."
That's the way the cookie crumbles," I said.
I asked Frances what she wanted to do about it, did she want to have an abortion or get married or just continue to live as we were?

She was non-committal to any of my suggestions and told me she needed and wanted time to think. From the day that Frances announced she was pregnant, things at the house began to go downhill very fast. Several times, Tony and I went out drumming but had no luck and came back with very little money or goods. I carried on in very much the same vane, which meant I went out drinking almost every night. I wasn't surprised when Tony suggested that we break up the partnership, as he would rather not have to share such small pickings. By that time I felt that I gained a good enough knowledge to go drumming on my own and agreed that a full share of a small pot was better than half a share of a small pot. We shook hands and agreed to go our separate ways.

Being as it was September and I knew my family would be down in Kent, hop picking, I asked Frances if she would like to meet them. She wasn't over the moon about the idea but did agree to come with me. We arrived in Five Oak Green late on a Friday afternoon; I introduced Frances to my mum and dad and my brothers and sisters. We were told that if we wanted to stay for the weekend we would have to sleep separately. After they had told us that Francis would be sleeping with my sisters in a hut and that I would be staying in a tent on my own, I told them that Frances was having my baby so we couldn't do any further damage if we slept together.
My mum looked like she was going to have a blue fit, she pushed me aside, walked over to Francis and said, "You must be some sort of bloody whore to let yourself get into that state." For a moment or two I thought she was going to hit her. She continued to say, "You can give up any idea that you're going to stay around here, among decent people."
Francis burst into tears, I took hold of her by the hand and led her back to the car and drove away.

On the way back to London the car broke down and as we weren't able to get fixed, we had to leave it and travel by taxi and a train the rest of the way.

I said to Frances, "As all my family are down in Kent we can stay at my parents house."
We slept in my old bedroom and didn't wake up until late on the Saturday. During the course of the different conversations we had that day and night, we both came to the conclusion that the odds were really stacking up against us. This was confirmed even more so when my brother Teddy arrived home on the Sunday afternoon and told us that we were taking liberties by staying in the house without permission. He started slagging off Frances so much so that I punched into him until he turned and ran out of the house. I thought that we would be able to stay at least one more night, but this wasn't to be the case. Teddy had phoned the police in Kent and told them to tell my dad that I'd broken into the house and was refusing to let him in. I was very surprised when in less than two hours of getting rid of Teddy my dad arrived and ordered us out of his house

Neither Frances or myself could understand the anger or bitterness showered on us by my family, I always knew that Teddy was my dad's favourite, and there were occasions in my life when I felt that my dad hated me. I asked him if we could leave our suitcase until we found somewhere to go and then come back and pick it up.
"Take your rubbish and piss off out of my house," he replied.
We picked up our case and walked out. While we were waiting on the platform of Stepney Green Tube station, I said to Frances, "September has always been my unlucky month. I'll lay odds with you that within in a week or two I will either be nicked or in some sort of very serious trouble."

Later that day, we went back to Tony and Babs' place, where we explained what had happened to us and asked them if they could put us up for a day or so, they agreed to let us stay until we could find somewhere else to live. They also told us that not long after we had left on the Friday, Babs had rented one of the upstairs rooms, to a family. As there were four of them she had given them our double bed, so if we wanted to stay, it would mean us having to sleep on two fold ups. I did feel grateful to them for the lodgings, but at the same time I felt very angry that they had given away something that belonged to me without my permission.

For some reason I can't recall maybe to go to the toilet or something, Frances left the room. While she was missing Babs gave me a letter that had arrived for her during our absence. Even though I could very plainly see that it was addressed to Frances, I opened and read it. It was from her friend in the Merchant Navy, via her ex-flatmate Barbara. From what I read it was very obvious that she had fallen pregnant to the merchant seaman, not me. I was totally unaware, until I read the letter that Frances had been writing to Barbara every week, telling her almost everything that was going on in our lives. After the way I had been treated by my family, then losing the car and having next to no money left; added what I had just read, I really felt at a very low ebb. When Frances came back into the room I confronted her with the contents of the letter. She denied that it could possibly be the other bloke's baby. For the very simple reason that I really wanted to believe I was the father, I accepted her explanation.

Tony said that as both him and Babs were very short of money he thought it might be a good idea if we went drumming the next day. When I agreed to do so, he told me that the new lodgers were also living on Poverty Street and that the husband wasn't averse to doing a bit of thieving. He then asked me would I mind if we took the bloke with us, I told him I had no objections. Later that night I was introduced to Billy Noble and his wife Moira, the new occupants of my old bed.

Early the next morning I was woken up by somebody knocking very loudly on the street door, when it became obvious that nobody else was interested in opening it, I did. At first when I saw the policeman I got a bit nervous and stayed that way, until I saw that he had Babs' son with him. Because of the way of life we were living, seeing a policeman that early in the morning came as quite a shock. I asked him to wait and made a hasty retreat into Tony's room feeling almost in a state of panic. Tony and Babs were having sex at the time, and were quite annoyed at my intrusion. When I explained that there was copper at the front door with Babs' boy, Tony told her to go and find out what that little pest had been getting up to. Before I could leave the room, Babs got out of bed and stood completely naked in front of me. Tony looked a bit embarrassed and told her to put her dressing gown on, after slowly taking her time to do so, she went to see what the policeman wanted.

It turned out that the boy, who was only about five years old, had got out of bed while everyone else in the house was still asleep and decided to go for a walk along Northend Road. When he came across an ice-cream shop with lots of tubs filled with various ice creams on display in the window, he'd lain on the pavement screaming and pretending to be sick until some kind soul bought him an ice cream. When he had eaten it, he lay down on the pavement again hoping that the same thing would happen a second time. Unfortunately for him the ice-cream vendor called the police. We could see that Babs was feeling very embarrassed as she promised the policeman that it would never happen again, he walked away smiling.

Before he had got out of sight, two blokes came running up and pushed their way into the house, one of them grabbed hold of Babs, who started screaming, "Loose me, Loose me."
I jumped on the bloke and forced him to let her go.
"Who the fuck are you?" I asked them.
Luckily while Babs was talking to the copper, I had got dressed, so I was now able to reach into my coat pocket and hold on to my knife, which I didn't pull out immediately, but was prepared to use if I had to. Babs explained that one of them was her husband. I felt rather uncomfortable about the situation, as I really didn't want to start fighting with a man who had just got out of prison and had

228

come to see his family. I didn't know this bloke but I had heard that he had been a small time villain, around the Fulham area.

When Tony came into the room, I explained to him what was going on, he looked at Babs and simply said, "Its decision time love." I think that Babs' husband had arrived with the idea that he was just going to move back in the house with her and the kids, as I thought, was his right. Tony was a villain and a thief, but he was never really a man who liked violence. I was full of admiration for him as I watched him conduct himself quite soberly, without showing any sort of fear. He told Babs that it was her choice and nobody else's who she was going to live with, while her husband who was at least a foot taller and three stone heavier than Curtis looked on.

After a lot of talking and tea drinking Tony, Billy Noble, and myself decided we would go drumming and hopefully, Babs and her husband would have things sorted out by the time we got back. I told Frances that I wouldn't come back until I had got sufficient money to pay a month's rent on a flat or a furnished room. I kissed her goodbye and walked up the street and waited at the corner of Northend Road. As I looked back I saw Billy Noble say goodbye to his wife and children and walk towards me, then Tony came out and followed him. Being without a car we decided to catch a bus over to Chelsea.

When we got to what looked a likely area, we selected a block of flats that we thought would house fairly well off people. As we were trying to loid open the first door we got disturbed by some people coming out of the flat above us, and had to walk away. Tony suggested, that when we got to the next block, Billy and me should wait outside and keep watch, while he tried his luck on his own. I told him that as long as he called us when he had gained entry, it was fine with me. While we were keeping look out, Billy and myself got involved with a chap who was trying to get his car out of a very tight parking space. I suggested that if we lifted up the back wheels of the mini that was blocking his car in we could pull it far enough away to allow him to get out. After pushing and pulling for some time we eventually made enough space for him to drive away.

Tony came down from the flats and told us that every door he'd tried, had been double locked with a Mortise, which had caused him to ruin his celluloid strip. Because none of us had thought to bring any extra strips, it meant we would have to devise other means of gaining entry. Feeling a bit down we walked off in the direction of Kings Road. Just as we turned the corner going in the direction of Sloane Square, five scruffy looking blokes came running along the street towards us. As they drew level two of them jumped on me and the other three tackled Billy and Tony. I managed to punch one of my attackers squarely on the jaw and put him down on his arse, as I was reaching into my pocket to get my knife, one of them said, "We are the police."
I said, "You must be joking, you're just a crowd of unwashed fucking beatnik's."
"I can assure you we aren't," the one on ground said as he held up his warrant card.

Tony was telling them to unhand him instantly! They were shouting, "We're the law, you're under arrest."
Tony insisted that they should still take their hands off him as they were wearing inferior clothing. I heard him tell them, "This suit cost me more than you can earn in a month you scruffy little bastards."
This really incensed them, they started kicking and punching into us and we started kicking and punching them back. The next thing I heard was a squealing of tyres, scraping alongside the kerbside close to where we were fighting and suddenly four large uniformed coppers carrying batons came charging at us.
Much to our delight they started to beat up our attackers, the one I had punched started screaming, "We are in the job! We are in the job!"

One of the uniforms who was wearing sergeant stripes, ordered all of us to line against the wall, which we did, whereupon the plain clothes coppers immediately pulled out their warrant cards and explained that they had been keeping us under observation for some time. What's more they were in the process of arresting us, for trying to steal a car and attempting to break and enter several dwellings.

The uniforms said they had been called out on a 999, to check on five suspicious looking characters, who had been seen entering and leaving several different basements! It was then that I attempted to walk away, thinking that while they were sorting things out and a having a jolly good laugh about the cock up the Wooden-tops had made, I could slip away unnoticed. I was making very good progress until Billy Noble shouted at me, saying, "Don't you fucking run away and leave us to take the blame."
Before I could take another step, both uniformed and plain clothes officers were all over me like measles. We were frog marched to the police car and then a driven to Chelsea police station which in those days was notorious for the good hidings that were administered to its various involuntary guests. It was well known to have the second highest reputation for cell beatings, the first being Leman Street.

Because we were held separately and out of earshot, I don't know in which order we were questioned. Taking a shrewd guess I think Billy Noble was most certainly the first, because when it came to my turn the policeman had a very comprehensive list of areas and addresses that Tony and myself had worked in. I denied all knowledge of ever having being near any of the places. I was told that I would be charged later that day and detained until the next morning when I would appear at the Magistrate's Court in King's Road. The next day, on the way to court Tony and I were handcuffed to two of the coppers that had nicked us, while Billy Noble was allowed to walk around unshackled. At the first given opportunity I asked Tony if he had ever discussed any of our previous jobs with

Billy? He said he had, and then agreed with me when I told him that I thought Billy had grassed on us about all the flats we had tried to do the previous day in the hopes that he would be able to save his own skin.

It was plain see that Tony's lips were badly bruised and swollen and he was finding it painful to talk. When I asked him how it had happened, he told me, that two coppers had come into his cell and asked him his name and address, which he gave them. Then one of them punched him in the mouth saying if you're Tony Curtis, I'm Burt Lancaster. It was a lifelong problem with him; no one ever believed that Tony Curtis was his real name.

When we arrived at Kings Road, they put all three of us in one cell at the back of the Magistrate's Court. During the time we were waiting, neither Tony nor myself spoke to Billy Noble. After about an hour or so one of the coppers came into the cell, and said that we were really lucky bastards, because the Magistrate on duty that day was such an easy touch for a sob story, we would most probably be let off with a fine. We were then led into the court and told to stand in the dock facing the bench. The Magistrate stood up, looked at us with disgust written all over his face and then walked out.
I asked Tony if he knew him. "I don't think so," he said.

A minute or two later another bloke came in and took his seat, he looked across at the policemen and said, "My colleague has had to step down in this case, because one of the charges against the three suspects is directly related to his place of abode."
I thought to myself, what fucking wonderful luck, not only had we had tried to break in to a bloody Magistrate's house, his best friend was going to try us for it.
I whispered to Curtis, "What odds will you give me, on this bloke being impartial?"
They read out a list of charges against us and asked if we were guilty or not. "Not guilty your Honour," Curtis and myself quickly

replied. Billy Noble told them he was guilty. Without warning Curtis turned and punched him on the side of the head calling him a stupid bastard.

In a matter of seconds, the police had jumped on Curtis and were holding the top half of his body over the side of the dock, with his arms forced up his back. The Magistrate was almost screaming, when he told us that he wasn't going to tolerate anymore of the lawless type of behaviour that we were using, in his Court. It didn't take long for him to make up his mind to deny our request for bail. He remanded us in custody until we would be brought up for trial at the London Sessions. Without further ado we were shipped off to spend our remand time waiting in Brixton prison. On arrival Curtis and myself told the M.D. that we were both epileptic and needed cells with soft furnishings, consequently we were both placed on the Nutters wing. The reason we claimed to be epileptic was quite simple, nutters were never expected to make up their beds or do any strenuous type of work and most of the time the screws regarded you as being off of your trolley and left you to your own devices.

On reception we were given blankets, sheets, a piss pot, and a blank letterform, which I sent to my mum. Also included in our reception goodies was visiting order that I sent to Frances, Tony sent both his letter and V.O. to Babs. It was ten days before Frances came to see me, she told me that no one had had the slightest idea that we had been nicked, or where we were, before she received my visiting order. She also said that Babs was now living back with her husband and Billy Noble's wife was sleeping with two men one at weekends and the other one during the week. She went on to say that she had absolutely no money and that she had walked from Fulham to visit me. This made me feel quite sick and totally inadequate, luckily in the next visiting box to us was a bloke called Harry Harrison who was being visited by his sister. I knew both them very well from the East End and I asked the sister if she would lend Frances the money for her fare back to Fulham.

She gave Frances a fiver and told me that I could pay her back whenever it was convenient, which I never did.

During the visit, Frances told me that she had left a letter at the gate for me and that it would explain what the true nature of her feelings for me were. Then she told me, that she would come and see me as often as she could. I felt pretty down as she walked away at the end of the visit, I stood back out of the box so could see her for longer. When I got back to my cell the letter was waiting for me. I sat down on my bed and began to read it; every line I read seemed to totally crush me emotionally. She had started it off by telling me that it wasn't my baby as she had already been a month or so pregnant when we first met. She went on to say that she was now back with the merchant seaman and was very glad that I had been arrested because it meant that I couldn't follow her back to Birmingham. The letter also told me not to write or try to contact her in any way, because if I did she would inform the police of the various jobs that she knew Curtis and I had pulled off. She also said for me to tell Curtis that Babs would do the same thing to him if he tried to contact her.

When you're locked in a prison cell alone with your emotions in the state that mine were in at that time, with an avalanche of crazy thoughts rushing through your brain, swinging from murder to suicide, the word agony doesn't come anywhere near explaining how you feel. I wanted to kill Frances, Babs and anybody else that I could blame for my rejection and incarceration. I stayed on my bed for three days and nights. The screws were very much aware of the mood I was in and left me alone.

Just after lunch on the third day, Curtis came into my cell and asked me what was wrong? When he had finished reading the letter, he looked at me, smiled and then said, "I have been expecting this to happen John, because it has happened to me every time I've been in prison. The only person that ever stayed true to me was my wife and I didn't want her."

PENTONVILLE JOHNNY

At that moment I wanted to be just like Curtis, no emotions, no regrets. I wasn't and over the next two or three weeks along with alcoholic withdrawals, I suffered from terrible nightmares and uncontrollable spasms of severe emotional pain. These are feelings that I have had on and off during my life and that I have never been able to come to terms with. We spent about six or seven weeks waiting in Brixton, I never heard from Frances again neither did Tony hear from Babs.

Time spent in prison seems to pass so slowly when you look forward to your release day or court attendance, but very quickly when you looked backwards at how long you've been there. Eventually we were given less than a day's notice of our appearance at the London Sessions. Sometimes, as I lay in my cell in Brixton I thought that if Tony had not punched Billy Noble until after we had got out of the dock at Kings Road, the entire matter may have been dealt by the Magistrates, who only had the power to give a maximum sentence of six months. Going up the steps as they call it meant that if we were found guilty there was no limit on the amount time they could deal out, anything from one day to life! My negative thoughts could always be depended on to take away any hope or confidence that might be trying to steal into my mind.

Travelling to the court we passed through many areas of London that I was familiar with. The comments coming from the rest of the passengers, about every attractive or unattractive woman we passed on the journey were mostly crude, but a few of them were very witty. Some of the blokes on the bus hadn't seen a woman for up to three months. The last woman I'd seen close-up, was Frances and that had been five weeks earlier. For the journey to the London Sessions we were handcuffed in two's. Good luck, was still riding high somewhere, but unfortunately not around me. My right-hand had been cuffed to an Irish bloke who was left-handed, who used that hand every time he needed to get his old chap out to have piss. I did explain to him in the best and politest way I knew, that if he had the misfortune to piss on my hand while he was holding on to his dick I would punch his fucking head in. I think the message got through, because the next time he went to the loo, he tried using his right hand and pissed all down the front of his trousers.

We arrived outside the Court just after nine, as we were being driven around to the back entrance, I couldn't help thinking what a magnificent building it was. Eventually the bus passed through two large wrought iron gates into a covered courtyard where it stopped. We were told to get off, and then escorted down a flight of stone steps, at the bottom of these, we were uncuffed and put into the smallest cells I had ever been in. Curtis, Noble and myself were put in together, which gave Tony and me our first chance to ask Billy Noble exactly what he had told the police, as we hadn't seen him since we parted company on Brixton reception. He assured us with tears in his eyes and took an oath on his kid's lives, that he hadn't said anything that would be detrimental to us in court. I asked Tony if he believed him, he told me he wasn't sure.

The holding cells were less than three feet wide and about eight feet long; the ceiling must have been fourteen feet high. They had obviously been designed to hold only one person at a time. There were two boards sticking out of the back wall, one to be used as a table and the lower one for sitting on, there was no other furniture so we took it in turns to sit down. There was a bell push to summon the screws if we felt in need of them. Because I had drunk a lot of tea before I'd left Brixton that morning and I was feeling very nervous, I needed to visit the loo. I rang the bell and asked the screw if I could use the toilet. He was one of the screws that worked on my landing back in Brixton and was quite used to walking away without checking when he told the blokes in the nick to go inside and bang their doors up.

I don't think he realised that these doors weren't self-locking because as he walked away he said to me, "When you've finished, go back to your cell and bang your door up behind you." When I came out of the toilet I went back to my cell and banged the door behind me. Obviously it didn't lock, so I waited until I thought that he and his mates were out of earshot. Then I walked around, to all the cells, looked through the door windows and asked the inmates if they would like their door opened, not one of them refused my offer. The doors were all secured on the outside by a sliding bolt, which slipped open both quietly and easily.

About thirty crooks started looking for ways to escape, no one actually got out of the court building but they were found to be in all the places where they shouldn't have been. The screw didn't have to be Einstein to guess who had released them. He and two of his pals took me into a cell, handcuffed my hands behind me and then punched me all over the place. They told me that, if I complained to anyone about the beating, they would charge me with attempting to escape. It was obvious that what they were saying to me was complete bullshit. I knew that if the newspapers, or the prison hierarchy, had ever found out that there were that many prisoners, some of them said to be highly dangerous, running around loose in the courthouse, all the screws on duty that day would have been severely disciplined if not sacked.

Some time after this little adventure, Curtis, Noble and myself were taken up a very narrow flight of spiral steps into court number one where the judge asked us if we were being legally represented. When we told him we weren't he asked us if we were going to represent ourselves, or if we would like a legal aid Barrister. We all accepted the offer of a free Barrister and then we were sent back to our cell to await a consultation with him. Eventually a screw came to the cell accompanied by our Barrister who was carrying a pile of papers. We were taken to an interview room where we sat around a very posh table, which the QC began spreading his documents over and then started asking us questions.

The files that he had spread out in front of him were our criminal records; he told us that the police evidence against us was so strong; we really had no alternative other than to plead guilty. I asked him how much he would be paid for defending us, he declined to answer but I knew that it would be the same if we pled guilty or not. I got the feeling that he certainly didn't want to go into court and defend us against the charges we faced. He kept telling us that if we put in a plea of not guilty, and then got found guilty, we would be given a more severe sentence, for wasting the Court's time. He then went on to say that apart from the seven police witnesses, who would be giving evidence against us there was also Billy Noble's statement. Tony and I looked at each other almost in disbelief, after witnessing the wonderful show of innocence that Billy had performed for us when we had confronted him in the cell earlier.

We were given his statement to read, it contained every word of our conversations and every detail of what we had done on the day of our arrest, he had also outlined what we had intended to do for the rest of the day, had we not been nicked. Noble asked the barrister if he could be tried separately from us as he intended to plead guilty to all the charges and give evidence against Curtis and myself. The barrister looked at us, I mean me and Curtis, and said Noble could most certainly be tried on his own and as he was going to give evidence that would definitely incriminate us, there was very little point in our pleading not guilty. We both agreed.

The Barrister suggested to us that he could put in a plea of mitigating circumstances and then asked us if there were any. I explained that I was unemployed that my girl friend was pregnant and we were about to become homeless, the barrister then said at least he had something to work on in my case. Tony told him that he was unable to work because he was an epileptic. Noble told the barrister that he could use any part of his statement that would help his case, he also muttered something about the police saying that they had promised to go easy on him for being so co-operative. We were then taken back to wait in our cell but not for very long because before many minutes passed we were called back into the dock. This time were taken into Court Two and came up before a different judge. I could see and almost feel the tension in Tony, who was standing between Billy and me. He whispered to me out of the side of his mouth, that he had been up before this judge in the past, and that he was a real mean bastard that hated housebreakers more than rapists or child molesters. This news made me feel really good, the clerk of the court read out the charges and asked us each in turn if we were guilty or not guilty.

Our barrister did a very good job with our pleas of mitigation, even I felt than none of us deserved more than a carpet (three months). The Judge however, had his own ideas; he started with Billy Noble, telling him, that he had gone out with the full intention of depriving some innocent homeowners of their property. And would have done so if he had not been arrested, but then like so many others of his kind he had tried to place the entire blame on his partners. He then went on to say, as a judge with many years of experience, he could see right through Mr Noble's plans. After further degrading Noble, he then turned his attention to Curtis describing him as an unfortunate individual who suffered from an inexplicable illness, which in no way gave any justification for his criminal activities.

Then it was my turn, "You sir have been a person with criminal tendencies dating back to nineteen forty-eight. You have a record of stealing and violence since your childhood, I can see no other way than a custodial sentence for all three of you. You will each go to prison for one and twenty months."
He went on to say; "In your case Mr Noble you can consider yourself very lucky."
We were taken back down to the cells to await transportation to whatever prison we were going to. The screw that had let me out to the toilet told me I would be going to Wandsworth, where some of his pals were going to be delighted to meet me. Suddenly I felt full of the joys of spring. Not only was I going to prison for the longest term I'd ever been sentenced to, there was going to be a reception party of hostile screws waiting for me.

I was handcuffed again but this time it was to a smartly dressed bloke who had been convicted of fraud and had been sentenced to five years. Knowing that he would be in nick longer than me made me feel slightly better, about my lot. Twenty-one months meant that my earliest date of release would be one year and two months away, which if you said it quickly did not seem so bad. Once again we were on the bus travelling through the streets of London watching life go by. The journey was made longer because the bus had to make pickups at another court somewhere in south London and at the Old Bailey. When we left the Bailey it was quite dark and several conversations had started between various convicts, as we now were.

The bus was a very old vehicle with shiny green leather, double bench type seats. The cons sat in pairs, the screws sat in various seats throughout the coach watching and listening. The bloke I was handcuffed to, told me that he had been grassed on by his wife and her boyfriend, he went on to say that he fully intended to get his revenge on them long before his release from prison. I asked him how he intended doing it; he looked at me and must have decided that I was someone he could confide in.
"She didn't get a quarter of the money I fiddled, and I am going to spend a good deal of what I have got left on a contract, with a man I know and trust to wipe them both out."
At first I thought this bloke had been seeing too many American Gangster films but when I looked in his face I realised that he was so consumed with hatred and resentment that he meant every word he said.

Finally we arrived at Wandsworth, even the poor view we had of it in the dark made it look sinister. When I had been in other prisons serving previous sentences, I had often heard cons say that Wandsworth had the worst reputation for bad food, dirtiness and sadistic screws in the country. As the bus passed through the large wooden reinforced gates I felt very lonely and alone, this was a feeling that I had experienced several times in the past and not always when I was entering prison. We were instructed to get off the bus and to form a queue in front of a small doorway that had a sign over it saying, "Reception." When the line was formed the bus was searched from top to bottom, and when it was given the all clear the driver was instructed to leave.

When the reception door opened we were told to go inside where we were unshackled and put into cubicles that were the same size as a telephone box and like most 'phone boxes around London they smelt of piss. There was no room to sit down and the only light that got in came through a small inspection spy hole that was cut in the door for the screws to see in. We were told to strip and give our clothes to the con standing behind a serving hatch at one end of the room. No one was in much of a hurry to give up their civilian clothes; it felt and looked like we were all hanging on to the very last vestiges of our freedom. Several screws came in and started shouting instructions. None of us new arrivals were actually standing inside the cubicles as we were supposed to be, which meant that I could see most of their faces, some of which were showing signs of sadness and great displeasure.

Among all the instructions that were being shouted at us was one that I was going to find almost impossible to obey, was to only speak when spoken to by a prison officer. Wandsworth still practised the Silent Rule, which meant that the only places inmates could talk to each other was either in their cells or on the exercise yards; and on the yards you were only allowed to speak to the person walking next to you. Smoking was only allowed in your cell. I looked around to say something to Tony about the rules but I couldn't see him. I went and changed my civvies for prison garb and then went back to my allocated cubicle, as I was getting dressed I saw Billy Noble come across the room and go in the box next to the one I was in, he had blood pouring down his face.

Tony had watched him go into the toilet and then followed him. Once in there he had given him a good hiding, which was something that I had very much wanted to do from the moment I had read his statement, and still fully intended to do at the first given opportunity. When I saw Tony he was looking ruffled but happy. I had been thinking along the lines that we might talk it over first and then do Billy when we got him on the wing. When I said this to Tony he told me that we might not be on the same wing as the treacherous bastard and he wasn't going to let the perfect opportunity that had occurred pass by. Several blokes asked me why Tony had done Billy, when I explained that he had grassed on us, as each of them got near him, they punched, kicked, or slapped him.

CHAPTER 11

Wandsworth prison was built in the 1850s and was originally called the Surrey House of Correction. Two of its most famous prisoners, though not at the same time, were Oscar Wilde and Ronnie Biggs. It was laid out with rows of cells radiating from a central circular unit, like spokes of a wheel, counting the basement each wing had four landings. There were two cellblocks, one with five wings and the other with only three. Each 'wing' was referred to alphabetically, A, B, C etc., and each landing numerically upwards, 1-4. On levels 2,3 and 4 there were walkways about a yard wide, where wire mesh was stretched like fishing nets across the central well. As in all closed nicks this was there for the safety of both screws and cons alike.

In the early hours of the morning we were moved from the reception area and put into holding cells located in the smaller of the two prison blocks, referred to as the G, H and K wing, this was only to be until we were allocated to our permanent accommodation. It had been a very long, busy day since we left Brixton, so as soon as I got into my bed I fell asleep instantly. I slept so soundly I didn't hear the wake up bell; therefore my first morning in Wandsworth began with my being placed on a charge of laziness. I estimated by pacing out from wall to wall that the cells in Wandsworth were eight foot wide by eleven foot six inches long and then I further guessed that they were about seven and a half-foot high. They were all painted the same; up to a height of three feet it was a dark green gloss, above that up to the ceiling was what looked like a mixture of yellow and brown which had come out as a sort of dirty putty colour. The ceilings were whitewashed with thick layers of distemper, the sort that flakes off as soon as it dries, so as of the moment they were decorated and from then onwards they always looked dirty.

After breakfast on the first morning we were told to pick up our bedrolls and piss-pots, then we were taken to the bigger block, which was the main body of the prison. Curtis and myself were given single cells next door to each other on E1, my cell number was fifty-six, Curtis had fifty-seven. Brixton had sent our medical records with us showing that we both supposedly suffered from epilepsy, this meant that the cells we were allocated were once again nicely situated in the middle of the nutter's wing. The only difference between our cells and the rest of the prison was that our cell floors were covered in a firm green rubber substance instead of the usual dirty old red and black earthenware tiles. They were each furnished with a three-foot cube shaped sack, made of very thick canvas and stuffed with coir which served as a table, a mattress made of the same material, which in my case was very well used and pissed stained, plus a smaller canvas cube for sitting on.

The metal piss pot that I had been issued with on reception, which I had found unusually acceptable and very clean, considering the filthy state of the rest of the prison, was taken away from me, and replaced by a plastic one. This unsavoury receptacle still had very visible signs of its last owner. As I looked at it, I thought bubonic plague would be mild compared to some the things I could catch if ever I had to sit on this thing! When I saw the even worse condition of the one that they had given Curtis I accepted mine without any further discussion. Along with everything else we had been issued with, there was a specially 'designed for nutters', plastic food tray and soup bowl, identical in shape to the metal versions, which the main body of con's used.

Quite a lot of them had more indentations in them than there had been when they were issued on to the wings; these were made when the cons used them as weapons against each other. A lot more thought and preparation had gone into the designing and making the bowls and trays than there was ever put into the food that got served on them. I am afraid to say that from day one, Wandsworth's reputation for dirt, inane discipline and bad food was proving to be very true. The way our meals were served was very similar to the army, large dishes of food were set up alongside each other on a hotplate come serving station, that were situated at the end of each wing. As the cons returned from their places of work, they formed a queue and were each issued with a tray and a soup bowl. After collecting the food they were banged up, for a two-hour lunch break. Unlike the ordinary everyday inmates, we of the nutter's wing weren't allowed to leave our plastic trays out to be washed-up by the kitchen staff, so without access to boiling water, our trays gradually got covered with an ever thickening film of cooking grease.

After lunch on the first day we reported as instructed to the P.O. in charge of our wing, who's name was Gearing which didn't even come close to rhyming with any of the names that the con's called him. We were then taken by another screw to the workshops. Curtis was put in the mailbag shop and I was sent into the sack shop next door, the work we did was very similar but sowing mailbags was a lot tougher on the hands than making sacks. Noble had been put on a different wing from us and must have been feeling pretty glad about the separation. Because of the way life was organised in the prison, we could well have served our entire sentence without ever seeing him but unfortunately for him, he was put to work in the sack shop in the next chair to mine. If I hadn't wanted to get my revenge on him so badly, I could have felt sorry for him. As well as giving him the sort of kicking I had promised myself I would, I was also going to make sure that everybody in the workshop knew that he was a grass.

When he saw me he turned and almost ran into the office of the screw in charge of the workshop, where he was asked what he wanted. The trustee con that worked in the office overheard the conversation and told me later that Billy had told the screw that I had threatened to cut his throat if he sat near me. The screw told him to piss off and sit down. We weren't allowed to speak but we could exchange notes and this is what I thought Billy was doing when he stuffed a piece of paper into my hand. I opened it and saw that it was a letter from his wife; he made a gesture indicating that I should read it, so I did. It wasn't the type of letter that I would have liked to receive from my wife while I was doing porridge. She had been to visit Billy in Brixton almost every week but had never told him what she was getting up to at home.

Somehow Billy had heard that she was sharing her bed with two or three other men and he had written to her asking for an explanation, her reply was in the letter I was now reading. She just simply said that as she was having Billy's baby it didn't really matter who she slept with because she couldn't get pregnant twice at the same time! This may have sounded a logical reason for committing adultery to her but I couldn't see it.

I passed the letter back to Billy and said, "You're a fucking fool as well as a grass, if you stand for that shit."

Moments later the discipline screw was standing over me and ordered me to stand up. He had pressed the alarm bell, which in turn had summoned the heavy mob. The biggest screws in the nick were on standby for emergencies, such as me talking! They marched me out of the workshop back to my landing. As I stepped into my cell one of them whacked me across the back and sent me sprawling headlong against the back wall.

I spun round as quickly as I could to face them but they had slammed the door shut before I could get to my feet. From outside one of them slid the peephole cover open and said that I would be charged with breaking the rule of silence. I felt relieved when he told me this, as I didn't have a clue why I had been treated this way. On the way back to the cell I had been thinking that the screws were going to get revenge on me for letting all the prisoners out at the courthouse. The next morning I was brought before the governor facing charges of laziness and breaking the no talking rule. I had heard that this present governor was a fair-minded man and that he would listen to me if I put up a defence against the charges.

The punishment block was in the basement beneath my cell, by comparison with what I could see on that landing, the rest of the prison began to look very inviting. I was marched between four officers two behind me and two in front so that there was no way I could go anywhere other than where they wanted me to go. It was very much like being on a tube train in the rush hour. When we arrived at a cell situated in the very corner of the basement, the two screws in front of me stepped into the cell and did an about-face, the two behind me pushed me directly into them, I felt like a human sandwich. The cell was brightly lit compared to the rest of the landing; it was furnished with a desk and a chair in which the Governor was sitting facing me.

The charges were read out to him and he asked me if I had anything to say in answer to them. I tried to explain that as it had been so late when I had got to bed on the first night, and that I had been very tired I just didn't hear the wake up bell. On the second charge I told him that, because it was my first day I hadn't been in the prison long enough to adapt to it. The governor said, "On the first charge of laziness, you will lose one days' pay. On the second charge, you will be confined to the punishment cells for three days, on a diet of bread and water, and if there are any further breaches of the rules, you will not be dealt with so leniently."

Due to the fact that I was in a special padded cell, as an 'epileptic', I didn't have to stay on the punishment landing. I served my three-day chokey diet in my own cell. The landing I was on was run by a screw named Thomas, he was also in charge of the inside gardens. Each day when he brought my bread and water he would ask me if I'd been talking to anybody and then walk away laughing. I did ask him why he felt that my downfall was so hilarious.
"You'll find out soon enough," he said.
When the punishment finished, I was given a proper prison breakfast, which I ate without thinking how bloody awful it was. It suddenly dawned on me that all the cons around me were openly having conversations with each other; the landing officer was looking at me and laughing again.

"What the fucking hell is wrong with you," I asked him in a loud, very disrespectful tone.

He looked at me and said "I won't put you on a charge of using foul language because I think the punishment you have just finished was totally unfair as the silent rule was abolished from all prisons at twelve o'clock on the day you were sent down."

I was working in the sack shop for several weeks, but no matter how hard I tried, I could not get the discipline screw to change my workstation, so I was stuck sitting next to Billy Noble. I got to know many of the cons that worked in the shop with me, some of them were very well known throughout the London underworld. Altogether there were over a hundred of us making hessian sacks. It wasn't what you would call difficult work, if you met your pre-set target, you could afford to buy toothpaste and sweets as well as the usual tobacco, matches, and cigarette papers. Now that the silent rule had ended the days in the sack shop seemed to pass quicker, we were able to have sensible conversations instead of all doing James Cagney impressions.

Very often, I would have newspapers given to me, where I could read all about the different crimes my fellow work mates who were sitting around me had committed, or their relations on the outside were still committing. I had a problem with my conscience when I allowed people to discuss some of the criminal activities they had either done or were going to do because I was aware that Billy Noble could overhear what we were talking about. I felt very uncomfortable, knowing how easy he had found it to drop Curtis and me in it. Every day I felt that I should tell the lads to be careful what they said and that he was a grass, but I was afraid that to do so may have meant, because he sat so close, nobody would want to talk to me.

Curtis came out of his cell one morning and told me that he had decided to appeal against the severity of his sentence. He handed me two sheets of notepaper, on which he had written at least twenty reasons why his sentence had been too severe. When I asked him what he hoped to gain by putting in an appeal.

He said, "Because the weeks we'd spent on remand in Brixton didn't count as part of our punishment, there is a very good chance of getting the equivalent amount of time cut from our sentence. Which would mean doing six weeks less porridge in Wandsworth, plus while you're waiting for the outcome of your appeal you are allowed visits every day."

I said," For a little bloke as ugly as you, you're quite bright."

He laughed and asked me if I was going to appeal along with him, saying, "If we both do it, it will increase our chances of success."

At the time I thought it was a good idea so I took his two sheets of papers into my cell and copied them down word for word. When the landing officer gave us some preaddressed Home Office envelopes, I posted them in the letterbox at the end of the wing on my way to the workshop, without having a clue how long we would have to wait for our results.

As all my relatives lived on the other side of London and there was no way that any of my family could afford to visit me more than once a month, if that, I don't know why I thought that having the availability of everyday visits was so attractive. I hadn't heard from Frances, who I had written to in the hopes that she would return my clothes and other belongings. I did explain to her in the letter that all she had to do was to ring my mum and let her know where she could collect them. The reason Frances was still in possession of my gear was because the last time we had travelled together, she had packed all our clothing and other belongings in my large suitcase for travelling convenience. This meant that apart from my prison garb, I only had the clothes I was wearing when I was arrested.

I continually mused over my appeal and began to convince myself that I was going to get out of prison much sooner than I thought I was on the day I got sent down. The landing screw Thomas was an evil bastard, at least twice a week he would come and tell me that

I was going to be released the next morning and to get my gear ready. He did this so often I began to get really pissed off with him. One day, Curtis and myself were taken to see the medical officer; I was called in first and was questioned about my epilepsy and the type of medication I'd been on before coming in to prison. I told him I'd been taking phenobarb three times a day for a very long time. After writing some notes he told me to wait outside of the surgery and send Curtis in. I did and then sat around waiting for him to come out again. When he did re-emerge, I asked him for more information on the different type of drugs I could say that I'd taken in the past to combat my make believe fits. Curtis said it doesn't matter what you tell him, he will only give you a limited dose of liquid phenobarb, served in an eggcup, once a day.

As I couldn't get back to the workshop, I went to my cell and lay on my bed to wait for lunch. While I was there a screw came in and gave me a letter with a Birmingham postmark on it. For a moment or two, I lived in the hope that Francis may have summoned up the decency to reply to one of my many written requests. I'm afraid my wishful thinking had let me down once again; the letter was from her mother, who I had never met or spoken to. I call it a letter, really it was no more than a nasty, threatening little note in which she said that I was never to write, or try to contact Francis in any way ever again. It also said, that it would be totally impossible even to think that a person like me could be the father of any child born into their family. As for my valueless belongings, Frances had no knowledge of them whatsoever. I felt very sick and angry. I went to the landing officer and explained the situation. After allowing him to read the letter, I asked if I could stay in my cell for the rest of the day as I thought it would be the safest thing for me to do. He made what he thought was a witty remark, laughed and said," Bang your door behind you".

Wandsworth like all prisons had a schedule that for many years actually ran like a very well oiled machine, at six o'clock every morning, seven days a week, year in and year out, a bell rang to wake up the inmates. Half an hour later when your cell door opened, you were allowed to go along the landing with your piss pot, washbowl and water jug to the toilets where you slopped out. In my opinion this was the most revolting, degrading thing that any man could be made to do. If you unfortunately occupied a cell some distance away from the ablution room, by the time you had queued behind a dozen or so other cons, to empty the contents of your pots into the open sewer, the stench got so foul; it felt like you were breathing in pure methane gas. You then went back to your cell and waited in the doorway with your enamel breakfast plate and drinking mug, plus a small plastic beaker for your tiny ration of luke-warm shaving water. At the same time as you were given breakfast, you were also issued with a razor blade and mirror.

Breakfast nearly always consisted of a thick dollop of Canadian pig food grade two, which was served to us under the pseudo name of porridge. This was accompanied by a thinly cut slice of bacon, that was almost see through, a small portion of beans, that were boiled in water just long enough to get rid of any acceptable taste. Along with those little delights came a square pat of margarine that tasted like it had be used for some industrial purpose before it became part of our diet, plus a quarter of an ounce of sugar and a pint of tea. You were then banged up again for a further hour, until you were allowed out for a less smelly sloping out session, and to hand in your razor blade. (The blade had to last a minimum of ten days). After you had finished the second slop out period, all inmates had to stand in their cell doorways until the Senior Prison Officer in charge of each wing instructed his landing officers to send us down to our workshops, it was a very regimental and historic practice.

I will never forget the first morning I started work in Wandsworth. Following the rest of the cons I walked along to the end of the wing and then straight across the centre, heading towards the wing opposite, which I had been told by my landing officer was the way to the workshop. The sound that erupted was almost inhuman, there were screams, whistles and bells, officers yelling, inmates cheering swearing and shouting insults.

The most polite repeatable one being, "Another fucking Wally bites the dust."

I thought for a moment or two that there had been an explosion or fire had broken out. Curtis who was following behind me thought the situation was hilarious and was one of the people making the most noise.

I had broken a rule that I was totally unaware of, which was that inmates were not allowed to walk over the very highly polished metal grill that covered most of floor space of the central area. The grill was buffed up every day by two cons for a minimum of four hours. It was about twelve feet across, about three inches in depth, shaped like an old-fashioned three-penny bit and honey combed with two-inch holes. It was actually a vent that enabled warm air to flow from the kitchens below, which went some way to warming up the cellblocks.

The chief officer sat in a box in the centre of the grill, waiting for people like me to make the same mistake that I had. He told me that if it ever happened again I would be charged with wilfully damaging her Majesty's property. I began to sense that somewhere, somehow there was a charge to cover every conceivable and inconceivable mishap that could happen to me in this prison. He also told me that before the day was out I should get my haircut and try to look like something that belonged to the human race. I was then told to carry on to my workshop. From then on I was always delighted when some other poor fool walked across the grill. This practice had been going on for a century or more.

During the evenings in my early days I would lie in my cell thinking about the outside world and how much I missed it, especially after lights out in the summer months when it was still daylight. I would often feel very melancholy. I would try to mentally recapture and relive the good times that I'd had, but most of the time I could only

PENTONVILLE JOHNNY

vaguely remember drunken escapades. The feelings of self-pity I suffered over losing my freedom were always worse at weekends when, apart from one hour's exercise in the mornings and the same in the afternoons, you spent the other forty-eight hours locked in your cell. I could read as many as four good-sized books over a weekend. After doing a couple of months what I call hard time, I decided that I would save up my phenobarb ration all the week and then drink it in one go on Saturday evenings. For several months this worked very well, I slept like a log most every weekend. I gradually began accept prison life and lost all the negative feelings that were creating my mental torture. And then as the days turned into months. I also got over the emotional pain that being in love with Francis had caused me.

One Monday evening just before cocoa time the landing officer opened my cell door and gave me an official looking envelope. Knowing that it was the long awaited result of my appeal I wasn't to keen to open it. It had taken them quite a few months to respond to my request for a reduction in my sentence. The envelope was addressed to my prison number, followed by my name; the contents read something like. Your criminal record shows that since 1948 you have proved to be a great deal more than just a nuisance to society. You have not shown the slightest regard for other people or their property. Therefore we feel that a 21month custodial sentence is an insufficient punishment. You will lose the time you have wasted bothering the court of appeal, your time spent on remand will not count as any part of your punishment, and you will serve a further twenty-one months to run consecutive to your current sentence. I felt sick, if I hadn't appealed, as of that day I would have had less than a year to serve, now I would have to do a total forty-five months and two weeks.

When I saw Curtis the next morning, it was obvious from the way he looked at me, that he had either got the same, or a very similar result. All the good intentions and dreams I'd had, to start a new and different way of life, when I received the more lenient sentence

253

that I had been expecting, immediately went out of the proverbial window. I wasn't going to put in the next bit of what was written in the appeal court reply because it really shows what sort of a bloody fool, this clever thinking wannabe gangster really was at that time; it now seems pointless to leave it out. So here goes. At the bottom of the document the judges had put an addendum that said, if our appeal forms had not been worded so identically they might have been looked upon as a serious request for leniency, and under a totally different light. It was these words in the document that were making me feel so angry with myself. Not once had I ever considered that the same judges would read both our letters of Appeal.

The word soon got round that we had lost our appeal plus the time we had spent waiting for it. It wasn't long after that I followed Billy Noble into the workshop toilet, grabbed his shoulder and spun him round and nutted him in the face. As he went down he let out the loudest girl-like scream I've ever heard coming from a man. I was just about to put the boot into his bollocks for the third or fourth time when the discipline screw come in with his cane (truncheon) in his hand, ready for trouble.
He said to me, "I haven't rung the alarm bell yet, if you return to your work station now, I will overlook what as been going on in here."
Billy Noble was crying, his tears were running down his face and mingling with the blood coming from his nose. During the scuffle his dick had slipped back into his trousers while he was still pissing.

I did as the screw said and went back to my seat, as far as I know Billy Noble was taken to see the medical officer. I never saw him again but I did hear about several different things that happened to him. One story that made me smile was how he'd got involved with a tobacco Baron who short-changed him on a tobacco swapping deal. Noble, being what he was, grassed on the Baron and then he asked to be placed on rule 41. Which meant that he had to spend the rest of his time in a protection cell, on a special landing among all the known sex cases and child molesters, totally segregated from the rest of the prison population. The only time that these people came into contact with the main body of inmates was in the bathhouse. This gave the screws an opportunity to leave them unattended and at the mercy of any of the ordinary cons who happened to be using the bathhouse at the same time.

I also heard that Noble had been mistaken for a nonsense case, and was raped by two very active bisexuals. Not only was he a grass, he was also such a coward that he allowed himself to become a sex toy for the two perverts for the rest of his sentence. I know what I heard about him was true because I knew both of his rapists. Not only did I not feel sorry for him, I wished that even more harm would befall the bastard, as I said I never saw him in person again.

The weeks turned into months the seasons changed but everything in the prison remained the same. There was always a build up of tension when it got close to Christmas. Some weeks prior to my first Christmas in Wandsworth, a German bloke who had killed a policeman was put in the death cell, which was directly opposite mine. Every day when the condemned man was taken out for exercise I could hear his footsteps as he walked along the landing. Why a man who was going to be hung within a couple weeks needed exercise every day still baffles me. When the news went around the prison that the German, whose name was Guenther Fritz Podola, had lost his appeal the entire prison seemed to go into a state of depression. Condemned men were only allowed out of their cells when all other prisoners were locked up, which was normally during the lunch hours.

On the day before Podola was due to be hung, I heard his cell door open as usual and then the footsteps of his guards, but not the familiar sound that he usually made. The glass in my peephole and been broken many years previous to my occupation. This made it possible for me to push the swing flap that covered it on the outside of the door, to one side and for a matter of a second or two I could see the people opposite. It became a bit of a habit with me to watch whoever was in the death cell take their first few steps towards the exercise yard. And then if I stood on my big canvas cube and pulled myself up to the far left, side of my window, I could see the condemned blokes exercising in their special yard. This was a separate court yard from the ones used by the rest of us, it was enclosed by four grimy yellow brick walls about 12 ft high, the area inside the walls was about 50 yards long and twenty wide. The condemned people were watched over by two screws inside the compound, while two more, stood guarding the double door entrance.

I couldn't see from either of my vantage, points exactly what had happened. The combined noise of the alarm bells and the shouting of the heavy mob as they ran along the landing past my cell and on out to where the German was on exercise, certainly made every inmate on the wing aware that there was some sort of trouble. When I heard them coming back towards the death cell I opened my peephole, and saw four or five screws dragging Podola along. One of them was actually kicking him from behind. They forced him to lie face down on the landing, then they pulled his trousers down, I saw one of the screws stick a hypodermic in the cheek of his arse. In a matter of seconds he was completely unconscious and totally limp. Then they picked him up and threw him bodily in the direction of his cell door. Back at the workshop, after lunch, it was the only topic of conversation. It was rumoured that the kraut, on hearing that his appeal had been turned down and knowing that he was going to be hung in the next day or so, had totally flipped his lid. He'd knocked out two screws, and then tried to have it away.

Before my time in Wandsworth, I had often read about and saw photographs of execution notices pinned to the outside of the prison gates, saying that the condemned person had been hung at such and such a time. And on many occasions in films I was led to believe that all British executions took place at precisely nine o'clock in the morning. This was all dispelled from my mind, because from my cell I could hear the trapdoor thump, whenever the hangman came in to test the apparatus, in preparation for an execution. I am certain, along with several other cons on my landing, when we heard it go thump on the morning they hung Podola, it was a lot closer to seven thirty, than it was to nine o'clock.

The wake up bell had gone off as usual, we had finished slopping out and were back in our cells eating breakfast or shaving. There was an uncanny silence throughout the prison. When the trap door made its fucking horrible sound, the entire prison erupted into a crescendo of cups plates and trays being hammered against the cell doors, windows and walls until it became almost deafening, the noise went on for what seemed like a very long time. Podola was hung on Guy Fawkes Day 1959 for killing Detective Sergeant Raymond Purdy. He was the last person in Britain to be hung for killing a copper.

When the noise finally got down to an acceptable level the screws began unlocking the cell doors. In that instance, everything in the prison fell back into its usual routine. The large clock on the centre struck eight o'clock and we were locked up again until it was time to go to work. I thought about all those silly films that I had seen where the convicted prisoner was granted a stay of execution at the very last minute, or within the last ten seconds of the eleventh hour. I'm afraid in poor old Podola's case a stay of execution, at the last minute, would have been about an hour and half too late.

The repository for the body, when it fell through the trapdoor was on the punishment landing, where several screws would be waiting to take it down. When the corpse had finished jerking about, they would release it from the noose, put it in some sort of receptacle, and then either wheel or carry out to be buried in a special walled off section of the prison grounds, that had been declared, unconsecrated. One year and five days later, on the tenth of November 1960, an almost identical procedure happened again when they executed Francis (Flossie) Forsyth and his mate Norman Harris. They had kicked a bloke to death for really no reason; other than to rob him of the very little bit of cash he was carrying on him. It said in the newspapers that both of them swung at the same time, Flossie in Wandsworth and Harris in Pentonville.

It became very noticeable that our landing screw was getting gate happy, he had done thirty years as a prison officer in Wandsworth and was due for retirement within the next year or so. Somehow this seemed to mellow him. By mellow I mean he had stopped being a very evil bastard and had become just a nasty bastard with evil intentions. I made an application to the medical officer to be allowed ordinary furniture in my cell and a change of Labour as I'd been working in the sack shop for over a year. When I told the landing screw about my request, he suggested that I might work on his garden party. The downside of this was that I would have to put up with his stupid, childish sense of humour at work as well as on the landing, but there was an upside, I would be working in the gardens all day and breathing reasonably fresh air.

With his help, my request for a change of labour was granted. The following Monday I was issued with a pair of leather boots and a rubber cape, old Thomas, seemed to be a different bloke once we got inside the garden work shed. He allowed us to smoke whenever we wanted to, if we were working in a part of the prison where there were no toilets we were trusted to go from one exercise yard to the next, unaccompanied and out of the sight of any screws. This newfound freedom presented so many opportunities to improve the quality of my prison life; I would have been stupid not to take advantage of every single one of them.

As it became known around the nick, that I was at liberty to visit most parts of the prison during the course of a week's work, many of my fellow inmates took the opportunity to use me as their postman. At any one time, I could be carrying five or six verbal or written messages. I didn't perform this service free of charge. My fee was two roll ups for a written message and one for a verbal. If I carried messages on a regular basis for the same people it would cost them an eighth of an ounce of tobacco a week for four messages, or a quarter for unlimited correspondence. When Curtis became the No.1 cleaner on our wing, it made things even more convenient because along with his own little deals he was able place any gear or messages that I passed to him into the appropriate cells above the punishment block. These could then be lowered out of the windows directly down to the unfortunate blokes they were intended for.

Very often the content of the written messages I carried could have been quite dangerous to me, on several occasions I could have been taken to an outside court to face some very serious charges. At one time I had previous knowledge of a very large escape plan. I also knew whenever anybody was going to get seriously hurt or murdered. All over the prison, inside the wings and around the gardens were hiding places for weapons, keys, tools, messages, money, and of course tobacco. I was given access to most of these places because I was trusted to collect and deliver anything. As I have already said I didn't perform these services for nothing.

One day I was told that I could earn three ounces of tobacco if I would place some small buttons into the locks of the doors and gates leading from the wings to the workshops. I didn't think twice about it, three ounces of tobacco, lent out to the right people would mean that I could be a Baron and have an even better quality of life, plus a bit more status among some of the inmates. On the day I was instructed to button up the locks, I told the garden screw that I didn't feel too well and asked him if he would let me on to the wing so that I could go to my cell and lie down
"Has little Johnny got a touch of the vapours," he mocked as he let me back on to the wing.
"Go straight to your cell and bang up," he said.

PENTONVILLE JOHNNY

"Yes cur," I replied, as he slammed the wing door behind me.

As soon as he had removed his key, I pushed two buttons into the lock and walked along the landing towards the centre, then crossed over to my own wing. The exit doors out of E wing led to the hospital, apart from medical officers and six or so inmates no one actually used them, but I did put the buttons in the lock as I had been instructed to. Then I went to my cell and lay down on my bed. Before many minutes had passed the alarm bells sounded and pandemonium broke out, the noise made it sound like there was a regiment of cavalry charging up the landing. At first I thought they were coming to my cell because someone had seen me put the buttons in the locks but to my relief they ran past.
I heard one of them shout; "The bastards have jammed this one up as well."
I laughed to myself and went to my cell door to see what was going on. There were 20 or more screws in a state of sheer panic because their keys wouldn't open any of the exits.

It very obvious that I hadn't been the only one involved in sabotaging the door locks, every wing from A. round to F had been got at. Someone had even put buttons in the Governor's office door, which was unfortunate for the con who had done it, because the screws knew that he was the only inmate who had been in or near the office that morning. There were screws running all over the place trying to find a usable exit. The next happenings I am going to write about were told to me by several different people, one who actually took part in them. The escape had been planned by two blokes, one called Henry Craig, whose brother Christopher was famous for shooting a policeman, and his mate Mad Tony. The arrangements they had come up with were for twelve cons to meet in the sack shop.

Only four out of the twelve people who intended going over the wall actually worked in the sack shop, which meant that the organisers had to convince eight other cons to go sick or make

260

up some sort of excuse not to go into work that day. Their empty chairs would then give the chosen ones somewhere to sit hopefully unnoticed until it was time to go over the wall. Only one out of the twelve people that had arranged to escape didn't show up.

When the allotted time came to make their bid for freedom came, two of the larger and more well known members of the escape gang, got up and positioned themselves at either side of the discipline screws observation box and then lifted him out. After they had done this they very politely asked him for his keys. I was told that he gave them up without a second thought, but asked if he could keep his house key back because his wife wouldn't let him in the house if he had to knock. A couple other members of the gang tied up the two screws in the office and told the discipline screw to lie down on the floor alongside them.

Then they took apart the mop head making apparatus, which consisted of a 15-foot long wooden plank, nine inches wide and three inches thick. Every two-foot along the plank there was an eight inch steel spike, each one being about an inch thick. When they stood it on its end against the prison wall it made a perfect ladder. One of the leaders of the escapees turned to the rest of the blokes in the workshop and asked if anybody wanted to join them. He told them that they would be most welcome, and that there was a lorry and driver waiting on the other side of the wall to take them anywhere they wanted to go.

Out of the hundred or so cons in the workshop only the original eleven went over the wall. One of them, who was a pal of mine in Civvie Street got to the top of the wall and in his excitement fell out of the prison and broke his ankle. It was the biggest escape in British prison history. Unfortunately all of them were recaptured within a very short time. After several weeks' excitement scanning the newspaper headlines, life in prison returned to normal. Several of the people who had helped to sabotage the locks were charged with aiding and abetting; some of them had their sentences increased by several years. I was very fortunate not to be one of them, old Thomas the garden screw quite often accused me of helping the escapees, but luckily he was to thick to prove anything.

The next incident, I got involved in was with a friend of Tony's, a chap called Denny Jarrett from Paddington. Denny was a well-known thief and hard case around north London, who the police wanted to nick very badly but they could never prove anything against him. That was until some nasty bastard grassed on him and also gave evidence against him in court. Denny got three years of which he had served two. On the day he was released some friends who were going to take him for a celebration drink, picked him up in a car but on the way to the pub Denny saw the bloke who'd grassed him waiting at a bus stop. He jumped out of the car, slashed the grass across the face with some sort of weapon and then almost kicked him to death.

He told me that he was just about to down his second pint when the Old Bill jumped him. For cutting the grass he was now doing another five years. He asked me if I could get him a yard or two of cloth, some chiv's, and a cell door key. I said I could for a price. We agreed the price and a couple of days later we exchanged the goods. That weekend, three blokes wearing Ku Klux Klan type masks unlocked a cell on the 4th landing of D wing, went in and cut the occupant all over his body, they then went very calmly back to their own cell. The con they cut could be heard screaming all over the nick, the only reason he didn't die was because the screws got to him in time

Denny Jarrett and his two pals were really unlucky because while they were chivving the bloke, one of them had slipped and cut Denny across the hand quite badly, without knowing it he had left a trail of blood from the grass's cell back to his own. Within two months Denny was sentenced to another 15 years for the attempted murder of the grass. Denny Jarrett was now doing 20 years with absolutely nothing to gain from his crime other than senseless revenge. When I talked about it to Curtis, we both agreed that it was very frightening to know how long you could spend in prison without ever seeing the outside world.

One Saturday morning I heard the cell door, on the opposite side of me to Curtis, being opened and then closed again. The bloke they put in there immediately began shouting and screaming.
"Please Lord, show them I am an innocent man, and tell them I never did it."
This went on continually until we were unlocked for exercise. When I saw the bloke, I felt quite sick, because I recognised him from the newspaper photographs I had seen of him. His name was Arthur Jones; he was the man who had been convicted of raping and then murdering a little Girl Guide.

I asked the landing officer why had he put the fucking animal next door to me and not on the rule 41 landing with all the other nonsense cases.
Thomas winked at me and said, "That's where he will be going next so don't get too excited." Later that afternoon I heard Jones's cell door being slammed open and what sounded like a real heavy scuffle. At first I thought it was the screws moving him to the other wing but changed my mind when I heard quite a lot of screaming and shouting and then footsteps running away. In the next instance Jones was walking up and down the landing outside my cell door ranting. "Please God don't let it be like this all the time."
When we were opened up for tea we found out that the screws had left Jones's door unlocked on purpose, allowing three cons to go in and beat him up. The only hitch in their plan was that Jones was a strong bastard and had very ably defended himself. In doing so he had given two out of the three blokes a good hiding, which was more than they bargained for. Every night for weeks, I could hear Jones crying and praying for something to happen that would prove him innocent.

In October 1960 a twelve-year-old girl named Brenda Nash went missing. Her body was found in a Hampshire wood in December the same year, Jones was arrested a week or so later, for an assault he had committed on another little girl. At that trial he was sentenced to four years' imprisonment. Reputedly, while he was in solitary confinement he had confessed to a prison officer, that he had killed Brenda Nash. He was then taken back to court and tried for her murder, the jury only took about seven minutes to convict him, and that in a nutshell is how he finished up in the cell next to mine, doing a life sentence.

I spoke to Jones on several occasions and asked him how he could live with himself knowing that he had committed such perverted and horrendous acts on children. He never gave me a straight answer and always insisted that if he could find the prostitute he had spent the night with, she would prove that he was innocent. Both Curtis and I asked him if he knew her name and if he could describe her. The name and description he gave us didn't fit any of the prostitutes we knew. Thinking about it, between us we knew nearly every prostitute in London. Several people warned me not to continue talking to Jones, because he was going to get done over. Some of the daft prat's who warned me off were about as dangerous as blind kittens. There were several attempts to beat Jones up but each time he managed to defend himself, I never saw him get seriously hurt. Eventually he lost his appeal against conviction and sentence and was moved down to Dartmoor, thankfully I never saw or heard of him again.

The next person to occupy that cell was a Welshman called Rondel. He was the bodyguard to the infamous property owner and landlord Rackman, who when he thought he could get a better deal on his properties or was offered an higher rent, would release rats and snakes into his present tenant's flats hoping to make them leave. The screws were definitely more polite to Rondel than they were to the rest of the prison population except one. That one being Frank Mitchell, known as the mad axe man, whenever he was brought up to Wandsworth from Dartmoor for reasons unknown to me. Everywhere Frank went in the prison two screws accompanied him. He would deliberately make them follow him over the iron grill in the centre. Both of the screws that accompanied him were big men and part of the heavy mob. I once saw him, as he was walking between the two of them, put his hands on their shoulders and take a firm grip of on them. Both screws went down on their knees in pain, one of them said to him, "Please Frank, don't show us up in front of the rest of the cons." He smiled and let them get up. He was one of the fittest and strongest men I ever saw. I never got to know Frank Mitchell very well but I did talk to him once or twice. On these occasions he asked me about the East End and we swapped newspapers.

I continued to carry messages and tobacco for the blokes on the punishment block, for a while the cell directly beneath mine was occupied by a bloke named Don Barrett. At the time he was a very good friend with several members of the firm. Often one or another of them would send messages to Don or Joey Maber, I always made sure that these messages were passed on word perfect and if there was any arrangement for a tobacco delivery, it was always sent down in mint condition and not tampered with.

Curtis had by this time requested and been granted a transfer to the smaller block, G, H and K wings, which was now being used for prison recreation and rehabilitation. This meant that your cell was unlocked in the morning and remained open until just before lights out in the evening. It didn't appeal to me one little bit; I hated the idea of mixing with other cons when it wasn't necessary. Around about this time there was a lot of construction going on in the prison, they were building a new workshop that was being attached to the end of D wing. It was being purpose built to accommodate the category A. prisoners. The thinking behind it was if there weren't any exits between the wing and workshop it would give the special watch lads far less opportunity to have it on their toes.

PENTONVILLE JOHNNY

Along with the new internal construction plans, the Home Office also decided that Wandsworth needed a new Governor. This job was given to a bloke named Guy Peyton-Walsh, who was the brother-in-law of Roy Jenkins, the Home Secretary of the time. It was rumoured that Peyton-Walsh had been disgraced when a high-ranking German Officer committed suicide to avoid being tried for war crimes at Nuremberg. Peyton-Walsh had been in charge of Nuremberg prison. He certainly did cut a dash whenever he walked around the prison yards wearing his pure white colonial suit and sports car flat cap

CHAPTER 12

For several weeks the punishment block got a lot busier, I was passing more and more tobacco and messages down through Don Barrett to the rest of boys. One day, for some unknown reason, the boys on the block were taken on a different route to the exercise yard. They were brought up the flight of steps nearest the centre, then led back along our landing, out towards the hospital wing and then around the outside of the wing to the yard. This was totally opposite to the way they had been going for years. Don said to me, "If we continue to go in and out this way and you leave your door open, it will be easier if I throw the boys messages into your cell rather than tying them to a piece of cotton. For some time this method worked quite well, the blokes were getting a good supply of tobacco and I was earning plenty for myself. For various different reasons, all unknown to me, there were several well-known villains sent down to the chokey block at the same time. This made the discipline screws show a bit more respect and drop their vigilance a little.

The slight relaxation of the regime resulted in an attempted escape. For some time while walking around the exercise yard some of the cons on the chokey block had been watching the laundry van come and go. As van drove around the inside of the prison it became very obvious that its roof was the same height as the perimeter wall. Always arriving and leaving at the same time each day, which coincided with the chokey block exercise period. One morning as the lorry drove close to the exercise yard Joey Maber and five of the boys overpowered the two screws that were guarding them and then dragged the lorry driver out of his cab. They reversed the lorry against the wall, then jumped up on the cab ran along the canvas roof and dropped over the wall into the street. I've known a lot of bad timing and unlucky happenings in my life but this escape was a classic, it was so doomed to failure it was untrue.

Whatever time they went over the wall, was not of their choosing and sadly it coincided with the time the screws changed shifts.

About 20 screws were walking along the street outside of the wall heading towards the main gate, when Joey and his pals landed on the pavement directly in front of them. I was told later that two of the boys had actually got as far away as Wandsworth Common where they came across Senior Prison Officer Gearing and P.O. Lawton, who they took captive and hung up a tree. If they hadn't stopped to do this, they most probably would have been at large for a lot longer than they were. All of them were back on the punishment block in less than half a day.

As most of them were already doing very long sentences, which they couldn't see the end of they felt that taking the chance of getting an extra year or two wasn't much of a deterrent. Several days later the same crowd overpowered two different prison officers. This time they tried to rip away the corrugated tin sheets that surrounded the scaffolding where the new prison workshop was being built. Once again their attempt was foiled. The same night, a con called Harry Jacobs and a chap that everybody knew as 'Rubber Bones' broke through the ceiling of their cell, which was on the 4th landing of D wing. When they got into the loft space they removed some roof slates, crawled through the gap, slipped down the roof on to the scaffolding and then went home.

When I had sat next to Harry Jacobs in the sack shop at the start of my sentence, he told me he was doing three years for stealing cars and exporting them to the Continent. He was one of those unlucky people you come across every now and then. His wife and best friend thought life and the world would be a much better place if Harry was permanently out of the way, just like the man I had been handcuffed to on the coach on my way to Wandsworth. Even though they were earning lots of money off of his schemes, they had somehow set him up and informed the police of his activities. He told me that he had acquired a very large amount of money from his dealings in the car trade, but had had to give most of it to the police in order for them to drop some of the more serious charges against him. It meant that the three-year sentence he was serving was only a fraction of what he should have got. At the time we spoke I thought here was a man who had successfully stolen and spent millions of pounds and he was doing less porridge than I was!

About a week later 'Rubber Bones' was recaptured in Covent Garden market and put directly onto the punishment block. It had now become a regular thing in the evenings that the boys on chokey and some of those in the cells above them, such as myself, would get up to our windows and have a chat. This way we could inform them what was going on in the rest of the prison and they would tell us things about themselves. We were all wondering what was going to happen to them for their two attempts at escaping. 'Rubber Bones' must have been listening to us because he joined in our conversation. When he was asked about his nick name, he told us that he was called rubber bones because he had once escaped from a prison by getting through the air vent in his cell, crawling up inside the cavity wall, out through another vent and over the roof.

It turned out that he had successfully broken out of five different prisons, each time using a method that no one else would think of, or was capable of doing. Unfortunately he was never able to stay at large for any length of time. He did tell us that Harry Jacobs had promised him a couple of grand to help him get out. This was more money than 'Rubber Bones' had ever had or seen in his life. As he only had a little time left to do of his present sentence, the money was the only reason he had gone with Jacobs. I asked him what he was doing hiding under a barrow, when he got caught. He told us that Harry Jacobs had promised to meet him in a cafe in Covent Garden to pay him the two grand. He went on to say that he thought Jacobs, instead of coming to meet him, had sent the old Bill. When he saw them coming, he had managed to squeeze himself out through a small toilet window at the back of the Café, but as he had tried to get away, he slipped and fell under a barrow and decided to stay there until he thought it was all clear.

'Bones' was a very amusing bloke, whenever he spoke he used cockney rhyming slang and for some time before he was moved his stories took all our minds off of our situations. The first window-to-window chat we had after 'Bones' had gone brought us all back to reality. The conversation that night was very brief. As I lay on my bed trying to read, memories of life on the outside were much more prevalent than they had been for some time.

It was several weeks before any of the boys on the punishment block found out what was going to happen to them. Eventually they were taken one at a time before a panel of visiting magistrates. This body of people were normally called a visiting committee or in prison parlance a V.C. They listened to the list of offences and evidence that was presented to them, and then went away to deliberate for a week or so. Whatever decision they reached was passed back through the Governors' Office to the offenders both verbally and in writing. It made very interesting window-to-window conversations each night as we waited for their verdicts, the jocular speculations about the committee's decisions that went on between us ranged from ten years to hanging.

One of the boys named George, who was a hard man but at the same time a very gentle sort of bloke, was the first to find out about the panel's decision. After the event, he told us how he had been taken from his cell to the Governor's Office, given a document from the Visiting Committee, and then taken to the laundry, where he was told he could read the paper. Before he had finished reading the first page, the screws jumped him, stripped off his shirt and trousers and shackled him face down on two planks of wood. Each plank was about eight foot long and bolted together in a figure X. The 'cross', was then leant at an angle, which caused him to put all his weight on his toes. At the top and bottom of each plank were shackles that held his arms and legs apart. They covered him with a thick sheet of canvas which had a square hole cut into it exposing his back from just above the waistline to the top of his shoulders, but protecting the kidneys and lower spine.

Once they had buckled the canvas into place one of the screws held the paper up so that he could finish reading it. It informed him that he had lost one year's remission and was to receive twenty-five strokes of the birch, which they had now begun to administer stopping after every fifth stroke for the doctor to examine his spinal column checking that there was no permanent injury. When they had finished they released him and brought him back to his cell. While he was telling us what had happened about twenty screws had very quietly sneaked down on to the landing, opened the relevant cell doors as fast as they could and overcame the rest of the blokes who were awaiting punishment. Each in turn was told that they had lost remission and were to receive between ten and twenty-five strokes of the birch.

In less than two hours they had received between them an extra seven years imprisonment plus almost a hundred and fifty strokes of the birch. The sentences were carried out so quickly that there was no opportunity for legal representation or appeal. All of them agreed that receiving the lashes was quite painful but the worst thing was the degradation of being stripped and beaten by a gang of blokes who were nothing but downright cowards. I never met a prison officer that I felt would stand and fight on equal terms. Gradually each of the boys were transferred to different prisons, all over the country and I never saw or heard of them again except for one, Joey Maber, who had been transferred to Dartmoor. The reason I heard about Joey was that when he got to Paddington station, he and the bloke he was handcuffed to decided they would make one final bid for freedom and ran off down the platform and along the railway lines.

About a hundred and fifty yards down the track his mate tripped over a sleeper and brought Joey down with him. Joey was brought back to Wandsworth and put before another V.C., which sentenced him to another long dose of porridge. Joey had initially come into prison doing five years. He had been given an extra two years for his part in the punishment block escapades and now with this further year he would serve the equivalent of somebody doing a ten stretch. After those blokes had gone the prison settled down to its usual boring routine once again. That was until one day when the garden party had to pass through the D wing exercise yard, on our way back to the garden shed. We were all very surprised to see the entire workforce from three of the biggest workshops sitting around the walkways in between the flowerbeds. I know that some of the rules had been relaxed but no one was ever allowed to stop walking during the exercise period.

In Wandsworth there was at that time one hundred and twenty screws to guard over seventeen hundred prisoners, all squashed into a prison built for less than a third of that amount. I had very often thought that if anybody had had enough influence to organise the whole of the inmate population into one unit against the screws, there would be very little chance that they could do anything to combat it. Now for the first time in British prison history we were having a sit down strike. As we walked across towards our shed some of the cons asked us to join them. They explained that they were striking against poor pay, the conditions of the cells and the workshops plus the very poor quality of the food and the mistreatment of inmates. For people who had wreaked some sort of havoc in all Four Corners of the world, this was a very peaceful demonstration.

A leading figure in the East End Firm asked me why I wasn't joining in, I explained to him that I was the E wing contact for the punishment block and working on the garden party gave me access to every part of prison. I told him that if I lost my job most of the prison grapevine would collapse and at least 70 per cent of the contraband and tobacco movement would come to a halt. Also I didn't want to go on strike. He laughed and said when we both eventually get back to the East End we should meet up with his brother and some of the boys for a drink in one of his clubs like we use to do. A few of the boys on the garden party joined in the strike but the rest of us went back to the shed from where we could see and hear what was going on. The heavy mob and the governor came out into the yard and promised that all the grievances would the given a fair hearing and that no disciplinary action would be brought against any single individual striker, if they returned to their cells without any further disruptions.

For the next week or so, only one or two cells were opened at the same time, even the cons that hadn't taken part in the strike were kept banged up. Only the yard and garden parties along with the kitchen staff were allowed out. We were responsible for cooking and distributing meals. Apart from getting fresh water and food no cons were allowed to interact outside of their cells at any time. If you were sick you were told to give your name to the landing screw and the doctor would come and visit you. Each afternoon the Governor and a number of screws, would visit a series of cells informing the occupants that because they had taken part in a totally unacceptable action they would lose three days pay and remission and would remain confined to their cells for the next fourteen days. Added to that was a further loss of library and canteen privileges. The cell detention was to allow time for tempers to cool and also impress on the cons that any further action against the prison authority would result in even greater punishments.

When the nick finally got back to normality we found out that over two hundred cons had suffered the same punishment and that Guy Peyton-Walsh had become the most hated and untrustworthy man in Her Majesty's Prison Service. I went on delivering tobacco and messages for whoever got sent to the punishment block, if they could afford my services. Curtis had now been on G.H and K wings for some time. Going on that block was supposed to be the reward for good behaviour and if you didn't apply for a transfer you would automatically be sent there a month or two before your earliest date of release. I always felt that the longer you spent out of your cell the more danger you were in of being nicked by the screws or grassed on by your fellow, well meaning inmates.

Late one night I heard what sounded like a fight going on in the punishment cell below me, there was a lot of shouting and swearing and a noise that sounded like sticks striking against the walls. There was some terrible screaming, I heard someone shout, "We are going to kill you, you bastard." Then a reply, "One of you fuckers is coming with me."

Just as suddenly as it started everything went quiet, I could hear the sound of footsteps running along the block and up the stairs and then a voice calling for someone to ring through for the Medical Officer.

The next morning, before breakfast, I was told to pack my kit as I was being moved over to the 'good boys' block before I went to work. When I asked why it had to be done so early, the screw told me it was because there wouldn't be anyone available to take me across at any other time that day. I was slowly and reluctantly packing my kit when I noticed no one else along my side of the landing had been opened up to slop out. The screw told me to get a move on as he had other duties to go to. I told him that while he was transferring me he couldn't be expected to do anything else, so why, all bloody the hassle. He then said that if I continued to be insolent he would place me on a charge and stop me going to the privilege wing.

"Bollocks," I said to him. "I don't want to go any way."

He got very strung up and agitated.

"OK," he said, "You're nicked,"

"Fine by me," I replied. "Shall I put my kit back in the cell."

"Yes," he said. "I'm fucking sick of smart arse bastards like you."

He banged me in the cell and stamped off like a spoilt little child who couldn't get its own way. The next voice I heard was the Principal wing screw giving my man a roasting, telling him not to be so bloody childish.

He went on to say, "This man must be transferred and the sooner the better, and then find some places for the rest of them as soon as possible."

The significance of all this didn't dawn on me until much later. Just before he unlocked my cell again I turned my back to the door, pretending that I was looking up at the window and hadn't heard what had been said. When I looked around, I could see that my man

274

was angry and embarrassed that his superior officer had undermined him, personally I was bloody delighted. I felt that anything that could make these bastards squirm should be made law.

I was put in a cell on G wing, where it was very obvious that the previous occupant had worked many hours scrubbing and polishing it. Curtis was once again the number one cleaner and came to visit me in my new cell. This was another first because prisoners on the main block were never allowed to go into any cell other than their own. When Curtis saw me furtively looking out of the cell door towards the landing he guessed what I was thinking. He assured me that visiting in cells was quite permissible on this block. After spending the time I had on the main block, this different regime was going to take some getting used to. He told me that the bloke who had occupied my cell previously was a poof and had had paint and polish sent in from the outside so that he could decorate it, just like his room at home. My cell was on the third landing; I unpacked my kit while I was chatting to Curtis. That morning for the first time in over three years I sat down at a proper table and had my breakfast off a china plate using a proper knife and fork, in the company of other people. After breakfast I reported to the end of the wing and was collected by Thomas the garden screw.

After lunch that day I was asked by one of the boys on the garden party if I was going to sign the petition that they were getting up the to send to the Home Office. When I asked what it was about he told me that they were going to ask for an investigation into the death of the bloke on the punishment block. At a first I felt very angry because I suddenly became aware that the noise I had heard the previous night wasn't a fight at all, it was a man getting beaten to death. In the past I had been the victim of two cell beatings. I knew from bitter experience that it was virtually impossible to put up any form of defence when three or more blokes were charging at you with a canvas shield the size of a single mattress held up in front of them. At the same time they used lead weighted, wooden clubs, attached to long leather thongs to whip you while they stayed safely hidden, behind their shield. The only sensible thing you could do to protect yourself was to back away quickly and then roll yourself into a ball, making sure that you covered all your vital parts. If they got you pinned up against the wall, while you were still in an upright position, they would cast aside the shield and with no holds barred, really get stuck into you trying to destroy your sexual manhood.

I realised why it had been so important for the screws to move me from above the dead bloke's cell. I found out later that all the other cons who might have been within earshot of the incident had been transferred to other nicks. The screws that worked on the punishment landing in Wandsworth had very little care or concern for prisoner's welfare or their lives. As a result of their working and living in a totally protected, closed shop environment, their mentality obviously made them feel above and beyond the law. I willingly signed the petition and told the boys that if they gave me a form, I would try and get some more signatures for them. That evening I collected about twenty signatures and would have got many more had I not been told by the screw to stop making a nuisance of myself to the other inmates? When I told him I really didn't think I'd been making a nuisance of myself, he said that he'd had complaints from one or two of the cons implying that I was forcing them to sign my paper. The next day I handed the form back to the bloke on the garden party who was handling the petition and thought no more about it.

Both Curtis and myself were getting very gate happy, it was now about 10 days from my release and even less for Tony, as he had not lost as much remission as I had. One evening I was walking back on to the wing after finishing work, when I saw Curtis carrying his kit and being escorted by two screws back to the main block. I asked him what was wrong; he said they had fitted him up. When I got onto the wing I asked one of the cleaners what had happened. He told me that Curtis had had a cell search commonly called a dry bath and screws had found a razor blade.

The next morning Curtis came back to collect the rest of his gear and I shouted to him, "Don't let them stitch you up any more Tony, otherwise you'll never get out this fucking pigsty."

The screw that was accompanying him stopped, walked over to me and asked me what I meant by 'stitched up'. I was very much aware that this screw hated all cons especially the ones on the rehab block; I tried to think quickly and choose my words very carefully when I answered him. It really didn't matter what I said to this man, because he was going to charge me with something - no matter what. About an hour later, he and another screw came and told me to pack my bedroll as I was on a charge of defamation. I asked them what it meant.

"You know what we mean.," he said. "You besmirched my good name in the prison service, you accused me in front of witnesses of planting evidence in a prisoners cell."

I said, "You must be fucking joking, I was only winding up my mate because I didn't believe that any one could sink so low as to do such a thing to a bloke who was less than a week away from his release date."

"It didn't sound like a wind-up to me" he said, "You will be up before the Governor first thing in the morning."

I was taken down on to the punishment block and put into a cell that was dirty and smelt of shit, the mattress was stained with years of piss, the electric light was the dimmest I had ever seen. I unwrapped my bedroll, made up the bed and was just about to lie down when the cell door opened. Two screws came in and asked me if I was going to break the rules and lie on my bed.

"Of course not," I said. "I have been in this place long enough to know what happens on this landing if someone breaks the rules. They could finish up dead."

I continued to say that there was no way I was going to break any rules with only ten days of my sentence left.

One of the screws was a real evil bastard who was believed to be the cause of more than one cons death. He always applied to do death cell duties whenever there was an execution. The last hanging during my time in Wandsworth was a bloke called Victor Terry who had come down through the trap but because of the strength of the muscles in his neck and shoulders his spinal cord had not snapped which caused him to swing around and gradually choke. The two officers that were on death duty with the bastard who was now in my cell told me how he had jumped up and caught Vic Terry around the legs and swung on him until he choked to death. He was also the one that we suspected of being the leader of the gang that had killed the boy on the punishment block, a couple of weeks earlier.

I asked the two screws if I could be put in a cleaner and less smelly cell. I got the answer that I expected as they walked out of the cell slamming the door behind them without speaking. The next morning while I was slopping out I saw Curtis, he managed to whisper to me that he thought we were going to be stitched up even more, but he didn't have a clue as to what we had what we had done to deserve it. When I appeared in front of the governor he asked me for an explanation. I told him that I was only winding my friend up and really did not believe that he had been fitted up. The Governor asked me whether I believed that any of his officers were capable of such devious tactics. It was the easiest lie I have ever told when I said, "No Sir."

He said to me, "You have only got a short time left of your sentence, and as you have had a reasonably good record for some time, I have taken that into consideration. You will lose all privileges and pay for the remainder of the time you will be here. Make sure you don't give me or any members of my staff any reason to further extend your sentence."

I turned round and was escorted back to my cell. I put the chair against the back wall and stood on it so that I could speak out of the window to Curtis. He told me that he had been given the same punishment.

A couple of hours later we were both taken and put in a cell on C3 along with another bloke who I had worked with on the garden party, he was the one handling the petition. He told us that the chap who had died on the punishment block had come from a large East End family. About a week before he died his mum had been to visit him, but when she was called back to identify his body she had seen cuts and bruises around his head and shoulders that hadn't been there on the day of her visit. I asked the bloke if there was any news about the petition, he told me that quite a few people had withdrawn their names, when I asked him why he told me he didn't know.

After lights out on the night before Curtis's release, the Deputy Governor accompanied by the Chief Officer opened our cell door. They asked Curtis and me to step out onto the landing. The Chief Officer was holding several sheets of paper, which I recognised as the petition form. First he pointed to a name on the form and asked me if it was my signature, I checked and said yes, then he turned to Curtis, asked the same question and got the same reply.
"Did you know this man personally," he asked us, meaning the bloke who had died.
We both said, "No."
"Then why, because of the suicide of a very unbalanced man, who you say you didn't know, are you jeopardising your freedom? Furthermore you are in the same instance, trying to cast aspersions on my officers, who have done nothing but put all their honest and ill rewarded efforts into serving you while you are in this institution."
Curtis said, "Surely with all the suspicion and gossip that has gone on among the inmates it would be good to have an investigation. So that everybody involved could be exonerated." I nodded in agreement.

The chief said, "Let's put it another way, both of the you are due to be released within the next ten days or so."
Curtis butted in, "In the morning Sir!"
The chief looked at us both and said, "If your names are still on this petition when I walk away neither of you will see the outside of this prison for the next two years or even longer, have a word with your friend in the cell. He has already shown very good sense."

As usual my mouth was working before my brain got into gear, I said out loud, "The fucking snidey bastard."
We looked at each other and decided that we valued our liberty far above our principles at that precise moment, each of us agreed for our names to be taken off the form. We went back into the cell where the bloke was laying in the lower bunk pretending to be asleep. I pulled him out of the bed and grabbed him by the throat. He squealed in a very high-pitched voice saying that he was sorry for not telling us about taking his name off of the petition but he had done it for the same reason as us. He had also been threatened with a substantial further amount of imprisonment if had he warned us what was going to happen. I realised that I had no reason to be angry with him because I had just done exactly the same thing under the same circumstances. My anger was really directed at myself for being such a moral coward.

The next morning Curtis was let out of the cell before we slopped out, we had now been close friends for over four years, each of us had tears in our eyes when we shook hands to say goodbye. But we were too 'manly' to cry. Just before he closed the cell door behind him he looked at me, smiled and said, " I've left my piss pot for you to empty."
Before I could catch hold of him he was gone and the door slammed up tight. The next seven days, as I waited for my release, seemed like they were the longest days of my entire sentence. I realised that because of what the Governor called my 'good record' I had served a year or more than I needed to. I was left with only six weeks remission out of a possible fourteen months. Finally the day came I went down to the reception and for the first time in over three years I put on my civilian clothes.

During the time I had spent in prison several fashions had come and gone. I went away in the late fifties and came out in the sixties! This meant that the clothes I had been wearing when I was arrested were now at least three years if not more out of style. As I walked out of the prison gate I breathed several lungs full of free air. I looked around to see if Curtis had come to meet me as he had promised, but he was nowhere to be seen. I asked the first person I met where I could catch a bus to the East End. Before he gave me the directions he said to me, "I hope you don't mind me telling you this mate, but if you walk for a while it will give the smell of the mothballs on your clothes a chance to lose some of its strength."

He smiled and told me that he had only got out of Brixton a week or so earlier. He went on to say that if I caught a bus smelling the way I did it would bring tears to the passengers' eyes and most of them would guess that I'd just got out. He then gave me the directions I had ask him for, wished me good luck and we went our separate ways. I walked about four miles in the direction that he had told me to go. I was thoroughly enjoying my walk, as I hadn't been able to walk for more than 100yds in a straight line all the time I had been inside. It was exhilarating and frightening at the same time, to see the speed of the traffic and the huge open space around me. I couldn't keep my eyes off of the women I passed. For three years or more I had seen men of all shapes and sizes. Occasionally while on visits I had seen their wives, mothers or sisters, and knew the cons would chop my head off if they thought I was thinking anything sexual about their nearest and dearest, so I thought it was wise not to spend too much time looking at them.

After a while I came to a bus stop, got on a bus and went directly upstairs to the front seat. I not only wanted to be free I wanted to see freedom. I wanted to exercise my every right as a person who had served his debt to society. I began to think back about the bloke that I had heard being beaten to death. I was really thinking should I go and see his family and tell them what I had heard on the night he died. Suddenly I was overcome with fear and a touch of panic. I hadn't felt like this since before I was nicked, I began to think that if I did cause trouble for the prison staff and got nicked I could end up back in Wandsworth and then I would never see the outside world again. In the past I had always alleviated this feeling of fear, and the negative thoughts that went with it, by taking a drink.

I thought to myself, if anybody in this world deserves to get drunk it must be me. After all, twenty-one months of the time I had been away, I wasn't entitled to do at all! I went straight to my parents' house, had something to eat and told them that I was going for a drink to celebrate my release. My mum said to me, "Don't get stupid drunk like you used to, John, because it's easier to get in trouble now than it was three years ago."

I caught a bus to Aldgate, went into one of the dives and ordered a double out of every optic along the bar to be put into one glass. I drank the first glass in two swallows and then ordered the same again.

The next thing I remember was waking up lying on a familiar wooden board in a white glazed room without my shoes. As I gradually came to I could feel that my face was bruised, I could see there was blood down the front of my clothes. For a while I thought that I had only dreamt that I had been released and I was still inside. Then I realised I was wearing my civvie clothes. My next nightmare was, what had I done to be in a cell again? I didn't have to wait long before a very happy looking policeman came into the cell with a cup of tea and a cigarette, which he gave to me.

"You certainly tied one on last night, didn't you?" he said to me.

I asked him what I was in for he said nothing much, just a simple case of a drunk and incapable. You were found lying in the middle of Commercial Road singing and offering to fight the drivers of any car or vehicle that tried to go around you. I felt ashamed and relieved. I was taken before the magistrate who asked me why I was drunk. I told him that after spending three and-a-half years in prison, I had gone out to celebrate my release and freedom. He fined me five pounds and told me that I would be celebrating my return to prison, if I appeared before him again. He banged his gavel on the desk and said, "Step down."

15 Stepney Green

George Reynolds Printing Factory

The Brewery Tap, Commercial Road

The Clare Hall, Diggon Street

PENTONVILLE JOHNNY

Stepney Jewish Dwellings

Thames Magistrates Court

The doorway into Vincent's Club in Baty Street

The shop front of what was once the chemist on
Aldgate Tube Station

PENTONVILLE JOHNNY

HMP Pentonville (Home Sweet Home)

PENTONVILLE JOHNNY

The Wall that the two Policemen hid behind —
The night I took my last drink.

The embankment where I tried to throw the copper
Into the Thames

The old office of Alcoholics Anonymous

CHAPTER 13

After having spent what I considered to be a long time in prison, it was taking me some little while to adjust back into civilian life. Having no idea what had happened to Curtis and being at a loss what to do or where to go, I just drifted back into my old way of life and started hanging around the East End dives again. There were still some of the old faces around who remembered me, but these were far outnumbered by newer people, most of whom didn't know or care who I was or where I'd come from. Although life among the people who frequented the dives was pretty much the lawless same as I had always known it to be, it now seemed to me that the new faces were of a lot lower moral standard. I know this sounds very strange coming from a person who had served time for housebreaking, violence and an assorted mix of other crimes. However, what I mean by lower moral standards is that the new girls working the streets were of a much younger age group than the ones I had known in the old days, and far more under the controlling influence of their pimps. Some of these girls weren't being allowed to finish hustling until they had reached a pre-set money target each night.

Before I went to prison, if the girls who worked for pimps were having what they called a slow night and got a bit fed up not earning any money they could decide for themselves to call time on the evening's proceedings. Always living in the hope that things would improve the next day. Most of the pimps I knew from the old school, as long as they could buy the occasional suit, enjoy their nightlife, eat and sleep in comfort, would allow their girls some dignity and would also show them lots of affection. I'm afraid this new breed of pimps were totally alien to me, the majority of them being drug addicts. They very unfeelingly treated their women just like moneymaking machines. I got to know some of these younger girls who told me they were being forced to walk the streets looking for punters for up to twelve hours a night. The choice they faced was either relentless soliciting or getting severely beaten. I never have understood the mentality of the women who went out and faced the risks of getting bodily harmed, even in some cases murdered, or catching every sort of venereal disease, and then freely handing over to some totally unworthy pimp their hard gotten gains.

I was receiving a small income from the dole office, which assured me that at least once a week I could remove myself from reality by getting drunk. If I was really lucky I could stay partially drunk for several days at a time. I rarely went to my parent's house during this period because now in the East End as well as several other parts of London there was a change in attitude towards renting accommodation. People from around the dives and their like were finding empty properties, calling them squats and legally moving into them rent-free. Landlords were suffering with financial problems because they couldn't get any return from the investments they had made in these places; it could take up to two years to get squatters evicted.

This meant that I could always find somewhere convenient to stay. I think the attitude about freely using other people's property came about with the drug culture, which was very quickly surging through the highways and byways of the London underworld. My observations at the time were whenever there was any cannabis to be smoked or booze to be drunk, people gathered together and enjoyed sharing the social side of it. This wasn't the case when cocaine or heroin became available. I got the distinct impression that most main line drug addicts wanted the people around them to share their addiction and their misery, but not their drugs. Whenever I tried hard or soft drugs I never liked the effect they had on me, so luckily I never got hooked.

Late one evening I was sitting alone in a café on Cavel Street, drinking coffee and having a quiet couple of minutes observing the other customers, when I was approached and asked by Doreen and Silvia, two girls that I had recently become acquainted with, if they could join me. Feeling delighted that they wanted to be in my company, I asked them if they would like any teas or coffees. Silvia thanked me but refused my offer, saying that she would only be staying for a couple of minutes, as she would be going out hustling. She also said that she was leaving Doreen in my care and hoped that I would look after her.

I knew that Silvia worked for a pimp named Dennis, who was the bloke that had warned me about the Maltese setting the police on me after the firebomb at Vincent's club. When Silvia had gone, just to make conversation, I asked Doreen if she had ever been on the game? She told me that Silvia had on one occasion persuaded her to give it a go but when she tried it she felt too uncomfortable with the feelings of shame and guilt. Plus she was also very frightened of the other consequences that could come of having casual sex with complete strangers. She went on to say that after being at it for a week, she had fully accepted that she wouldn't be able to live that sort of life and felt that she could never do it again.

During the course of our conversation, Doreen told me that she was staying in a flat with Silvia, but occasionally she went to visit an Irish bloke for a couple of nights, this was while her regular chap was away driving his lorry. She also told me that her husband was doing 18 months in prison and their three children were staying with his mother. She asked me if I had any girlfriends, I told her that at that moment in time I wasn't going out with anyone. She then asked if I would like to go with her to see her children at the weekend.
I said, "Won't either of your boyfriends get upset if I'm seen going about with you?"
She said, "It wouldn't matter what they thought because the driver would be at home with his wife and only very occasionally did they get the opportunity to sleep together." She went on to tell me that she wasn't very keen on him in a sexual way and that; she just liked being in his company when they were out and about. And the same went for the paddy bloke. I said to her, "You seem to lead a very complicated way of life." She laughed at me and asked if I would like to simplify it for her.

I told her I would be very happy to go and see the children with her but I may have the wherewithal to pay for any travelling expenses. Don't worry she said I will have enough money to cover all the expenses when we take my kids out.

"In that case," I said, "I would be delighted to come with you."

We met up on the following Saturday morning and caught the tube over to Islington. On the way there, she told me that her husbands' friends and relations called her Dolly. When we got to the block of flats where her mother-in-law lived she asked me if I would mind waiting downstairs while she went up to get the children? I said it was no problem and sat down at the bottom of the stairs to wait for her.

Some time later she reappeared looking very tearful and disturbed. When I asked what was wrong, she said," Because my husband doesn't want me any more, I have just had to agree to put my two youngest children up for adoption, and allow my oldest daughter Kim to live with her Grandmother permanently. Out of the three of them, I will only be allowed to see Kim, and even then only on the condition that I give at least a weeks notice."

I could see that she was upset, but not anywhere near as upset as I thought a mother should be, who had just had her kids taken away from her.

She said, "Come on let's go back down the East End and have a bloody good drink."

While we were travelling back on the tube, she related more of what had happened in her mother in laws. She told me that while she had been in the flat, a girl she and her husband had been friendly with had arrived and dropped quite a bombshell. It seemed that this girl had been carrying on with Dolly's husband for nearly two years and was now having his baby. On his release from prison they fully intended living together until he was free to marry her, which in my mind made any relationship Dolly may have thought she still had with him very much a thing of the past. During the short time I had spent getting to know Dolly I had often wondered how she became separated from her family and seemed to be drifting aimlessly around the East End. I never asked her about it because I just assumed that she was marking time until the husband got out and then she would resume family life with him and the kids.

I didn't feel that Dolly was showing the sort of emotional distress that a normal mother and wife would do in her situation, but as I didn't know her very well I accepted that maybe she showed her feelings in a different way, I don't know what way. All I do know is that if it had been me in her place I would have completely fallen apart or gone into a raging temper.

When we got back to the East End, Dolly bought several bottles of wine, which we took back to Silvia's flat and drank like it was going out of fashion. We spent most of the night drinking and having sex, which in my book was about the next best thing to heaven. Around about six o'clock in the morning Silvia came home with Dennis. We still had a bottle and half of wine left and they supplied several joints of cannabis. As I've said before, cannabis only ever made me feel hungry, and usually ruined any effect that I got from the alcohol. A couple of hours later I woke up feeling ravenous and as there was no food available in the flat, I was forced by my hunger to go in search of something to eat. I dressed quickly and quietly and then made my way to the nearest cafe, where I ate a king sized fry up.

It was about a week before I went back to the cafe in Cavel Street, I was hoping to see Dolly, but at the same time felt that due to her complicated way of life, it wouldn't be the end of my world if I didn't. Dolly was an attractive girl just under five feet tall with natural black hair, which was unusual because her eyes were green. Although I fancied her quite strongly if I hadn't seen her again, I wouldn't have lost much sleep over it. I was just downing my third cup of tea when Silvia's pimp, Dennis, came into the cafe and joined me. He immediately began reminiscing about the morning we had spent together drinking and smoking pot with the girls. He also told me that I had made a very good impression on Dolly, which prompted me to ask him what sort of good impression. He said that for two days afterwards she hadn't said a word that wasn't followed by my name.

"She hasn't stopped talking about the fact that you went with her to see her children and it hadn't bothered you in the least that you might have been seen with the wife of a very well known Islington villain."

This surprised me because I thought I knew most of the villains around London, if not personally I certainly would have known them by name. When Dennis told me Dollies' husband's name it never rang any bells, then or since.

Dennis went on to say that Dolly had told him that she been searching for me around the clubs and cafes for the last three days or so, as she had something important to tell me. When he got up to leave I pressed him to have another cup of tea; I wanted hear a lot more about why an attractive woman wanted to see me. Mainly due to the fantasising I was doing about the reasons she would have for seeing me, my ego was surging up through my mind and almost bursting at the seams. While we were talking, Dolly and Silvia arrived and came over to us. Dolly said to me, "Would you mind coming for a walk along the street with me because I have something very private to tell you."

As we walked along Cavel Street towards Commercial Road, I was suddenly overcome with a very uncomfortable premonition that whatever important news, message or question Dolly had in mind to tell or ask me, wasn't going to be very pleasant.

"Look John," she said, "I don't know how to say this but I must tell you about something I caught from the Irishman I've been seeing."

I asked what she meant by something she'd caught?

"I've got a venereal disease called gonorrhoea and I'm very sorry but I think I've passed it on to you."

This was the very last thing that I could have guessed she was going to lay on me, it was something completely new and totally alien in my life. Occasionally around the dives and during my stays in different prisons, I'd heard of people catching a nasty dose of the gun, but I never really understood what they meant, nor had I ever seen or felt any reason to question them about it.

At that moment in time being told that I had been given it, made me feel extremely frightened and very lonely.
"What exactly do you mean, when you say that you have passed this disease on to me, why did you do it?" I asked her.
"I'm very sorry," she said, "I really am, but at the time we had sex, I had no idea there was anything wrong with me. I certainly wouldn't have slept with you had I known. Other than that, I don't really know much about it. I've been to a special clinic and the doctor there told me that I should tell everybody I have slept with in the past four weeks, to attend the clinic, as soon as they possibly can, in order to prevent the disease spreading any further."
"How many people have you slept with in the past month?" I asked her.
"Apart from Paddy you're the only one," she replied.

I felt so angry. I tried to recall some of the bad things I'd done in my life, I had been pretty evil and totally immoral but I couldn't think of anything I had done to deserve my being in the situation that Dolly had put me in.
She said," Can we stop walking for a while and look at each other?"
At that moment in time, looking at her wasn't exactly what I had in mind. I was totally ignorant of what gonorrhoea was and what it was capable of doing to me. I felt physically and mentally afraid and wanted to lash out at her. She was actually crying, and at the same time saying that she had fallen in love with me, and was hoping that we might form some sort of a relationship together. I couldn't believe what was happening to me. I fancied her and I had spent a very enjoyable night and day in bed with her. I had also felt very comfortable in her company on the several occasions we had met up and chatted in the café's. At that moment, however, standing on the corner of Commercial Road and Cavel Street, as I was looking directly into her face, my head filled with the idea that she had given

me a life threatening illness. I couldn't think of anything else, other than committing a very justified murder.

I could feel a rage boiling up inside of me and knew that I should get away from her as soon as could. She went on to say that the doctor had told her that gonorrhoea was a very painful illness, but in most cases it would only take one course of treatment to cure it. We walked back to the cafe where I said goodbye to her, still feeling that I should get as far away from her as I could get and as soon as possible. That night I went back to my parent's house and told my mum what had happened. I'm afraid that she was as ignorant as I was about my situation. She told me to catch a bus up to the West End and go into one of the all-night steam baths and stay there steaming myself for as long as took to get rid of it.

Sorry mum, I said," I don't think it works like that. I have been told that there is a clinic Turner's road that specialises in venereal diseases but it doesn't open until nine o'clock in the morning would you mind if I stay here until then."

She said she didn't mind in the least, as long as I kept all my clothes on and only drank out of one cup. She also told me that, after I'd been to clinic I must come back home and give her my clothes to destroy, which she would do along with the cup I had been using. That way no one would be any the wiser as long as we didn't say anything. I agreed and said I would like go to bed. This brought a strong sound of disapproval from her.

"I'm sorry son," she said. "I really cannot let you use the bed clothes because if we have to burn them as well, I can't afford to buy new ones."

I really began to feel angry and got very short tempered with her.

"Where to you want me to stay, outside in the bloody yard?" I shouted at her.

She was equally blunt, "I'm very sorry John but if you had got yourself a proper job and mixed with decent people, all the misgivings, trials and tribulations that you bring upon yourself and me and your dad, would have no part to play in our lives."

PENTONVILLE JOHNNY

My mood swung from anger to self-pity I felt very sorry for both my mum and myself. She was so right when she told me that everything I did was my own fault. No matter how much pity I showered on me, I was the only one I could blame. Knowing this, I still didn't think that any of the things I had done in my life, warranted someone giving me what I still thought was a death dealing disease.

After my mum went to bed I sat on a chair listening to the radio hoping that one of the loneliest nights in my life so far, would pass very quickly. As most people know, wishing and reality are poles apart. The next morning found me standing outside the door of the V D treatment clinic a good forty-five minutes before it was due to open. I still find it impossible to describe all the thoughts and feelings that went through my mind from the time Dolly told me what she had done to me, until the clinic door opened at nine o'clock the next morning.

In this modern age, it would be illegal for me to voice a description anything like the one I would have used back in those days. All I can say is that the person who opened the clinic door was wearing a white uniform that looked like it been supplied by the local tent hire company. His opening words to me were, "Has my little darling developed a nasty little blooby knob. Come inside my lovely and take out your little Willie out and show it to your old Auntie."
To say that this bloke was gay would be grossly understating the word. I was beginning to feel more embarrassed about showing him my private bits than I was about my reason for being there.

Go into that cubicle and take your clothes off from the waist down he told me. I did as he said, a couple of minutes later he came into the cubicle wearing rubber gloves, grabbed hold of my dick and squeezed it. It made me feel very sick when I saw what he was forcing out of the end of it.
"Oh dear we do have quite a disgusting little dribble don't we," he said, "Other than that it is a very attractive looking little weapon."

This bastard certainly knew out to rub salt into a very embarrassing wound.

I said to him, "Look you fucking pervert, I have caught this disease through no fault of my own, and was hoping that you could come up with something that would help me to get rid of it. I would also very much appreciate it if you to stopped doing your best to degrade me all the time!"

"Don't worry my lovely it will only take a little prick that's not much smaller than the one you already own, to clear up all your little misdemeanours," he said as he pointed at my dick.

I thought to myself, I've had enough of this fat bastard and his sexually insulting innuendoes. I also thought that the bloke wasn't taking my situation as seriously as he should. He was coming very close to making me lose my temper, which in turn meant that he was in grave danger of being lumped up the side of his head with what ever I could lay my hands on. Suddenly he changed and became very apologetic saying," I'm very sorry my lovely, I have just realised that you're not one of my regulars in fact I don't remember seeing you here before. Also I realise that you don't really understand what's wrong with you!"

At last I thought to myself this prat's come to his senses.

"Let me explain," he said. "Gonorrhoea is one of the mildest forms of venereal disease you can get, but one of the most uncomfortable. I can assure you that one injection is all you will need to be completely rid of it. You may not believe it but some people come here as often as five or six times a year. But I can assure you that none of them have ever died from a dose of gun after they've have received my treatment."

The sense of relief that came over me, once his words had sunk into my brain, was beyond belief. All the hours I had spent mentally torturing myself suddenly meant nothing. All the resolutions I had made to become a better person were forgotten. The enemies I had planned to take with me to the Promised Land didn't seem so bad. Even Dolly began to look like a nice person again. Before I left the clinic the bloke told me that as I had only very recently contracted the disease, it hadn't had time to run its proper course. Which meant even though I'd had the treatment it would still get progressively worse over the next few days He also said, that the worst part was still to come, and that it would be very wise and a lot less painful if I didn't drink too much. Because urinating was going to be a problem. He very firmly told me that both sex and alcohol were off the menu for at least 14 days and if possible I should bathe every day to make sure that my old chap stayed clean.

As I walked down the road away from the clinic I suddenly felt that my entire past life had all been very worthwhile and the best part of my existence was still to come. I felt very good about myself for several hours. How great it was to know that I had a future. Everything was going along fine and dandy, until I needed to have piss; it was then that I that found out exactly what the gay nurse meant about not drinking too much. You can believe me when tell you that pissing while I had gonorrhoea was the most physically painful thing that I had experienced in my short life. It felt like pieces of broken of glass were being pushed down the tube of my penis. Once again the desire to kill someone came back into my mind, I said to myself if I ever see that Dolly woman again I will definitely do her some sort of injury whereby she will carry a painful memory of me for the rest of her life.

Fortunately for her, because of the embarrassment I was suffering, I had decided to stay away from the dives and café's around Aldgate, at least until the gonorrhoea had cleared up. For a while I hung around a cafe called the Silver Star, which was situated further eastwards down Commercial Road, very close to Brewery Tap Pub where I had first started drinking. The people that frequented it were much younger than the normal crowd I ran with; some of them were actually the younger brothers and sisters of a lot of my old school friends. I didn't think so at the time but hanging around the Silver Star every night until it closed, was like being on a training programme, preparing the youngsters for life in the Aldgate and Soho dives.

Like me the kids in the Silver Star were always on the lookout for some sort of fun or excitement. Despite their age, most of them smoked pot and took pills like it was the only reason they had for being on earth. I also found that none of them were averse to sharing my wine when I eventually started drinking again. The owner of the cafe was a Greek who I had got to know when I was the tea boy at the Glendale Cabinet Company, which was situated directly behind the café. He was pretty open-minded about most things and knew very well that the only reason we bought tea or coffee was so that we could use the cups to drink our wine out of. Although he turned a blind eye to our drinking he drew a very strong line on people smoking weed or taking drugs on his premises.

Varying in age between 16 and 23, about a dozen or so of us started going around together like a pack of wolves, creating all sorts of havoc. Early each evening we would meet up in the Silver Star and then go to the off-licence bar of the Royal Duchess pub where we would buy as many bottles of wine as we could afford. If at any time we didn't fancy going back to the café, we would seek out other suitable places where we could drink wine and smoke cannabis, unseen by members of the public and undisturbed by the police. Between us we devised various methods of drinking the foul tasting cheap plonk, hoping to discover how to stop ourselves throwing up when our bodies wanted to reject it. My way was to take several deep drags on a cigarette and then swallow as much as drink as was humanly possible in one go. One of the other lads came up with the idea that if you drank it very slowly in small sips, not only could you keep it down, you would stay pissed much longer.

After some of these clandestine drinking sessions we would walk the streets looking for any sort of trouble we could find. Very often we would start fights with complete strangers for no other reason than they may have looked in our direction. At other times we would let some of the girls who were part of our clique walk a short distance in front of us, wait until some bloke or blokes looked or made a pass at them then the girls, as prearranged, would claim that they had been insulted. It was like Christmas had come early if we could find and beat up some Pakistanis or Indians. We became very unpopular, I would go so far as to say we were despised, even among the people that knew us, because they could never be sure when or if we were going to turn on them. I really loved the effect that the cheap wine had on me. The other thing I relished equally if not more was that the gang looked on me as their leader.

One evening after picking up our usual wine quota we went back to the Silver Star, with every intention of doing the things that had almost become ritualistic with us. By now the owner had made it pretty obvious that he didn't like or want us hanging around in his café, but we knew that there was nothing he could or would do physically or otherwise to eject us from his premises. Very reluctantly, to avoid any confrontation, he tolerated us, most probably hoping that as soon as we had finished our drink we would leave. On the particular evening in question it was very different because, much to my surprise, Dolly and a couple of her friends came into the cafe.

She walked over to me and said "I have been trying to find you for weeks, have you been deliberately avoiding me?"
I said, "I haven't, but then again neither have I been looking for you."
"Didn't our night together mean anything to you," she said.
The small amount of wine I had drunk just previous to her arrival hadn't yet had sufficient effect on me to make me think or want to do anything evil to her. I replied, "One night in bed with you, left me with all the pain and suffering that I will ever need thank you."
She said," Please John it really wasn't my fault! I had no idea what was wrong with me, but I can assure you there's nothing wrong with me now or will there ever be again, if I can possibly help it."
From out of her shoulder bag she produced a large bottle of vodka and said, "There's nobody using Silvia's flat tonight why don't you and your mates come back for a drink."
The size and contents of the bottle made it an invitation too good to turn down.

With Dolly's friends and mine crammed into the furnished rooms there wasn't much room to do any partying, so using the bed and the floor plus the only two chairs we just laid and sat around drinking and talking into the very early hours of the morning. The gathering didn't break up until two of my friends, who were both very drunk, decided to stagger off home. After they had gone the rest of the people gradually drifted away until there was only Dolly and myself left. I climbed on to the bed laid down along side her and within minutes I fell into a sort of drunken, stoned unconsciousness.

When I came to, I felt very hung over and immediately blamed it on mixing good vodka with cheap wine. Dolly was already up and about, when she saw that I was awake she began to apologise once again for giving me what she now called the clap. I said it didn't matter any more because I'd had the treatment and everything was fine. As this was the first time we had been alone since she arrived at the café I took the opportunity to ask her why she had been looking for me. She told me that she fancied me and would like to go around with me on a regular basis.

I said, "I'm sorry but I don't want to hang around the dives in Aldgate any more."

She said that it wasn't because I hung around those places that she wanted to go out with me. After we had drunk several cups of tea and talked some more, she got back into bed, where we stayed until the following day.

When we finally struggled out of bed, we went to the cafe in Cavel Street for breakfast. During our time in bed she had told me that she was no longer seeing the lorry driver or the Irishman, and that she had come to accept that her marriage was over. She went on to say that she'd been back to her mother-in-law's and collected all her belongings, which she had now left for safe keeping in a house belonging to a bloke, called John Silver. Immediately she mentioned the bloke's name, my knowledge of his reputation told me that she would never see her property again. John Silver was notorious around the area for promising to look after people's property and then selling it as soon as their back was turned. This man had once taken a woman back to his house for sex, after the deed was done and she had unwittingly fallen asleep, he took all the clothes she had been wearing and sold them to the local nearly new shop.

When anybody confronted John, he would come up with such wonderful, almost tearful stories of how he could do nothing else but trust the people who told him they needed his help and give them the keys to his house. He often said that it was because he had been unfairly inflicted with the curse of deafness; the people he befriended would take advantage of him, coming back while he was asleep or out and steal whoever's belongings he had been entrusted with. John would go into such vivid details of how he was going to disable or kill the very low lives that he had, at one time, thought were his good friends. Now because of them, and only because of them, he was being confronted with the very serious situation of losing another highly valued genuine friendship. He would even tell his stories of misfortune to people knowing full well that they had heard them all before and knew they were all bollocks. Curiously the people he said he lent his keys to never stole any of John's personal possessions.

When I saw how upset Dolly was getting while John was giving her one of his fantasy explanations of how some no good bastard had got into his house and stolen her suitcases. I butted in and told him that if her property wasn't returned by the next day I would set light to his house, with him locked inside it. He said to me "Surely John, you of all people must believe me, because you are more aware than most of how unlucky I am." I looked him straight in the eyes, grabbed him by the lapels of his jacket and said, "I know how very unlucky you are going to be, if she doesn't get her stuff back."
For the following week or so we called round to John's house every day, as well as searching all the cafes and dives, but had no luck in finding him or tracing Dolly's gear. It seemed like he had completely disappeared from the face of the earth.

Dolly and I would occasionally stay at Silvia's flat; who I thought was unaware I was using the place. That was until late one night when she came home and without turning on the light took off her clothes and got into bed with me. Thinking that it was Dolly, I turned over and put my arm around her, tweaking one of her nipples as I did so. She immediately let out one almighty scream, jumped out of bed and called me a dirty lesbian whore. It wasn't until she switched on the light I realised my mistake. I assumed that both of us had thought that the other one was Dolly. Silvia switched off the light got back into bed saying, "could you please continue where you left off before I so rudely interrupted you".

I said, "We had better be a bit careful because Dolly could come in at any moment."

She or my Dennis will have to knock, which will give us enough time to get dressed."

I said, "You're not exactly Dolly's best friend are you?"

She came back at me with, "When a women's in bed with a naked man the only best friend she's got, is between her legs, so hurry up and put what you've got between yours, between mine!"

I muttered something like I am only here to serve and then did what we both wanted to do.

When I woke up the next morning I began to wonder why Dolly hadn't come home all night. I didn't have the slightest idea where Dolly may have gone or who she would be with, which made me feel a bit reluctant to go searching for her. After another session of sex with Silvia and some guilty mental deliberation about it, I decided I would go and look for Dolly. The first place I thought of to try was in the cafe in Cavel St, as it had become one of her favourite haunts. When I got there I spoke to a chap called John Scott, who told me that he had been talking to both Dolly and Silvia the previous night. He said, "When Silvia was leaving to go out hustling, she had told Dolly not to leave until she came back for her."

At first I was a bit confused and asked him to repeat what he'd said, once again he told me that Silvia, had told Dolly to wait for her in the café, and not to leave until she got back. "What time did Sylvia go out to work?" I asked him.

"About midnight," he replied. Feeling even more confused, I thought to myself how could a woman ask her so called best friend to wait for untold hours, knowing full well that she wasn't coming back and intended spending the rest of the night in bed with the said best friends' boyfriend. I began to wonder if the drink was dulling my brain. For some time Sylvia had been dropping hints and flirting with me, often saying how nice she thought it would be if we made love and also saying what a lucky girl she thought Dolly was. Because it was said quite openly between us in a very jovial manner and in Dolly presence, I accepted it was meant as a joke. In reality, Sylvia wouldn't have needed to use such a deceitful trick to get Dolly out of the way, if she had been a bit more up front with me, about her intentions.

After searching for several hours around all the cafes and dives without any success, I was told that after waiting most of the night Dolly had eventually left the cafe, saying that she was going up Commercial Road to look for Silvia. From then on, no one had seen anything of her. My feelings for Dolly by this time were not exactly feelings of love or deep affection. I just liked her company but deep feelings or not I was beginning to get a bit worried about her, so much so I even checked the two local hospitals. I felt sad and glad at the same time when I didn't locate her in either of them. Eventually I gave up searching and made my way back to Silvia's place, hoping that Dolly might show up there.

The welcome I got when I arrived back there was far less than cordial. Silvia's pimp, Dennis, met me at the door and greeted me by saying, "My fucking whore as been sleeping around for free and she tells me you're one of the people she's slept with."
I said "I'm sorry Dennis but I wasn't the instigator of that little get together."
Then I told him what had gone on and how Silvia had deliberately got Dolly out of the way for the night. Dennis thanked me for being honest with him and then invited me into his room for a drink. The

strong smell of cannabis hit my nostrils long before I saw the three new age pimps sitting around the room smoking it. Silvia was sitting in the corner looking very ruffled and upset.

She looked at me and said, "I suppose he's now conned you into telling him that you've fucked me."

I realised that this was exactly what had happened. Knowing Dennis's reputation as well as I did, I should have known that no girl in her right mind would admit to doing the dirty on him.

In the next instant Dennis was standing over Silvia, holding a can of hair spray in his hands, with the nozzle aimed at her face. When she realised what his intentions were, she let out one very loud wounded animal like scream. The next thing I saw was one of the most horrific scenes I think I have ever witnessed. Dennis pressed the nozzle, which released a jet of cellulose spray directly into Silvia's face and eyes. At the same time he flicked his gas lighter into the path of the escaping gaseous fluid, which had the same affect as a blowtorch. It all happened too fast for me to stop him. The resulting flame completely engulfed Silvia's head' her hair started to burn. It looked to me like her head had exploded, her screams were more than just spine chilling, everybody in the room apart from Dennis, suddenly became very sober. I jumped up and grabbed a loose pillowcase and clumsily attempted wrapping it around her head.

Looking at Dennis I said "You're one fucking crazy bastard, no woman deserves this sort of treatment."

I could see from the look on his face that he was getting some sort of sexual buzz out of it. I had seen and heard a lot about weird people and their strange fetishes but this was the first time I had ever witnessed real sadism first hand.

He said to me, "Why are you getting so fucking upset, don't you remember the dozen or so people that you burnt down in Vincents' club? You seemed to enjoy doing that, I thought you would more than love watching me do this to her."

I felt very sad and ashamed that anybody could think that I was capable of getting sexual pleasure from burning a girl's face. Making me recall the firebomb incident as he had, started me thinking about the consequences the innocent men and women had suffered as a result of my crazy actions several years before. Up until that moment, I had never felt any kind of remorse or any other uncomfortable feelings about setting those people alight. Now, watching this poor girl's suffering close up brought me into a very real, emotionally painful state of awareness.

Knowing that she was in terrible pain, the only thing I could think of that would relieve it quicker than any pill, was alcohol. I remembered there were still two bottles of wine left under the bed in one of the other rooms. Before I got back to her, I'd almost finished drinking the contents from one of them. By this time, the three pimps had decided to go walk about, leaving only Dennis, Silvia and myself in the house. When she took the pillowcase off her head, I could see that her hair was singed down to the surface of her skull. Her face was covered in blisters that seemed to be growing as I was looking at them. I offered her the full bottle of wine but she was shivering and shaking so much she couldn't hold on to it.
She looked at me and said, "If you had kept your fucking mouth shut this wouldn't have happened."
I looked at her and said, "It certainly wouldn't have happened if you had kept your legs shut."

Both Sylvia and Dennis asked me to leave and not come back, and also to tell Dolly that she was no longer welcome. I stood up, looked at them and said, "How the fuck, can you blame me and Dolly for what has gone down here? I think the both of you need to see some sort of shrink because you're completely out of your fucking skulls."
Feeling the effect of the wine starting to overtake me I walked out of the house thinking that it would be much safer if I put some distance between us. I knew in my mind that if I were still in their company when the full effect of the alcohol hit my brain I would become quite capable of and have no qualms about setting fire to the both of them.

When Dolly walked into the Silver Star cafe a week or so later, I was more than a little pleased to see her looking both safe and well. When I asked why she had disappeared, she told me that when she had got fed up waiting for Silvia to come back, and had decided to walk along Commercial Road to look for her. As she was crossing the junction of Christian St Road and Turners Road the police had arrested her for soliciting and taken her to Leman Street police station. The next morning she was put up in front of the Magistrates at the Thames Court, who sentenced her to seven days in custody, which she had served in Holloway Prison.

She told me that she felt the Magistrate had been lenient with her because the police had somehow got their wires crossed, and had mistakenly told him that she was still supporting her three children, plus it was her first offence. When he was passing sentence on her he had said that he felt the shock she would get from a short spell behind bars might help her to mend her ways. I said, "If you were only walking along Commercial Road looking for Silvia and not doing anything wrong, why the fuck should you be sent to prison."

I couldn't believe that she thought she'd been dealt with leniently for something she hadn't done!

She said, "Maybe it's a punishment for the times I've done it in the past." She smiled and completely changed the subject by asking me what I had been doing for excitement.

I told her about sleeping with Silvia, and also what Dennis had done to her as a consequence. Dolly said she already knew about it but she was glad that I'd been up front with her. She was now talking and acting as though we were a couple and I felt glad that she felt that way.

She said, "I don't think that I can ever go on the game again and you haven't got the job, so what are we going to do about renting somewhere to live that we don't have to share with every Tom, Dick, and Harry?" I really didn't have a clue what life was all about when you became a couple I had no idea about any of the responsibilities that went with this sort of partnership. My earlier experience living with Frances hadn't exactly been a learning curve.

CHAPTER 14

Most of my assumptions in those days turned out to be wrong, whatever I thought or imagined people wanted of me was always the opposite in reality. Dolly would have liked a stable relationship in a furnished room or flat and maybe a part time job. She didn't tell me this, so I took it for granted that she just wanted us to carry on in the same way as we had been. Which meant that when she talked about finding somewhere permanent to live I thought she was thinking of some time in the distant future. So for several weeks we skippered around various squats and sometimes slept in the waiting room on Liverpool Street Station, which afforded us a certain amount of warmth on cold nights. Each day we would go to the public baths where we would spend hours just lying in the tubs of water until it got too cold. Most evenings we hung around drinking in the Silver Star or some other café.

One evening whilst Dolly and I were sitting with several other people in the Cavel Street Café, doing our usual thing of disguising our wine drinking by pouring it into teacups, John Scott came into the café and whispered in my ear.
"Don't look out of the window right away, John, but I think the vice squad are waiting outside to nick you for living on immoral earnings." Because I had never taken any money from Dolly, immoral or otherwise, the shock of what he'd said, caused me to lose my breath for a second or two. I had always believed that pimping from a woman, (or poncing as it was called it in the East End) was a totally spineless way to acquire money. Not only was Dolly not on the game, the money we were living on was coming from my signing on the dole and little bits and pieces of gear I was stealing whenever an opportunity came my way.

It was common knowledge among the pimps and their prostitutes that there was a legal requirement for the vice squad to keep a suspect under observation for a minimum of four days and nights. Part of their brief was that they actually had to see a pimp taking money from his prostitute partner. I knew for certain that Dolly had never given me any money, in public or in private. Most of the people around that area, who had known me for any length of time, knew that I would never become a pimp. I also felt sure that the Vice Squad officers were aware that pimping wasn't my game, as I knew one or two of them from the times they had arrested me in the past. Nevertheless, I also knew that no one in my living memory had ever received a not guilty verdict when they were brought up before a judge on charges that were laid against them by the Vice Squad. Whatever the coppers in that mob didn't know or hadn't seen they simply manufactured.

In those days the Magistrates at the Thames Court, like most of their colleagues in the other halls of justice spread around the East End, would totally ignore anything the person in the dock had to say in their defence. Over the years of trying pimps, prostitutes and petty criminals the Magistrates' Court proceedings had become very standardised, and being sent to prison was a mere formality; a forgone conclusion. Firstly the accused would stand in the dock and plead not guilty to the charges, after which whatever police squad was dealing with his or her case would be asked to present their case. Usually this would consist of mostly conjured up evidence bolstered up with totally off the wall verbalisations, such as, "The defendant said you've caught me bang to rights officer, it's a fair cop". The Magistrate would then give the offender a long, severe bollocking about morals plus half a stretch in the Ville.

Dolly and I decided that it might be better for us if we split up for a while and both kept a low profile. I told her that I would go home to my parents and maybe she could find someone to stay with, outside of the East End. We were both hoping that if we dropped out of sight for a week or two the Vice Squad might forget about us. We were also hoping they hadn't had us under observation long enough to arrest me as soon as I walked out of the cafe. I really didn't want to be seen with her anymore because she was now a convicted prostitute, even if the conviction was trumped up. Although very unjust it still meant that any man seen in her company for any period of time would naturally be branded a pimp by the Vice Squad.

Of all the disgusting things I'd done to get money for booze, even once a robbing a cripple, I still felt that taking money from a prostitute was totally immoral. Most of the people I knew around the cafes and dives thought that I wasn't the full shilling whenever I spouted out my views on the subject, some of them laughed at me quite openly. One of my friends asked me who the bloody hell I thought I was to talk about morals with my chequered history. The real reason behind my thinking this way was that my dad had never let my mum go out to work for a living. He had always drummed it into us as we were growing up that the woman should stay in the comfort of the home, and it was the man's responsibility to go out and earn the money to keep them.

Over the years my brain had somehow translated this into you must never take money from a woman under any circumstances. I also felt that it would be the ultimate disgrace I could bring to my family if my dad or mum ever read in the local paper that I had been convicted of living off of the immoral earnings of a prostitute. Most of my life up until then had been dominated by their, Victorian way of thinking. A lot of my parent's values have stayed with me but I am afraid the majority of them fell by the wayside during my life's colourful passage. Dolly and I planned to stay apart and only contact each other through friends and maybe have the occasional secret rendezvous, from that moment on our relationship was meant to be all very cloak and dagger.

I have always been amazed at the difference between theory and reality. All the wonderful plans we had laid down in the café that night came to absolutely nothing. When we met quite by accident a couple of days after we had started our separation, Dolly told me, now that she had seen me again; she had decided that she wasn't going to stay away from me. If I did get arrested, she would come to the court and explain to them that I wasn't a pimp. I'm afraid she was very naive in those days and really didn't have a clue how the system worked. As I have said previously, I knew all to well that if the police in our area said you'd done something wrong, no protestations on earth would prove you hadn't. Try as I might, to explain this to Dolly I couldn't get through to her that what she was hoping to do, at that time and in those circumstances was quite ludicrous.

I slowly began to realise that Dolly was one of the most stubborn people I had ever met. Once she had made her mind up that we were going to be together, there was no way that she would allow anyone or anything to separate us. At first I found it quite flattering, but as time passed, living with the fear that I could be arrested for something that I hadn't done or ever intended doing, I found mentally disturbing and thought very seriously about breaking up with her. Strangely at the same time I was having these thoughts, I knew I my feelings for her were running very deep. Once again we started hanging around the Silver Star, which by now had acquired a very wide spread reputation for being an illicit booze and drug den, this along with all the young apprentice pimps and pro's made it a real in.

Dolly and myself were looked upon as role models, whatever we did the younger people hanging with us emulated. Once again we roamed the streets, like a pack of wolves looking for prey. By this time the gang had grown much bigger, which meant that we feared nobody, we were firm believers in the safety in numbers cliché. The wanton undeserved attacks we made on innocent people made that part of Commercial Road and several of the streets surrounding it, including the local park come cemetery and Church yard, a no go area for most people. Even the police only came around in teams of three or more. Our reputation, thankfully stayed very localised which meant that the senior more serious villains, or the governors as we called them, never came to regard us as a threat

PENTONVILLE JOHNNY

One day Dolly said to me, "John, don't you think that we are getting too old to be running around with these kids, doing the sort of things we're doing. People hate us. Even people we don't know dislike us intensely on sight and what are we getting out of it? A couple of bottles of cheap wine and a reputation akin to leprosy! If you and me are going to stay together I want more than this out of life. I am going to find a room or flat outside of the area and a long way away from these kids. If you want to come with me you are very welcome and I really want you to, but I'm afraid I can't continue living the way we are now." She had chosen her moment well, because for the first time in many months I wasn't totally under the influence of alcohol and what she had to say registered in my partially wine sodden brain. I was now in my mid twenties, which was another thing she pointed out, along with the fact that I didn't own one single article of clothing that I hadn't slept in or been sick over.

Dolly was as good as her word. She went off and got a furnished room just above where the boundaries of Stepney and Bow met. When she came back to the cafe for me she said, "The room is lovely, but I don't think you'll like the situation very much." I didn't understand what she meant until I saw that our new home, at number 109 Bow Road, shared a wall with Bow Police Station, and was sighted about thirty houses up from the Kray's twins Double R Club. The room Dolly had rented was at the back of the house overlooking the garden. If I lent out of the window and looked slightly to the right, I could see the police cell windows all standing level with my observation point. As I was looking around the place I heard Dolly laughing. She said to me, "At least I won't have to go far for visits if you ever get nicked."

We stayed in that room for some time; Dolly started doing the things that housewives do, like shopping and cooking. As we now had a permanent address it meant that I could claim dole money as a married man. For quite a while I managed to stop drinking, and we went through a period of time where we both enjoyed being together and away from the other side of the East End. I stole a television and had Radio Rentals put in one of their piped music boxes, which cost the princely sum of a pound a month. Dolly wasn't the best cook in the world but she certainly knew how to fry chips. For some time chip sandwiches were all we lived on.

Our newly found happiness came to a sudden halt about seven o'clock one morning when there was a very loud thumping on the room door. Dolly called out; " Who is it." "It's the Police, open the door please! Someone shouted back to her. "What do you want?" she asked.
Feeling afraid and very disappointed I whispered to her, "I think the vice squad have caught up with us."
She whispered back to me, "If I tell them to wait until I get dressed it will give you chance to jump out of the window."
Before either of us could make a move the room door, which we had got into the habit of leaving unlocked, was pushed open and in walked a very large policeman holding a sheet of paper up in front of him. He asked me what my name was. When I gave him a false one he turned the piece of paper round and held it up for me to see. On it there was my photograph under which, in bold print was my name and last prison number.

"Could you please get dressed and come with me," he said.
"Why." I asked. "What have I done wrong?"
He looked at me and said; "Some time back you were arrested for driving a van on the motorway near Birmingham without the necessary licence or insurance. When you were taken to court you were given a fine of £100 of which, Ten Pounds is still outstanding. This piece of paper in my hand is a warrant for your arrest, which I will discharge if you pay me the money." I was so relieved to hear that this was all the copper wanted. I asked Dolly if she had £10. She said, "Sorry John, I spent my last couple of bob buying our food."

The copper said, "Come next door where I am sure we can sort something out."
I followed him into the Police Station and was put into one of the cells that overlooked our garden. After what felt like forever, I shouted for the copper and asked him how long it was going to take before they let me out.
He said, "I'm very sorry John but if you haven't come up with the money by tomorrow morning we are going to have to send you back up to the Birmingham Magistrates' Court, who issued you the fine in the first place."
I said, "You are going to send me in some sort of transport with at least two old Bill for company on a hundred and sixty mile round trip because I haven't paid a Tenner fine. It doesn't make fucking sense." He came back at me with one of the oldest cliché in the book, "The law is the law!"

I couldn't believe that I was looking at Dolly through a cell window as she stood in the garden of 109 talking to me. She said that she thought she would be able to borrow the Tenner quite easily, as it would only be for day or two. We could pay it back when we received our dole money. I told her that she would have to be very quick about it, because I had overheard the copper telling his mates that I would be the first case up in the Birmingham court the next morning, she promised to do her my best for me. After we had finished saying our goodbyes and swearing our undying love to each other, I climbed down from the window, picked up the grotty little blanket, laid down on the wooden planks come bed and fell asleep.

At about half past six the next morning the duty sergeant unlocked my cell door and told me my mum had paid the fine and I was free to go. As I was walking out past him he said, "You're a very lucky man to have two women that care so much about you, some people don't have one."
I suppose what he was saying held some sort of deep meaning for him, but I am afraid it went right over my head, as I was in

too much of a hurry to regain my freedom. Over the next week or two my mind became very preoccupied trying to fathom out how the copper who nicked me had found out where I lived and exactly what room door to knock on. Without realising it I put Dolly through some totally unnecessary mental torture, as I had assumed that it was her that had given our address away.

Eventually when she couldn't take any more of my sullen moods and snide comments, she told me if I didn't stop being so bloody nasty she would leave and wouldn't come back until I had regained my senses. The fact that she threatened to leave jolted my emotions and made me realise how much I had come to care for her. Up until then I had considered her to be just somebody I shared things with and on my part, not always equally. I apologised for my behaviour and asked her if there was any way I could make up for it. She said that there was a way for me to compensate her but she would wait until I had got over the apologetic mood I had adopted. My mind filled with curiosity wondering what sort of penance I was going to have to pay for my nasty behaviour.

About three days later Dolly asked me if I still felt like doing something to make up for torturing her, I nodded, smiled and thought this is where she lowers the axe.
She said to me, "I can that see you're smiling but I've been with you long enough to know that you don't t trust me very much and that you're suspicious of what I'm going to say next." Once again I nodded in agreement. She told me that on the night that I had been taken into the police station she had lain in bed all night thinking about her daughter Kim.
She then said, "What I want is for you to come with me to see her because I really do miss her so much."

After the way I'd treated Dolly about the Police finding out our address, I thought this was a very small penance to pay; in fact I was quite looking forward to meeting Kim. Dolly had often spoken about her although she never made mention of the other two children. I actually felt that she had completely forgotten that they existed. We got dressed and walked to Mile End station where we caught the tube to Islington. On the way there, I told Dolly that this time I wasn't going to sit waiting at the bottom of the steps like some bloody Dick head. She answered by saying that she had been hoping I would go up to the flat with her, as she was and had always been very nervous whenever she had to deal with, or be around her mother in law.

Whether my presence helped or not I don't know, but on the visit everything went very smoothly between Dolly and her mother in law, who very gracefully allowed Kim to come out with us for several hours. Unfortunately, while we were out Kim showed quite openly an extreme dislike for me and there was nothing I could do to win her around. I could see that being in the middle of the situation was making Dolly feel very uncomfortable. As we walked away after leaving Kim back at her grandmothers, Dolly fell into a very sad state of depression, which continued throughout the following week. There was absolutely no consoling her, until I eventually suggested that we could go back and bring Kim to live with us. As the words were falling out of my mouth, I could feel myself worrying that making a big decision on the spur of the moment like I had could be a very big mistake

Dolly told me that she didn't need me with her when she went to collect Kim. Although I did volunteer to go with along her, she insisted it would be much better if she went alone for the simple reason that if there was any trouble she, could easily walk away, where as if I was there I might start fighting with the people. Which wouldn't be the best of first impressions to inflict on her daughter. I tried to convince her that I wasn't like that, but after she had finished reeling off a list of people that I had fought with in the past, after making solemn promises that I wouldn't, she convinced me that she was right. Dolly was becoming very aware of my unstable character; she'd also developed the ability to tweak my conscience whenever there were things she did or didn't want me to do.

When Dolly and Kim eventually arrived back some hours later I surprised them by having a bed made up for Kim, who was about three years old. I had got the bed from my mum it was one of those foldaway camping things. I never told Dolly about any of the action that the bed had seen when I had used it in my tent during my Faversham days. She assured me that Kim had promised to like me. Up until this day I have never discovered how you make some body like someone when they simply don't. We sat down to eat the first meal we were going to have as a family and once again reality came rushing into my head. I was now expected to become a father as well as a husband, without having the slightest understanding what the two words meant.

Dolly started talking about moving closer to a school, so that when Kim came of age, she wouldn't have so far to go. She also she told me that when I next signed on the dole I should make a claim for child allowance. Over the next couple of days Dolly couldn't stop showering me with all the wonderful benefits that would come my way because I now had a daughter. The idea of making plans for the future came as quite a shock to me; I was beginning to feel a bit trapped and very uncomfortable along with a large portion of jealousy. Apart from when I was a kid alongside my brothers and sisters I'd had absolutely nothing to do with children in any way shape or form until Kim arrived. I suppose I was lucky in one way because she had outgrown using nappies and she was a very competent walker. Looking at the situation I found myself in I began to feel emotionally trapped and very frightened.

Like so many other times in my past, a fear born of ignorance took control of my mind; I couldn't see a bright side ever appearing in my life again. I felt too young to be a dad and I certainly was too immature to carry the responsibilities of being a husband or even a live in partner. The thought that I would be stuck in a single furnished room with a wife and daughter for the rest of my life sent uncontrollable waves of fear through my mind. Yet, something somewhere in my make-up told me that it would be the most cowardly thing I could do if I deserted Dolly and Kim.

When I decided to talk to my mum about it, the first question I asked her was how she felt when she discovered that she was going to spend at least 20 years of her life, doing nothing else but attending the every want and need of a kid. My mum was always ready with the answers that I never wanted to hear.
She said to me, "This might be the making of you as a man. It might be the best thing that you have ever done in fact I think it is. Kim is a lovely little girl and you will have lots of fun and lovely feelings as you watch her grow up."
I'm afraid that my feelings of insecurity were preventing me from seeing all the pleasures that being a dad, held in store for me. I was thinking that it was getting very near time to put my running shoes on.

While I was at my mum's, Dolly had gone to do some shopping down Burdett Road Market, where she met an old mate of mine and invited him and his wife and their daughter to our room. Coincidentally the daughter was exactly the same age as Kim. My mate's name was Norman Sullivan, I'd known him back in my Cable Street and Soho days when he had been at least as much, if not more, of a tearaway as I had.
After the initial surprise of meeting him again and the usual greetings had been exchanged he looked at me and said, "I never, ever thought that you would settle down with a family. You were always the one that most people thought was born to be hung. Even my wife who you most probably don't remember tells me that you once broke her heart."

At that instant I couldn't recall meeting Norman's wife before, I would have sworn on a stack of Bibles that I didn't know her. Her name was Eileen and she told me that we had been camping on the Isle of Wight together, with the Oxford House group from Bethnel Green. As soon as she mentioned the Isle of Wight my memories

313

of her came flooding back. I remembered that one of my old my probation officers had taken me, along with several other boys in his care, on a two-week camping holiday to Freshwater Bay. As the thoughts of what Eileen and I had got up to went through my mind. She said, to Norman you already know the story about John and I. As it all, happened such long time ago and before he met Dolly, I don't think either of you two will mind if I tell it again. I'd love to make him squirm a bit. Norman who was looking a bit embarrassed said, "We're all adults get on with your story."

She told us that it was on the Isle of Wight I had started going around with her when we were both in our early teens. She said that I'd spent the first three days of the holiday trying to convince her what wonderful memories she would carry for the rest of her life, knowing that I was the first bloke to shag her. I'd been so persistent that she finally gave in and let me do away with her virginity. Dolly joined in the conversation at that point and said she knew that all the things that Eileen was saying about me were true because I was about as romantic as a plank of wood. While Eileen had been relating her story, I remembered who she was. I could always remember the incident but not the girl. I should have because I'd continued seeing her when we got back to the East End. She lived with her parents not far from my mum, in a flat directly above my old school mate Alex Warren.

For a while in my younger days I had worked at the London Hospital students' hostel, which in its day was a very grand institution consisting of three floors of very small bed sitting rooms with one bathing cubicle to every four rooms. On the ground floor there was a very large common room furnished with expensive, genuine leather furniture, which was randomly spread out over the extensive wooden parquet floor. Part of my job, as porter, was to polish both furniture and floor at least once a week. I carried out both these duties in the early evening, not because there was any ritual or any specified time for doing the job. It was simply because a very attractive blonde girl used to walk past the front of the building at the same time every evening, who I very much enjoyed having little sexual fantasies about.

Like many other jobs I had cocked up in my short life, this one was no different. A little bit of over indulgence and too many days off with hangovers soon brought about a situation whereby my services were no longer required. It was almost a year after losing that job that I went to the Isle of Wight and met Eileen. After our first three-day wrestling match and the completion of my conquest, we stopped and gave ourselves time to breath and talk. During this rest period, Eileen told me where she lived. I was more than a little surprised when I discovered that she was from the next street to the students' hostel. When I first invited myself into her tent I didn't realise or recognise that she was the girl who a year earlier had been the subject of my fantasies.

And now here I was in her company once again and I still hadn't recognised her. She must have thought that I was some sort of dim wit. Looking for a way out of this slightly embarrassing situation, I luckily assumed that maybe it might not have occurred to her that each time we met or crossed paths her hair was a different style and colour. Anyway that was the excuse I used for my bad memory. When I looked back at what had gone on between Eileen and myself, I thought, you fucking idiot, fancy letting a beautiful girl like her slip out of your grasp. We spent a most enjoyable evening reminiscing and exchanging similar light hearted stories during which, both the children had got on to our bed and fallen asleep. We all drank very sociably that night and promised to do it again soon, but we never did.

After that evening the fear and several other hang ups I'd been carrying around in my head, concerning my situation started to diminish. I slowly began adjusting to this completely strange way of life and at the same time, against my better judgement, I started to enjoy it. Even my parents were adopting a more kindly attitude towards me. They treated Kim exactly the same as they treated any of my sisters' or brothers' children. All the good things that had been happening and were still happening to us, during this sort of honeymoon period, certainly helped to make the day that our landlord told us he had to evict us from the room, feel like one of the blackest days of our lives. He said he was very sorry but under the new housing act, having a child above the age of two and two adults in one room was considered overcrowding, and had become an offence.

I think because all three of us had began to accept each other and had more or less settled down into a very cosy little routine, the notice to quit, coming out of the blue as it had done, shook us down to our boots.

After the landlord had gone, Dolly turned to me and said, "If you were any decent sort of a man you would have got us a proper place to live months ago."

She said it with such bitterness and venom in her voice I could hardly believe my ears. I thought that, like me, she had been enjoying the past couple of months; I was so positive she had I told her so. It didn't matter what I said; she wouldn't let the subject drop. She started telling me off for not having a job, and then pointed out a million other little things she'd suddenly discovered I had wrong with me.

She ranted and raved at me for nearly an hour until I was on the very verge of either strangling her or walking out never to come back. Before I knew what had happened she picked up the frying pan, which was almost full of very hot oil and freshly cooked chips, and threw them across the room in my direction. I don't think she had any intention of catching me with them but I just saw red. I felt there was no need for her over the top behaviour. I picked up a carving knife from the table, raised it above my head and threatened to kill her if she didn't stop screaming at me.

The next thing I knew was that the landlord and the bloke who lived in the next room were wrestling me to the floor.

I said, "You two must be soft in the head if you think that I would do her any harm. I was only trying to stop her nagging." Looking at the landlord I said, "It's not my fault you've decided to chuck us out into the streets."

He said, "There is no way I'm going to throw you out on the street. You can stay as long as it takes you to find somewhere else to live, but as long as you do stay here, you will not repeat any of these noisy scenes."

Dolly told him that she was very sorry for causing all the disorder, but it was because she had been so happy for the first time in many years, and the thought of having to leave and go back to her old way of life had absolutely terrified her.

During the time we had been together Dolly had told me that her parents had separated when she and her two brothers, Fred and Reggie, were very young. She said that her and the younger of her brothers, Reggie had been raised together in a children's home in Chobham, Surrey. Neither of her parents had ever shown any interest in the children. In fact Dollies' mother had treated her very much in the same vein that Dolly was now treating Kim's younger brother and sister. This grotty furnished room had become the only stable place she had known outside of the children's home. I could never have guessed in a million years the devastation she felt when she thought this place, and the little bit of security it had afforded her, was being taken away.

The landlord said we could take as long as we liked to find somewhere else to live, but by law he had to give us a formal notice period. I asked him if he could make it for a minimum of at least three months, he said it wouldn't be a problem. I thanked him and explained that there was a very good chance that we would leave before the time was up as my cousins' husband, Gerry Crawley, had told me he could get me a very well paid job de-scaling industrial boilers. The landlord said, "There's absolutely no need to explain anything to me, as long you abided by my written notice".

Jerry Crawley was married to my cousin Kathy Macdonald. They lived in Burdet Road, which wasn't very far from 109. He was a great big bloke who was most of the time very gentle, however, when he came across anything that frustrated him, through lack of understanding, he would lash out. His motto in life seemed to be 'If you don't understand it, bash it!' At the first given opportunity I went to see him and explained the situation I was in and asked him if the offer of the job was still good. He looked at Kathleen and both of them burst out laughing. When people do this to me I usually get very angry or paranoid but with Kathleen and Jerry I knew they weren't taking the piss. When I asked them what the joke was, Jerry said, "I'm sorry John but it has been over a year since I offered to get you the job."
I must have looked at them in complete disbelief because they both assured me that they hadn't seen me for at least eight months and the last they'd heard about me, was that I'd left the East End to live in either Kent or Paddington.

Kathleen said "Don't worry about it John, Jerry still works for the company and I'm sure if you meet him early tomorrow morning he will get you a job. But I am warning you now! If he does get you a start, don't stop at any pubs on the way home or you will have me to answer to. I've got enough problems with him when he goes out drinking on his own."
"Surely Kathleen, you don't think I would lead your poor Gerry astray," I said.
"Neither of you two piss heads have ever needed any body to lead them astray. I'm just warning you not to go drinking before you get home, and I mean both of you."
She said all this with a very knowing expression on her face. Most of the people in my family are very loud cockneys and can be heard having a conversation from a very long way off, but I'm afraid to say that Kathy Mack was the loudest member of my entire clan. Even when she tried to keep her voice down, people a hundred yards away thought she was talking to them.

Bright and early the next morning I was outside their door waiting to go to work for the first time in years. Both Gerry and Kathleen had thought that there would be absolutely no chance of me showing up and were more than just a little surprised when I did. Not only had I showed up, I was almost an hour early. Gerry and I walked to Stepney East station and the caught the tube out to Epping where the yard and Office of a company called Boiler Maintenance was located. Jerry took me into the office and told the man in charge that I was his wife's cousin and that I had lot of experience working on ship's boilers. He asked if was it possible for me to replace his usual mate.

The man in the office introduced himself as the Billy the Boss and asked me what was the largest boiler I had ever worked on. Before I could answer Gerry interrupted and said he thought that the biggest one we had worked on together was on board the Queen Mary. Without stopping for breath he began to tell the biggest cock and bull story about the job we had done on the old tub, as was his description of the Queen Mary. After listening for a short while Billy the Boss raised his hands in surrender and said " So he's never worked on boilers in his life!

We all laughed. He then looked at Gerry and said, "You will be totally responsible if he fucks up."
He went on to say, "I must tell you Gerry that I feel very happy for your last mates wife because she will be over the moon to hear that you two have split up, she might even get the chance of seeing him sober. Now take your wife's cousin and go to the Wonderloaf factory in Welwyn Garden City where you will find three boilers that need de-scaling and several of their water circulation pipes replacing. Hopefully this will keep you both busy and out of my hair for at least 10 days." We left his office and went to a lock-up shed in a corner of the yard were we were instructed by the yard foreman to load about five very long lengths of air hose into a small van and hitch up a mobile compressor to it's tow bar.

After a very uneventful journey, we arrived at the Wonderloaf factory where we were greeted by a little roly-poly bald headed poof, who both directed and escorted us to the boiler house where he started getting very excited and animated. He told us, that he felt having two lovely young men like us put in his care was like having a gift from the Gods. I could see that Gerry wasn't very comfortable around this type of bloke. Under normal circumstances Gerry, who feared nobody on this earth and was certainly one of the hardest men I'd known in my lifetime, would make sure that whoever was making him feel uncomfortable was put firmly put in their place, either verbally or physically.

It was obvious in this situation that Gerry wasn't sure of himself and the more uncertain he became, the more the gay bloke kept making cheeky suggestions to him. He kept spouting out these innuendoes until he left us in boiler house. I felt rather glad that the bloke had decided he fancied Gerry and not me. In those days, I also felt very uncomfortable in the company of gay men. I thought that walloping them would be the same as hitting a woman. Most of the men I had grown up with in the East End didn't go in for violence against women. I was sure that Gerry's reactions would be the same as mine, if this bloke actually started making any uninvited physical advances towards him. Without using violence neither of us would know how to handle the situation.

It turned out that two out of the three boilers we were going to work on were still going full blast and the other one hadn't been switched off until very late the previous night, which meant it was still full of boiling water. Gerry explained to me that there were two sides to the internal workings of boilers. One side held the water and was called the white side, the other was the black side, simply because it was the side where the fire created all the soot. We immediately set about draining off the thirty or so thousand gallons of boiling water. As it flowed along the purpose made gully the steam rising from it caused the temperature of the boiler house to soar to almost a 150 degrees.

The way my body instantly began to pour with sweat made me feel very uncomfortable, it was the hottest and wettest I had ever been outside of having a bath. I asked Jerry if he had got any extra working clothes as I only had the ones I stood up in. He told me that when you were working inside boilers it wasn't necessary to wear any clothes.

He added, " But if you're a bit shy you can put on swimming trunks or use your underpants."

He then suggested that we ask the funny little bloke if he had any spare boiler suits. As it was compulsory for all the employees of the factory to wear them Gerry said he thought the little bloke might have some spare ones tucked away somewhere. I thought it was a good idea and suggested to Gerry that as the bloke seemed to fancy him, he would be more forthcoming if he was the one that asked him for the gear.

When we asked one of the bakery staff where we could find Roly-Poly we were directed to a small cupboard come storeroom. Roly-Poly's little eyes shone with glee when he saw Gerry, and actually looked fit to burst when he found out that Gerry was actually looking for him.

"Come to my little room and tell me what I can do for you," he said, when we told him what we wanted. He again invited us to his little room saying "Come inside, come inside, I sure I will find something to suit you lovely boys."

I could see that the standing space inside the storeroom was about the size of two telephone boxes, and was surrounded by shelves stacked from floor to ceiling with linen. Gerry tried to stop about a foot outside of the door, but I pushed him into the room. This brought him so close to roly-poly they were almost touching; I had never seen Gerry looking so uncomfortable.

I quickly stepped back out of the storeroom and closed the door behind me leaving Gerry and roly-poly in what I thought could become a very compromising situation. I turned the key in the lock, but before I had released the handle on my side of the door it began to turn rapidly backwards and forwards which made it very clear to me that Gerry was panicking.

I heard him say to Roly-Poly, "Look mate, if you come anywhere near me I will punch your fucking head in, so just keep your distance."

Then he shouted to me, "If you don't unlock this fucking door now, when I do get out of here, I'll fucking kill you. I am fucking sorry now that I ever got you the job, everybody told me you were no fucking good but I stuck up for you. Now I know they were telling me the truth. Open this fucking door you skinny bastard. Please let me out!"

He went from threatening to menacing to begging and back again with each request.

I knew that if I let him out at that precise moment, being in such a state of panic, he would have done me a serious injury. I walked back to the boiler house laughing to myself and thinking I would give him time to cool down. Unfortunately for me two of the women factory workers had gone to collect some linen from the store and let him out much sooner than was safe for me. By now he had become a raving lunatic. Even more so because he believed that the women thought he had been up to something sexual with Roly-Poly. Luckily I saw him coming and managed to hide on a gantry up above the boilers. From my, vantage point I could see that he was in such a bad temper there were tears streaming down the sides of his cheeks. I was beginning to feel that my little joke had backfired.

The two women who had opened the storeroom came into the boiler house and asked him who had locked him in. I heard him trying to explain to them how he had only gone in there to get a boiler suit and he wasn't like what they were thinking he was like. He was really trying very hard to convince them that nothing sexual had happened between him and Roly-Poly. I knew Gerry always had trouble talking to women about sex and the more he tried to convince them that he wasn't an homosexual, the deeper and more confused his words got until eventually I couldn't stop myself laughing out loud.

"Come down here you skinny bastard," he said to me. "Tell these girls that I'm not a poof."

I said I would but only on the condition that he kept control of his temper.

"I promise I won't do anything to you," he said. "Just tell them what you did to me."

I climbed down from the gantry making sure that I didn't stand within arm's length of him. I looked at the girls who were both very attractive and said to them, "Isn't it strange how you think you've known someone all your life, but when it really comes down to it you realise you don't know them at all especially in a situation like this. I don't know how I'm going to explain this to his wife, my poor cousin! That he actually asked me to lock him in the cupboard with the little roly-poly bloke

Gerry looked like he was going to explode, he didn't know what to do or say, especially when one of the girls tumbled that I was winding him up.

She said to me, "When I saw you both arrive this morning I really fancied him. But now I can't put into words how disappointed I felt when I saw who he was in the cupboard with."

"Please John tell them that I am not a poof and that I didn't ask you to lock me in the cupboard," he said.

I looked at him and said, "Well, if that is what you want me to say then I will say it."

"It's not what I want to you say, I just want you to tell the truth okay!"

I said "I would tell them the truth if you can explain what you had been doing in the cupboard for more than an hour before you raised any alarm". I could see the veins on the side of his neck begin to swell with temper. I decided that enough was enough, but I hadn't taken into account the girls' sense of humour. They began to wind him up even more. The last thing I heard them say to him

as I made a very hasty exit, was, "Do you go with both men and women? Are you what they call AC/DC?"
Poor old Gerry became totally lost for words; I decided to make myself scarce for at least an hour. This I did and spent a pleasant time wandering around the factory introducing myself to the various members of staff, who I met along the way. Eventually I went back to the boiler room where I found Gerry and the two girls still talking only now he was in a much better and calmer frame of mind.

When the girls left we started taking the side plates off of the boiler to see if it had cooled down enough for us to start working on it. Although the boiler had actually been closed down for almost twelve hours when we took the plates off, the internal temperature was still too high for us. Gerry told me to rig up a cold-water hose and then climbed the ladder and started hosing down the inside of the boiler. It still took several hours before it became bearable to work in. We then set up the compressor just outside of the boiler house door, attached the air hoses and pushed the working ends of them inside the boiler.

The entrance into the boiler was a circular hole less than 18 inches across, which made it rather a tight squeeze. It meant that we had to enter head first, and exit feet first. It soon became very apparent that what Gerry had said about not needing to wear any clothes to work in was true. Both of us were very soon in the nude, which really delighted roly-poly when he put his head in through the boiler door to say that he had made us a cup of tea. The first thing Gerry did was to drop his air hose and cover up his manhood with both hands. When you're working with air hoses, you should never let go of them before the supply of pressurised air is switched off. If you do lose your grip, the pressure of the air being forced through them turns them into lethal weapons. They immediately take on a life of their own and start whip lashing around with such ferocity that the metal vibrating hammer, head, which is attached to the end of them, can become quite capable of inflicting very serious injuries or worse.

So here we were imprisoned in a very small space getting very close to a state of panic brought about by the fear of getting hammered to death. Gerry acting all very coy covering up his nuts to stop the poof from seeing them, I was feeling rather embarrassed and didn't know why. The poof was blocking our only means of escape, and Gerry's compressor hose was flying around at great speed doing its best to kill us.

I looked at Roly-Poly and shouted, "If you could take your eyes off our bollocks for a second or two and climb down the ladder it would greatly reduce the chances of one, if not both of us, getting seriously hurt or killed."

"Oh dear," he said. "Am I being a nuisance, and there was me thinking that you would both like a nice cup of tea and some jam doughnuts."

Somehow Gerry managed to grab hold of his air hose with one hand while still keeping the other one firmly planted over his private bits. I don't know what he thought was going to happen to them if they were exposed to the elements. Eventually we decided that we had done enough work for the day and once again Roly-Poly looked overjoyed when we sorted him out to ask him where the showers were. I felt almost sure that he wanted to hold Gerry's hand when he showed us the way.

For my first day's work in a very long time I had really enjoyed myself I couldn't believe how easy it had been to wind Gerry up. Travelling back on the overland train before we had to change on to the underground we both agreed that it had been a very funny day. By the time we got on the tube it was the rush hour, all the carriages were overcrowded with bowler hatted men and lovely young office girls. We were both standing very close to each other, enjoying being squashed from all directions by these smartly dressed, lovely looking ladies. Without any prior warning I was suddenly overtaken with a very strong, uncontrollable urge to fart; which didn't exactly come out with slippers on. Several of the girls looked disgusted but quite a few of them laughed.

I looked straight at Gerry and said, "Do you know that there is a time and place to do that sort of thing, or were you brought up somewhere uncivilised."

On several occasions earlier that day I had thought that he was going to explode but looking at him now I was amazed at how the human body could turn so red without being cut open.

Just then the train stopped, when the doors opened several of the people that were around us got off and stood on the platform staring back into the carriage at Gerry. Once again I had embarrassed him so much he couldn't speak and when he did finally manage to get out the words.

"It wasn't me," they came out so high pitched he sounded like a soprano choirboy When the doors closed he managed to say to me, "If you pull any more strokes on me, relation or no relation, I will break your fucking jaw."

Being the sensible sort of lad I was I promised him that I wouldn't do anything else to upset him. We sat down opposite each other in the seats that had just been vacated by the people who had beat a hasty retreat from the disgusting noise and smell they thought Jerry had made.

As we travelled across London Gerry unfortunately nodded off, because he looked like he was really enjoying his nap, I didn't bother to wake him up when we reached our stop. When I met him the next morning, he told me that the train had reached the end of the line before he was woken up by a porter, who told him that he was lucky that hadn't locked it up and parked it on the siding for the night. He threatened me again saying, "If you even think of pulling the slightest stroke on me today I will make sure that Billy the Boss gives you the sack." Taking an account of how much I had pushed my luck the day before I decided not to overdo it again.

CHAPTER 15

I worked with Gerry for several months; we cleaned and repaired boilers in some of the most prestigious hotels, private and public buildings throughout the south of England. Unfortunately neither of us heeded Kathleen's warning about our drinking. I am afraid due to the large amounts of booze we consumed I was unable to save enough money to put down a deposit on a new place to live. This made life in our room at 109 pretty unbearable. Dolly continually searched through the local papers looking for accommodation but each time she came up with somewhere she considered was suitable for us, I wouldn't have enough to pay for it. She was getting very annoyed and very fed up with my broken promises. Much of the time I found it was better to stay out as late as I could, living in the hope that she would be asleep when I got home.

If I did arrive home at a civilised hour, feeling full of the joys of spring, I knew full well that as soon as I stepped over the doorstep, Dolly would be waiting with the address of some flat or furnished room for us to go and see. On the rare occasions I felt like this I knew that it wouldn't be long before all my good feelings would be replaced by a defensive, ill-tempered mood. Personally I felt that by going out to work and supplying Dolly and Kim with money for food and lodgings I was doing something wonderful. I would often ask her, if she was ever going to get her husband to donate something towards his daughter's upkeep. Making this type of under handed comment, always left me feeling very guilty, knowing full well that I had agreed to live with and support them both without any terms or conditions.

That year, was one of the coldest winters we had had since records began, it turned our room into the very worst of environments for a child to be in. The fireplace had been solidly bricked in long before we ever moved in. The power sockets were the double round pin types, several years out of date, which meant that the modern electric fire I had stolen, with its three-pin plug, was useless. Even when I took the plug off and tried to force the bare wires into the socket holes using matchsticks to hold them in place only resulted in the entire house being without electricity for three days.

Dolly and Kim stayed in bed under the blankets most of the time just to keep warm. The longer the discomfort continued the more the guilt I felt increased. I was fully aware that the situation we were in was entirely my fault and my responsibility. I knew that if I hadn't spent so much money boozing and having such a good time, we could all be enjoying a much better and warmer standard of living. On several occasions my befuddled little brain would tell me that if I took a bottle of wine home it would ease the tension and make our situation seem less real. It never dawned on me that this type of logic was not entirely sane. My mind always told me that the reassuring effect that alcohol gave you, was a feeling that everybody would surely enjoy experiencing, no matter how dire his or her circumstances.

Our luck started to improve when Dolly read in the local paper that there was a vacancy for a live-in porter to be second in charge of building maintenance at the Stepney Jewish Dwellings. The dwellings, which I had known all my life, were made up of three separate blocks of flats situated behind the last park in Stepney Green. Not having a clue what building maintenance work consisted of didn't for one instance deter me from applying for the job. Like always, I found it very easy to lie about the things I didn't know. As luck would have it the Superintendent of the flats had even less knowledge about the job than I did. He didn't have the slightest idea whether I was being truthful or not when I told him about my fictitious years of experience in building maintenance. The other thing that went in my favour was that his wife was a very good friend of my mum's.

I was interviewed for the job on a Friday afternoon and on the following Monday morning I started work as the number the two porter in charge of building maintenance. As there was only one other Porter this meant that I was at the very bottom of the ladder, which suited me fine. I knew enough about myself to realise that, outside of Dolly and Kim, in no way did I ever want take any form of responsibility. At this time in my life I had become a dab hand at blaming other people for any misfortune that befell me. Also, the lack of confidence that I had suffered in my earlier, pre-drinking life was continually resurfacing and was now taking larger amounts of booze to keep it at bay.

My mum was quite delighted when she heard that I had at last got what she called a proper job, especially one were she thought that she could keep an eye on me. The job consisted of several very boring routine tasks. Most of our time was spent assembling drain rods with hooks on the ends and ramming them up the rubbish chutes because the tenants insisted on trying to push large amounts of rubbish into very small apertures, creating continuous blockages. The majority of the people who lived in the flats were third or fourth generation Jewish families. The largest percentage of them were very nice people and treated their new porter with respect, but as I am sure most people know, in every walk of life there are some real arrogant, pathetic bastard's. Believe me Stepney Jewish Dwellings had its fair share of these.

The word Porter meant something totally different to this little minority. I felt that the description of Porter they carried around in their heads was interchangeable with the word slave and very lowly slave at that. Some of the things those people expected me to do, were beyond belief. For example on a Sunday afternoon when I was off duty someone, somewhere would by accident or mistake throw something of value down their chute. Realising what they had done they would then come knocking on my door expecting me to immediately drop whatever plans I had for the day and start combing through yards and yards of the most foul smelling rubbish to find their misplaced item. On many occasions outside of my working hours they would think nothing of summoning me to clear their blocked waste pipes or toilets. From the likes of these people the chores were always demands, never polite requests.

Taking all things into consideration, for several months things went very well, Kim started at the local school and Dolly got a job as a copy typist, which she had been trained for while she was growing up in the children's home. My wages included rent-free accommodation, which was a very nice one-bedroom flat on the first landing. The only drawback was living opposite the superintendent who never accepted that off duty meant I didn't have to work. He grew fond of telling the tenants to knock on my door to let me know that he had given permission for me to go and do whatever job they wanted done. The other porter lived in the second block of flats on the third floor, which was very convenient for him when it came to extra curricula duties. He never did any. I didn't mind helping the people although it was sometimes very inconvenient.

Very highly skilled tradesmen using the best of materials had built the blocks of flats, which made up the dwellings; nothing was spared in their construction. The flats were similar to many other Jewish settlements that the trust owned throughout London. They were very recognisable by their unusual red bricks and very ornate cast iron safety railings, which were embedded in the concrete on each of the landing floor, safeguarding the tenants from falling over the balconies. I was told that the original benefactors were a very wealthy tribe of Hebrew people, who had set up a trust fund to build and maintain the dwellings so that the less fortunate Jewish families would be given priority when it came to occupying them. They were also assured of reasonably priced controlled rents.

Getting this job and working the set hours seemed to put some discipline into my life I don't know how it happened but for several months I didn't drink nor did I seem to miss it. With the two of us working we managed to furnish the flat quite nicely. As well as doing the maintenance, part of my job was to attend the communal bathhouse every other Friday. This duty actually started on Thursday mornings when I lit a small industrial boiler, which would supply the hot water for 10 bath cubicles. Thursday was ladies day and was attended by one of the lady tenants, who received a small token payment and expected to get tips to make the money up to a reasonable day's pay.

The little experience I'd had, on boiler maintenance, really held me in good stead around the bathhouse. I had learnt how to keep the boiler at a constant very high temperature, which meant that the tenants were delighted not to have the hot water rationed out to them, as it had been in the time before I did the job. Most of them showed their gratitude in the tips they gave me. Life seemed to go from strength to strength. The time I had spent in my younger days, learning to hang wallpaper and paint was also paying off, because I was being asked to do private decorating jobs around the flats. Once I even tried my hand at repairing a television set, but sadly that ended with the same result as plugging in the electric fire back at 109.

The flats were situated about 500 yards from my old school and lots of my old mates still lived in the area around them. As well as those, some of the people living in the flats had also been at my school. One girl I remember was Maureen Harrison who was the daughter of Russ Harrison the senior porter, who had worked in the flats for over 30 years. At school Maureen had always purposely given the impression that she was from a far superior class of people than the rest of us. I never really knew why but she had always treated me with contempt. Now that I was her dad's understudy and knew about her true upbringing. I never missed an opportunity, to remind her about all the airs and graces she had put on at school. At first she treated it as a joke but as time passed she realised that I was working out the childhood resentments I still held against her.

One day she came into the workshop and told me exactly what she thought of me. Unfortunately Dolly was sitting behind the workbench, out of Maureen's line of sight. It took all my strength to pull them apart and I am afraid that poor Miss Harrison got very much more than she bargained for. Her dad reported the incident to the superintendent who in turn reported it back to me and I told Dolly. As it had gone full circle, we both thought that was going to be the end of the matter, but a couple of days later we found out that there were going to be repercussions. Several of the women, who had become very friendly with Dolly, started giving her the cold shoulder when she met them. It soon became obvious that the Harrisons had been talking about the episode to all and sundry because even the people, who Dolly had only been on 'see and nod' terms with, were now acting like she didn't exist.

One evening after work she came into the flat and began crying very bitterly, she said these people were treating her like dirt and it wasn't fair because none of them really knew her. She told me that she had felt a lot happier living at 109, at least there she didn't know anybody nor did she want to. I explained to her that this was only a job and as soon as it was possible I would find another one and somewhere else to live. This seemed to cheer her up; she said to me, "Why don't we go down the local pub for the evening because all we've done since we've lived in this flat is worked hard and watched television."

Thinking about all the rows and problems we'd previously had because my drinking, the idea of going to the pub being suggested by Dolly, hit me like a very agreeable bombshell. After we had finished our evening meal, Dolly put Kim to bed, and made sure she fallen asleep before we left. For the first time since we had moved into the flats we went out for a social evening. The name of the pub we went to was the Clare Hall situated on the corner of Diggon Street and Stepney Way. We went into the public bar, ordered our drinks and sat at a table alongside two other people, who we had seen around but had never spoken to. When we introduced ourselves and started talking, they turned out to be a really nice couple.

Some four or five drinks later I could recall the feeling the effect of the alcohol over coming me. It felt so good after being dry for as long as I had. I had almost forgotten the wonderful feeling of supremacy that it gave me. As well as completely cancelling any emotions, the booze now flooding through my veins made me forget that I could feel physical pain. It filled my head with wit and sarcasm, which I used as I felt each occasion needed. The return of all these good feelings was accompanied by a slight feeling of resentment that kept popping in and out of my brain. Why had I denied myself this pleasure for so long? Dolly said that she could see a television in the other bar and asked if I would like to go around and watch it with her. At that moment in time if she had asked for a pile of gold I felt quite capable of getting it for her. We went into the saloon bar and sat down at a table from where we could see the television I don't remember what was on.

Why they charged an extra penny for the drinks because we were sat an inch or two on the other side of a see-through partition, in exactly the same type of seats, drinking exactly the same beer from the same pumps, has always remained a mystery to me. We stayed in the pub rather longer and later than we had intended to. On arriving back at the flat we were greeted by the Superintendent, who informed me that it was my week to stay on call.
I said, "I'm very sorry. I just don't know what you're talking about and I really don't give a fuck. So why don't you piss off to bed and in future if you ever have anything to say to me please confine it to my working hours."
I unlocked my flat door and went in slamming it very loudly behind me. Dolly made a cup of tea, we sat down and I turned the volume of my radiogram up as loud as I could and played my entire, large collection of West Indian Blue Beat music.

At lunchtime the next day the Superintendent came into the workshop and told me that he was very upset with my language and behaviour, and had it not been for his wife talking him around, he had seriously considered sacking me. The man couldn't have picked a more opportune moment to talk to me because the withdrawals from last nights' booze up were making me feel very rueful about my insults and actions. I was puzzled about why and what had come over me to make me say the things I had and by doing so I had put my home and livelihood in jeopardy. Grudgingly I searched for the words of apology I thought would appease the man the most.

Over the following months I became a regular in the Clare Hall, most nights in the week I went on my own but on Saturday nights I took Dolly. We very quickly became friends with the landlady, her staff and some of the customers. In the public bar there was a regular little firm of card players who also enjoyed the darts and domino scene whereas television sports fans tended to stay in the saloon. I frequented both bars according to whatever mood I was in. Within three months of our first social night out I was drinking almost every day in both the evening and the lunchtime sessions, not very heavily because I couldn't afford it, but very regular.

At first I would try to get into the company of the people who bought rounds like my old mates back at the cabinetmakers. This could mean if I had judged the situation right I could get away with only buying one round of drinks and then hopefully drink for the rest of the session on them. In the beginning it worked very well but like my old pals, each little circle of drinking buddies I joined very soon tumbled what I was up to. In the public bar one night because it was early and most of the regulars hadn't arrived, I started drinking with a flash little bastard. I didn't like him very well but when it came to drinking, I really didn't care who paid for my booze.

This particular bloke had always struck me as a nasty, snidey piece of work, an opinion I shared with most of the punters in the Clare Hall. He was always bragging about everything he did, his ego was so inflated he would tell us totally outrageous things about himself, expecting us to believe every word he uttered. For instance, he once said he had so many suits he could change every hour into a different one and a not put the same one back on for a week. This might have been very true but no one had ever asked him to tell us about it and no one was very interested. There wasn't a car in the world that he hadn't driven, and not an accident that he hadn't managed to walk away from totally unscathed.

On this particular evening I listened to his repetitive bragging about his many conquests with women, he went as far as to say that any woman married or not that had ever walked into the Clare Hall between certain ages he had either shagged or they had sucked his cock. Drink or no drink this prat was getting right up my nose, so much so that I asked him if he had taken a University degree in talking bollocks. This didn't deter him in any way he just ranted on about his sexual prowess and activities. Eventually I couldn't take his constant, inane babble any longer. I walked away from him and out of the public bar but not before telling him that I was pissed off listening to him. He just didn't get the message he followed me into the saloon bar and asked me if I thought he was telling lies. I said, "Yes, as a matter of fact I think you talk complete bollocks all the time." He looked at me and said, "You, you're nothing but a fucking wanker."

The amount of booze I had drunk hadn't had very much effect on me otherwise I'm sure my reaction to his insult would have been totally different. I just slapped him around the side of the head like you would a naughty little boy and told him to go and play in the road because there was some heavy traffic due to go by. He ran out of the pub like a scalded cat, threatening to do all sorts of nasty things to me, when and if ever he saw me again. I sat down, ordered another drink, turned on the television and watched the evenings' programmes. The rest of the night went without incident; as usual I drank too much, but felt in very good spirits when I left the pub. The next morning I woke up in a lot of pain one of my eyes wouldn't open, there was blood all over my pillow, my wrists, knuckles, and arms were covered in cuts and bruises. I found it almost impossible to move without creating even more pain; my mind went into a complete turmoil how could I get all these injuries without knowing who or what had caused them.

When Dolly opened the door of the bedroom and saw that I was awake she said, "Thank God you're still alive, the Doctor told me that if you didn't wake up in the next hour or so they were going to put you in hospital."
I looked at her and asked if she knew what had happened to me.
She said, "I'm sorry John I don't, all I do know is that two blokes from the Clare Hall carried you home. When the Superintendent saw them helping you up the front steps he called a Doctor, who came and attended to all your cuts. One of the blokes told me that you had been fighting with somebody outside of the pub."

It was several days before I was feeling fit enough to go back to the pub. In my mind I felt very confident that whatever injuries I had suffered, the person who had inflicted them on me was going to be ten times worse off. I asked Pat White, the landlady of the Clare Hall, about the fight, she said surely you must remember what happened. She looked across the bar and shouted for Terry, her live in lover, to come over to us. When he did she told him to explain what he had seen happen to me. The next five or ten minutes felt more painful, than all the injuries I had received from the beating I'd taken.

Terry told me that as I walked out of the pub door, the bloke I had slapped earlier that evening came up behind me carrying two sets of marital art chain sticks and attacked me with them. His first onslaught caught me across the back of my head and shoulders knocking me to the ground. Although I had managed to get up once or twice, each time I got to my feet he beat me back down again. Terry also said that the bloke was so expert with the tools he was using that before anybody could get outside to help me or stop him, he had rendered me unconscious and was cutting me to pieces with every blow he landed.

Terry went on to say, "I'm very sorry John but the bloke was so quick. I couldn't do anything to save you until it was too late."

It is true to say that I felt more mentally shattered in that ten minutes than ever before, because it was the first time that I had actually come off second best in any one to one violent confrontation I'd had whilst I was under the influence of drink. The emotional pain and disappointment that I was suffering was immeasurable. I kept asking myself over and over again how could this happen, how had this bastard got through my alcoholic armour, why wasn't he frightened of my reputation as a hard man; didn't he know about my not feeling any physical pain when I was drunk. My mind was in a complete turmoil because someone had penetrated my physical barriers and my faith in the fact that I would always be safe as long as I was wrapped in the arms of booze. This belief was the closest thing I had to a religion. The four horsemen of the acropolis were saddled up and galloping full tilt around my head. For several days, terror, bewilderment, frustration and despair were my only feelings. For some time I was both mentally and spiritually lost.

My mind went into in a state of total disbelief about the fact that my best friend and closest ally, booze, had let me down. In desperation I began mentally searching for a way to repair the loophole the bloke had blown in my safe little world. I decided that revenge was going to be my only salvation. I became very determined to find this bastard and give him a severe beating in a very public place hopefully the saloon bar of the Clare Hall. Having no idea where he came from or went to, I decided to wait until he showed up again. It was during this period of time that Pat White's barmaid Sally told me that she thought I depended on drink far too much. This comment pierced my mind like a dagger. How could anybody possibly depend on drink too much, especially if they drank for the reasons I did. My false bravado told me to tell her that she had got it all wrong, and to prove it I wouldn't drink for a month. When I ordered my next drink, I made sure that everybody in the pub could see that it was a pint of orange juice. I felt that if I was going to be a hero, all and sundry around me should know about it. I tried to carry on in the same manner as always, but somehow drinking orange juice really didn't quite cut the mustard.

My intended month off of the booze lasted half way down the very first pint of orange juice. I knew then and there that I would never be able to stop drinking. I realised that I would always need alcohol to give me a few precious hours of freedom from the person I really deep down thought I was. Mentally I was very much aware that I had always been, and still was, a very weak frightened immature little boy. Up until then I could live with my deficiency because I had always been able to rely on the change that booze brought over me. After the beating and coming to terms with the horrific realisation that I wasn't infallible under the influence of drink, I tried my very best to stay on a mentally level plateau. I rationed myself to what I thought was the right amount of drink that it would take to give me the effect I both wanted and needed. I wasn't aware that trying to stay drunk had become a compulsion, I don't mean drunk and stupid I mean drunk and still in control. To achieve this I drank stronger beers and then went on to spirits. Try as I might I could never maintain any kind of level playing field or work out the exact dosage to maintain my intentions.

For weeks I went in to Clare Hall hoping I would catch the flash prat, so that I could repair my reputation and regain the respect I felt that I had lost from my fellow drinkers. Earlier in the year Pat White asked me if I would work behind the bar over the Christmas and New Year holidays. When I started it felt like manna from heaven, once again I felt all my blessings had come at once, just like when the juvenile magistrate told me I was getting probation. To be allowed behind the bar of my favourite pub, there wasn't a good enough cliché to cover how I felt.

The superintendent of the dwellings had threatened me so many times with the sack and then not doing so, I started to believe he was incapable of getting rid of me. One day when he came into the workshop I caught hold of the him by his shirt front pushed him against the wall and threatened to kill him and his wife if ever he jeopardised me or my family's position. Knowing that this man was physically inferior to me and mentally afraid, I decided that there was nothing to stop me working full-time in the pub and spending as little time as possible at my proper job.

Out of the blue Dolly dropped the bombshell that she was several months pregnant, and the baby was due in November. We sat down and had a long conversation about having an extra mouth to feed and in my devious way I used her condition to justify working in the pub over the Christmas holidays. I went into a long and detailed explanation of how the extra money, I was going to earn would cover all the expenses a new baby would cost. The picture I painted about all the wonderful things that my extra financial income would pay for looked very good in my mind. Dolly had other ideas, she said, "The money you earn now doesn't pay for what you drink and I know from past experience that the more money you get the more you will drink."

She went on to say that she thought the only saving we could definitely make was if she didn't come out with me on Saturdays and I gave the money I would spend on her at home. This sounded like a great idea. At that moment in time I felt so pleased that I'd decided to live with such a sensible person. Life was beginning to look perfect I had a full-time job on a part-time basis, I had a wife that in the very near future would be permanently indoors and I was going to become a barman with access to unlimited free drink. Obviously Pat White the landlady wasn't aware that she was going to be the supplier of my complementary alcohol.

My son John was born in November on the very day the doctors said he was due, cigars and booze flowed liked it was going out of fashion that evening. For the following ten days I became the model husband. I attended every visiting session with the proverbial bunch of flowers or box of chocolates that was expected of all good fathers, but unlike all the other good fathers mine were stolen from outside of the wards that I passed by on my way to the maternity unit. For about a week after Dolly came home, I walked around like the cat that got the cream, showing off my new son, I even started putting more hours in on my day job.

One morning late in December, I began thinking about how lucky I was and decided to celebrate my good fortune. With this in mind I went into the pub and started drinking an hour or two before we opened to the public, it was one of the biggest binges I'd had for a very long time. It continued throughout the Christmas, until it culminated on New Years Eve with a tremendous, tragic climax. I was already three parts cut from the lunch hour piss up when we reopened for the evening session at 7 o'clock. I had been topping up most of the day while the pub was closed. This became very obvious to Pat White who wasn't at all happy about the prospect of having a drunken barman serving her customers, on one of the busiest nights of the year.

She made me a big mug of black coffee and told me to go and lie on her bed for and hour or two, as I left the bar I stole a quarter bottle of Scotch and drank it in two swallows. After lying down for what seemed like forever I decided I would go down and entertain the customers in a way that they would never forget. I felt that the people in the saloon bar deserved to be treated to a naked version of the Can Can. Carrying a large joint of beef, which I had found cooling off on top of the oven in Pats' kitchen, I took off my clothes and left them in a heap at the foot of the stairs and made a very grand entrance. I skipped across the floor, jumped up on the bar and started parading up and down with my nuts swinging akimbo, doing the famous French dance, whilst singing jingle bells.

By this time the bar was full of the usual regulars, plus their relatives and friends who had come visiting for the holidays. The entire place turned into bedlam, everybody began clapping to show appreciation for my efforts. At this point I got down like a dog on all fours and began eating the meat. One dear very frail old lady decided that she would like to have a dance with me and pulled me off of the bar. I really was in no condition to rock and roll and I'm afraid as I tried to spin her around I sent her careering across the floor. She went down and slid across the floor until her head came into contact with edge of the brick built fire surround. She looked up at me and tried to get to her feet but unfortunately she fell down again, I knew if I tried to help her, I would fall over as well so I left it to her friends to help her.

I went back out through the private door and got dressed, then made my way very unsteadily along the outside of the pub to the public bar, where to my drunken delight I found the big mouthed flash bastard that had beaten me up. Because of what he had done to me and how that he had done it, I had started carrying a chain, which was about 2 ft long with half-inch links and very heavy. I was delighted when I realised that the bragging little bastard couldn't escape from the bar without having to face up to me, which I had learnt from people who knew him, wasn't his style. The entire bar fell into silence it was like an old western movie. Most of the customers knew from what I had been saying would happen if ever I met this prat again that this was the moment I had been waiting for. The tricky little bastard tried to dive through my legs; this made things turn out even better than I thought they were going to. I punched him, kicked him and bit him. I knocked him around that bar like he was a rag doll and when he couldn't stand up anymore I propped him up against the bar and lashed into him with the chain.

The next thing I remember was being woken up on what I thought was New Years' Day. Dolly was offering me a cup of tea and not looking very happy. I told her that I had some good news that would cheer her up and began telling her how I had taken my revenge on the flash Bastard.

She said, " Stop talking, John, and listen to me."

Due to her tone, the hairs on the back of my neck began to bristle. I felt a familiar sense of impending doom, come over me.

"Hurry up and tell me what's wrong," I said to her.

Once again she looked at me in a very sorrowful way, "Come on," I said. "Tell me what's wrong."

"I don't know what to say, she said. "The police have been here looking for you but I told them that you hadn't come home."

"What the fuck are you talking about?" I asked her.

"Listen to me," she said again. "The woman you knocked down in the pub died and the bloke you beat up is in the intensive care unit of the London Hospital. The police want you for murder and attempted murder."

I'd never felt more scared or lonely, or ever more sober than I did at that moment.

I said, "Surely the police didn't come around here and not look in this bedroom."

"They have been here twice a day for the last three days."

"What ever are you talking about" I asked her. "I only had the fight last night.

"John," she said, "You've been missing for four days."

The reality of the situation was totally beyond my comprehension, where had I been? What had I done? Who had I been with? The most important question I asked myself was why couldn't I remember any of it? I had suffered this type of drunken blackout before, but never for more than a couple of hours at a time. Dolly began to cuddle me and told me that she loved me and then went into an uncontrollable, shaking and crying fit.

I got myself to the pub as soon as I possibly could and asked Pat if I had been there in the past three days. She told me that she hadn't seen me since I had helped to put the bloke I'd beaten up into an ambulance. Like a lot of other people, she didn't believe that I had no memory of what had happened in the past four days. She did however tell me that the old ladies' two sons had been in the bar when the incident occurred and that they had explained to the police that their mother's death had been an accident. It was quite a relief to know that they couldn't charge me with her murder. However, I will never forget the guilt, emotional pain and mental anguish that I felt at causing the death of that lovely little old lady. It took me many years to come to terms with it. I will always remember that New Years' Eve, because it nearly became the last one I would ever have seen out side of prison. Pat also said that she thought that I should go and hide out somewhere until the bloke in hospital either got better or died.

Faversham seemed like it was the perfect place for me to go. Harry Swan and Mary were having domestic problems but were still just about managing to hold on to a very fragile relationship. Harry did me a great favour and put me up for two weeks. It took me that long to summon up the courage to ring Pat and ask her what the situation was. She told me that the bloke was almost fully recovered and was due to be discharged from the hospital at the end of the week. I caught the first available train back to London and went straight to the hospital. After searching through nearly every ward in the place I finally found the little bastard. When I confronted him with the fact that when he had done the cowardly thing of beating me up from behind, I hadn't gone anywhere near the police. But now it was his turn to be hurt and not from behind, he wanted to get me arrested.
I said to him, "Getting me nicked won't help you to get better any quicker."
He told me that he hadn't reported me to the police and neither was he going to, and he was quite willing to forgive and forget about it all, as long as I promised him that all our differences had been settled. On receiving that bit of good news, I decided it was time I went back home to Dolly.

After knocking very loudly for several minutes on my front door without getting any response, I decided to go to the workshop. I hadn't been there very long when the superintendent came down from his flat and told me that I'd only got two weeks left of the month's notice, that he had given Dolly, in writing, during my absence. All in all I felt that the New Year was going along very swimmingly. During the first three weeks of January I had been wanted for two capital crimes, plus I had become hated by the families of a dear old women and the snidey little bastard, none of whom I knew. I had been down to Faversham, one of my favourite places and couldn't remember very much of what I had done there. Knowing my luck, whatever I had done wasn't going to be good. I had lost both of my jobs and in another fourteen days I would lose my home as well. Sometime over the Christmas period, someone had told me that I had also successfully managed to upset several members of the Kray twins firm.

Taking all things into consideration, being very much aware that I was now fully responsible for a very hysterical wife, a stepdaughter, plus a new born son, and carrying the uncomfortable knowledge that a great deal of my immediate future life was going to be spent living on poverty street. I just couldn't wait to see what other goodies the rest of nineteen sixty-five was holding in store for me.

CHAPTER 16

For the following two weeks life was absolute hell, Dolly and myself fought like cat and dog; she blamed me for everything. Our relationship was in such a bad way I don't know why we didn't split up. Two days before the end of our notice period the superintendent asked me if I had been able find any alternative accommodation. Due to the permanent state of anger I was living in my reply was loud and threatening. I told him in no uncertain terms that I hadn't bloody well found anywhere else live, and that I didn't have the slightest intention of leaving our flat until I had. If he thought any different or was nursing any ideas of making my family homeless he was going to be a very disappointed man.

Once again I had firmly planted my two feet in my big mouth. Like so many times in the past I had jumped the gun, which I found out when he told me his reason for coming to see us wasn't to make sure that we were leaving the flat, but to say that the company had decided to re-house us. He told me that we were going to be allocated a two-bedroom ground floor flat in Flower and Dean Street, which was a little street that ran between Commercial Street and Brick Lane. As if by magic the atmosphere in our present home completely changed, Dolly became a different person, the strain that I had been under, caused by my guilt and all the Christmas incidents, just drifted away.

About a week later we loaded all our goods and chattels on to Wally Welford's open back truck and, looking very much like the Clampits, we drove to our new home. After collecting the keys from the rent office we went to see what sort of flat we'd been given. To say that it was dirty would be one very big understatement. I think because it was late in the afternoon and the daylight had faded, it helped us not to see too many faults in the place. Because the area was known to have more thieves living in it than there were in Wormwood Scrubs, while we were unloading our furniture we left Kim on the truck to make sure nobody stole anything while we were going in and out.

Dolly instructed me where she wanted the furniture put, which bedroom was going to be ours and which one was Kim's. After several hours of trial and error we finally got some sort of order into the place. Using the excuse that I knew the neighbourhood better than Dolly, I volunteered to go and get some tea, sugar and milk; my real intention was to get a drink in the local pub, which was called the Frying Pan. It was a grotty little place that I knew quite well, when I was a kid my gran had lived in the next street to our new flat. During our childhood days, my dad had sent my sisters and me to visit her every Sunday morning. Her idea of a visit from her grandchildren meant the three of us waiting outside the door of the Frying Pan throughout the entire lunchtime session, while she got drunk.

My dad's two sisters were still living in the same block of flats, where my gran had lived, so on the way to the pub; I thought it would be a good idea to drop in to see them. Giving them first hand the good news, that their least favourite nephew was now living only one street away from them. If anybody could have seen the looks on their faces when I dropped this wonderful piece of information in their laps, they would have thought that I had told them they had been stuck down with leprosy. My aunts really only ever cared for my eldest sister, Kathleen, my second sister Jeanie they tolerated but me they despised. I couldn't blame them because for several years I had only ever gone to see them when I was drunk and never missed an opportunity to insult them.

The Frying Pan wasn't the dingiest pub in Brick Lane but it came very close, it was one of the very few pubs that still spread sawdust on the floor and looking around at the customers anyone with half a brain could see why. The first person I spoke to after I'd ordered a drink looked like he hadn't moved from that spot for many years. Trying to be polite and strike up a conversation I asked him if he remembered my gran. He looked at me and said,

"Why don't you fuck off. If you think I'm buying you a drink just because you have spoken to me you're very sadly mistaken." I stood back and was about to swing a punch at him when the barman intervened and said, "That man stands there every day drinking pints of bitter until he shits himself, if you start a fight with him you will very sadly regret it."

When I got back to the flat several hours later, not drunk but definitely feeling a bit merry, without the tea, sugar or milk, Dolly looked at me and said, "Are you never going to change? Is drink always going to come before the welfare of your family? Don't you care about us."?

I told her that I hadn't been drinking in a pub, that I had gone to see my aunts, who had given me a couple of pints.

She said, "What little regard your aunts have for you is common knowledge, there's no way on this earth that they would give you a drink. Not only do you put your drinking before us, you lie to us about it as well."

Before I had a chance to say anything in my defence, she added, "Don't make any more of your false promises, if you're going to do something just do it and that way you won't be such a disappointment to us, or to yourself."

Angry isn't a big enough word to cover how I felt. This sort of conversation cropped up more and more in the months that followed. Drunk or sober I could never give a truthful answer, to even the simplest of questions, I didn't know how too.

Without being very conscious of it I had drifted into a stage in my life where I hated being told the truth about me. I very often asked myself, why couldn't people just take me as they found me, why did they always think that I should be different. I had become totally incapable of being myself; I was terrified of people finding out that if I didn't have sufficient alcohol in my system I was frightened of most things in this world, My vivid but unbalanced imagination told me that I was the hero in my Walter Mitty daydreams, but in reality I was living proof of the Jekyll and Hyde syndrome.

It wasn't long before Dolly found a babyminder for our son and had started Kim at the local school, then she went back to work in the City. This time she had a far better job at one of the largest stockbrokers in the world. Every month she would receive a financial bonus on top of her salary. On these occasions I would always make sure that I was there to meet her. I did explain to her that I felt it was my duty to protect her from being mugged, as a lot of people knew about the monthly bonuses that the staff received. One time she said to me, "The only person I am in danger of being mugged by is you John." Because she was smiling when she said it, it made it easy for me to pass it off as a joke.

Thinking that I should play some part in making our lives more comfortable I took a job as an assistant service engineer in a tea packet-making firm, my title was Bag Tackler. This was the first time I had worked with women since I had been sacked from the Gin Factory in the Minories. It wasn't the best paid of jobs but it was the only one that didn't require references. The other and most important advantage it had going for it was that it was only a hundred yards or so from a well-known pub called Dirty Dicks. Where they sold wine in sensible schooners, not silly little glasses, which was very much appreciated by all the city gents I drank with while they waited to catch their commuter trains out of Liverpool Street station.

One Friday evening the foreman asked me if I would mind working the next morning, as it would be easier to carry out some rather urgent and difficult repairs on a broken down machine whilst the factory was empty. I readily agreed because it meant I would be paid the overtime rate of time and a half. Thinking about the extra money I would have in my wage packet the following week seemed to justify my going into Dirty Dicks and rewarding myself for sacrificing my pleasure time, as I called every weekend. I felt more than just a little bit upset when I arrived home and found Dolly in floods of tears and our flat in total disarray.

From the way Dolly and Kim were looking at me, I got the distinct feeling that whatever had happened to them and the flat must have something to do with me. I didn't have a clue, all I knew was that I felt very tired and wanted to go to bed.

I said to Dolly, "Whatever I have done can we leave talking about it until I get home from work tomorrow afternoon as I am going to do some overtime in the morning, I will need all the sleep I can get."

Dolly flew at me like a wild thing, screaming, spitting, and kicking and, unusually for her, swearing. Trying to hold her off to protect myself from being scratched to pieces while asking her whatever was wrong all at the same time was proving to be very difficult. Eventually she calmed down and began to tell me what I had been up to, like several times in the past she told me about things that I had done, that I genuinely had no recollection of doing.

This time even I couldn't believe what she was telling me when she said that I had come home late on the Friday night very drunk almost incapable of standing up but very carefully nursing two bottles of wine. I had gone to bed, slept for about an hour then got up again and gone out; I had done this without speaking to either her or Kim, however I had managed to drink the wine. I have no memory of that weekend I can only go on what Dolly and the other people who were involved told me later. The fact of the matter was that I had turned up for work on the Saturday morning as promised and worked most of the day on the broken machine, carrying out a very expert repair job without any supervision. When I left work I went to see my parents where I behaved in a very normal manner going with them to the 'Pie and Mash' shop in Cambridge Heath Road.

The next thing I knew it was Monday night and Dolly was telling me that I had been to work again that day. I was now standing there trying to defend my self against her onslaught, which as of yet she hadn't told me the reason for. I was still in total disbelief when she said that I'd lost my temper and deliberately smashed our flat up just because she'd asked me if I had any housekeeping money for her. Just like in the film I'd had a Lost Weekend. I asked a lot of people about those missing days, every one I spoke to who had seen me over that period of time said that I had seemed completely sane and sober. From then on whenever I came out of the many blackouts I had, my fear was much more intense as I was now fully aware of the sort of violence I was capable of inflicting on people without any conscious knowledge. I may even have murdered someone and be facing the consequences of having committed a capital crime I had no recollection of!

One day a friend of mine told me that the G L C were looking to hire a team of labourers to do the ground work in preparation for building a block of flats. Without giving any notice to the bosses of the tea bag-making factory, I decided that it was time for me to change jobs. The site I went to for an interview was on Cambridge Heath Road, just opposite a park where as kids my mates and me used to go paddling. The park was once the grounds of a mental home that had been changed into a workhouse and was now a library/come museum. It was still lovingly known as Barmy Park as we had dubbed it many years previously. Wearing a suit that I was looking after for a mate who was in prison, I arrived at the site office looking a lot cleaner and smarter than I had done for a very long time. The Clerk of the Works, who conducted the interview, invited me to sit down and asked if I would like a coffee.

I said, "Yes thank you," thinking this was a very civilised way of employing a labourer.

He went on to ask me what other sites I had worked on and without hesitating for breath, I reeled off the names of at least ten different Building Companies that I had heard of.

"Good," he said, "I feel that I can confidently leave you in charge of this site."

To say that I was flabbergasted was another one of those under statements, this man had obviously mistaken me for somebody who was either starting or applying for the General Foreman's job. When he told me how much the salary was, it was just too much for my devious little mind to tell him the truth. I thought to myself if I can last a month I will earn more than I've earned in the past year, it would certainly be a lot more than I would be getting if I told him I was only a labourer. He told me that the furniture for my office would be arriving that afternoon and the telephone would be connected the next morning. He issued me with a bunch of keys, which he told me were for my office door and the labouring gangs changing hut and canteen. He said that there were a dozen men coming from another site and if I needed more, I could ring the local labour exchange, whose number he had written on my blotter pad. So far I hadn't said a word other than to thank him for the coffee and reel off a list of company names that I hadn't worked for. My mind was still contemplating what I was going to do with all the money they were going to pay me.

The Clerk of the Works picked up his coat and hat, wished me the best of luck, walked out of the office, got into his car and was gone. Throughout the entire interview I hadn't said more than a dozen words. I sat down on the packing case that was acting as my desk until my furniture arrived, trying to take stock of my situation; common sense had gone completely out of the window. I was sitting there thinking, "What the fuck am I supposed to do next." Just as this thought was passing through my mind, a bloke came in and told me that he and his gang had arrived and wanted the keys to their changing hut.

He said to me, "I see they have slung you in at the deep end, they haven't even given you a proper desk."

As he was saying this he began unrolling what looked to be like a set of maps. I thought to myself, "If this Pratt asked me to read what I assumed were site plans, it's going to be the shortest job I've ever had."

Just like Clerk of the Works, this bloke didn't stop talking; he just assumed that I understood every word he said. I hopefully nodded

351

in what I thought were all the appropriate places. "Okay boss" he said to me, "What end of the site do you think would be most convenient to start digging the trenches?"

I looked out of the window and pointed, asking what he thought about the area over that side. He said to me "I can see that we are going to get along like a house on fire, because that is exactly where I had in mind."

"Good," I said, "I hope you don't mind me telling you this but I have had one of those mornings that really hasn't worked out as I expected it to. I feel very much like I need a drink."

"Don't mind me, gaffer," he replied, "I know exactly how you feel, I've been a ganger for 20 years and I am perfectly capable of looking after a little site like this blindfolded. So if you want to take the rest of the day off I can assure you everything is safe in my hands."

When I had worked with people like this man in the past, I'd always found that they were capable beyond their knowledge. They were so delighted and satisfied with being left in charge they didn't care about promotion, titles or even money. I think these are the people that keep the wheels of industry spinning. All the keys that the Clerk gave to me, I passed on to Nobby the ganger. I felt that he was going to be my saviour, until such time as I was confronted by anyone who could test my knowledge of the building game. I was absolutely right; it was six weeks to the day when the Clerk of the Works brought a party of inspectors into my office. They were very a official looking bunch of people who asked me to give them a guided tour of the site and work in progress, as well as pointing out any deviations I'd had to make to the site plans.

I tried to explain to them that as Nobby the ganger was more hands-on than I was he would be far more capable of showing them around and explaining the intricacies of the various jobs than I could. That was my first mistake because one of the jumped

up, officious little bastards said, "Good, then you can stay here and explain why the job hasn't reached the time targets we set." I looked at the Clerk of Works and said, "I didn't realise that you had set any time targets."
He said, "Surely you've seen all the targets on every page of the plans."
"You mean those targets," was all I could think of to say. When it came right down to the basics, I couldn't tell you if the site plans were the right way up or not. If I'd put my entire knowledge of map reading to work for a week, I still wouldn't have been capable of finding the right page in an A to Z London street guide.

Before I knew it nearly every member of the visiting team of inspectors, had reached the decision that I wasn't a very capable general foreman. They told me that if I wanted to remain employed by the G L C, I would have to accept demotion to labourer and be transferred to another site; the choice was mine. For a minute or two following the confrontation, I was left alone with the Clerk of the Works, who I could see was feeling very uncomfortable. He explained to me that if I had been able to give them just one or two right answers they would have let me keep the General Forman's job. It turned out that the bloke they had interviewed and given the job as General Foreman had been due to start work at the same time I had arrived for my interview, but as he didn't show up, the Clerk of Works assumed that I was he. They had taken six weeks or more to find out their mistake. It was pointless trying to argue any sort of case for myself so I just accepted their decision.

On the following Monday I reported to the new site as instructed, I walked into the office where I introduced myself to the General Foreman, "Oh yes," he said, "You're our new ganger."
Once again I thought to myself, "It's going to be better money than labouring."
Due to my being temporarily on the sobriety wagon, I managed to keep this deception up much longer than the first one. The

site was within walking distance of my flat, which meant there were no travelling expenses involved. Life was really looking up, Dolly was getting a very good salary plus bonuses and I was much better off by a good few quid each week, plus the profit I made from any stock that I nicked off of the site. At a very rough estimate during the time I worked there I think each of the 100 flats we were building had to be supplied with at least three times the amount of plumbers fittings that they really needed. Lead and copper piping in those days fetched a lot of money.

When I first started working on this site I went home for lunch which; Dolly would prepare before she went to work each morning. It was actually less than half a mile to my flat; my only problem was I had to pass the ever-open doors of two very inviting pubs. This was a temptation that I couldn't overcome; in less than a month I'd started drinking again. The pub that tempted me back on the booze was called, The Alma, and was located on the corner of Handbury Street less than fifty yards from the site entrance. The owners were a Polish family who spoke little or no English, which suited me fine, because I thought that talking during the limited time I had available in my lunch periods was a great waste of drinking time.

The job was going along very well, it reminded me of the camaraderie I'd found in my old days back at the Glendale Cabinet Company. Opposite one side of the flats we were building, was a row of little terraced houses where some young housewives lived. It wasn't very long before, in response to our catcalls and whistles, we were being invited in for cups of tea by some of the more carefree of the women. I got very friendly with a girl called Maureen, the mother of two children, whose husband very conveniently worked for a bookmaker's on the other side of London.

The relationship that followed was always a disaster waiting to happen. She was a very willing and active participant in all kinds of sexual goings on. For a time, in those days, I thought and acted like a control freak; if any person, male or female allowed me to have any sort of mental or physical hold over them, I would never miss an opportunity to exploit it. Maureen was no exception. Every lunchtime I would go into the Alma, drink as much as I could in the time allowed, and then invite anyone that was interested to come back to Maureen's house for afternoon sex sessions. She told me that the only reason she took part was because she liked me so much

In one of my meaner moments I said to her, "If you care so much about me you won't mind if we have sex in front of your husband,"
She told me that she would love to and if I went round that evening it would be fine. At about eight o'clock I knocked on her door, which was opened by her husband, Norman.
He said to me, "You must John,"
I nodded. He then invited me in saying that Maureen had told him that I was coming round for a chat.
"I think we are going to have more than a chat," I said.
"What do you mean?" he asked.
"Surely she's told you that I have come round to demonstrate to you, how many different ways there are to fuck a woman," I replied.
As I was talking to him I could see that he was getting into a real state of despair and disbelief, it was obvious that he wasn't capable of defending himself or his family. From the way he looked at me I felt that this wasn't the first time that Maureen had done this sort of thing to him. I began to think that it was all a mistake and that I shouldn't be there. Then the reality of the situation began to excite me and I couldn't stop. Maureen came into the room and said to her husband, "I suppose John has told why he is here."
Norman nodded to her and then started crying.

I couldn't bring myself to feel sorry for this man, in fact it was just the opposite, I became angry with him for not having any backbone. I wanted to humiliate him in every way I possibly could for being such a coward. I told Maureen to take all her clothes off, which she did without blinking an eyelid. We then went through every kind of sexual act that we could think of. Finally I sat on an armchair and made her perform oral sex on me, with her naked private parts in full view of her husband who was sitting opposite us.

I said to him, "Why don't you give her one up the arse while she is doing this to me."

Looking straight at me through his tears he said, "She's always told me that she doesn't like it that way."

The effect of the drink was beginning to wear off. I began to feel a bit ashamed of myself and told Maureen to get dressed and make some tea.

Norman said to me, "People like you will always do what you want to people like me, as we will never be able to summon up enough courage to stop you. But one day you'll look back at what you have done to my marriage, and if you have one shred of decency or moral fibre left in your body, you may suffer some sort of remorse, hopefully it will make you feel like I do now."

At that moment I felt more degraded and humiliated than the man sitting opposite me would ever guess or know. There wasn't the slightest vestige of any drunken feeling left in me; I had absolutely nowhere to hide my guilty, remorseful thoughts. I had done some very evil things in my life but at that precise moment, I couldn't think of anything worse. My mum had had a brother also named John, who had died in a lunatic asylum after spending many years locked away. As I stepped out of Maureen's house, I started taking stock of what I had just done in there and the many other similar disgusting things I had taken part in, in my past. I thought to myself, "This must be the sort of behaviour that got my Uncle John his life sentence in a nut house."

I didn't drink for several nights following the episode with Maureen's house. No matter what I tried I couldn't rid myself of the shameful feelings nor could I stop Norman words continually going around in my head. I really wanted to be absolved of what I done, even if it meant being declared insane like my Uncle. I would have become quite willing to accept it. When I thought that I couldn't take any more punishment from my conscience and was about to confess it all to Dolly, or anybody that might understand how I felt, I met Tony Welford. I hadn't seen Tony for some time, when I tried to explain my feelings he told me to stop talking bollocks and to come for a drink.

Within ten minutes of being in the pub, all the shame and degradation I'd been going through was lifted and I had very little or no recollection of why I had felt like it in the first place. On Monday I returned to work, went to the pub for my usual liquid lunch and was in bed with Maureen all that afternoon. For several weeks I kept topping up with drink, which stopped my mind from going on any other guilt trips. Myself and three other members of the site gang drank similarly, which meant that after lunch the building site became almost inactive because none of us were capable of carrying out our duties.

The Alma was now staying open longer hours, because more and more people wanted to drink later, and we couldn't see any reason to disagree with the landlord's plans. During one of these late afternoon sessions, I met a girl named Joyce Robinson. I say met but what really happened was, I was in the saloon bar playing a noisy game of darts, when the landlord told me that a young lady in the public bar wanted to buy me a drink. I put my darts down and went around to the public bar, to find out who was going to buy me a drink. The only woman in the place looked like a replica of Dusty Springfield. I was very surprised when she asked me if I was going to accept the drink she had offered. As I have said many times I was never one to say no to a drink.

I asked her if she knew me, as I certainly didn't know her. She said that she thought I was a friend of her boyfriend, Maltese Tony.

I said to her, "I know lots of Maltese blokes called Tony but none of them, would I ever call a friend."

She asked me my name and said it really didn't matter whether I knew him or not as we were now talking to each other and that had been the object of her exercise. What will you have she said, and at the same time suggested that I try one of the very strong Polish spirits which the pub was famous for. I'd often looked along the range of optics and wondered exactly what the bottles with the unpronounceable names had in them. I thought now was a good time to find out, I think I will try a large one of those I said, pointing to a bottle labelled Zubrodca.

The landlord told me to drink it very slowly and not to have too many until I got used to it. He explained that it was made from a mixture of very strong Polish spirits and herbs, with a piece of buffalo grass floating around inside every bottle. I didn't have a clue what all this meant, but just like when I went into the army I chose to ignore the Landlords warning. Five large Zubrodca's later I was totally out of my brain. Once again I had discovered the real meaning of life. I fell deeply in love with Zubroca and got to quite like Joyce Robinson. That night I took her back to Maureen's, where we spent the entire night in bed together, very much to Norman's delight and Maureen's disgust.

The next morning I realised that I had spent all my money, which meant I couldn't afford keep myself topped up. Most people might think this wasn't much of a problem, or maybe no problem at all! To me, it meant going through withdrawals and the return of my sober, guilty conscience. I really couldn't understand why this was constantly happening to me. I tried several times to summon the courage to talk about it, but when I felt sufficiently brave enough, nobody seemed to understand. Nobody wanted to be burdened down with my guilt problems and feelings of loneliness.

PENTONVILLE JOHNNY

When I saw Joyce waiting at the site entrance the next lunchtime, I was more than delighted. My brain clicked into gear and came up with at least 10 good reasons why she should lend me some money. Before I could present her with any one of these reasons, she opened her handbag and produced a bottle of whisky. Smiling she invited me to join her for a liquid lunch. The next morning I woke up in Kim's bedroom with Joyce lying face down on the bed next to me, both of us were naked. Suddenly the door flew open and Dolly came in carrying a leather handled dog chain, which she swung around her head and lashed Joyce across the arse instantly cutting open deep a wound.

Dolly lashed into Joyce several times before I could stop her. Every time the chain made contact with Joyce's body it tore bits of her flesh away, there was blood spurting all over the three of us. There was so much screaming and noise that our neighbours came to find out what was going on. Joyce managed to cover herself with a blanket, hoping it would give her some protection and then she told Dolly that I had threatened to beat her up, if she hadn't come home with me. This made Dolly go into even more of frenzy. For the next couple of minutes, whenever Joyce tried to speak Dolly set on her again. As soon as there was a lull in the action I asked one of my neighbours to call an ambulance.

Before he went to make the call he looked into the bedroom, and said to me this looks like a scene from a Hammer Horror film. Every time Dolly had caught Joyce with the dog chain she had opened up such large wounds I thought that she would die from the loss of blood. Looking into Dollies' face, I could see a lot of emotional pain and anger.
She said to Joyce, "No painted face, fucking slag, like you, is going to break up my marriage."
As she was saying the words, she hit Joyce across the chest, which unfortunately for her was naked and exposed. This caused both of her tits to start bleeding. I had in my time inflicted lots of injuries

to many different people, but seeing these wounds on a woman really made me feel quite sick.

Just then there was a very loud knock on the street door, to my relief, it was an ambulance driver and his mate, carrying a stretcher. I told them to come in, which proved to be a big mistake. A couple of days earlier we had adopted an Alsatian dog, hence the dog chain. On seeing the first ambulance man the dog went crazy and took a large a bite out of his leg, which caused both men to leave the flat in rather a hurry, refusing to come back. Joyce seized this opportunity to wrap herself in the blanket again and chased after them, leaving the flat door slightly ajar. Dolly seeing Joyce leave, decided she would have one last go at her but unfortunately our neighbour chose that moment to put his head round the door, and caught the blow full in his face.

I thought to myself at least Joyce will have some company on the way to the hospital, I went back into the bedroom got into Kim's bed again and fell asleep. I don't know how long I'd slept, before Dolly woke me up and asked me, if I'd been with any other women since we had been together. I was feeling very pissed off because what she had done to Joyce, had cut off what I thought was going to be my weeks' supply of booze. I said very casually that there had been hundreds, she called me rotten bastard and then walked out of the room. When she came back about a minute or so later she was carrying a frying pan full of sizzling hot fat, which she held above my face. I could hear it spitting and bubbling.
She said to me, "Now tell me about these hundreds of women and remember there won't be any more after the skin gets burnt off of your fucking face when I pour this hot oil over it."

Still feeling muddled from the previous nights' drinking and the events of the morning, for a second or two I struggled to find what I thought would be the words she wanted to hear. My brain was under more pressure to come up with a quick response than it had ever been in my life. It must have been divine intervention that made Kim start crying at that very moment. Whatever it was, it gave me the opportunity to remind Dolly that if she burnt me to death she would go to prison and there would no one to look after the children. Apart from that, she would be seeing me off for something I had only been joking about.

I said, "I'm very sorry about last night but I was so drunk, I just didn't know what was happening and that girl must have taken advantage of my condition just to get somewhere to sleep."

As I was speaking I could see Dolly's face start to relax, my brain kept telling me to think up more excuses, if I could talk long enough the oil might cool down. My next thought was that that could take hours.

"Come on Dolly," I said, "You know if I hadn't been drunk, this wouldn't have happened, where would I ever find the time to go out with other women, you must know that I care too much for you to even consider looking at anyone else."

This seemed to work the Oracle; Dolly started to cry and took the frying pan back to the kitchen. I thought to myself if ever there was a time or situation when a man had earned and deserved a stiff drink this was it.

I got out of bed dressed stole some money out of Dolly's purse and went straight to the Alma pub where I drank five or six large Zubrodca's as fast as I could. The next thing I knew I was waking up in Maureen's' bed, with the General Foreman from the building site standing over me, telling me that I was no longer going to be employed by the Greater London Council. I sat up and punched him in the face. Very much to my surprise, he turned and ran out of the house. As I was still fully dressed I just walked out and went back to the pub where to my amazement, I discovered that I'd been missing for another three days with no recollection of how, who, where or what I'd done.

As I approached my flat later that day I could see that the door was slightly ajar. I don't know what made me do it, but I just took a run at it shoulder first and barged it all the way open with such force it almost came off of its hinges. With the little amount of Dutch courage I had mustered up from the couple of pints I had drunk on my way home, I was ready to tackle any situation. The uppermost thought in my mind was I had burglars or the like. I don't know how many times I've said that I was surprised to find, but I'll say it once again. When the door flew open I was very surprised see my flat and its entire contents absolutely in chaos. My furniture had been thrown all over the place, there were blankets and sheets in the living room, a torn pillow stuffed down the toilet, the living room furniture slung into the bedrooms and kitchen.

I called for Dolly and the children but there was no reply. I sat there in a daze for several minutes until Dolly walked in with both children when she saw the flat she just broke down and cried. I was so relieved to see them safe, the shock of what had happened to my flat seem to pale into insignificance. Dolly asked me have you got any idea, who would want to do this to us. Right at that moment I could think of hundreds of people that hated me but certainly wouldn't smash up my home up. Checking around we found that both the electric and gas meters had been robbed which was really sickening because it meant that we would have to repay the stolen money.

The one good thing about this robbery was that we wouldn't have to buy the dog any more food because the burglars had taken the fucking thing with them. When I used to go drumming with Curtis, at the slightest sound of a dog we would lose interest, even if it meant that the Crown Jewels were at stake. I knew whoever had robbed my flat certainly wasn't scared of big Alsatians, but then, apart from the money in the gas and electric meters it was the only other thing of value we owned that could be stolen. It didn't take us long to tidy up, we soon realised and they really hadn't done much damage or broken anything, they had just scattered things around to make it look like it had been done by kids. It wasn't long before the entire clientele of the all night cafes and dives got to know about the robbery. Most of them thought, it was hilarious that the burglars had stolen my guard dog.

One Friday afternoon a couple of weeks after the flat breaking incident, I was sitting having a drink in the Alma, when Joyce Robinson came in and told me that her Maltese boyfriend, was looking for me, with every intention of seriously hurting if not crippling me for life. As I was pretty drunk, I really didn't give a fuck what his intentions were. She had in the past told me who he was, so drunk or sober I never considered him any sort of threat, unless he had a gang with him. I drank my beer, grabbed her hand and walked over the road to Maureen's' house where we went to bed. She told me that and her boyfriend had stopped her carrying the bottles of alcohol. This really disappointed me because the fact that she might have had some booze on her was the only reason I wanted to be with her that afternoon. She was still covered in bruises and stitched up cuts from the beating Dolly at given her.

I asked Maureen to go and get a bottle of Polish vodka from the Alma and to tell them I would bring the money in later. Very much to my surprise and delight the landlord trusted me, and gave her one of the biggest bottles of vodka I had ever seen. I remember feeling very drunk when I left Joyce and Maureen. I also know that I was carrying the bottle of vodka at the time, or at least half of it. My next recollection was arriving home with a bottle of whisky, opening my front door to be greeted with an almost identical scene as I had witnessed a week or so earlier. The difference this time being Dolly was sitting in the flat with the children.

I looked at her and said not again, surely they must know by now there is nothing here of any value. Dolly looked at me and said, "Don't pretend you don't know about this, I've called the police and I'm going to tell them exactly what you have done."

Once again I was totally baffled. In my mind I had only been out long enough to have a couple of drinks in the Alma and spend a bit of time with Joyce and Maureen.

Dolly said, "Don't try and play the innocent with me, you know you did this as well as I do. Don't blame it on the drink because you weren't drunk, you just ripped this place apart like a bloody animal, I wouldn't mind betting it was you that did the last supposed burglary."

I was completely flabbergasted, this time the flat had been totally trashed, the fridge door had been ripped off its hinges, the gas meter and the oven had been torn from the walls. There wasn't a single chair that could be sat on, all our bric-a-brac and mirrors had been junked, and the place was reeking of gas. I could hear it hissing as it was escaping from the broken pipe where the meter should have been attached. There wasn't a single cup, saucer, plate or dish that hadn't been smashed; everything was piled the floor of the living room. Several of Dolly's dresses had either been cut or torn, there was tea and coffee and bloodstains all over the walls and ceilings, which I'd spent some time carefully decorating since the trouble with Joyce. I really was incapable of taking it all in.

"Whoever would want to do this to us?" I asked Dolly. The look on her face was one of sheer hatred and desperation.

"Why are you looking at me like that," I asked her. "What's wrong with you. What are you accusing me of now? I've only been out for a couple of hours, you were here when I left and you're still here now that I've come back."

She screamed at me, "You fucking lousy bastard, you know you did all this. You know that you terrified the kids and me. You know that you have embarrassed me so much that I can never return to my job. You are the lowest object that breathes air on this earth."

Dollies words were hitting me like bullets, apart from when she beat up Joyce I had never seen her looking or acting like this.

"Please," I said. "Tell me what I've done wrong. Please start at the beginning and tell me word for word what you are accusing me of and why have I lost you your job."

Once again she looked at me like a wild thing, "You know. You know what you've done," she kept saying. "You know what you've done."

And I kept saying, "I don't, I don't, I don't please tell me."

Eventually she looked at me and said, "Can you really and honestly look me in the face and swear on your children's lives that you do not know what you have done."

Without any hesitation, I agreed to take any oath or make any promise that she wanted me to; I was begging her to tell me what had happened.

"Please Dolly, please tell me what I've done this time," I pleaded.

She looked at me and said, "Are you really telling me you don't know that the blood on the walls is yours. Are you really expecting me to believe that you don't know how you got the cuts on your head and arms."

I raised my hand to the back of my head, quickly pulling it away again when it got painful. Very gently I felt it again, and realised she was telling me the truth because there were cuts on both the back of my head and my arm. The realisation that the blood spread all over the walls, ceiling and my clothes belonged to me, made me feel a bit numb.

"Could you please start at the beginning," I said to her. "Tell me what you think I've done and please explain to me why I should want to smash up my own home."

With a face as black as thunder, she looked at me and laughed in my face. For a brief moment, I thought, that she had been making it all up. I tried to smile at her but she immediately went on the attack again and started swearing at me.

"You haven't got the right to smile at anything, nor should you ever have again, after the way you have terrorised me and the children."

I was beginning to feel angry and at the same time thinking that I had done something so bad it had driven the poor woman completely over the edge.

The next thing she said to me was, "Don't you even dare to think about losing your temper because I will tell the police to take your way forever."

"Don't talk bollocks," I said to her. "Just fucking tell me what happened?"

"Ok." She said. "Let's start at the beginning. You left the flat at 12 o'clock on Friday do you remember that part?"

"Yes," I said, " I do."

She then said, "Do you remember telling me that you wouldn't be home until Sunday."

I told her I couldn't remember what I had said.

"Do you remember I gave you £15."?

"Yes." I remember that I said.

"Good." She said, "If you don't interrupt me any more I will tell you everything that you're pretending not to know."

"You kissed me goodbye and said you were going off to see Tony Welford."

"That's true, I remember that bit but why do you keep saying on Friday?"

"Because today is Sunday, John." She said.

I realised then that I had had another one of those three-day blackouts, where I functioned like a sober person without any knowledge of doing so. I remember cadging the 15 quid and telling her that I was going to call for Tony Welford and instead of doing that I decided to go to the pub where I met Joyce and then went on to Maureen's'. Twelve o'clock was the time I'd said goodbye to Dolly, because she had to go back to work. In fact she had only come home in her lunch hour to meet me in order to make sure that I was definitely going away for the weekend. That part was all so clear and vivid in my mind, I just couldn't understand where the next two days had gone.

Once Dolly had started talking about it she became very determined that she was going to tell me every grubby and gruesome little detail about the weekend. While she was at work on the Friday morning, one of her mates had invited her to send John and Kim to stay with her and family down in the country for the weekend. Dolly had jumped at the chance of having a free weekend without me and the kids around, in fact she was so glad she invited her supervisor and three girls from her office round to the flat for Saturday afternoon tea. This was something she would never have considered doing had she known I was going to be anywhere near the place. The reason she had been so generous and given me 15 quid was because I had told her that me and Tony Welford were going down to Faversham to see Harry Swan.

Somewhere along the line I'd spoilt all her plans because unbeknown to her, not only hadn't I gone to Faversham. I can only assume that I must have got so drunk on the Friday night I had gone home and into Kim's bedroom where I fell asleep until late on the Saturday afternoon. When I got up I went into the living room where the supervisor, Dolly and the girls were sitting eating sandwiches and having a friendly little chat. To really put a tin hat on things, apart from being stark naked I stood in the middle of them and pissed in the fireplace. Dolly, who had no possible reason for lying to me, told me that as I was pissing it splashed up the supervisor's legs, plus when I had finished pissing I turned around to face her friends, making sure that they could all see my block and tackle. After that display I just calmly went back to bed.

When I pictured the scene in my mind, I really wanted to laugh but remembering I was still in the situation where my flat had been completely wrecked and I didn't know how, I managed not to even smile. I desperately wanted to know what had happened. Dolly continued, telling me how her friends had got up and walked out within seconds of me leaving the room and then, when she came into the bedroom to tell me off, I just went completely berserk and started tearing the place apart. During my lunatic actions Dolly had attacked me, cutting my arm with a knife and hitting me on the head with a bottle. She said after doing all the damage, I got dressed and walked out the door and as I passed along the street under our window, she threw the bottle, which caught me on the back of my head. She told me, I just walked away and didn't even turn around to see what had hit me. Even to this day, I have no firsthand knowledge or memory of anything that occurred over that weekend.

Two of the girls from Dolly's office came around on the Monday evening to find out why she hadn't gone to work. When they saw me, they both laughed, one of them told me that the supervisor was so embarrassed at what I done to her, she had promised to take them out to a very posh place for dinner if they in turn promised never to mention what had happened. I asked them if they thought the supervisor would buy me a dinner if I promised never to talk about it! They assured Dolly that no one would say a word when she returned to work. I felt so relieved when she agreed that she would go back the next morning. I still wonder about that weekend and where I got the nice bottle of Johnny Walker Black Label, I arrived home with.

CHAPTER 17

I decided that I would stay at home for a while repairing the flat, I put the Black Label on the mantelpiece, unopened, thinking that at least I didn't have to go out if I needed a drink. About a week or so later Tony Welford called round, he told me that he had been with me for some of the of time over that weekend and that we had visited a few clubs in the west end and around the Paddington area. I asked him if there had been any trouble. He said you must be joking we went to least half a dozen places and in four of them you either attacked the doorman or one of their punters.
I said to him, "Tony don't talk bollocks. How could I do all that and still be here smashing up my flat?"
He told me that our tour of the clubs was on the Friday night before I went home.

"Look Tony," I said, "Are you sure you're not fucking winding me up?"
"On my life, John", he said. "I'm not joking."
He went on to tell me the names of three of the doormen that I had fought with. When I heard the names a shudder of fear ran through me. I thought to myself, I really hope none of them know where I live. I knew for sure that without the courage of a drink in me, anyone of these people could and would tear me apart. Gradually the fear spread through my entire body, I began to shake and silently ask God to relieve me of my feelings.
Tony said, "Don't worry about it now, just' drink some of that Black Label."
It took half of the bottle before I began to feel any effect. Tony left saying that he would see me the next day.

Try as I might, I couldn't achieve the full internal shield of protection that I would normally have got from drinking half a bottle of Scotch, something totally different was happening to me. I was feeling physically drunk but still mentally aware of what was going on, the fear that booze usually kept at bay was still floating

369

in and out my mind. I knew that Dolly hadn't forgiven me for smashing the flat but at least she was still with me, and I still had the children. I was trying to take some comfort from the thought that all three of them cared for me. The feeling I was suffering was a sort of very acute loneliness, which I had felt in the past but it had never been so intense or taken so long to pass.

I drank the remains of the Black label, which gave me enough courage to walk down Brick Lane. I was thinking that if I threatened a few people, someone would return the gear they had nicked from my flat in the first burglary. Everybody I approached denied knowing anything about it but said they would spread the word around that I was looking. I told them that I was angry and would kill somebody if I didn't get my stuff back. As I wasn't getting the effect I was looking for from the booze, I made sure that the people I threatened were the ones who were pretty harmless. What was really bugging me was one of the suits that had been taken was the one I was supposed to be looking after for my mate in the nick!

I was absolutely flat broke and feeling totally paranoid about not getting the right effect from the booze. My brain told me that it was the whisky's fault because it wasn't strong enough, not like the Polish spirits. The next thing that clicked into my mind was a wish that I had the money to get some of that really strong vodka. I decided to go back to my flat and wait for Dolly to come home. My hands were shaking and my legs didn't want to support me, the fear that I wasn't going to get home was almost overwhelming.
As I was walking or rather stumbling along a bloke came up and said, "John, if you go to the address on this piece of paper you will find most of your gear, would you like me to come with you in case there's any trouble."

"No," I said, "Don't worry about it. I'll go later when it gets dark." If I had been in my usual drunken state, I would have found a suitable weapon and immediately gone round to sort the bastards out. Mentally I felt that by not taking up his offer of support I had somehow exposed my true inner fears to him. I was really worried that this bloke might have discovered that I was trying to cover up my fear, not of him or of the people that had my gear; I was just terrified of everything.

I said to the bloke, "I feel a bit cold so I'm going to run back to my flat."

I really don't know what he thought as he saw me staggering and veering off in all directions, trying to pretend that I was running. At the time, my brain was telling me that I was travelling along like a sprinter, but my eyes were showing me that I was almost falling over with every step I tried to take

It must have taken me the best part of an hour to travel the quarter of a mile to my flat; in that time I had seen and felt every horror from small rodents to green monsters. I lay in my daughter's bedroom for several days. Some time later Dolly told me that I hadn't always managed to get out of the bed to go to the toilet, but when I did on my way there and back she could hear me mumbling and praying to God for help. She told me that I kept kneeling down beside the bed asking for forgiveness and begging for someone to explain what was wrong and asking why did I feel the way I did, then I would go into crying fits. Gradually the intense fear subsided I began to feel better, still very frightened but a lot better. I began eating the occasional slice of toast.

I never allowed Dolly or the children to open the curtains; I just couldn't face the streets. The loneliness and the inexplicable fear were gradually overtaken by the more tangible fear of reprisals from the people I had had trouble with on the weekend of my last blackout. I continued to sleep in Kim's bedroom with a sawn-off shotgun and a large bayonet for company. I put four bolts and a chain on the front door. Dolly did point out to me that the hinges the door was hanging on were actually broken and if anybody gave it a little more than a gentle push the door would fall off. Somehow my brain told me this wouldn't happen. She also said that I should see a psychiatrist to get some kind of help. Every day she continued

371

to go to work and take the children to whoever was looking after them. The hours I spent alone were almost unbearable, every sound in the flat and every noise that came in from outside sent fear racing through my body.

For a short period of time, previous to above events, I had started hanging around with two real snidey characters. One of them was married to the sister of a old schoolmate of mine, the other one called Joey was a sneaky, ferretty looking little bastard, who always carried a small, opened penknife wrapped in his handkerchief. Whenever he was faced with any sort of confrontation, he would take out the hanky, pretend to blow his nose, manipulate the knife into the palm of his hand and try to stab or cut who ever he was arguing with, usually catching them across their face and eyes. Some of the dives in Cable Street and along Commercial Road had been closed down by the police, which meant that the majority of the night people, having been deprived of their regular meeting places, were now frequenting similar haunts in Brick Lane. It was in one of these places I had originally met, Joey and Paddy.

One day, during the time of my fear inflicted incarceration there was a knock on the flat door. I stood behind it, held my breath and listened, not moving until I recognised the voices of Joey and Paddy. I opened the door and let them in; because I hadn't seen them for some time I thought it was a social call. As I was offering to make them a cup of tea I lost control of my nerves and went into some sort of shaking spasm. Paddy and Joey must have thought my sudden bout of shivers were due to my fear of them, because the two spineless bastards started talking to me in a very aggressive manner. It turned out that they had come round to turn me over for something I'd said or done to them about a month previous. Together they couldn't fight their way out of a paper bag and yet here they were challenging me in my own home. Something that in my sober mind, I would never have considered doing if there was, the slightest chance that children could possibly get involved. In my book of morals the sort of argument they wanted with me, was a street matter.

I went into the bedroom picked up the shotgun and bayonet and then came back into the front room, and asked them who wanted to be shot and who wanted to be stabbed? It gave them such a surprise Joey dropped his handkerchief, which as usual contained his penknife. My brain was back in gear, these two cowards were ready to cut me to pieces and I couldn't fathom out how or where they had summoned up their courage from. It didn't matter because I was now holding the trump cards.
I looked at them and said, "Before you die, tell me what this is all about and tell me the fucking truth."

Paddy told me that on several occasions while I had been hanging around with them they had wanted to do away with me. The reason being that every time they planned to do anything, I'd fucked it up by getting pissed. They went on to say that someone had told them that I was in my flat in a very bad way, almost on my last legs. With this in their minds they had decided it was too good of an opportunity to miss, not only to get their revenge, but also to take me out of the game altogether. Had they come a week or so earlier they could have achieved their goal so easily.

All the old bollocks and Jack the Lad attitudes they had come into my flat with were now gone. They weren't begging me but it was very close to it, when said they were very sorry for what they had done and asked if I could forget all about the matter. They will never know the sense of relief I felt, when they put that suggestion to me. I knew that there was no way on this earth that I could summon up the courage to pull the trigger of the gun. I had managed to stop shaking long enough to put on a little act of bravado, I said " if at anytime in the future they even think about having a go at me you'd better apologise, then I told them to fuck off. As Joey bent down to pick up his penknife and handkerchief I kicked him in the head. Both of them were trying to get out of the door at once, I did manage to cut Paddy across the arse as they ran away.

I just had enough time to close the door behind them before my nerves gave out altogether. Within a matter of seconds I was shaking from head to toe. I felt so mentally, physically and spiritually lonely. I couldn't believe what I'd just done without a drink in me. I looked through the curtains into the street to make sure that they had gone. As I was doing so I saw a kid who was a friend of Kim's. I tapped on the window and signalled for him to come to my front door, when he got there I gave him my last 10-shilling note and asked him to go to the off-licence to get me a bottle of V.P. wine. He looked at me and said thanks for the money but if you want a bottle of wine you can go and get it your fucking self. With that he ran away with my ten bob. I couldn't believe it, I had just kicked and cut two would be villains, and now this little bastard had turned me over as sweet as a nut. I just stood there looking out of my door, knowing that I was to frighten to go after him. Try, as I might, no matter how desperate I got for a drink, I couldn't summon up the courage to leave my flat. I also that knew there was no way on earth, that neither, Dolly or Kim, would bring one home for me.

Two days after the kid ran off with my ten bob, Tony Welford decided to show his ugly face once again and much to my to my absolute delight he had half a bottle of Scotch with him.
Dolly looked at me and said, "You have just started to look human again John, why do you want to start drinking?"
I looked at her, then at Tony, who said to me, "Surely you're not going to let a woman tell you what to do."
"Not on you're fucking life." I said.
I put the bottle to my lips and swallowed more than half the contents. The burning sensation at the back of my throat, the wonderful regeneration of my courage, felt beyond fantastic. Only someone, who drank like I did, would know what that experience is like.

When Tony left at about two o'clock in the morning, I felt on top of the world, because he had told me that he had been winding me up about the trouble with the doormen. He said he'd never believed that I suffered from blackouts and had been testing me to see if it was true. For the first time in weeks I went to bed with Dolly and fell contentedly asleep, even when she left for work the next day I still felt good. I had made up my mind that I was going to walk around the area just to show my face and to prove to people I was still around. Theory is a wonderful thing but fact is a different matter. I managed to get to the address I had been given where my gear was supposed to be. I knocked on the door and felt really sick when the person who answered it turned out to be someone I'd been a close friend of for most of my life. Someone told me later, he needed over thirty stitches in the wounds that my bayonet made across his face and neck.

When I got back to my flat, I felt like I had run 20 miles. Once again the fear began overtaking me, I knew the only solution was to have a drink but I didn't have enough money to buy one. My mind kept telling me, go out and get a drink, you really do need a drink. So, why don't you go out and get one, why are you letting a little matter of having no money get in the way of what you need, depriving you of that nice safe feeling. You've got a shotgun and bayonet; they should get you all the drink you need. And then reality would take over; the fear would tell me that without a drink in me I couldn't summon up enough courage to walk out of my own front door.

That night, after Dolly had gone to bed and the children were asleep I sat on my armchair in the living room with the lights out thinking to myself, "How can I get enough money to buy sufficient drink to last me for the rest of my life. How many drinks would it take to maintain the level of courage I needed to live the life I wanted? Why couldn't I be like Kray twins or my cousins Philly Snooks and Jerry Crawley, they were men who people respected for themselves not because they were drunk, or needed drink to live." I gradually convinced myself that I could become a gangster; I would go round the pubs and clubs with my gun and demand protection money from the Landlords.

I was totally convinced that this was possible; I was just about to get up and put the light on when I heard footsteps on the landing outside my street door. I could hear the familiar voice of Joyce Robinson pleading.
"Tony don't go in there because he has got two young children, just come with me and leave it until we see him in the pub."
Then I heard a voice with strong Maltese accent say, "No, I've got to give the gun back tomorrow. I will kill him and his wife and children for what they did to you."
The next thing I heard Joyce say was, "If you loved me Tony, you wouldn't be risking spending the rest of your life in prison away from me."

All my determination and resolve to be a hard man come Gangster melted like a snowball in a fire. I was suddenly paralysed with fear; I fell down on my knees and curled up behind the door. I cried and sobbed and prayed. I mentally apologised to everybody I had ever hurt, promising God if he let me live I would do nothing but good things towards all humanity. I wasn't cold but I was shivering from the feeling of sheer terror. I lost control of my bowels and bladder; not one single ounce of courage remained in my body. The fear was total. The only other feeling I had was contempt and hatred for my cowardice. The words that Maureen's husband, Norman, had said to me when I was abusing his wife in front of him, rang so very true. People like me do things to people like him, because he couldn't stop me. As I lay behind my door that night, I knew exactly how he felt. I was powerless to stand up like a man to defend myself against a bloke half my size. I lay on the floor soaked in my own piss and shit until the next morning.

I still don't know if I really heard those people, nobody tried to get in my flat.

When Dolly came into the room the next morning and found me, she said, "I'm going to get a doctor before you die." "Please," I said to her. "Don't bother with a doctor just get me a drink, I really do need a drink so very badly. If I am going to die please let me die happy." As sick as I was I was still playing games and using whatever feelings she had left for me to manipulate her into to doing what I wanted. Less than an hour later I was up washed and clean with half a bottle of vodka running through my veins. My mind told me once again that it had all been a mistake, just a very bad nightmare, nothing much to really worry about. I was bound and very determined that nobody would ever find out what I went through behind my street door that night.

My resolve that it would never happen again became so strong I couldn't believe that I was capable of doing some of the things I did to make sure that there was always a drink available to me. One night I made my way over to a dive in Cable Street, where I got in the company of two Liverpool blokes I had met in Soho some years earlier. They told me that they were watching a seaman, who had come up from London docks and picked up a prostitute that one of skousers was pimping off of. She had somehow informed them that the seaman was carrying loads of money. The plan they had formulated was for the girl to take the man down an alley pretending that she was going to have sex with him, then the two skousers would jump him and relieve him of his money, in the trade this was called mugging.

They invited me to join them and share the money four ways, I felt quite delighted to be asked. Two large drinks and five minutes later we followed the girl and the turban wearing sailor out of the club and down through several back alleys. The two boys seemed to be hanging back which made me think two things firstly they were losing their bottle, and secondly we had better jump on the bloke very soon. When we reached what I thought was a perfect spot to do the mugging, I told them to hurry up and do the dirty deed before the girl and Seaman could turn the next corner. I ran up behind the bloke grabbed him by the shoulder and swung him round to face me, at the same time I caught hold of his jacket lapels and dragged him towards me, saying, "If you give us your money we won't hurt you." I said.

"Alright, alright," he said, "Please don't hurt me. I will give you my money."
I thought, this is an easy way to make a living. If I could get the girl to be my partner in crime, my financial problems would soon be over. The Seaman took a step back and reached inside his coat. I was now holding on to one of his lapels, with my other hand outstretched palm upwards, ready and waiting to receive his money. From inside his jacket he pulled what looked like the biggest knife, I'd ever seen.
He grabbed me by the throat and said, "This knife is a religious object, and I'm not allowed to put it back unless I take some blood. I will consider that your blood runs through every thing you have in your pockets."
The man relieved me of seven player cigarettes and a box of Swan Vesta matches plus 25 bob in cash. I asked him if he would leave me enough for my bus fare home.
He looked at me and said, "You wouldn't have left me mine," then he was gone.

For a brief period of time after that episode I started going back down to the Batty Street dive with Tony Welford, who had convinced me that a mixture of cannabis, amphetamines and lots of booze were all we needed, to have a wonderful life. By this time the West Indians had take over most of the dives and café's. I really believe that during this period, the people who frequented that square mile of the East End could have stayed as high as kites just from the fumes the Jamaicans exhaled. No matter where you went around the area, day or night, the sweet smell of hashish would grace your nostrils. There seemed to be far less violence and a lot more loving and dancing going on. The Batty Street dive now used the light coming from the jukebox to illuminate both of its clubrooms. Sometimes even this was covered by a blanket, which meant the only way you could tell if anybody was in the place, was by the loud inhalation noises made by the people as they sucked on their glowing reefers.

After several days and nights of drinking pints of bitter mixed with Vodka, I decided that the best way to make money was to become a bank robber. I had the gun all I needed was a couple of partners. It all seemed so simple and for the life of me I couldn't think why I'd never thought of it before. I took myself off down to the Alma to find some likeminded people who I thought might want to join with me in my new career. After downing two more pints of bitter I saw two blokes I knew quite well, arrive in the other bar, when I called for them to join me they weren't too keen on the idea but soon changed their minds when I offered to buy them a drink.

When they came into the saloon bar I made sure that we were standing well away from anyone who might overhear our conversation. I had just finished telling them all about my plans to become a bank robber, emphasising every detail of how simple it was all going to be. I could see from their expressions that I was holding their interest. Just then, very unfortunately for them, I let off the loudest and wettest fart I could ever remember doing, followed by a very uncomfortable feeling of a warm, damp, thick liquid running down the backs of my legs. The smell was more than a little offensive and was obviously totally unpalatable to the noses of my two would-be partners in crime. They quickly stepped away from me each wearing a look of utter disgust on their faces.
One of them said to me, "John, if you shit yourself while you are just talking about robbing a bank, whatever are you going to be like if we actually do one."
They both drank up and told me they would give the matter some very serious thought.

I began to get touches of what the junkies called the horrors, these that brought on by not having enough alcohol or drugs in my system. When I could feel them coming on I would run home, often leaving Tony Welford in one or other of the clubs. I never explained to him why I did it; I think he just accepted that I was more than slightly nuts. It was on one of those nights when I was feeling very uncomfortable and paranoid and just about to run away that I met a girl called Rita. She could see that I was having some sort of problem and said to me, "Why don't you come back to the house."

"What house?" I asked.

She told me it was a place that was very friendly, where anybody was welcome and not just for a short visit, but they could stay as long as they liked. She said there was always plenty of drink and 'stuff' available; it sounded like heaven to me.

Rita took me to a three-storey, yellow brick terraced house just off of Christian Street Road, which at first sight looked derelict. She pushed open the street door and shouted up the stairs to say that everything was okay and still in a loud voice informed whoever was there, that she was bringing in a friend who was looking for a good time. I suddenly thought, maybe she thinks I am a punter that's looking to pay for a bunk up. I told her that I wasn't there for that reason.

She said, "My dear boy, never for one second did I think that you were. I'm part lesbian and tonight I fancy a woman, some other night you might get lucky, and I do mean lucky."

We went up a flight of narrow wooden stairs, walked along a short landing back towards the front of the house and into a room that was very brightly lit, which surprised me because from the street you couldn't see any sign of light or life at all.

There were several people in room, two of who I'd never seen before. Rita asked me if I needed any introductions, I pointed at the two people and said, "Who are they?"

She looked at me and said, "Nobody important, or at least nobody you should be concerned about." One of the people I had referred to came over and shook my hand and told me his name was Billy Jennings then he pointed to a girl and said, "They call her Dirty Doreen."

Sitting in a corner of the room was an African bloke that had I known in my old days when I was working on the door of the St Louis club. What I remembered about him wasn't only the tribal scars on his face, but the belief that he carried in his mind, which was that, if ever he were knocked to the floor or ground in a fight he would die. Over the years I had known him I had seen him do battle with some of the hardest men in London, he was never once put down. Unfortunately, he never won any of the fights either. I saw some very tough characters completely exhaust themselves trying to knock him out.

I turned around to see the man who was standing behind the door when I came in. It turned out to be my old adversary, Bobby Silver, the bloke who had stolen Dolly's suitcases when she first arrived in the East End.

Before I could grab him he held out a bottle of wine and said, "In the case of your girlfriend losing her belongings, I really was robbed. Maybe this can help make up for it."

He was holding the one thing that I really needed at that moment. I accepted his olive branch and at the same time thought that I could always find him again. There was a bed, a sofa and four single armchairs in the room. The windows were covered up with very thick old army blankets nailed into place around the frames.

The house wasn't exactly filthy but it wasn't very clean either, everything you saw was just about touchable. All around the room there were saucers filled with different coloured pills which Dirty Doreen told me to help myself to, after she had finished describing the different reactions that each pill should have on you. I thanked her very much and told her that I was quite satisfied to drink the wine. She said that's no problem at all and from under the bed she pulled another three bottles of the same cheap wine. I asked Rita who paid for it all.

She said to me, "Don't worry about it. When you come into some money you can make a contribution."

This arrangement suited me right down to the ground; I pulled up a vacant armchair, carried all the wine over to it and settled in.

For the next month or so I didn't leave those premises, I found an empty bed on the top floor which I claimed as my own. Sometimes I would share it with Rita or Doreen and other times I would share it with Rita and whatever girlfriend she brought home. I don't remember ever having sex with any of them. This was mainly due to two reasons, the first being I didn't fancy any of them, the second, I was too pissed all the time. This didn't seem to bother anybody and it certainly never bothered me, as long as the wine kept flowing, I didn't care about anyone or anything.

One-day I woke up to find Tony Welford standing next to my bed, saying, "John, don't you think it's time that you went home to Dolly and kids. More importantly don't you think it's time that you took a bath and changed the clothes you're wearing? I haven't seen you for a month or more and your still wearing the same clothes. Don't you feel any shame."?

"Look, Tony," I said to him, "I have at last found a place where nobody gives a fuck what I look like or what I smell like. They don't even want to know my name."

He said to me, "They are such great people they've all gone away because they know it won't be very long before your dead."

I didn't have a clue what he was talking about. I thought, it was less than an hour ago when Billy Jennings had come into the room and asked me if there was anything I wanted. He told me that there was nothing he wouldn't do for me all I had to do was ask.

I remember saying to him, "Billy, I haven't had a drink for hours so if you think that much of me, go and get me some liquid of life, or in other words a bottle of fucking wine and hurry up about it."

Then I must have fallen asleep until Tony woke me up. Somewhere in my foggy brain I realised that it was raining and I was getting wet.

Tony said, "I met Rita downstairs. She told me that you haven't been out of this bed for over a week and so far the only thing you haven't done in it is shit but even to do that you've stayed in the room, you really have turned into a dirty stinking tramp."

I looked around the room and in one very fleeting moment of sanity I knew that what he was saying was true. I had used that bed like a tortoise uses its shell; only a tortoise would have kept itself much cleaner. I had stayed in that bed after any living thing would have had the good sense to leave it. The room looked and smelt like a cesspit. I felt so ashamed and was suddenly struck with more guilt and fear than I had ever felt before. I looked at Tony and told him to fuck off and let me die in peace.

He said to me, "I will make sure that you fucking well go home if it's the last thing I do. I don't know why or how you can just let it your wife and children suffer, the pain of not knowing whether you're dead or alive. To show that I care for you and them, I'm going to make you want to go home."

He went out of the room, slamming the door behind him, calling me all the worst names he could think to put his tongue to. Even if I had wanted to I couldn't summon up the courage or energy to leave that bed. The next thing I knew was the smell of smoke and then the sound of fire engine bells. There were firemen running all over the place with hoses spraying water all over me; it was the cleanest I'd been for weeks.

Tony came back and said, "I really wish you had died in the fire rather than having to watch you slowly rot away, you're not even 30 years old yet you poor pathetic bastard I don't suppose I'll ever see you again." Then he walked out.

Sometime later Rita came in the room and told me that two friends of mine were downstairs waiting in a car, they had told her to ask me if would like to go for a ride with them.

I said, " I'm very sorry but I am waiting for Billy Jennings to come back with my wine."

She looked at me and said, "I love you very much John and so did Billy but I'm afraid you won't be seeing either of us again."

"What the fuck do you mean."? I said to her. "Why won't I be seeing Billy Jennings."?

"Because he's dead." She answered. I couldn't believe her, Billy was only twenty years old.

"How did it happen, was it an accident. Did he get run over?" I asked her.

"No," she said with tears in her eyes. "A fucking big African promised that if Billy had sex with him he would give him some money to buy your wine."

My brain was more confused than ever. "How the fuck did he die?" I asked her.

"That is exactly how he died," she said. "He got shagged to death trying to earn the money to get your so precious fucking drink." As she turned to walk out the door I asked her to wait and told her I wanted to go with her.

Somehow finding out about Billy had given me the courage and strength to leave what I thought was going to be my deathbed. She was telling the truth, downstairs there were two people I knew sitting in car waiting for us. The first question I asked them was, did they have any money because I desperately needed a drink. They both said they had enough money for what I wanted but didn't have a clue where I was going to buy drink at that time of night. Don't worry I told them there's a little man on Charing Cross Embankment who will have exactly what I need, you just give me the money.

We were travelling along the Embankment in the direction of Big Ben when one of the boys said to me, "Look there are two girls

over there that I'm sure we could pull, if you and Rita wouldn't mind getting out of the car and walking the next couple of hundred yards."
I really didn't think I was capable of walking two yards let alone a couple of hundred. I felt totally empty, totally devoid of any emotional or physical feelings. I was terrified and desperately lonely down to my soul. At that moment in time the only thing that was keeping me on my feet was the thought that I was going to get a drink of what I truly thought had become the liquid of life, the only reason I had to live for.

I put my arm around Rita's shoulder, using her as a crutch, feeling that all my bodily strength was gone. I could quite clearly see the bones on the backs of my hands sticking through the skin. I could smell the stench of the shit on my clothes and body my brain was telling me if I could get that drink I could be anybody I wanted to be and do anything that I wanted to do. I could become the big time gangster that I'd always desperately wanted to be. I could be a proper father to my children. I could be a proper husband when I married Dolly. Finally and at long last we reached the coffee stall at Charing Cross station, I pointed to the bloke and told Rita to give him the money for half a bottle of Scotch, which she did. When she got the bottle she opened it took a sip and then passed it to me.

The first mouthful was too much for me. I instantly threw up; it felt like someone had put a blowtorch in my mouth.
"Please give me a cigarette." I said to Rita, "I must take a few drags to help me hold the whisky down."
She lit up two cigarettes and passed one of them to me. I took several drags on it and then tried to drink some more Scotch, this time it stayed down. The meaning of life started to flow through my body once again. I began to shake, vomit, drink and smoke all at the same time. Rita was half carrying me, half dragging me, to where the boys had parked the car.

Desperation alone was all that was keeping me going; I didn't know where I was going. I just knew that I needed to get to the car and sit down. We were within twenty yards of it when two policemen, stepped out from behind a wall, walked over to me and asked where I was going. I had just sufficient drink in my system to give me the courage to tell them that it was none of their business and to fuck off and find some child molesters. One of them was only a cadet in his blue band flat cap the other one, I think I recognised but I'm not sure.

The non-cadet said to me, "You're nothing but a fucking turd and my God you even smell like one."
I looked at him and said, "If you weren't wearing a uniform, I would take you in those trees and knock your fucking head off."
He removed his helmet, gave it to his partner and then started pulling me towards the trees saying, "Come on hero, lets see what you are made of, it still smells like shit to me."
 Rita started pulling me in the other direction telling me to ignore them because all they wanted to do was get it back to the nick for the night. I struggled out of his grip and walked away intending to get into the car. One of the boys was holding the back door open for me and said, "It's not worth it John, let's go back down the East End."
I said, "OK," and lent forward to get in. The next thing I knew and felt was a very sharp pain at the base of my spine, which sent me, sprawling into the car. I realised that one of the coppers had kicked me

As I landed I saw one of those old-fashioned wind-up, triangular car jacks on the floor. I picked it up by the neck and climbed out of the car on the opposite side to where the two old bill were. I ran around and hit the first copper right over the crust. Luckily for him and for me, he had put his helmet back on, which I think saved his life but it didn't stop him going down. When I saw he wasn't getting up again I decided I would throw his cadet sidekick over the wall into the River Thames. As I have said many times, theory is wonderful but fact is a totally different matter. While I was trying to drag the cadet over the road, the 'hurry up wagon' arrived full of policemen all dressed in nicely pressed ready for work uniforms.

They picked me up and threw me at least ten feet through the air. I landed face down in the back of the wagon. I remember being punched and kicked for what seemed like an endless period of time. I also remember having my head pulled back by the hair and seeing the copper I had hit with the car jack draw back his boot and kick me full in the mouth. I spat out my two front teeth and what looked like a pint of blood on to the floor of the police van. I don't remember anything after that, apart from being in a cell and curling up to stop myself from being beaten to death. I think every copper on duty in the nick that night punched, kicked or spat on me. The only thing I could think was if I'd had the time to get enough drink down me, this wouldn't have happened, I don't remember much more. Gradually as the little bit of effect I had got from the booze wore off and I my regained my awareness I began to feel a great deal of fear and pain.

When I came up before the Magistrate the next day, my eyes were so badly bruised and swollen I could hardly see. As well as my missing teeth, my nose had been broken and was spreading across my face. I had a dislocated shoulder and every part of my body was discoloured with bruising. Because of the way I had been living on alcohol and not much else for the past lord knows how long, I now weighed less than 7 stone soaking wet. Before I appeared in the Court the Police had made a deal with me, which was very simple. They wouldn't charge me with the more serious charge of Grievous Bodily Harm, only a minor one of Assault, on the condition that I agreed to plead guilty and not bother going 'up the steps' for a trial by Jury. That way the Magistrate could deal with it that morning and I would be back home in no time, they told me. When I got into court, those nice policemen had certainly charged me with 'Assault' but they had added on the words 'With an Offensive Weapon'.

I was given six months and taken to Pentonville Prison, where on my arrival I was immediately taken to the Hospital Wing. Where the Medical Officer informed me that along with all my obvious injuries I had several broken ribs. They patched me up and then put me on D1, the Dossers' landing. D1 was where Alkies from Itchy Park and the homeless cardboard city dwellers resided. They were put straight onto that wing without changing their louse ridden clothes and just left until they finished their seven or fourteen day sentences for 'Drunk and Disorderly' or 'Drunk and Incapable'. And there was I, in the prime of my life, being put on the Dossers' wing. Feigning indignation I asked the landing screw why I was being put on D.1. He said, "Well John, just stand back and take a good look at yourself. Where else could we put you?" I was twenty-nine years of age and really didn't understand what he meant.

I was put in a cell with a West Indian geezer who was stone raving bonkers and another chap who was gay, as it's called these days. I went straight into the DT's. I was thrashing about, shivering and screaming but the screws on that landing had seen it all so many times they had grown used to it. They moved the other two blokes out and left me alone for about three days, as was their usual practice. They had become experts in that sort of detoxification.

While I had been waiting in the cells of the Magistrates court to go to the Ville, Dolly had been allowed down to visit me.
She had said, "Can't you see what drink has done to you John?"
What she said or meant didn't really register with me at the time. I thought that drink was the only thing I had left going for me, but after a couple of days in the nick suffering from withdrawals, I began to give it some very serious thought. Along the lines of, if I hadn't been looking for a drink so badly that night I wouldn't have been on the embankment or anywhere near it. I also knew for certain that if I hadn't been drunk, I wouldn't have been so lippy to the Old Bill.

After the initial period of DT's, due to the withdrawals, I began to think more clearly. I could see how far down I had gone in the thirteen years since I had taken what I had considered to be my first adult drink. Thoughts about my Uncle John who had died after spending most of his life locked in a mental institution came into my brain. I asked myself was his insanity hereditary. Not knowing what to do for the best I put my name down to see the prison psychiatrist in the hopes that he could or would throw some light on what was wrong with me. Maybe he could even explain why I drank like I did. In those days my dishonesty was so ingrained that if I had owned two very accurate watches, I was incapable of telling anyone the right time

It took all the courage I could muster to go and see the psychiatrist, whose name was Merrydown, how appropriate! Any apple grower will know the most famous name in cider. I tried desperately to tell him the truth, but it was hard. I had always found it was so much easier to live in a fantasy world rather than to be honest. His questions seemed to be a load of bullshit. To ask a man of my age, 'Did my Mum and Dad still live together?' 'Was I in a stable relationship with my wife?' 'Was I still this, that, and the other?' 'What happened when I was a kid?'
When he'd finished questioning me, he said. "It's obvious that you drink for pleasure."
I asked him to repeat the word.
"Pleasure is what I said," He told me.

"When you come to near the end of your sentence, I'll give you some Aversion Therapy."
I didn't know what Aversion Therapy was, but I did know that the psychiatrist was pissed all the time he worked in the nick. I didn't bother to ask him to explain. I thought here he was, an educated man, pretending to be able to treat the minds of the mentally sick, namely people like me, but he couldn't help himself. My next thought was, I know what to do when I get out, I'll go back to Dolly and I'll learn to control this bloody drinking. I'll drink like my

brothers. I'll only drink on Saturday Lunchtime and Evening, plus Sunday Dinnertime and that's it. I won't let it get out of control ever again.

When Merridown dismissed me, I walked to the end of the wing where I stopped to wait for a screw to take me back to my workshop. While I was standing there, I started to read the prisoners' notice board, which was hanging on the wall outside the Landing Officers' room. Whenever I had done porridge in the past, I had never wanted to be part of any of the official associations or knitting classes if I could possibly avoid it. My preference was to go to the library and take out several books, do whatever deal I could for my bit of tobacco, then go into my cell, close the door and read my time away. That's the way I did my bird, which meant I didn't usually pay any attention to notice boards, but unusually this time I did. The notice read:

If you've got a drinking problem ask the Welfare Officer to put you in touch with Alcoholics Anonymous.

The title 'Alcoholics Anonymous' didn't register, but Drinking Problem did. I certainly had one of them. I decided to do as the notice suggested. Early the next morning I put my name down to see the Welfare Officer. I began thinking about Alcoholics Anonymous. The only thing I knew about it was a film, called 'I'LL CRY TOMORROW.' From that I had got the impression that AA was full of rich old birds with more money than brains that had nothing else to do with their lives other than to get pissed.

On the following Thursday evening a screw opened my cell door and told me to go the end of the wing, which I did. As I was waiting I looked across at another group of cons that were lined up on the opposite wing. Among them there were blokes I'd known for many years. With my vivid imagination still strongly in control of my mind, I naturally thought that these people looked on me as the villain I had always tried to project. When the screw on the centre, shouted out my name then said, " Alkies this way," my blood ran hot and then cold with the shame of it, but it was too late to turn back. I hung my head and quickly made my way across the centre into the meeting room, which was made up of two cells knocked into one.

There were two other cons already waiting in the room, both of them were right iffy, you wouldn't have trusted them to look after a dead dog. Just the three of us, I was regretting that I had put my name down because I knew if any of my old mates ever saw me mixing with these two, even the slightest remnants of any street credibility I still had in my life would be gone forever. Luckily just as I was going to walk out, two civilian blokes arrived and introduced themselves as Johnny and Bill. Johnny was a Florist and Bill had his own painting and decorating business.

Johnny introduced himself as an alcoholic and then told us his drinking history, and then Bill related part of his. At first I didn't trust either of them. It wasn't until much later I realised how lucky I was. Bill's story was similar to mine, but most of Johnny's story was like a mirror image. So much so that I thought they were both policemen who'd seen my records and were using parts of them to get my trust by masquerading as drunks. I thought they were living in the hopes that I'd start telling them about myself, and all the crimes I'd never been caught for. My still befuddled brain told me if I opened my mouth I would finish up having another twenty or so years added to my little bit of porridge.

After the meeting I went back to my cell with a couple of tailor made cigarettes and a small folded card they'd given me. I sat down on my bed and read what was on the front page of the card, it was a copy of 'The Serenity Prayer', a prayer that Johnny the Florist told me was recited at the end of all civvie AA meetings. Within ten minutes I'd learnt it by heart. Having time to think about what had been said at the meeting, I began to realise that some of the things that John had told us, especially about the fear he suffered, couldn't be written down in my or any records because I'd gone to such pains to hide the fact that I was frightened. Also some of the people he mentioned in his story I actually knew, I realised then that if the illness of alcoholism as they called it, was John and Bill's problem, it surely must be mine.

Suddenly I felt warm. It wasn't a warm glow or anything supernatural, I just felt warm with the sense of relief that I may have found out what was wrong with me. I'd always known that there was something wrong. Now I had been presented with a possible answer. If these blokes were claiming to be alcoholics, then I must be one because I'd gone so much further down the drinking scale than either of them. Sitting in my cell recalling what I had heard at the meeting, I suddenly felt that I had found the strength and ability to declare that that part of my life was over. I couldn't wait for the next opportunity to get back to the meeting room and talk to John and Bill again.

The following Thursday night I went back but this time I met two different people. There was a Jewish bloke called Joe from Tottenham. His was a totally different story, but it had a similar ending. This was a man who had earned a lot of honest money in his life, he'd had factories, dozens of employees, partners, a wife and kids but he'd still finished up shaking and shivering on his kitchen floor. Just like I had shaken and shivered out in the cold, or in police stations and prison cells. The third week a little roly-poly Scotsman named Mick came in to speak. After listening to him for thirty-five or forty minutes I was almost convinced that I wasn't an alcoholic, because I hadn't done a quarter of the things he had.

After attending seventeen AA meetings, the day of my release came. As I stepped out of the security of Pentonville, what felt like a knife of fear hit me? The old feelings, which I had always fended off by taking a drink, descended on me. I was shocked at the realisation that these feelings still existed within me. All the security of the prison and the meetings had led me to believe that it was going to be easy not to drink; yet here I was faced with a very desperate urge to do just that. Why I didn't go running into the nearest pub I don't know for sure. I think it was mainly due to the fact that I had promised to ring, Bill who had trustingly given me his phone number so I could make arrangements for him to take me to an AA meeting that night.

I rang Bill and was very disappointed when he told me that he couldn't meet me because both he and his wife had got the flu. However, he had arranged for a bloke called Howard to meet me at Stepney East tube station at six thirty. It got very cold as I waited for this complete stranger to show up. From where I was standing I could see the lights of a pub and as the time passed they began to get brighter and more and more inviting. The taste and smell of the liquid of life kept drifting up my nose and through my imagination. The Serenity Prayer tumbled out of my mouth at least a hundred times until eventually a Morris Thousand car pulled up in front of me.

Howard introduced himself and a girl called Olive who was in the car with him. He told me that they had both been sober for six months. He said he would be taking me to a meeting at Chapel Street, just off Tottenham Court Road, in Soho. That's what he said he was going to do. I still think to this day, I have never had a worse or more fearful car journey in my life. Whenever I came out of prison I always felt nervous of the speeding traffic but Howard was the most incompetent driver I had ever ridden with, and somehow due to his incompetence we finished up in Ilford, which is completely in the opposite direction to where he intended taking us. At my first civilian meeting I heard, with a great deal less swearing than I was used to, the same despairs and hopes and shared experiences that people had told me about in the nick. Howard was my first contact in Civvy Street he took me to my first AA meeting outside of prison. Sadly he died in 1998.

He gave me a directory of meetings aptly called a 'Where to Find'. He told me that there were a couple of meetings in it he really didn't think I should bother with because he felt they weren't 'my type of meeting'. This seemed strange to me as Plaistow Bill, Mick the Tick, Johnny the Florist and Jewish Joe had all told me that AA was pretty much the same all over the world. Plus they'd said how welcoming and friendly it would be when I found my way around in Civvy Street, and yet here I was, out of prison only one day and I was being told that there were some meetings I shouldn't go to! I just thought; I'll have a look at them anyway.

After the meeting they drove me back to my flat and came in for a cup of coffee. I could see that both Howard and Olive were quite nervous at the prospect of hanging around in the area where I lived.
On the stroke of eleven, Howard said, "We must be going now hopefully we'll see you around the meetings."
When they had gone I said to, Dolly, who was still recovering from the shock of me arriving home sober, "Those two people have waited until this time because they think I can't get a drink now the pubs are closed."
I got the distinct feeling they thought that I was going back on the piss.

It so happened, that, just as they were leaving. Tony Welford arrived with a bottle of Scotch sticking out of his pocket. Talking to Howard sometime later he told me that he never expected to ever see me again because he'd seen the bottle. He hadn't got the slightest idea how I felt.
When Tony came in I said to him, "I'm off the booze, so I won't be helping you to drink that." Tony looked at me and said, "Thank God for that because you're a fucking pest when you drink!" Once again I had it confirmed in my own mind that I was an alcoholic. At my first civvy meeting I was christened Pentonville Johnny

Most of the next day I spent with Dolly and the kids trying to build bridges and repair some of the years of emotional damage I had caused. In my own usual ignorant way I naturally thought that after a few apologies, some cuddles and kisses, and a bag of sweets all the sad and bad events in our past life together would become bygones and forgotten and forgiven and in no time at all we would be back playing happy families. With all the bonding and making amends I considered that I had done during the daytime, I decided it might not be a bad idea to go to the meeting, that I should have been taken to if Howard hadn't have been such a bad driver. Once there I would tell everyone I met how I had done the programme as it had been suggested I should. All was well in my world once again.

I arrived at St. Patrick's Church hall in Soho about 30 minutes before the meeting was due to start. Having unwillingly spent the last of my money on my tube fare I wasn't feeling in a very sane or sociable mood. All the way there my mind had been racing. Rationalizations were bouncing around inside my brain like spilt ping-pong balls on a stone floor. One of the most reoccurring thoughts I was struggling with, was that I wasn't an alcoholic and that any person who drank like I had should surely be able to control the amount they drank and when they drank it. And then in a matter of seconds another brainwave would bring to light some of the horrors that overtook me when ever I'd even thought about trying to control or stop my drinking.

It was almost like someone walking along side of me was having these thoughts I nearly convinced myself that I had never tried to control my drinking so how did I know I couldn't.. Images of what it was like immediately before my last prison sentence were also paying the occasional visits to my thought processes. Thankfully when I had arrived at St Patrick's there were already several people in the meeting room with tea and biscuits on the go. .Two cups of tea and four biscuits later I struck up a conversation with two members. One was a chap called Ken the other was a lady called Una, although both of them seemed like a very nice people I was immediately on the defensive.

I began wondering to myself if I should or should not tell them that I just been released from prison. I thought I would be rejected completely if ever they found out even the slightest detail about my criminal past. When they asked if I was a new member I told him that I was and that I had been sent to the meeting by Jewish Joe from Tottenham who was my sponsor. Ken immediately said, you must be from Pentonville. I don't really know what my reaction was to his statement but I must have shown some sort of outward sign of embarrassment, because he immediately came back with there is nothing to be ashamed of if you have been in prison due to alcoholism.

I was really glad when the meeting filled up with more people and we were invited to take our seats, I sat as far away from Ken and Una as I possibly could and hoped that they wouldn't tell anybody that I was an ex-con. The chairs were arranged in schoolroom fashion about ten across and five or six deep we sat with our backs to the entrance which meant that anybody arriving late would come in at the rear of the meeting. Facing us raised on a small platform was a table that had a navy blue silk banner draped over and around it. The banner was embroidered in gold letters with the words, I am responsible.

From the top table a very smartly dressed man introduced himself as Eddie the group chairman and Secretary. He welcomed the members and then enquired if there were anyone newcomers. As this was my second meeting in Civvie Street I didn't put my hand up, however my new found friend Ken decided that he would introduce me. At that moment in time I wanted the world to disappear, I wanted to fall down a big hole filled with booze and never be seen again... My irrational mind took the opportunity to tell me that I should have gone to the pub and got drunk first and then come to this bloody hell hole.

To my surprise Eddie welcomed me and seemed very genuine in his welcome, once again negative thoughts raced through my head, they won't be this welcoming when they find out who or what I am and what I have been. Eddie then went on to introduce the lady sitting next to him she then introduced herself by saying I am Sheila and I am an alcoholic. I don't know how to describe my feelings when this woman introduced herself as an alcoholic. I thought that was the last thing in the world I could ever have guessed her to be. Because looking at her as I was she looked everything but a drunk. She actually looked to me like the very attractive wife of a wealthy suburban stockbroker. She was certainly wearing the very expensive clothes and all the trimmings that go with that role in life, and nothing remotely resembling my vision of how a drunk should look.

When she started relating her drinking story to us I found it very difficult to believe that this woman had spent 20 years in prison. By the time she finished half an hour or so later, I had lost all my inhibitions and reservations about telling people that I had been in prison. Not only was I not worried about telling them about my incarcerations, I felt quite innocent after listening to the list of crimes this woman had committed. The thing that really impressed me most about her, however, was the fact that she was five years sober.

After the meeting I was invited to join the members for coffee at the Kenco coffeehouse which was just around the corner from the meeting room. When I explained to Ken that I had no money, he shrugged his shoulders and said we didn't ask if you had any money, just for if you wanted a cup of coffee. My mind jumped straight back into the past, and to other times I had gone with people to café's without any money and thought nothing of bumming of off them all night and day. And now here I was supposed to be a reformed character, doing just the same thing sober. When I told Ken what I was thinking he simply shrugged his shoulders again and said you will be able to repay us when you do the same for other new members in the future.

Later when people started to leave the coffeehouse and head of home. I was left on my own again. It wasn't long before the sense of well-being that I'd acquired over the past couple of hours began to slip away to be replaced with by the more familiar ones of loneliness and aloneness. It was less than half a mile to the tube station, but with the negative thoughts going around my brain it seemed to take forever to get there. Once again the battle of sanity versus insanity was raging inside my head.

When I arrived back in the East End the negative side of my personality was really in charge. I could not think of anything else but the effect that alcohol would have on my system and how it would give me the ability to overcome all these stupid negative emotions. Fortunately I was too late to go to any of the pubs so I made my way home to Dolly and the kids. I don't know how you register the degree's of surprise, but the look of amazement on Dolly's face when I arrived home not even smelling of alcohol was a wonder to behold.

She told me that this was the longest period of time I had been voluntarily without alcohol in all the years we had been together. Even I was surprised and once again I started looking at my past and tried to summon up a memory of any alcohol free times I had had. At that moment I could not think of any period of time, not even a day when I hadn't taken a drink. If my eyes were open, and I wasn't in prison, hospital or sick in bed I drank and had been doing so since I was in my early teens.

When Dolly and the kids went off to bed I had time to think about the past evening and how most of the people I had met had been sober for varying periods of time. Thinking about some of the individuals I had a feeling that if they could do it so could I. Suddenly, the feeling of warmness that I had felt in my cell, after attending my very first AA meeting, returned and I knew that I had a chance to stay sober if I became a regular attendee and a committed member of Alcoholics Anonymous.

I just fell totally in love with AA, and some thirty odd, sober years later; I am still in love with it.